THE GARDEN BOOK

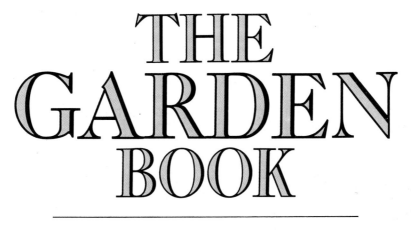

THE GARDEN BOOK

JOHN BROOKES

Crown Trade Paperbacks
New York

For JHR

The Garden Book was conceived, edited and designed
by Dorling Kindersley Limited, 9 Henrietta Street,
London WC2E 8PS

Project Editor David Lamb **Art Editor** Steven Wooster
Editor Anthony Livesey **Designer** Julia Goodman
Managing Editor Jackie Douglas **Art Director** Roger Bristow
American Editor Marjorie J. Dietz

Published by Crown Publishers, Inc.
201 East 50th Street, New York, New York 10022. Member of the Crown Publishing Group.
Originally published in hardcover in Great Britain by Dorling Kindersley Limited
and in the United States by Crown Publishers, Inc., in 1984.

Crown Trade Paperbacks™ and colophon
are trademarks of Crown Publishers, Inc.
Library of Congress Cataloging-in-Publication Data
Brookes, John, 1933-
The garden book
Includes index.
1. Landscape gardening. 2. Landscape architecture.
3. Gardens / Design. I. Dietz, Marjorie J. II. Title.
SB473.B725 1984 712'.6   83-23181

ISBN 0-517-58948-6

10 9 8 7 6 5 4 3 2 1

First American Paperback Edition

Contents

Foreword

I have tried to write a book not for setting-up home but for setting-up garden, though I think the two are inseparable. The process applies to both the owners of new, unmade gardens and those who have established gardens with which they are unhappy. In whichever of these positions you find yourself, I cannot overemphasize the necessity of immersing yourself in the theories of design and styling before setting forth to devise your own solution, to peruse the book logically from the beginning so that the basic philosophy of garden planning is not neglected in your understandable enthusiasm for the final horticultural result. Unfortunately, the horticultural industry encourages a disregard for a preconceived garden plan – witness the lip-service most garden publications pay to design. Even books supposedly written on the subject do not allow garden design to progress beyond the 1920s. In no other field of design are we of the modern world so blind. Arguably, the garden is one's private antidote to modernism and progress, the place where the individualist in us all makes his last stand, introducing all manner of emotional overtones and fulfilling totally impractical aspirations. And why not? But the modern world need not necessarily be banned from the garden. Economic factors that have put a high premium on any outside space, and new construction and surfacing materials, demand useful and attractive garden designs to suit.

I suppose the grass is always greener in your neighbor's garden and, by the same token, many Continental ones embody for me much from which we in the British Isles can learn. Conversely, Continentals love the large gracious gardens of the British Isles that are open to the public. In the United States and Canada, the quite different climatic zones have of necessity influenced garden design and plant selections. More recently, American landscape design is responding to the reality of smaller properties and a demand for low-maintenance plantings. Shouldn't we seek some essence from all these influences, but conditioned by the practicalities of location?

A view of herbaceous planting in the walled garden at Denmans, West Sussex

WHAT TYPE OF GARDEN?

Your outside space, its location, orientation,
climate and soil

The modern garden in the light of gardens past

Introduction

While many of us might not conform to what convention would have us wear for a particular time of day, or for performing a particular function, we all appreciate that for a special evening out, jeans, for instance, would not be appropriate. You would not normally go fishing in a suit either, or garden in a dressing gown, although all these garments would cover us adequately. Choosing the correct garment allows us to perform most comfortably, whether it be dancing, fishing or digging. The cut and fit of the garment matters as well, for the best tailored clothes go on for ever, being made of good material and being designed to fit the wearer.

The way in which you clothe the area around the house is subject to the same discipline as choosing a garment to wear, according to what you want of it, how it will be used and how it will serve the house which sits in the middle of it. Gardens which are well made and individually styled will work best for the user.

The type of garden that you evolve for yourself should depend on the demands you make of it. Long before setting pencil to paper to produce a plan from which to work, let alone setting spade to earth, you must ask yourself what it is that you want your garden to do for you and your family.

As soon as the word "garden" is used, common sense is often ignored. Pictures of lawns and grottos and ponds start to cloud the issue and we are soon going to the supermarket in an evening dress or "mucking out" in a dinner jacket. Get back to reality, forget the stately layouts that you might have seen and think about the type of garden that you really need. Your type of garden must depend on you and your family's lifestyle. This will provide much food for thought, for the permutations of possible requirements among even a family of four, considering their diverse ages, and various likes and dislikes, are endless.

You might not be able to afford to pave terraces or build walls in order to fulfil your plan in one operation. This is unimportant as long as you get the plan of action correct and work slowly towards its completion as and

Creating style, *below left. Traditional English architecture with mellow stone walls and leaded windows is emphasized by a traditional garden. The same stone has been used for the steps, and plants allowed to smother and soften the whole. The gray foliage of Leucanthemum sp. blends with the stone while red climbing roses provide contrast. Below, in completely opposite style, a crisp, modern approach has been used to tie in the building and plants of this house. Japanese influence is strong, with sliding glass doors allowing the inside and outside to merge.*

when it is possible to do so. Whether you can afford to construct all the garden or not, it is essential to start to use the site according to your plan – storing wood, building the rubbish heap, walking a certain path or siting the dustbins, for instance.

The good garden plan will also provide a setting for your house. Many homes will have more than one garden, with an area in front and an area to the rear. These areas have totally different functions, as different as those of a kitchen and a sitting-room, and their characters should reflect this. The front garden is usually a place for display, whereas the rear garden is essentially an area to be used and viewed by you and your family throughout the year.

Your garden design will obviously depend on your individual taste, and how you have designed and decorated the inside of your house, for the garden will often become an immediate extension of it. Your taste may be traditional or it may be modern; you might like masses of plants or be very spartan in your choice. But the initial controlling influence on your plan is the location of your garden – town, country or the vast suburban areas in which most people live. It is the first factor to examine in detail.

The rear garden, *above. Unlike the public display of the front garden, the rear garden should be thought of as a private, outside room used as an extension of the home in summer. Consider the variety of uses to which* *you and your family will put the garden and try to include as many as possible in your rear garden plan.*

Where is your garden?

Gardens with a similar layout can feel completely different depending on their location. Enclosed town gardens will seem much smaller than the same size garden in a more rural, open setting. But it is the very fact that you have a private, outside space within a tight urban mass that makes the town garden so attractive to use in the summer, and to look at throughout the rest of the year. In the town garden, planning must be influenced by the proximity and feeling of the buildings which surround it and by whether the garden is overlooked.

The hazards of the walled town garden include a lack of light throughout the year, making plants reach upwards and inwards to gain the most from it. Shade might come from surrounding buildings or from an overhanging tree growing in a neighboring garden. Conversely, the walled garden might be a sun trap and become far too hot for limited periods.

Taking these factors into consideration, the design for an enclosed town garden should be very simple, with the object of making an outside room furnished with permanent sculptural groupings of plants. In front of these you can contrast bright masses of annual plants, grouped and arranged in pots. You might consider some form of overhead canopy too, for seclusion. The character of the town garden should be quite different from that of gardens in any other situation and should not be a reduced version of the country model.

Gardens of a larger size – and they usually are in suburban locations – have greater demands made of them. Couples tend to move outwards from city centers as their families grow, giving themselves more space.

Vegetables might be included in the garden plan to supplement the table, and any open space will eventually be used for children's play. Whereas the design of the town garden promotes passive enjoyment, the suburban family garden design should provide for more active enjoyment with enlarged terrace areas for play as well as entertainment. The planting of such a garden will at first be limited to the screens required to give privacy, and only as the children of the family grow up will it come to include more specialized decorative groups.

While country gardens may be large, there is now a general movement to make them more manageable. The increasingly wide spectrum of pursuits which a family can now undertake inhibits time spent working in the garden. Weekenders in the country often prefer to enjoy the countryside, rather than achieve an immaculate plot by Sunday evening with the prospect of starting again the following Saturday. The whole outlook on rural gardening is now far more relaxed. The area of the garden which requires moderate maintenance might be restricted to the house surround, with alternative and less demanding treatments used for the garden beyond the house or cottage.

Town, suburban and rural locations are often indivisible, one flowing into the other. My concern is for the smaller garden area within any of them. Often the only difference between the locations is climatic conditions, or the altitude at which they are located, for the standardization of modern building has meant that new houses and their plot size are often similar anywhere. It is easy to end up with a standardized garden to match if you are not conscious of its location.

Rural garden, *right.*
This Swedish cottage yard epitomizes relaxed country gardening. The seemingly casual arrangement of poppies and marguerites has been allowed to self-seed among the small elements of random paving.

Urban gardens, *below.*
The tiniest gardens in town, even on roofs or balconies, can be magical. They provide an escape from bricks and mortar and a link with the natural world beyond the city.

Suburban garden, *left. Out of the city center, more space means less intensive gardening and more space for garden activity. The sunken area in this suburban garden allows for a sheltered meal table, usable for many months of the year. Changes of level provide casual seating places for less formal entertaining.*

11

Climate and weather

The climate and weather of a location will have a major influence on its character. They will have molded the vernacular style of building and where wood and stone are available locally they will have been used traditionally for constructing walls, paths and fences. Indigenous herbage will have been used for hedging and infills, giving gardens a particular local quality. It has only been the development of the modern garden center that has changed this by offering universally available modern materials. It is sad that gardens north and south are now paved in similar materials, and are stocked with a similar range of alien plant material. Only more extreme climatic conditions prevent this universal approach and encourage a garden molded by its environment.

When considering what any particular climate will support horticulturally you can do no better than to look and see what is supported naturally and in agriculture, in rural and suburban situations, and, of course, what is growing in other gardens. The main climatic factors which influence plant growth in an area are its altitude and the intensity and length of its winters. An area's horticultural possibilities can also be greatly affected by wind. Wind off the sea, for example, will be salt-laden in diminishing amounts up to five miles from the coast. The range of plants which can stand its full blast is quite small.

Climatic conditions can also vary enormously from garden to garden. The presence of surrounding buildings, or trees, or a combination of the two, might inhibit the number of sunlight hours that the garden receives. In summer, when the sun rides high over obstacles there will probably be more than enough light even if bright sunshine is limited to only part of the day. But in the winter,

when the sun is lower in the sky, direct sunlight might not reach the garden for months on end.

Trees and buildings can funnel prevailing winds and cause considerable damage, although open fences or hedges can be sited to counter the force of the wind by filtering away its strength. A solid barrier, like a wall (which in other circumstances can do so much to promote plant growth by retaining the sun's heat) simply increases wind turbulance and is inappropriate as a wind break.

Homes and gardens which are comparatively close to one another, but one on a hill top and one in a valley bottom, will experience considerable differences in temperature in both winter (due to frost) and summer (due to wind). Frost is an important factor to consider on a local basis. You must remember that cold air flows downhill like water. If your garden happens to be in the way, any solid barrier will trap the cold. It is possible to deflect the flow of cold air with well-thought planting, though. Gardens in valleys, or otherwise below hills, are likely to be in frost pockets, causing their micro-climates to be surprisingly cold. Frost will remain in a frost pocket until dispersed by wind or sun. Such a situation may be lethal to spring-flowering fruit trees.

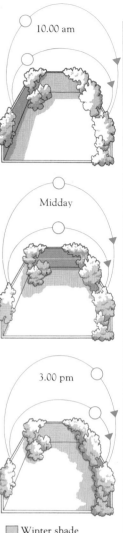

10.00 am

Midday

3.00 pm

Winter shade
Summer shade

Sun in walled gardens, *above. Only the central portion of an enclosed garden is guaranteed direct sunlight the year round. The low arc of the sun in winter dramatically increases the areas of shade through the day.*

Frost-trap *Cold air, like water, runs downhill into valley floors and basins where it lies.*

Temperate climate garden *Adequate rainfall and mild winters allow for an amazing abundance of wide-ranging plant growth.*

Mild winter garden *Boxwood will not survive the coldest New England winters, but is used farther south and along the Coast.*

Hot climate garden, *left. Desert-type sun and lack of rain can produce striking examples of gardens molded by climate. Architecture, garden layout and choice of plants which can stand intense sunlight and possible drought, combine to reflect the spirit of place strongly.*

Cold climate garden, *below. This Continental woodland garden nestles beneath a plantation of poplars. The informal use of shade-loving plants merging with the established trees beyond, combines with the steeply-pitched roof line of the house to suggest a place of shelter against heavy winter snow.*

Aspect and site

The reasons which govern why we live where we do seldom include the suitability of a site for the creation of a garden. Access to place of work, proximity to relations, the suitability of the house and the potential of its internal space are the more usual concerns. When moving home, a pleasant view might be considered an advantage, or a property's closeness to the sea, but only the *size* of the garden is likely to be advertised as a feature of the space outside. Often you will have to adapt what you have bought from a previous owner, or, if you move into a newly built home, to start from scratch on a new site.

Even a brand new site can have encouraging features under the builders' rubble. Look for a change of level within the site, distant views, or even the shape of a neighboring tree in relation to your own plot. All can be used in your ultimate design. Older, established gardens will have existing vegetation with which to work. Small urban gardens, including basement areas, will have surrounding walls to establish the character of the garden, and with luck a little vegetation too.

The type of soil which you inherit – if there is any at all – will affect the character of the garden too (see p. 16) for certain plants prefer an acid soil, others a more chalky or alkaline one. The consistency of the soil will either allow it to warm quickly, encouraging early spring growth, or cause it to remain cold and sticky for longer and thereby slowing down plant activity. All too often a new

Dramatic aspect, *left. An Italian garden terrace in an established orchard setting exploits a magnificent view of the valley below. The simple line of an encircling granite block wall is all the garden design necessary in a site of such unusual aspect. In practical terms, the wall will shelter the seating from drafts blowing up from the valley floor far below.*

Considering aspect, *below. The dwellings illustrated have opposite aspects, the top with house front facing north, and the bottom with house front facing south. A rear seating area has been well-positioned in each garden to catch the sun.*

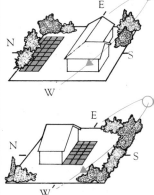

plot has a meagre layer of topsoil, perhaps only a dusting of it over clay compressed by building work. If you are moving to a new property, this problem is well worth checking since the removal of clay and its replacement with a more fertile topsoil can be an expensive operation and only possible if there is easy access.

The aspect of the house will rarely influence your choice of home but it will have a significant effect on the type of garden that you can make. The ideal aspect in much of the northern hemisphere is open to the south-west, gaining full benefit from long summer days. Remember that a sunny, south-facing frontage gives you a shady, north-facing rear garden, and while many plants will grow in the shade, your terrace will have to be a distance from the house if you want to sit in the sun. In hot climates, an area of reliable shade near to the house might be desirable.

There are very few aspects which present insuperable problems to garden planning, but frequently too little consideration leads to a plan which makes the garden difficult to live with. Tall planting or building in the line of the sun's regular path, for example, can cast shadows which restrict plant growth and give the garden a cold feel.

A garden on a slope often allows a good view, but if you are contemplating a new, steeply sloping site, and wish to work the garden, remember that retaining walls (see p. 120) may be necessary to create level areas in the garden. Such walls can be very expensive to construct well. Another problem to beware of, is that sites which fall towards the house may well produce drainage difficulties (see page 103), especially in winter.

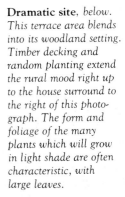

Dramatic site, *below. This terrace area blends into its woodland setting. Timber decking and random planting extend the rural mood right up to the house surround to the right of this photograph. The form and foliage of the many plants which will grow in light shade are often characteristic, with large leaves.*

Analyzing your soil

The type of soil in your garden will be a guide to the type of plants that you can grow, provided that other variables, such as drainage, weather and the amount of sunlight that the garden receives also suit the plants you choose. Having said that, most soils which are in good condition, (in gardening terms, in "good tilth"), will grow most plants. Soil condition depends on its texture, and this can always be improved with the addition of organic matter. Only extreme soil types are particularly difficult.

The basic factor leading to regional differences in garden type is the soil. It has been formed over millions of years by the breaking up of the rocks of the earth's crust, so it is the nature of the underlying rock that influences the type of soil above it. For example, older, igneous rocks, like granite, and also sandstone, tend to form slightly acid soil, while limestone and chalk rocks will produce an alkaline soil (see below).

The texture of the topsoil – the bit we garden on – is determined by the size and consistency of the particles which make up that soil, and the presence or absence of organic matter in it. A clay soil is composed of very small particles packed so closely together that it retains moisture even in warm weather. It is often, therefore, a cold and sticky soil, but if it does finally dry out in hot weather it will crack. A sandy soil is composed of far larger particles than a clay one. It will drain well and warm up quickly in spring, and is therefore known as a warm soil. However, the line between draining well and draining too quickly is a thin one. A soil that drains too quickly will be a poor one as all the nutrients normally held in solution around each soil particle will leach away. The ideal soil, as far as texture is concerned, is a loam, consisting of a mixture of slightly more sand than clay particles, and with a high organic content.

The incorporation of organic manure in either a clay or a sandy soil will improve its condition enormously, not only by improving its texture but also by feeding the soil. The crumb-like consistency of well-rotted manure will bind together the particles of a loose, sandy soil, or divide up the fine grains of a sticky clay one, while the bacteria it contains will activate either soil type to promote plant growth. To test your soil for organic content, examine it closely and pick up a handful, running it through your fingers. Ideally, it should be of a crumbly consistency, neither too spongy and sticky nor too dusty. It should look dark in color and should also smell sweet.

As well as its sandy or clayey nature, a soil is judged by its relative alkalinity or acidity,

two opposing conditions. The relative alkalinity or acidity of a soil can be measured against a scale which has become accepted by gardeners and is known as the pH scale. This runs from pH0 to pH14 with pH7 as neutral. Plants grow in soils within the range of pH4.5 to pH7.5. A soil between pH5.7 and pH6.7 is ideal for the majority of plants. Above this reading the soil is too alkaline, and below it, too acid. A chalky soil has a high calcium (alkaline) content and will, therefore, have a high pH reading. It can be made more acid by adding heavy dressings of organic material, such as farmyard manure or compost. When adequately manured, a chalky soil will become quite fertile.

A peaty soil is at the other end of the pH scale, being acid. Unlike other soils, peat is derived from plants and is therefore organic itself. Occurring naturally, a peaty soil will often need to be drained. It can be made more alkaline ("sweetened") by adding lime in the form of ground limestone. A dose of 2.25 kg per 9 m² (5 lbs per 97 ft²) will raise the pH between 0.5 and 0.75 of a point. Bought peat has usually been sterilized and will therefore contain little or no food value, but it will still condition a soil by improving its texture.

To test your soil for alkalinity or acidity in America, a sample can be submitted to your county extension agents for analysis. Otherwise you can use a home testing kit, many types of which are readily available on the market.

Each soil type has a range of vegetation which will thrive upon it, from the smallest herb through, in many cases, to forest trees. The presence of any of this range on a virgin site will be a guide to the soil type. Neighboring gardens, too, will tell you what grows well there. For example, in many parts of Europe the rhododendron growing is a sure sign of an acid soil, and forms of viburnum usually indicate chalky (alkaline) ones. Birch, pine, gorse and broom usually indicate a light, sandy and often acid soil.

It is one thing to improve the texture and drainage characteristics of your soil and to make it suitable for healthy plant growth but it is a wasteful process to spend much time and effort trying to change the soil type of your garden completely in order to grow a particular range of plants that is alien to your locality. If necessary, you can use containers to hold a special soil type for plants that are not happy in your local soil.

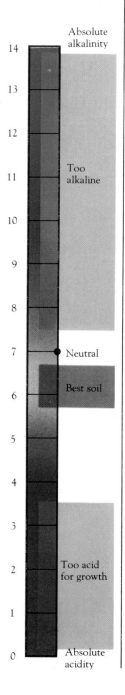

pH scale and values
The pH scale indicates alkalinity or acidity about the neutral value of pH7. Soil is usually acid or alkaline and has according characteristics. Soil testing kits are available which simply assess the pH value of your soil by measuring the hydrogen ion concentration in a suspension of soil in distilled water.

Absolute alkalinity

14
13
12
11
10
9
8
7 — Neutral
6 — Best soil
5
4
3
2 — Too acid for growth
1
0 — Absolute acidity

Too alkaline

Recognizing soil type from natural vegetation

Although soil type can be modified by the location of a site (sun or shade, and slopes, will alter the water content of soils), certain types of plant are attracted to and flourish in certain soil types. Plants which have seeded themselves in a garden plot, therefore, can be a good indicator of the soil type which you are to inherit with a plot.

Willow herb (*Epilobium* sp., fireweed in the United States), for instance, grows in a fertile, moist soil, as do nettles. Wild blueberries are standard vegetation on acid soils, which are usually sandy or peaty and poor. While ferns are adaptable plants and can be found growing on wet and dry soils, they mostly indicate a heavy, damp soil, suggesting clay. A sure incidator of a wet soil is the buttercup (*Ranunculus* sp.). It is often seen in low-lying garden corners and across poorly drained lawns. An alkaline, chalky soil is often the chosen home of saltbushes (*Atriplex* sp.) and yerba mansa (*Anemopsis californica*)

Willow herb – fertile soil

Heath and heather – poor, acid soil

Ferns – heavy soil

Buttercups – wet soil

Dog's Mercury – alkaline soil

A garden's uses

In the main, historic gardens that survive are those that have best met the requirements of the grand families for whom they were built, with their expansive life styles. That historic layouts have survived is a tribute to their architects, who not only fulfilled the requirements of their patrons but also created gardens of beauty that have proved worth preserving. The clue to their success is an understanding of the life and times of the families involved.

To tailor your own site to your requirements you too will need to analyze your family's needs and recognize that this is a continuing process. As the individual members of your family grow, so their interests and their resulting demands of the garden space change.

Before thinking about the trees and shrubs you would like to include in your garden, consider the practical aspects of your outside living space. These are usually centered on the service door from the house. Think of rubbish storage and access to it, of the compost heap, of gas storage if it is necessary, of a clothes drying area, and a place to store surplus household furniture, garden tools and machinery. All these areas will need to be serviced by hard, dry paving, preferably lit at night. This paving might link to a garage, or a workshop, or a glass-covered area perhaps, even a conservatory. Think about winter use as well as summer, and night as well as day. Some areas will need an electricity or water supply. A terrace for summer sunbathing, entertaining or for family meals outside should be an extension of these functional areas as well as the house.

Think where you might like a herb area (which ideally should be near to the kitchen entrance) and a vegetable plot. The size of a vegetable plot is an important consideration. Just how much time can you afford to devote to vegetable growing? Remember that vegetables will be cheap in the shops at the times of year when you will have to spend most time growing your own. Perhaps you only need to provide salad crops, or to grow soft fruit or even just a fruit tree. Whatever you decide, tough service paths to a vegetable and/or fruit growing area are vital.

The type of garden that you create within this framework will depend on the many possible demands that can be made of an outside space. Will children play in it, first perhaps in a sandpit but later football or tennis practiced against any available wall? These latter activities will mean that planting must be limited. A barbecue space will be useful to entertain the family throughout the summer and a further terrace which serves it might also be useful for table tennis in summer, and for more sunbathing and entertaining space. The growing, prosperous family might need a second garage space, or space to park a boat perhaps through winter or a camper.

As children leave home, parents often want to garden the area more, increasing its horticultural content. The addition of a greenhouse and a cold frame can be a means of extending this activity. Such detailed horticultural interest frequently lasts into retirement; then the maintenance of a detailed layout starts to take its toll, and areas of high cultivation can be reduced again.

Productive gardens
Vegetable gardens and herb gardens are demanding but very rewarding if your interest lies in using plants to produce food, spices, essences or medications. Well-planned sections of gardens, or indeed gardens devoted to vegetables or herbs, can be beautiful, as in the examples below.

Entertaining gardens, *above. Gardens made to serve their users must sometimes contain areas for active entertainment. For adults this often means an area for preparing and cooking outdoor meals and for children a sandpit can have endless attraction. There is no reason why such features should not be a bonus to the garden, as in this example.*

Relaxing gardens *If what you want from your garden is a place for relaxation that requires the minimum of upkeep, then this, too, is within your reach if you take the trouble to plan and build the garden well in the first place.*

How gardens have changed

The modern garden is very much a product of mundane practical considerations for, in the main, the space available is small and the design tempered by the time and money which is necessary to realize it. Gardens in the past were fewer, more spacious, and generally used for more gracious living. Moreover, such gardens were worked by staff. Those gardens which remain and which we visit, once served prosperous families, but running concurrently with them, and now lost to us, was always the laborer's cottage garden. Until the nineteenth century there was little connection between the two social extremes. Only after the Industrial Revolution in England did a middle class emerge which sought to copy grander gardens, albeit on a much reduced scale. The laboring cottager became urbanized, and he too gardened though with produce more in mind than decoration. These two developments converged to produce the garden which typifies suburbia.

A parallel horticultural development, starting in the eighteenth century, had provided an ever increasing choice of plant material, first collected from all corners of the world and then worked upon and hybridized by plantsmen to supply the clamoring horticultural market. Publishers provided volumes (and still do) of weekly and monthly journals to foster this market, and gardening societies were formed to exchange plants and information on their culture. This need for horticultural fact gathered real momentum with the formation of the Royal Horticultural Society in the mid-nineteenth century.

A lack of available labor to maintain the detailed garden altered the course of its development throughout the early twentieth century. However, it was not until the 1950s that any inspired new thinking changed the form of garden layouts in England. The spark which ignited new thought on garden planning originated in the sunny, open-air climate of California, where various streams of thought and circumstances converged to make this change.

The early Californian garden was of Spanish origin, arriving by way of Mexico. This was a garden of shaded patios and cooling sprayed water epitomized in the famed Moorish gardens of the Alhambra in Granada, Spain. A new ingredient was added to meet the twentieth-century requirement of living outside, centered on the swimming pool the fashionable venue of outside life in that climate. The horticultural content of the new garden was low, since the climate limited it. However, when planting was attempted it was often maintained by the Japanese labor which was so abundant and cheap in the 1920s and 1930s on the west coast of the United States. Some essence of the Japanese artistic tradition was inevitably added.

Tradition dies hard, *below. A 16th-century Flemish garden, portrayed in idealized form by Abel Grimmer. The design is attractive and crops abundant but a large work-force is needed.*
Right, view of part of the garden at Sissinghurst Castle, Kent. Though a 20th-century construction, it is traditional in design and requires as much detailed husbandry as its 16th-century precursor.

Japanese traditions had previously influenced the Modernist schools of architecture, painting and sculpture in central Europe. These had migrated to America in the face of Nazi antipathy and came to affect the design of gardens both in the pattern and use of new materials, paralleling the influence of new house designs as well. The best of the gardens which resulted are those of Thomas Church which he completed in the 1940s.

After the dull days of the Second World War, this sparkling emergent style strongly influenced European landscape designers who were employed to enhance new building. The new style, however, had to take on a form more suited to the climates to which it was transferred. In Germany and Scandinavia, for example, the limitations of the winter climate restricted the range of usable plants, and a concern for shape and form outweighed the original demands for color.

In the United Kingdom, where the climate favors a far wider range of plants and the horticultural tradition is strong, the consideration of garden structure beneath the plants was much more discreet. Far more of a stimulus to considering design of the garden was the need to provide small, serviceable gardens for young, growing families on the new housing developments of the 1960s and 1970s. That the realization of even sensitive plans often produced mundane results is a criticism of the emergent garden center which has encouraged standardized materials for universal usage, and brought about the demise of the specialist grower and his discerning range of plant material. The suburban plot has been reduced to a depressing sameness wherever its location.

A marked concern for conservation and building in the vernacular style now spearheads a new approach to the garden, followed by the decreasing time available for garden maintenance because of the ever increasing spectrum of alternative interests. For those who are horticulturally concerned, and there are many millions, the garden will always be a place for growing plant collections, but for the millions more who are not it must become a usable home extension, but outside – a place designed to fulfil a cycle of family requirements furnished with plants. It is plants that will contain and articulate this outside room, giving it style and character. The hard materials for walling and paving must, of course, suit the style and location of the house that the garden serves.

The object of looking at gardens in history is to see how each evolved at a certain time, in a certain place, for the particular use of the family which owned it. That they survived at all is a tribute to their conception, and most of all to their maintenance through the years. A garden is a moving, growing entity and to maintain it in a particular style is an ever growing discipline.

It is at this point that there is an increasing realization that much of our current garden thinking is styled to an outmoded tradition. Does the owner of a small garden want to have to cut a lawn twice a week? And for the small family, with a supermarket nearby, are not bought lettuces, clean and packed, to be preferred to those grown by themselves? Then again, what of holidays and weekends – who maintains and waters the produce?

The undoubted charm of the eighteenth-century garden, which has been aped for so long in garden design, in town as well as country, is being superseded by a new approach, based on usage and available time. However, the modification of planting techniques, such as the mixed border or ground cover planting, is not enough if the underlying design concept is wrong.

And are we right to perpetuate the horticultural approach as a suburban ideal? What is wrong with longer, rougher grass, with plantings of subjects more naturally suited to their surroundings? We have been conditioned to the merits of perfected artificiality and seek horticultural excellence as the only yardstick of a garden's being, when the aspiration of an average gardener's personal paradise is far less discerning and, on a realistic level, a much more relaxed place.

Japanese style, right. *A garden at Okayama, Japan, in which plant forms and colors are sensitively combined with abstract shapes, creating a satisfyingly timeless composition.*

New styles demand new gardens, *below. A 20th-century garden designed by Christopher Tunnard within an earlier garden design. The lines and materials of a new house necessitate designing a new garden appropriate to the changed conditions. Bottom, the Dewey Donnell garden at Sonoma, California, designed by Thomas Church in 1948. The swimming-pool has been brilliantly interpreted in abstract form and works well with the landscape seen beyond.*

Inside-outside living

At first signs of sure sun in spring we (in northern latitudes at least) throw open windows and swing doors wide. Animals and children move naturally from indoors to out and the garden comes into its own as a usable space, realizing a potential which has been lying dormant all winter.

My own basement flat in London had a simple sliding glass door and through most of the summer, from early morning until evening, it was open, linking the small garden with my studio, and making urban life considerably more bearable. When the door was closed, the garden still gave enormous pleasure, even through the winter, when a solitary brave little winter-flowering cherry (*Prunus subhirtella autumnalis*) performed for months on end.

An inside-outside design is one where there is visual interaction of the inside of the house with the garden throughout the year. The link is effective from the depths of winter, when floodlit snow, for example, can look spectacular from the comfort of a warm sitting-room, to mid-summer, when easy coming and going can make the garden an extension to the home, for eating, for play and for entertaining.

The tradition of providing for outside living within a home originated in climates where sunshine is predictable. It started with the tight, enclosed courtyards of the Islamic world in a style which overlayed a previous tradition of the ancient Roman courtyard, or *atrium*. These two sources fused in the Moorish patio of southern Spain, which is a central well of light, enclosed by the stories of a dwelling – an arrangement not dissimilar to the medieval English courtyard. During the summer, much outside living takes place in such patio gardens. They are surrounded at ground level by open colonnades and furnished as a living-room might be, for daily usage. But rather than catching the sun, these outdoor rooms remain cool, being shaded from the sun by the surrounding high walls of the house. A simple central fountain cools the air and the noise of the trickle permeates the building.

This inside-outside Moorish way of life moved with the Spaniards to South America, to Mexico and latterly to southern California, where an enlarged version of the Moorish garden style provided a secluded surround to the fashionable swimming-pool-orientated life of the 1920s. New forms and constructional methods of Modern architecture emphasized light inside the house and allowed for easy movement in and out.

These are the roots and influences of a new interpretation of the garden as an area which extends the inside of a home outside. In summer, such a garden has a physical and visual link between inside and outside space – a link which is enforced by a use of similar flooring materials for both in and out, the use of indoor plants where possible, and furnished external terraces. If you can match colors too, inside and out, the bond is strengthened to give a feeling of increased size.

On the following pages you will find examples of successful designs which link inside with outside and so effectively increase the living area of homes. Some tend to take the feeling of internal decoration outside to balconies or patios, while others bring the style of the garden indoors. Your success in making the link between inside and outside in your own home depends on your willingness to use materials of both indoor and outdoor decoration inventively. And while an opening door allows the easiest movement between inside and outside, views in and out through windows provide similar opportunities for linking inside with outside increasing your use of the garden.

Conservatory feel, *right. Elegant though casual outside living is the theme for this conservatory-type grouping. Foliage complements upholstery, while hard flooring allows for watering through summer.*

Mediterranean terrace, *left. In hot, sunny climates, simple solutions for outdoor seating areas are often successful. The shade provided by a pergola engenders the feeling of total relaxation in summer months.*

Linking inside with outside

When there is nothing but glazing separating room and garden, you have a special opportunity to use the space of the adjoining garden fully. In summer the two are physically linked when you open garden doors. The sense of space remains through winter if the garden is well co-ordinated with the room and itself presents strong visual interest. Garden lighting will continue the effect after dark. An example of converging inside and outside spaces is shown in the photograph, below, where one end of a living room has glazed access to a paved terrace used for casual meals outside in summer. Alternative approaches are shown in stylized diagrams below.

Existing living/garden room *This relaxing room has a large expanse of glass which opens on to a terrace used for dining.*

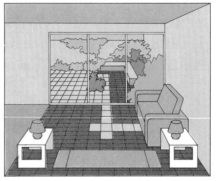

Alternative A, *left. A fully paved garden ideal for entertaining. The concrete slab ground patterning runs from outside, across the threshold, and into the room, linking inside and outside seating areas. Brick paving and matching colored walls emphasize the link.*

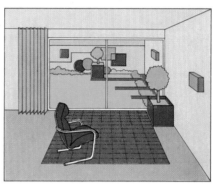

Alternative B, *left. Here, the space outside is designed for visual effect rather than use. The composition is abstract, using broad masses of a single plant, contrasted with clipped trees in square tubs. A mural draws the eye to the far wall beyond a ground design of lawn and paving brick.*

Terrace room, *left. The architect of this town house has used every available inch of space for an occupant who enjoys airiness and plants. Above, outside, is the roof terrace; below, inside, a music room. Both areas are equally full of plants.*

Relaxed outside dining, *right. The proportions of my own dining-room have been extended outside by the use of overhead beams stained to match the woodwork of the folding doors. The same styling is present in the garden furniture.*

Enclosed urban privacy, *right. A jungle of foliage outside your garden door, as in this example, has the effect of obliterating the rest of the world. Such an approach creates an outside living space of mood, atmosphere and fine detail.*

Rural space and light, *below. In complete contrast to the urban inside-outside plan, right, the space of a rural garden, below, allows a crisp, almost spartan approach. The uninterrupted garden view and large area of glass allow enough sunlight to illuminate the design inside perfectly.*

PLANNING
YOUR GARDEN

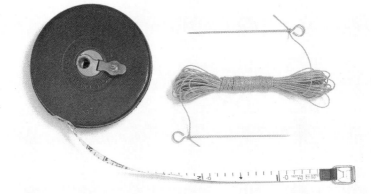

Assessing size and shape

Having estimated a site's potential and decided what you, the user, actually want from it, it is time to put some hard facts about the area on to paper so that you can start to produce a design to work to when constructing and then planting the garden. The first step is to take a blank sheet of paper, or graph paper if you prefer, and start to measure up, or outline survey, your site.

Start at the house. Most houses are built to a regular plan with angles at 90 degrees, so measure up the dimensions of your house working around it from face to face, taking running measurements to the windows and doors as you go, as shown opposite. In this way you will produce an accurate outline of the dwelling.

If you live in an older house which has many odd corners, or ancillary outbuildings, you might find it easier to seek out the deeds of your house. These will include a fairly detailed outline drawing of your property and you can use this as the basis for your measurements. If you have had any architectural work completed you might have a copy of the house plans ready drawn.

Once you have measured up your home, carefully draw up its measurements to a working scale. The scale should be at least 1/100, but preferably 1/50 for the smaller garden. Allow enough space to add the garden boundary around your house outline. The next procedure is to measure the garden. Go outside again and measure lines, or offsets, at 90 degrees to the house to the boundaries of your outside space. If necessary, mark these offsets on the site with string so that you can move down them and take further offsets, again at 90 degrees, to any existing features which are within striking distance. Then work around the lengths of the perimeter of the site, noting the measurements as you go.

If any elements within your garden are left "floating" on your layout and cannot be located by taking 90-degree offsets, take measurements to them from any two points already located. When you draw up your survey you will be able to use a pair of compasses set in turn to each of the pairs of measurements to establish the exact position of such features. This process is known as triangulation (see opposite).

Having established the positions and dimensions of the boundaries and major features of the site, work down in scale measuring the size and relative positions of smaller features including details such as the girth of a tree trunk and the span of overhanging foliage. Note also any internal walls or fences, any steps and manhole covers. Be as accurate as possible to make your survey worthwhile.

You will need to measure and plot any changes of level which may exist within your plot so that you can plan steps or retaining walls (see p. 119). Mark the positions of the top and the bottom of the level change to start with. If the change of level is great, you might need the help of a surveyor, who will quickly give you some spot levels to key points in the garden relating back to a datum or zeropoint, usually coinciding with a threshold into the house. For smaller changes of level, it is possible to take your own measurements by the system known as boning (see opposite). To do this, use a builder's plank, or a light aluminium ladder. The idea is that you measure the vertical descent of the slope against the plank or ladder which is held out absolutely horizontal from the top of the slope. If you cannot reach the bottom of the slope in one go, you can work your way down quite lengthy gradients plank- or ladder-length at a time, adding fall to fall to find the overall drop.

Mark clearly on your survey the direction of north as this will determine the ultimate pattern of the garden. Mark too the scale of your survey since it is all too easy to forget it.

Equipment for surveying and drawing your plan
The simple measuring and drawing equipment shown here is necessary for drawing up an accurate outline survey and then going on to make your garden plan.

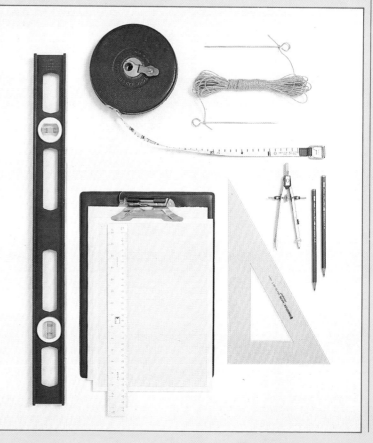

Making an outline survey

A simple survey, like the one shown right, shows all the relevant details of an existing plot, providing the owner with a basis for a new design. It has been drawn up to a scale where one unit of measurement represents a hundred units in the garden. If you can draw your complete garden on to your paper to a scale where one unit represents a smaller number of units in the garden, then do so.

First make a rough sketch of the area on which you can record measurements out in the garden. Ask someone to hold the end of the tape for you, or secure it to the ground with a skewer each time. As you measure offsets from your house to the boundary, make a note of any useful measurement along each one (running measurements).

Having filled in as many measurements as you can, you are ready to draw up the survey, turning your rough sketch into an accurate plan with ruler, set square and compasses.

Triangulation

Measure from any two points which you have already fixed (such as house corners) to any feature which is not within easy reach of a 90° offset. Set your compasses to the measurements required in scale, and make two intersecting arcs to locate the position.

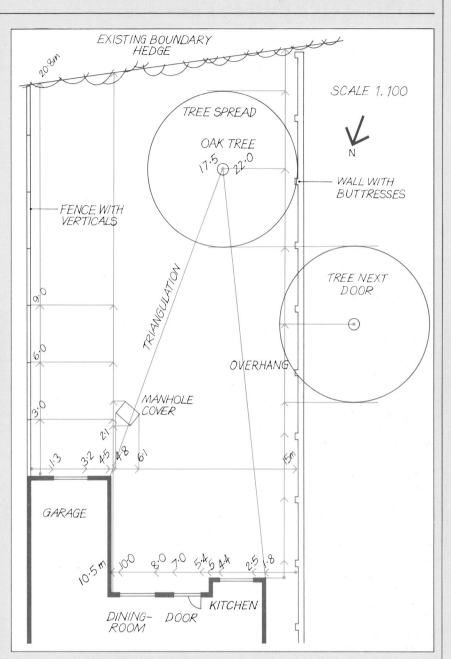

EXISTING BOUNDARY HEDGE

20·8m

TREE SPREAD

OAK TREE

17·5   22·0

SCALE 1. 100

N

WALL WITH BUTTRESSES

FENCE WITH VERTICALS

TRIANGULATION

TREE NEXT DOOR

9·0

6·0

OVERHANG

3·0

MANHOLE COVER

2·1

1·3   3·2   4·5   4·8   6·1   15m

GARAGE

10·5 m   10·0   8·0   7·0   5·4   4·4   2·5   1·8
                                        5

KITCHEN

DINING-ROOM   DOOR

Measuring gradients

To survey a simple slope, a good practical way of boning, or judging the gradient by eye, and so measuring it, is to use a pole exactly one meter long, a plank and a spirit level. Nestle one end of the plank into the ground at the top of the slope and prop it horizontal using the meter pole, sliding it along under the plank as necessary and using the level. The slope falls a meter over the distance from the anchored end of the plank to where it meets the meter stick. Measure this distance. If necessary, repeat the process, moving the end of the plank down to the mark of the first meter stick. Add the vertical measurements and then the horizontal ones to find the overall gradient.

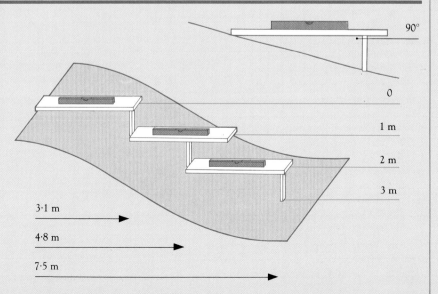

90°

0

1 m

2 m

3 m

3·1 m

4·8 m

7·5 m

Line and pattern

Most people will recognize and relate to a garden which has been laid out formally, others will appreciate a freer-shaped, "natural" layout. In both cases the style of the garden is enforced by the way in which the plants have either been clipped to conform, or allowed to ramble, but the essential character of the design depends on its underlying pattern.

The lines which you use to produce the pattern of your garden plan will eventually mark the edges of the contrasting areas of the layout, whether these are for use as paths and service areas or for ornamental use as lawns and planting areas. Lines which run away from the viewer will make a site appear longer, and if you deliberately converge these (making a path get narrower for example) you will make the garden appear even longer. Conversely, lines which run horizontally across the view will give a site breadth.

Some patterns are static in feeling, others will appear to have movement in them, as can be seen in the examples of pattern below. We should be able to produce the right pattern for the right job. A garden with room for a focal point within its boundaries, or which has a view, will accept a pattern with movement in it. Lines in the pattern should lead the viewer to the view or the object. It is wrong to impose a pattern with movement on a garden if there is no goal for the viewer. Without some focal point his eye will wander aimlessly. On the other hand, a small walled garden area which has no outside interest, needs a patterned layout which will hold the eye within the site, so its design should be static.

There are permutations within these basic rules of course, the same effect being possible using curving lines as well as straight ones. The type of pattern which you use as the

Choosing a pattern

There are endless permutations of pattern, most of which can be adapted for garden planning. Those suggested here are drawn on a square grid so that they are all bound by the same scale. (You will eventually make such a guiding grid for your own garden, as on page 38.) Some of the patterns are in pairs showing positive and negative versions.

Static checkered

Static formal

Abstract

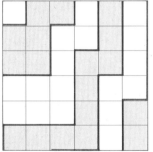

Dynamic

Static abstract

Dynamic diagonals

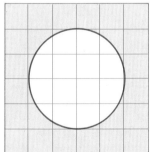

Static formal

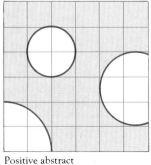

Positive abstract

Negative abstract

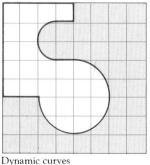

Dynamic curves

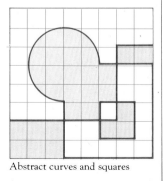

Abstract curves and squares

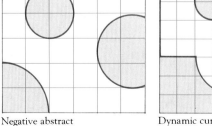

basis of your garden plan will depend on its suitability to the site, considering levels and views, and the period of the building it adjoins. A modern abstracted design, for example, would probably be unsuitable for an eighteenth-century house, while a modern, semi-detached house seldom requires a symmetrical, formal plan.

Remember that small elements, like bricks or granite blocks, can be used for quite intricate patterns, while larger elements of stone or concrete block, are mostly suitable for larger, or simple layouts, if they are not to need expensive cutting. Simpler shapes, too, are easier to fill with plants. Odd corners are seldom easy to fill with any garden medium – hard or soft. But having said that, it is better to think of a pattern first, and then decide how to describe its lines and fill it in. It is too easy to become bogged down at the start in plants and materials and how to use them. The patterns shown opposite illustrate a few possible choices on an idealized square plot. As yet, no decision has been made as to what the lines enclose (paths, planting, lawns or terraces), but each pattern creates a different feel and so will make a different garden. Your garden will have its individual shape and it will have its own character established by many variables, particularly your dwelling. You must try to emphasize this character through the lines you use to make the underlying pattern of your garden.

Dynamic pattern,
The bold lines which formed a simple pattern of interlocking circles, drawn boldly as the basis for a design, are very evident in this impressive garden. They now mark the boundaries of lawn, paths, steps, a plunge pool and planting.

Shape and texture

The lines which you have chosen to create your garden pattern will perhaps produce a satisfactory drawing in plan form. But the ultimate shape of that plan will only emerge as you take it into the third dimension, by planning the heights of different elements, be they walls or changes of level, or soft plantings of trees or shrubs. With these you build up the real shape of your garden so that it becomes a pleasant place to be in.

But what makes one plot a pleasant place to be, and another not, are the shapes and proportions of the grown masses of planted greenery that hold and surround those areas which we use to walk on or lounge in. Further, the shapes and proportions of these planted and non-planted areas can either complement or vie with the other three-dimensional shape on the site – your home.

These proportions, and whether they balance or not, are obvious in older, more mature gardens, where the planted masses –

the trees and shrubs – are established and in front of you. What makes garden planning such a difficult art is that you must try to imagine the planted areas as they will appear in years to come while planting twigs now. It is difficult to grasp that even planners of the great English landscape parks of the eighteenth century had the same problem. They could reshape the landscape in the manner of "Capability" Brown, making lakes and shifting vast areas of earth, but they had to plant out their rolling parks with tiny trees which we see in their maturity more than two hundred years later.

Planted masses, of course, are not the only means of giving a garden shape. Walls, fences, raised beds, even built-in barbecues, mold the proportions of the smaller garden. The materials which you use will affect the feel of the garden considerably, reflecting or absorbing the light, or giving either a hard or a soft finish. However, within each planting

Composing on a small scale
Every grouping of elements in your garden should receive the same attention, however small the scale. Points of interest can be created with simple compositions that contrast shape and texture, like the one shown below. Plants of various shapes and textures are contrasted with a smooth stone or concrete ball.

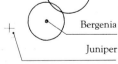

Phormium or yucca

Concrete ball

Bergenia

Juniper

Balancing shape and texture *The plan of this urban garden is bold and simple, holding the eye. The garden presents a green picture from the various levels of the house that it serves. While the firm shape of the design is softened by foliage forms, it is still strongly evident. A weaker layout would have become merely a collection of plants.*

Molding space, *right. In this layout, plants have moulded the space that we peer into through the shadow of foreground planting. The feeling of three-dimensional containment in a garden is important, and it is this aspect which makes a garden an effective retreat.*

area, you must eventually compose groupings, as you will see in the chapter on planting design (see p. 167). The shape of each mature plant and its components (leaves and stems) is not the only consideration; its texture and the quality of light which it reflects or diffuses are also very significant. Consider and compare a rhododendron leaf with that of a camellia, for instance. The rhododendron leaf is flat and dull while that of the camellia is bright and shiny. Multiply this difference by the number of leaves on an average bush and the total adds up to a considerable contrast. Deciduous species (those that drop their leaves in winter) will obviously have less all-year impact, but the appreciation of the tracery shapes and the texture of their bare branches and shoots is an acquired pleasure in winter.

The garden in three dimensions

The shape of your garden is largely created by three-dimensional effects. Space can be molded by the siting and subsequent growth of trees, shrubs and smaller plants. The two examples, below, show how the same site can be manipulated to create totally different effects.

That on the left, termed formal, has a grouping of foliage that holds the eye, the masses of trees and shrubs balancing each other.

That on the right, termed informal, has a grouping of foliage that leads the eye around a central mass and suggests hidden extensions to the garden. In both gardens, foliage (mass) balances the open area (void).

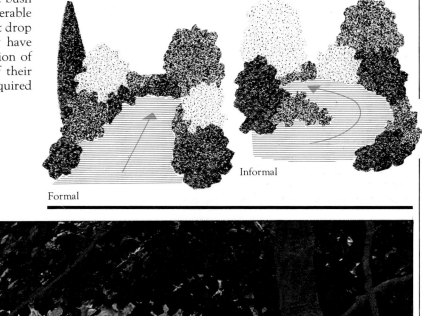

Formal

Informal

Color

Bright splashes of color, which every seedsman's catalogue would have you use, will only last for a limited period, for most plants actually flower for no more than one month in the year. Primarily, you should be concerned with more subtle color – the hues and tones of permanent foliage which last the whole year through. The foliage colors of both deciduous and evergreen shrubs and trees are remarkably varied, and, when well selected, will provide interest and cutting material throughout the year.

The "walls" of your outside room should be a background mass of subtle color. Seen in these terms, you will see that if this color is too strong it can become a disruption to the herbaceous or annual color that you might want to place against the background.

The colors of indigenous flowers are fairly low key in Northern Europe, with soft spring colors giving way to pale early summer ones which intensify through the months until the mellow tones of autumn appear. Harder, hotter flower colors originate in sunny climates, where their intensity is enhanced by the strength of the sun's rays. Be guided by nature and beware of man's interference. Plant breeders and hybridizers now strive to produce the most bizarre-colored varieties from even the simplest subjects. If

Subdued tones, *below. Compare the soft tones and beautifully blended foliage forms of this planting, with the striking blue border opposite. While the initial impact of the soft planting is not so dramatic, the subtle tonal range of this grouping creates a longlasting attraction.*

Theory of color
You should plan colors in the garden with the same care you give to decorating your home. To understand color, it helps to differentiate between hue (a pure color) and tone (a shade of a hue). The relationship of hues can be shown simply on the color wheel, below. The wheel has a warm half (magenta, red and yellow) and a cool half (green, cyan and blue). Hues next to each other on the wheel generally harmonize, while those opposite each other contrast.

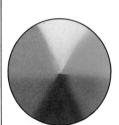

Color wheel

Color harmony

Color contrast

Powerful warm colors, *right. The effect of this strong grouping of* Achillea, Helenium *and* Hemerocallis *is restful, despite the power of its warm colours. The secret lies in restricting the choice of colours to hues from a narrow sector of the colour wheel.*

there is a market for black roses, for example, then cultivators will produce them. Such plants are particularly difficult to use in juxtaposition with others, if they are not to dominate the scene.

Color outside should be used and controlled to back up the function and feeling of the garden, with herbaceous and annual color continuing the effect of your chosen foliage shrubs. Bright yellows and oranges, for example, are stimulating and are ideal in conjunction with a lively activity area. Softer colors, blues and pinks for instance, with a touch of purple or white, will produce a tranquil, calming effect. Both bright, stimulating colors and softer, recessive ones can be used in an area, but the effect should not be a pepper-and-salt one with both types mixed indiscriminately. Locate the strongest

colors within the foreground, and allow the colors to become paler with distance. A brilliant patch of color in the middle of a distant view is bound to be a visual disruption, as well as having a foreshortening effect.

So think carefully of the mood which you intend to underline with color, and when a selection of plants is to be seen against a backdrop of existing vegetation, grade the colors to compose the arrangement. The metallic blues and dark greens, contrasted with silver and gold in an average conifer selection, only produce tasteless discord.

Striking contrasts
The color impact of this border is breath-taking. Pinks and blues predominate, with gray in the selection of herbaceous plants and touches of lemon and white to enliven the whole. The border relies totally on color for its success but it has little form, with no bold foliage to subdue the color contrasts.

Evolving a framework

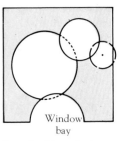

Window bay

Furnished with your original survey (see pp. 28–29) and some basic ideas about designing a garden (see pp. 30–35), it is time to produce your own garden pattern, but to do this you need a framework to guide your design. No design, from that of Concorde down to that of the smallest piece of jewelry, is a random shape plucked from the air.

The most useful framework to use is a grid of intersecting equally-spaced lines. The spacing of the lines of this grid (its "modulation" in design terms) must usually depend on either the structure of your house, or on the boundaries which surround your plot. Study these structures closely, for your purpose must be to relate the scale of your grid to the scale of one or the other, or perhaps both, of these influences.

You might find that the external structure of your house suggests a strong, regular division of space. Look at the house wall facing on to the garden. If it has a formal design, for example, there will be a recognizable rhythm of the measurement which divides its doors and windows. These intervals might suggest the spacing of your grid. Modern houses are often built of pre-fabricated units which will similarly suggest the spacing. Many houses, however, have weaker, asymmetrical designs. If this is the case, it is better to look elsewhere for the scale of your grid.

Walls and fences are usually constructed in a regular pattern with vertical supports at regular intervals, in concrete, wood or brick, infilled with wood or brick. Such a boundary can provide an ideal starting point as you can use the post or pier interval as the spacing for your grid. Many sites will have little else to indicate a framework for the final plan.

To draw your grid, lay a separate piece of tracing paper over your original survey and, ensuring that you are working to the same scale, extend lines across the site starting from your reference points, either at 90 degrees to the house, or to the boundary, whichever you have chosen. Using the same interval which separates each of these lines, overlay another set at 90 degrees to the first set, covering the site with squares.

This square piece of tracing paper should now be used as a guide for positioning elements and creating patterns in your garden. Any pattern which you evolve within these guidelines will have a scale relationship either to the building which it surrounds and serves, or to the fences or walls which bound it. If you later reinforce this relationship by constructing your garden in materials which match those of the house or boundary, house and garden will inevitably link strongly and your design will support a variety of treatments when it comes to infilling the pattern.

When you come to draw the pattern that will be the basis for your garden plan, use the grid as a guide wherever possible, coinciding right-angles with the intersections of the grid lines and using the spacing of the grid as radii for any circles necessary. Although it is best to follow a grid where possible, to achieve a positive and bold plan, you can use your guiding grid in a flexible way. You can divide the squares of the grid in equal proportions, or even turn it through 45 degrees, to accommodate specific features.

Interlocking circles, *right. The pattern of this walled garden is a series of interlocking circles, inspired by the projecting bay window of the adjacent house, as can be seen in the diagram, above. The raised circle is edged in brick and surfaced in gravel with random planting and rock grouping.*

The grid as ground pattern, *below right. Although a grid should be used as a temporary overlay to guide your pattern, here it has been used as the finished pattern of a garden plan. A small area of the garden has been divided into three boxes of contrasting paving and uniform ground cover planting.*

Making and using a grid

The garden frontage of the house, shown right, has some interest, particularly in the projecting wing. However, more dominant is a boundary wall with piers spaced at 1.8-m (6-ft) intervals and these have provided the spacing for the guiding grid of a garden plan. The grid lines do, however, coincide with the important features of the garden elevation of the house as well, making this grid particularly successful. The beginnings of a pattern have been drawn on to the grid, circles and squares being included with equal confidence. It is unlikely that all the existing features of your garden will fit a grid exactly but it is important to establish a discipline for your plan that will encompass most elements of the layout.

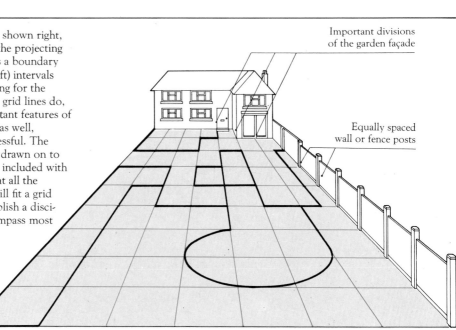

Important divisions of the garden façade

Equally spaced wall or fence posts

Linking house and garden, *above. In this urban garden the guiding grid has emerged strongly, linking the garden to the house façade rather than the public garden beyond the balustrade.*

The plan

On to your grid, which now overlays your basic site survey, you can next prepare to mark the areas that you have allocated for particular functions: the terrace to catch the sun, the vegetable area conveniently near to the house, an accessible area for rubbish bins, a greenhouse, an area of water, the soft fruit area and so on. Their positions will be influenced by convenience, the necessary positions of service paths and any safety precautions necessary for children. However, first you must consider the position of the sun in summer and winter, and prevailing winds, and make sure that you are neither blocking a particularly good view beyond the site, nor conversely, allowing too little room to plant a screen to hide a nasty one.

The positioning of these areas will sometimes suggest an overall pattern for the garden, or at least the run of the designated hard-surfacing. If no shape is forthcoming, evolve a pattern along the lines shown on pages 32 and 33, considering your preferences for regular or curved shapes. Always bear in mind, however, the contrasted effects which differing patterns create and their suitability to your site.

Often the area in which you are working will indicate the sort of pattern needed. A box-like garden, for example, surrounded by walls, will probably need a hard, straight-edged pattern which reflects the character of the site. You can later soften the whole with bold planting to achieve a balanced overall design. Curves generally need more space. Too large a circle within a square, for example, leaves corners which, in garden terms, are both hard to build and later to infill. Certain areas will of course require certain shapes. Although it is possible to cultivate vegetables in a circle, for example, straight rows are much easier to tend.

It is important to realize that all the parts of a garden design must work as a balanced whole, with no left-over corners and with positive balancing negative. The finished design should be clean and open, buildable, and ultimately workable. To achieve this clean, open plan, you must work within the discipline of your grid. Stick to its squares, fitting in angles at 90 degrees. Fit circles into the grid so that they run cleanly into each other and connect with the line of the house or a boundary. You might decide to turn the grid through 45 degrees and plan on the slant from your house and boundaries, or you might decide to divide the squares of your grid in half, thirds or quarters to facilitate a particular shape. But however you manipulate it, your guiding grid will provide an underlying strength to your plan. Your pattern will be positive, with bold sweeps to

Stages of the plan

The finished plan of your garden, shown as stage 4, below right, is achieved after completing stages 1 to 3 as carefully as possible, following the advice on pages 30–31 and 38–39. With this enclosed court-yard garden, stage 1 shows how a guiding grid can be evolved from the position and size of the garage, and the front and kitchen door-ways. Stage 2 shows the grid extended to cover the whole area and notes added on site conditions and potential features. Lines coinciding

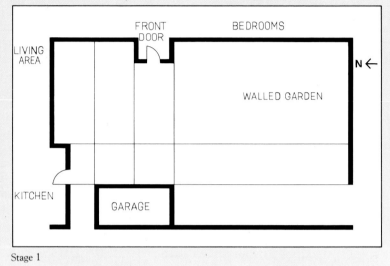

Stage 1

Stage 2

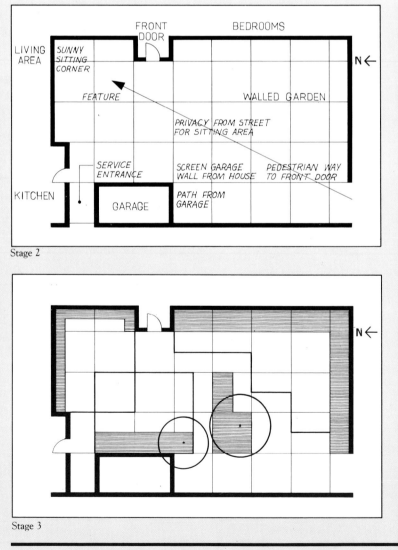

Stage 3

with, or bearing a relationship to this grid will ensure that the features of the garden will eventually bear a strong relationship to the house and garage.

Stage 3 involves the choice of pattern and areas to be planted, surfaced or otherwise given some sort of feature. As the finished plan emerges, decisions such as what type of paving and whether there should be changes of level have to be made. Planting will need further planning (see p. 168).

curves. There will be no weak, wiggling lines in the pattern and when the grid is removed and you draw up your final plan, the pattern will stand on its own as a meaningful shape, broadly encompassing differing functions and areas of activity.

Using a grid to help your design will work for any size of garden and for any style, whether you prefer straightforward traditional patterns, or those which are abstracted or flowing. Try to visualize the garden in a sort of patchwork pattern, with areas of cultivation, of lawn and of paving, rather than inhibiting yourself by too rigid a layout of paths which leave awkward, left-over plots. Your garden should be dominated by areas of attraction which are served by hard surfacing.

Your final working plan will be a two-dimensional guide. Its success will depend on how you have been able to imagine the three-dimensional results of your plan – a procedure that becomes easier as your experience of plants and garden materials grows. The sketched projection, below left, is a representation of my mind's-eye-view of the shape of this garden.

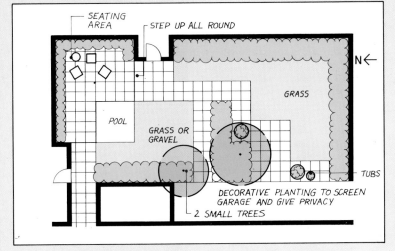

Stage 4

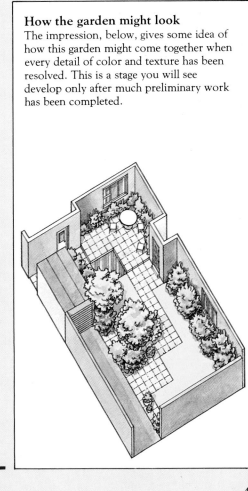

Visualizing the plan
The success of your final plan will depend on imagining the three-dimensional results. Always plan bold masses, resolving the detail as you come to know garden construction and plants.

How the garden might look
The impression, below, gives some idea of how this garden might come together when every detail of color and texture has been resolved. This is a stage you will see develop only after much preliminary work has been completed.

Well-designed gardens

Each garden illustrated in the following pages has been chosen as an example of successful garden planning. They show how the "rules" of good garden design have been used to produce gardens of individuality and character. Each garden is a composition in itself. What makes the compositions satisfying in each case is the effect of hard materials offset by softening planting and the enlivening influence of some sculptural element, often a simple pot or a group of boulders. Each, too, has a theme or a focal point, whether it be water, an outstanding tree or some other eye-catching feature.

The balance between structure and plants in a garden is difficult to achieve, for the horticultural content of a garden constantly changes with growth. Even when established, the balance has still to be maintained by pruning and thinning plants. In the following gardens, the balance is achieved, and its maintenance helped, by a simple garden plan – a crucial factor common to most well-designed gardens. Their outlines, in whatever material they are realized, can be appreciated even if the plan is thickly planted.

Gardens can be appreciated on a number of levels: from a design standpoint, from a horticultural standpoint and from an entirely emotional one. Emotional reaction to gardens is personal, while horticultural appreciation depends on knowledge and an interest in gardening. The appreciation of design, however, is an expression of personal likes and dislikes of a particular composition, for we all react differently to colors, patterns, shapes and textures. Once in a garden the senses of smell and hearing also play a part – the scent of a particular flower, the rustle of bamboo leaves, the singing of birds and the movement and fall of water affects all of us differently. The garden is one of the few art forms that can stimulate all our senses.

Unhappily, we cannot speak with the owners of these gardens, so the nuances of the compositions might elude us. We can only study them, seeking to understand how the elements and their arrangement are successful. But in seeing the use of line, pattern, shape, form and color in the following gardens, remember that your own garden must be planned to satisfy you and your family, and not necessarily others, so aping effective layouts will not be successful. It is up to the gardener to be his own designer, but looking closely at pictures of other people's designs can be an inspiration.

Water garden

This pool, the bridge and all the other, smaller components of the group work together as one sculptural unit and must give enormous pleasure to its owner throughout the year.

The pool is a rectangle, crossed by a timber bridge at right angles to it. The bridge structure is of softwood horizontals laid across metal braces. It is important that such a bridge, with no handrails, is wide enough for the pedestrian to feel safe. One edge of the pool is let into a bricked terrace, laid in a basket-weave pattern with a brick-on-edge surround. The treatment of the concrete pool at this end is informal, with rocks and boulders descending into the water.

The key plants are foreground fescue grass (*Festuca ovina glauca*) with the sword-like leaves of *Phormium tenax* beyond. In the foreground there is *Bergenia beesiana*, with its big, evergreen leaves. The far side of the pond is decorated with a sumach tree (*Rhus typhina*), while to the left of it the distant jar is highlighted against a bamboo (*Arundinaria* sp.).

In design terms the plan is quite formal, but subtle touches such as the counterpoise of the urns and the well-considered plant groupings make the arrangement appear pleasantly informal.

Key
1 *Miscanthus sinensis*
2 *Typha maxima* in pool
3 *Arundinaria* sp.
4 *Rhus typhina*
5 *Festuca ovina glauca*
6 *Phormium tenax*
7 Annual nasturtiums
8 *Bergenia beesiana*

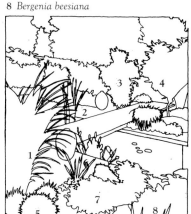

Deck garden

We tend to think of gardens as always being seen from ground level, but many gardens, especially in towns, are seen from above and need both a strong ground plan and plants with large leaves so that one can be appreciated through the other, as in the example above.

The garden, or outside room, illustrated here is constructed in timber and furnished with plants. The sunny part of the garden, against the house, is decked to form both a terrace and a surround to a small pond. The terrace provides a junction between house and garden. Built on to the deck is a low bench seat, which is backed by a herb bed. From this decking, one steps down into a private, outside dining-room, screened from neighbors, with planting areas contained by stained wood retaining walls, which match those of the decking.

The foliage that shades the garden is *Aralia elata* on the left, with *Rhus typhina* on the right. In the right foreground are the gray-green leaves of the perennial *Macleaya cordata*. Water lily pads are contrasted with rushes and water iris in the pond.

This is a designer's garden, for few others would be so restrained in their selection of forms and leaf shapes. A detail of interest is the concealment of the pool edge by the decked terrace. The pool container itself could simply be of fiberglass. Notice also the pleasant small-scale ribbed effect of the stable tile surface to the lower garden. The lesson to learn from this garden is the quiet calm that such a disciplined layout can produce.

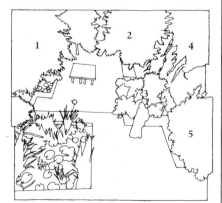

Key
1 *Aralia elata*
2 *Rhus typhina*
3 Small bed of mixed herbs
4 *Polygonum baldschuanicum*
5 *Macleaya cordata*

Suburban garden

This small garden is one in a row adjoining terraced, single story houses, built so that the wall of one house becomes the garden wall of another. Against this wall, a planting area has been retained with U-shaped pre-cast concrete blocks, and another adjoining row used to form a permanent garden bench, which can be provided with cushions in summer. This area looks into a small, private, paved space, bursting with plants and culminating in a single millstone fountain feature, set among boulders. The boulders are laid in a concrete saucer so that the overflowing water is retained and pumped back up through the center of the millstone. Pergola beams successfully divide the garden and frame a view to the small area beyond. A subtle detail that deceives the eye as to the size of the area is a mixing of paving materials. A coarse aggregate concrete block has been used and a pattern of granite works its way through them.

The planting is full and areas of planting interlocking with paving give movement to the garden, and this again makes it appear larger.

Key (plan joins split image)
1 *Miscanthus sinensis*
2 *Picea abies*
3 *Ligularia stenocephala*
4 *Kniphofia* sp.
5 *Arundinaria nitida*
6 Mixed planting including *Pinus mugo*
7 *Koelreuteria paniculata*
8 *Lavandula augustifolia*

Sunken garden

This small, sunken garden makes a handsome and secluded sunbathing area and can also be used for entertaining. It could work in either town or country, at ground level or on a roof. The designer has created a world on its own and, although the central space is open, the area is full of detail. The sympathetic use of hard materials, contrasted with softening plants, has created a visually satisfying balance.

The beds surrounding the central brick area are bounded by pre-cast U-shaped blocks used on their sides. They are wide enough to serve as bench seats. The stained timber detailing of the pergola, fencing and decking path hold the design together, while the subtly placed stones and an old millstone provide low key sculptural features. Such a garden layout would be hard and unsympathetic without a generous planting. The selection of plants is mainly evergreen for year round interest, though the deciduous weeping silver birch (*Betula pendula* cv.) makes an attractive feature even without its leaves.

Key
1 *Pinus sylvestris*
2 Mixed shrubs including azaleas
3 *Berberis* sp. with *Sambucus* sp. behind
4 *Betula pendula* cv.
5 *Armeria maritima*
6 *Lavandula augustifolia*
7 Brick paving in basket-weave pattern
8 Old millstone
9 Stained softwood timber decking

Long, thin garden

The long, thin terrace site is a difficult shape to design satisfactorily. Some gardeners mistakenly try to resolve the problem by reducing a larger garden layout in scale to fit the site. This, however, creates small, unrelated patches of interest within too confined an area, whereas on a larger scale areas of grass or other surfacing would have held the concept together.

The designer of this 18 × 6 m/59 × 19 ft garden has taken the site as a whole and created a serpentine meander through it, providing an outside "room" for family use and another for play at the far end. The two are linked by strong architectural planting, which contrasts well with the hard paving materials and camouflages neighboring houses, to provide a real extension to the house.

A low seating wall of U-shaped concrete units also divides the two areas. The foreground space is paved with pre-cast concrete blocks, which run to the sanded play area. The latter is retained by timber sections, set in concrete.

The plant selection will look well throughout the year. Clumps of bamboo, sustained by, and combined with, tall summer grasses, are used to provide evergreen screening to the fence. The small tree with a sculptural quality on the left of the concrete seat is a cut-leaf sumach, *Rhus typhina laciniata*. In the middle distance is a shade-loving, large-leaved *Hosta glauca*.

The success of this small garden design stems from the balanced but generous arrangement of hard textures with soft planting infill, and a simple, yet positive, working layout.

Key
1 Sandpit
2 Herbaceous plants with roses
3 *Rhus typhina laciniata*
4 *Cotoneaster simonsii*
5 Paving interspersed with brick
6 Azaleas, *Arundinaria* sp. and trailing plants

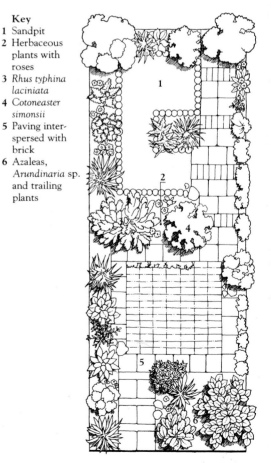

Shaded water-garden

Two raised areas of water make a visual center for the small, shaded town garden, shown above, that backs on to the rear wall of a neighboring dwelling. The design perfectly illustrates how to make a virtue out of necessity.

The layout is an abstract pattern of interlocking rectangular shapes in brick, though with the addition of a change in level. The plan culminates in a terracotta bust, offset by the painted, neighboring wall.

This simple subtlety in design works so well because it combines a carefully conceived modern plan with traditional materials that provide an attractive feature – the raised pools. The edges of the pools also provide casual seating. Planting in such a location is difficult because of shade and dripping rainwater from the over-hanging trees, but ferns and mosses (growing on the left) do well in these conditions, as does bamboo. The positioning and form of the foreground shrub, a cotoneaster, offsets the shape of the pools. The only hard material used is brick.

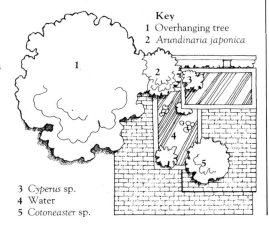

Key
1 Overhanging tree
2 *Arundinaria japonica*
3 *Cyperus* sp.
4 Water
5 *Cotoneaster* sp.

Front and rear town garden

The pattern of the small rear garden in this Milanese example has been turned at an angle of 45 degrees to the house, to work round a pear tree and thereby make what would have been a dull little garden into something quite unusual. There are many interesting corners which are not only servicable but make stimulating, abstract patterns of wood and water, centered on pieces of metal sculpture. The whole is designed to be appreciated not only from within the garden space but from the house.

The designer has used only two materials in its construction, giving the layout added strength: wooden block paviers and disused railway line ties and large, rounded cobbles. The cobbles have been used in such a way as to deter small children.

The railway ties have been used to form retaining walls, a bridge and a bench seat, and to provide an attractive end "wall" which also serves to screen a rubbish area by the far boundary. Unplanted, such a hard treatment might be thought overscaled, but when fully planted the relationship between hard and soft materials is fully balanced. Much of the planting is evergreen for year round interest, with bold clumps of foliage working with the ground pattern – fatsias, camellias,

bergenias, rhododendrons and variegated *Hedera colchica* have all been incorporated with ferns (which are not evergreen) in the shaded corners. The rampant climber, *Parthenocissus tricuspidata veitchii* grows through the far boundary fence and provides brilliant color in autumn.

The frontage to this house is narrow but it is full of interest. The color is warm and welcoming and the garden plan is essentially a path straight to the door, but circulating round a large piece of sculpture. The same sort of wood blocks have been incorporated as in the rear garden, but they have also been used with granite blocks.

Key

1 *Parthenocissus tricuspidata veitchii* on fence
2 *Iris pseudacorus*
3 *Ilex* sp., rhododendron and variegated *Hedera colchica*
4 Large pear tree
5 *Fatsia japonica*
6 *Yucca* sp., *Chamaerops humilis*
7 Camellias, *Hydrangea macrophylla*
8 Pots of bulbs and summer bedding

Rear garden

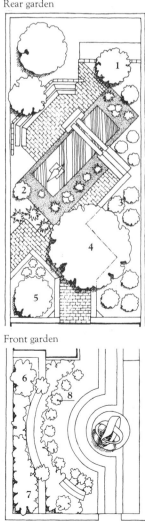

Front garden

Above and top, rear garden
Right, front garden

Park-side garden

Most of the gardens illustrated in
this section are of European
origin. Their designs are impeccable
– designs that work in a constructional sense and in the use of
plant material in conjunction with
the layout. There is, however, a lack
of variety in their planting since
cold continental winters inhibit
many plants that can be grown in
the British Isles and regions of
similarly mild winters.

It is the abundance of plant material
in English gardens that cold climate
visitors find so attractive. Then,
too, there is a more relaxed approach to garden design in the
British Isles. This comparatively new garden in central London
illustrates both points.

The setting is grand and monu-
mental, for the crescent of houses,
of which this is one, are of early
19th-century origin though with
obvious 18th-century influence.
Any gardening in the shadow of this
type of structure calls for a strong
layout if it is not to appear insignificant. The plan is therefore a
simple checkerboard of brickwork,
on the scale of the house, infilled
with stone paving or grass. It was
originally intended that the grass
area should be of consolidated
gravel, but the designer's client
thought that grass, a continuation of
the ground medium of the communal garden beyond, was more
appropriate. To strengthen the
bond with the communal garden,
balustrading crosses the garden so
that the two appear to be joined.
The planting, though heavily shaded
by trees, is full and, in the traditional English manner, is a bold
mixture of masses, seemingly
bursting from their confining beds.

Key
1 *Laurus nobilis*
2 *Cordyline australis* in pots
3 Old pear
4 Mixed planting in light shade

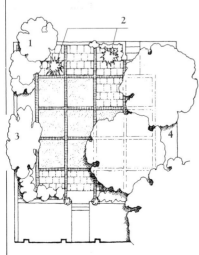

GARDEN-BY-GARDEN GUIDE

Gardens of different shapes, sizes and styles with
alternative possibilities for their design

*Alternative suggestions for plants in cold climate
gardens are included*

Small walled garden

You can grow an extensive range of plants in a small, walled garden, particularly if it catches the sun. The garden illustrated below is a good example of what can be achieved within a limited space. The view is from the upper story of the house, showing the garden's profusion of flower color. The high view-point also shows how the terrace is divided from the rest of the garden.

Both treatments opposite show the space opened up to provide a broader view of the planting when the owner is sitting on the terrace or within the house at ground-floor level. In the top suggestion the pattern is turned at 45 degrees to the house, so that a meander is created in the design; the end of the garden is lost but the eye is led to a piece of sculpture.

The lower suggestion is a more formal design but the view is again stopped, this time by a pergola running across the area. An arresting feature is provided by a timber bench surrounding the tree sited half-way down the lawn. Both designs provide a paved edging so that foreground herbaceous material can overflow.

Enclosure and abundant planting *This garden has old-world charm with its mass of flower color and its feeling of seclusion. The terrace is enclosed and has a relaxed feel with plants allowed to spread into the jointing of the random stone.*

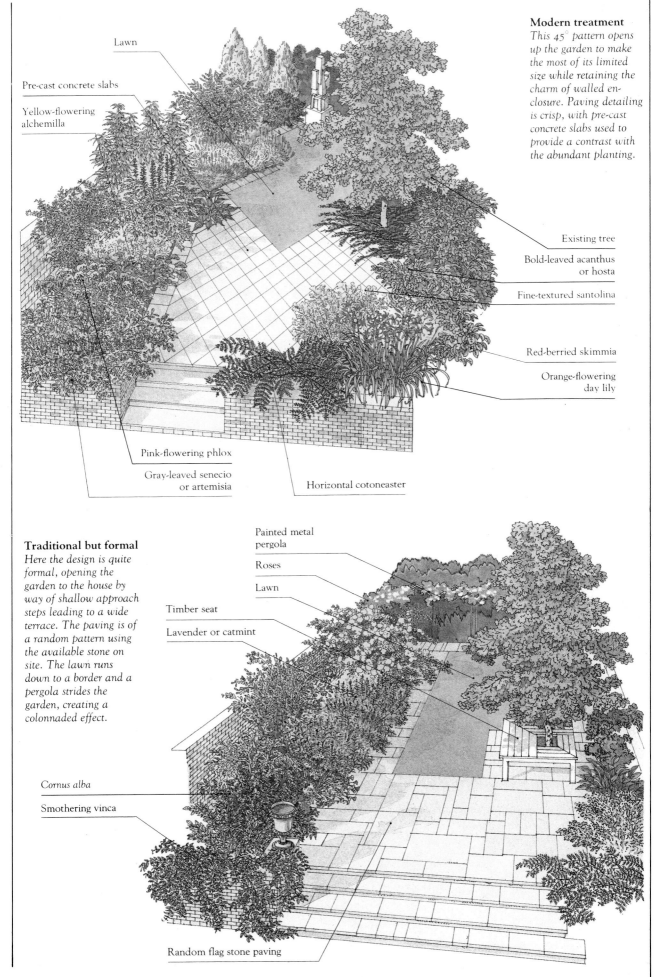

Lawn

Pre-cast concrete slabs

Yellow-flowering
alchemilla

Modern treatment
*This 45° pattern opens
up the garden to make
the most of its limited
size while retaining the
charm of walled en-
closure. Paving detailing
is crisp, with pre-cast
concrete slabs used to
provide a contrast with
the abundant planting.*

Existing tree

Bold-leaved acanthus
or hosta

Fine-textured santolina

Red-berried skimmia

Orange-flowering
day lily

Pink-flowering phlox

Gray-leaved senecio
or artemisia

Horizontal cotoneaster

Traditional but formal
*Here the design is quite
formal, opening the
garden to the house by
way of shallow approach
steps leading to a wide
terrace. The paving is of
a random pattern using
the available stone on
site. The lawn runs
down to a border and a
pergola strides the
garden, creating a
colonnaded effect.*

Painted metal
pergola

Roses

Lawn

Timber seat

Lavender or catmint

Cornus alba

Smothering vinca

Random flag stone paving

Spacious room outside

The garden to this house is a true outside room, for it connects directly to the building and is the only outlook from the windows. Vegetation provides shelter and privacy, so that the space is conducive to outside use.

The garden is slightly sunken, so that there is a step down to it from the boarded decking that adjoins the house. Beds, surrounded by brick paving, have been arranged to provide a small flower garden. Such a layout might with equal effect have been employed as a herb garden or, if the gardener were interested, a model vegetable garden.

The treatment in the top example, opposite, enlarges the decking area, which now projects into an area of water. Stepping stones cross the pool to a sitting bay, which is covered with a timber pergola over which a Russian vine grows. Planting includes a proportion of evergreen, with yellow spring-flowering *Cytisus* sp. and *Genista* sp.

The proposal below comprises a progression of brickwork bands, with tightly-packed granite paving between. Planting, which includes gray-leaved *Santolina* sp. and *Senecio* sp. with purple-leaved *Berberis* sp., runs through the pattern bands to give a staggered effect. The garden culminates in an L-shaped bench, facing towards the house. Tubs of blue-flowering *Agapanthus* sp. punctuate the design.

"Window" planting areas *The shape of the garden beds and the brickwork employed in this design resemble the wall and windows of a Romanesque church when seen from the house.*

Including water and a pergola, *right. In this proposal, the decked terrace has been extended to project into a pool. The pergola encloses an intimate space for summer use.*

Plan

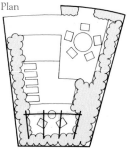

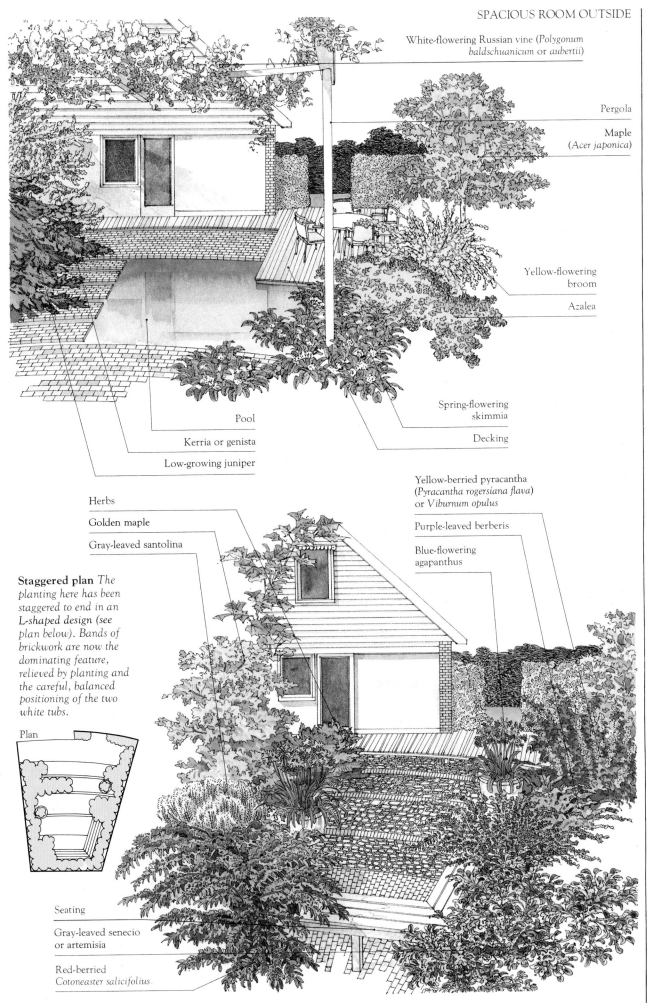

White-flowering Russian vine (*Polygonum baldschuanicum* or *aubertii*)

Pergola

Maple (*Acer japonica*)

Yellow-flowering broom

Azalea

Spring-flowering skimmia

Decking

Pool

Kerria or genista

Low-growing juniper

Herbs

Golden maple

Gray-leaved santolina

Yellow-berried pyracantha (*Pyracantha rogersiana flava*) or *Viburnum opulus*

Purple-leaved berberis

Blue-flowering agapanthus

Staggered plan *The planting here has been staggered to end in an L-shaped design (see plan below). Bands of brickwork are now the dominating feature, relieved by planting and the careful, balanced positioning of the two white tubs.*

Plan

Seating

Gray-leaved senecio or artemisia

Red-berried *Cotoneaster salicifolius*

55

Town garden with a backdrop

This town garden ends by the rear wall of a garage, which has been made the backdrop and focal point of the layout by extending a pergola from it to cover a decked terrace. The pool on the left has a raised stone surround; general surfacing is of granite blocks. Plants include foreground *Ilex* on the right, which face the large leaves of *Vitis coignetiae*. Bamboo (*Arundinaria* sp.) and Portuguese laurel make up much of the remainder of the planting.

The top layout opposite has a strong gridded pattern, which harmonizes with the proportions of the pool and garden. The ground pattern is composed of precast concrete slabs (the color of the stone pond surround), with an infill of brick to match the garage construction. Most of the existing evergreen planting remains, but a low species of *Cytisus* is included at the end of the pond. The Russian vine that masks an ugly height transition with neighboring buildings at the end of the garden in the existing design is replaced with a contorted hazel (*Corylus avellana* 'Contorta'), backed with pyracantha.

The garage in the lower proposal remains the focal point in the design but it has been further incorporated into the layout. Planting to screen the garage includes *Malus floribunda* on the right hand side, with evergreens in front; on the other side of the garden, behind the pond, are grouped *Rhus typhina*, with *Viburnum plicatum* in front. Perennial planting before them includes iris, and aster for autumn interest. At the rear of the garden, hellebores are planted in the shade, with small-leaved golden ivy that will grow up to cover the garage. The garden is then furnished with tubs of bright annuals and bulbs for early spring effect.

Backdrop as a feature
This garden terminates at the rear of a garage and in the existing design the roof of the garage has been extended to become a pergola over a decked terrace. The idea is a good one and works well to provide a private seating area within a small garden.

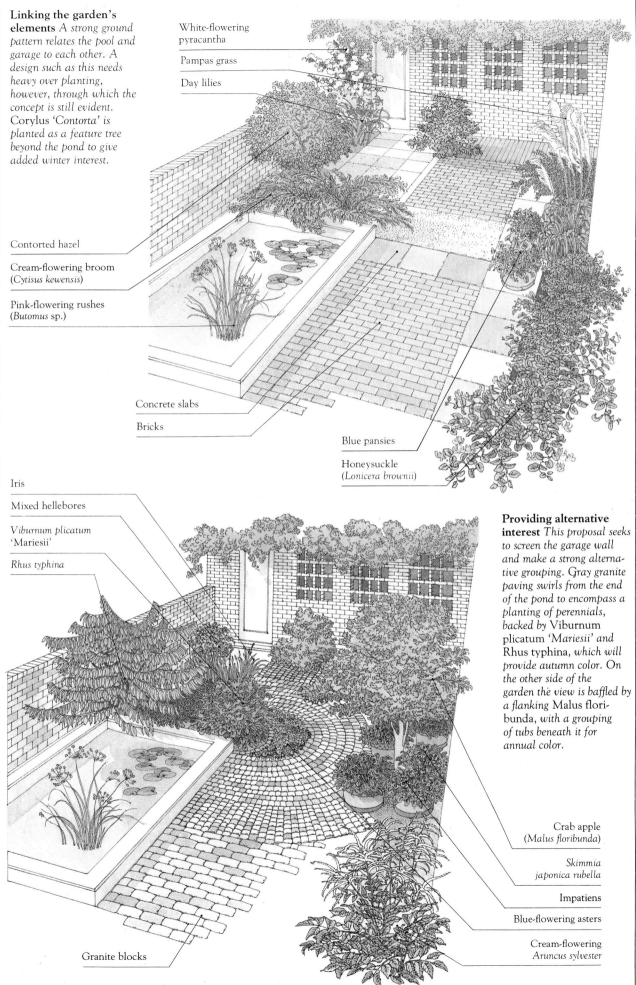

Linking the garden's elements *A strong ground pattern relates the pool and garage to each other. A design such as this needs heavy over planting, however, through which the concept is still evident. Corylus 'Contorta' is planted as a feature tree beyond the pond to give added winter interest.*

White-flowering pyracantha

Pampas grass

Day lilies

Contorted hazel

Cream-flowering broom
(*Cytisus kewensis*)

Pink-flowering rushes
(*Butomus* sp.)

Concrete slabs

Bricks

Blue pansies

Honeysuckle
(*Lonicera brownii*)

Iris

Mixed hellebores

Viburnum plicatum 'Mariesii'

Rhus typhina

Providing alternative interest *This proposal seeks to screen the garage wall and make a strong alternative grouping. Gray granite paving swirls from the end of the pond to encompass a planting of perennials, backed by Viburnum plicatum 'Mariesii' and Rhus typhina, which will provide autumn color. On the other side of the garden the view is baffled by a flanking Malus floribunda, with a grouping of tubs beneath it for annual color.*

Crab apple
(*Malus floribunda*)

Skimmia japonica rubella

Impatiens

Blue-flowering asters

Cream-flowering
Aruncus sylvester

Granite blocks

Woodland garden

The cultivated section and wild areas seen from this garden are clearly defined by the strong line of the hedge that divides the two. Natural woodland acts as a backcloth for the plant forms within the man-made garden and so creates a sense of seclusion and contrast.

In the proposal opposite below, the garden is made completely open to the woodland beyond with the removal of the distant garden planting, so that features are made of the silver birches (*Betula* sp.) and the trunks of the oak trees (*Quercus* sp.). The shape of the lawn is softened so that the cultivated grass disappears into the shadow of the woodland, with an outpost of "wild" garden planting (foxgloves) on the right. In spring, bulbs and later bluebells will grow in the areas of rough grass. With careful lighting, this garden could look magical at night.

When a boundary line must be defined, such an open solution is not feasible. In the proposal opposite above, silver birches have been established nearer the garden to link the natural woodland and the cultivated area even though the boundary hedge remains. Additional planting of wild grasses to the right repeats the original foreground planting but otherwise the distant garden planting has been removed to allow woodland and garden to blend. The far boundary is a single wire that allows a view through to the woodland.

Even though the woodland may not be part of the property, it is the "borrowed landscape" (features beyond the confines of the garden that provide visible background) of the garden. Few town gardens have so spectacular a backdrop as this but you can often reveal a view of a church tower or a neighbor's tree, simply by clearing the foreground. In attempting to create a view, however, be careful to maintain the privacy of your garden.

Contrasting garden and backdrop *The small, raised bed, the rectangular shape of the lawn and the shapes, forms and flower colors of the plants chosen, deliberately separate the existing garden from its woodland setting. The cultivated garden appears to be a protected, exotic area.*

Disguising the boundary When a boundary line is absolutely necessary in such a setting, woodland planting can be introduced into the garden to soften the division between garden and surrounding woodland. Here the dwarf, fastigiate conifer has been removed from the foreground raised bed to allow a clear view of the nearest silver birches.

Wire boundary line

Wild grasses

Repeated grass

Wooden container

Assorted alpines

Removing the garden boundary Here the boundary hedge has been removed to open the view to the woodland and to allow the garden to flow naturally into tree shadow. The foreground grasses and the raised bed – a feature of the "cultivated" garden – have been removed to make way for plant forms that extend the woodland feel right up to the house.

Foxgloves

Silver birches

Sedums

Areas of rough grass

Alchemilla mollis

Pinks

Mimulus or Veronica sp.

Entrance garden

The entrance to a house can give clues about its occupants. Two factors influence this. As a general rule, the bigger the garden the less welcoming it appears, much as a large office with a single occupant seems intimidating. The second and most crucial factor, however, is the peripheral planting. If it is low and well-spaced, allowing an uninterrupted view to the house, the effect is welcoming. Conversely, tall, bunched planting that encloses the house gives the impression that the owner is unsocial. However, privacy may well be what you seek and this has been achieved in the garden below. The composition of structures and planting works throughout the year, with a mass of foliage established to hide the greater part of the house. An urn on a plinth makes a feature that points out an entrance way and marks the way to the narrow, but perfectly adequate, entrance path.

An isolated characteristic that will give a welcoming feel to your home is a wide access path, such as that shown in the top proposal opposite. The wide path has been enhanced by the use of alternate paving textures while the vertical line provided by conifer planting helps integrate the house with the garden. Other planting in this proposal is a mixture of the existing scheme with some new plants. The low-clipped hedging and ground cover masses to the left of the path have been retained, for example, while horizontal-growing junipers now edge the path on the right to emphasize the new width.

In the lower proposal, the entrance path has been opened out completely. Steps have become platforms, the shapes of which are repeated in ascending masses of clipped boxwood (*Buxus* sp.). To counteract the strong structure of the approach, multi-stemmed birches have been incorporated to soften the planting and to increase the scale of the design.

Private entrance, *below. If you seek privacy, this massed planting is effective and gives year-round cover and interest. Planting roughly balances the area of forecourt and the well-detailed path. Since the house is purposely masked and the entrance path is not deliberately linked with the front door, the effect suggests seclusion.*

Widening the approach, *right. The feeling of hospitality is strengthened by wide steps that give the pathway more importance in comparison with the low hedging on both sides of it. The fastigiate conifers that replace part of the original massed planting have the visual effect of joining the house to the garden.*

Reddish-purple maple

Low-clipped barberry

Fastigiate junipers

Horizontal-growing juniper

Low, shrubby pine

Small-leaved ivy

Spiky yucca

Random paving

Horizontal-growing juniper

Welcoming effect, *below. The effect here is very welcoming, for now the entrance path has been opened out completely and consists of platforms rather than steps. Both the use of a single paving material, brick, and the raised bed of scarlet impatiens, take the eye straight to the entrance way.*

Multi-stemmed birch

Raised bed with scarlet impatiens

Clipped box

Cobbles

Basket-weave brick paving

61

An enclosed corner

There is usually one favored corner in a garden, however small, that catches the sun the whole year round. You are lucky if your house is sited at such an angle that this corner is adjacent to it. Many have to make a sitting place to catch the warmth at a distance from the house and such an example – an enclosed corner – is shown below.

The ground rises 450 mm (18 in) into a corner formed by brick wall. In the existing design shown in the photograph, railway ties have been used to make the stepped levels into the corner. Stone slabs cross the levels and also provide a base for the timber seat. The warm tones of the brickwork are repeated in the mass of low shrub and perennial species. These mingle on the different levels to produce a patchwork of color. Such a country-garden-style mass can soon get out of hand, however, if the ground-covering species are not rigorously thinned each autumn.

The two alternative treatments for such a corner, illustrated opposite, show how sharply contrasted moods can be created by the selection and the location of plants to complement new structural elements. Any alternative treatment must be tempered by the existing conditions of the corner. You must choose plant species that like both warmth and a dry aspect because the foundations of the wall will soak up moisture. Bear in mind also that the strong root runs of certain species make them inappropriate for planting too close to walls.

The treatment you choose depends very much on the location of your garden. The summerhouse corner might best suit a town garden for it is crisp in its detailing, while the Japanese-style garden would be suitable anywhere if the style harmonizes with the rest of the garden.

While the existing country-garden selection of plants is of low, circular, colored forms, the summerhouse planting has a combination of larger circular forms contrasted with the stronger forms of evergreens and the summerhouse itself. The Japanese composition is altogether linear and, though low key in color content, has great visual interest throughout the year because of the strong forms of the plants used.

Country-garden corner *The existing country-garden corner is more random than the alternatives suggested opposite. Its effect depends on a massed carpet of aromatic prostrate perennials and shrubby herbs. The shrubby material includes thymes of various colors, low white lavender and fastigiate rosemary. Perennial gold creeping veronica forms a base for the tiers of wallflowers. Purple and silver variegated ajuga feature strongly. Much of the planting is evergreen, giving continued interest through the seasons.*

Summerhouse corner *The stepped levels to the summerhouse are in brick to match that of the walls. The canopy itself is tiled and the timber structure painted white. The lower level of loose gravel is planted with self-sowing perennial alyssum, while the shrubs and climbers are full and rounded to soften the hard lines of the walls, paving and building. The colors are soft; white, gray and a touch of blue.*

Fastigiate conifer

Ceanothus or dwarf Korean Lilac

White rambler rose

Large-leaved climbing ivy or clematis

Warty barberry or cistus

Low-trailing *Vinca minor*

Engineering brick

Spiky white-flowering libertia or day-lilies

Gravel

Spiky phormium or yucca

Japanese effect *The Japanese layout depends on the contrast between structural lines and the shape and form of plant material. Planting includes a craggy sumach, fronded bamboos and the drop of the branches of a small weeping willow which are repeated by wisteria flowers in season. The stepped levels and the seating platform are made up with railway sleepers but the infill is of cobbles. These elements combine with a water container to make a zig-zag of incidental interest.*

Weeping willow or 'Red Jade' crabapple

Craggy sumach (*Rhus typhina*)

Large-leaved bamboo

Blue-flowering tree wisteria

Railway tie

Loose cobbles

Low bamboo (*Arundinaria* sp.)

Large-leaved hosta

Luxuriant rural garden

This old garden runs parallel with the house and slightly above its base level. Instant character is provided by the dominant old apple tree at one end, which plays host to a profuse rambler rose. Shrubs on the right, facing the house, have become large and include a good proportion of evergreens.

In this situation, the gardener who wants to redesign his garden should accept the surrounding planting but rethink that at ground level. A modern layout would be discordant; far better to extend the old feel of the garden by turning it into an ecological area in which insects and birds are encouraged to find a home, and this is the purpose of the proposal, opposite top. For the young family especially, there is much to be said for a garden in which berries attract birds and various planting provides a sanctuary for small creatures. In my ecological garden a saucer-shaped pool has a stony

beach running down to the centre of it, giving access to the water; a grass path surrounds the pool and beyond, under the apple tree, a grouping of grasses provides good, natural protection for small creatures.

Alternatively, this garden could be revitalized to enhance its old world feel. More of a feature is made of the apple tree in the lower design by surrounding its base with a bench seat painted white. The right-hand side planting has been thinned and then extended. Perennials include traditional plants of phlox, aster, lupines and delphiniums together with low-growing herbs such as sage, chives and rue.

Traditional feel *The charming existing garden has reached a full-blown maturity with all of its plants grown to large proportions. There is a fine line between a mature garden and an overgrown one and any revitalization should be carefully considered if the original has charm.*

Ecological garden, *right. This version of the garden is planned to be attractive to wild life. The surrounding planting of grasses and berrying shrubs, such as Cotoneaster sp., is to attract birds, while flowering perennials will encourage butterflies and other insects. Foreground planting includes bold masses of Sedum sp., Helleborus sp. and Iris foetidissima for winter interest and to provide animal food.*

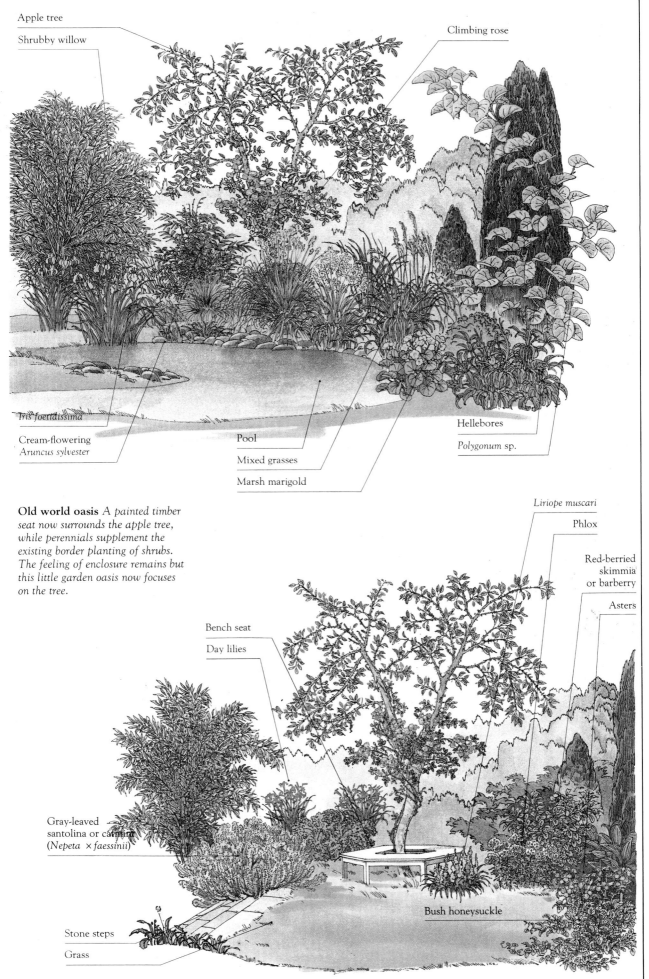

Apple tree

Shrubby willow

Climbing rose

Iris foetidissima

Cream-flowering
Aruncus sylvester

Pool

Mixed grasses

Marsh marigold

Hellebores

Polygonum sp.

Old world oasis *A painted timber seat now surrounds the apple tree, while perennials supplement the existing border planting of shrubs. The feeling of enclosure remains but this little garden oasis now focuses on the tree.*

Liriope muscari

Phlox

Red-berried
skimmia
or barberry

Asters

Bench seat

Day lilies

Gray-leaved
santolina or catmint
(*Nepeta* × *faessinii*)

Stone steps

Grass

Bush honeysuckle

65

Small courtyard garden

This modern atrium-type house has a central courtyard overlooked by all its rooms. From the existing planting of ferns and Japanese anemones (*Anemone japonica*), one would assume that it receives little light. The central shrub is a *Forsythia* sp. and all the plants are growing in gravel.

The existing garden area has been treated to provide an all-year visual feast. Such an enclosure, if it is to be treated as a garden, can be very exciting, for the conditions here are quite different from a normal exposed site. The courtyard has a micro-climate with still air warmed by heat from the house in colder weather. If it also receives sun, the vegetation in this environment can be exotic. A temporary roof in the winter would give extra protection.

The alternatives, opposite, treat the enclosure as an outside room for children's play or a water fantasy. The plan for a play area makes supervision from the adjoining kitchen easy and I have extended the tiled kitchen unit on the garden side of the window as a standing for plants and provided a small table at which children could sit. A sandpit could eventually be turned into a small pond. The rest of the area is paved, but slightly sunken so that the surrounding step becomes a seat, protecting the glazing from wheeled toys.

An entirely different feel has been achieved in the second possibility by making the whole enclosure a mirror of water, reflecting light into the house. The pool is lined with the same tiles as the kitchen and the water flows through individual tiles raised up on integral pillars.

A central feature is a bed of white *Iris laevigata*, with an underplanting of weed to keep the water clear. A few brightly colored koi carp, a mass of simple fountain jets or underwater lights for night-time will all help to bring the area to life.

A courtyard garden *In a courtyard garden such as this where plants are so minutely observed from all angles, it is asking a lot of them to provide continual pleasure and interest throughout the year. Strong and exotic plant forms pull this off though. Here ferns provide strong leaf shape against grasses and cobbles on a shingle bed.*

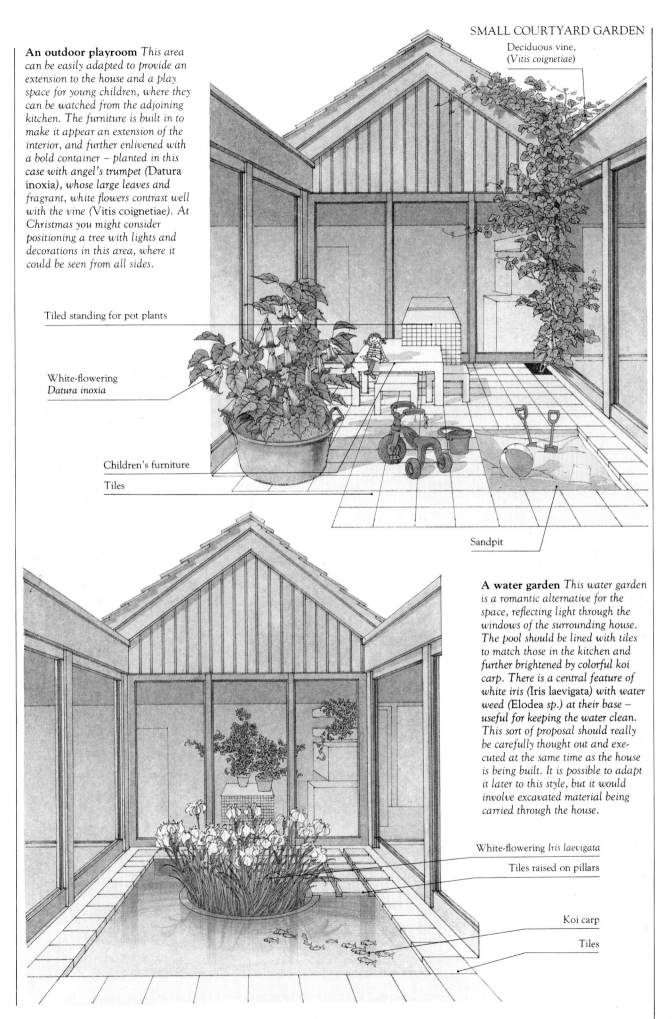

An outdoor playroom *This area can be easily adapted to provide an extension to the house and a play space for young children, where they can be watched from the adjoining kitchen. The furniture is built in to make it appear an extension of the interior, and further enlivened with a bold container – planted in this case with angel's trumpet (Datura inoxia), whose large leaves and fragrant, white flowers contrast well with the vine (Vitis coignetiae). At Christmas you might consider positioning a tree with lights and decorations in this area, where it could be seen from all sides.*

Deciduous vine, (Vitis coignetiae)

Tiled standing for pot plants

White-flowering Datura inoxia

Children's furniture

Tiles

Sandpit

A water garden *This water garden is a romantic alternative for the space, reflecting light through the windows of the surrounding house. The pool should be lined with tiles to match those in the kitchen and further brightened by colorful koi carp. There is a central feature of white iris (Iris laevigata) with water weed (Elodea sp.) at their base – useful for keeping the water clean. This sort of proposal should really be carefully thought out and executed at the same time as the house is being built. It is possible to adapt it later to this style, but it would involve excavated material being carried through the house.*

White-flowering Iris laevigata

Tiles raised on pillars

Koi carp

Tiles

67

Divided rural garden

This typical English garden was probably made 40 or more years ago, for the surrounding trees are mature. Gardens at that time were usually divided, with lawns and flowers near the house and a greenhouse and possibly a small vegetable garden beyond. Such an arrangement can produce extremely attactive results when the elements of the garden are linked by luxuriant foliage and when there is adequate dry paving connecting the various sections of the "working" garden – the vegetable and herb area beyond the greenhouse – to the house.

The two accompanying views, opposite, show how such a garden could be altered, though still within the original context. The top proposal is for a paved herb garden,

working well with the greenhouse. A lattice plan of brickwork is infilled with further brick panels, alternating with brushed concrete. A raised brick pond is a focal point in the concept. The beds are filled with herbs, while the foreground barrel contains chives for a variation in plant forms. This layout makes the garden a lovely, scented place in summer, busy with bees, and will also provide an attractive, enclosed area in winter.

The lower design is a layout suitable for a modern cottage garden. The angles of the greenhouse roof have been repeated in the foreground metal arch and then again in the staggered pond and the path leading through the garden. This angularity is contrasted with soft, flopping herbaceous plants.

Separate lawn and greenhouse areas
View of a traditional English garden of the inter-war period, with grass at the rear of the house leading to a transitional greenhouse area with a vegetable patch beyond.

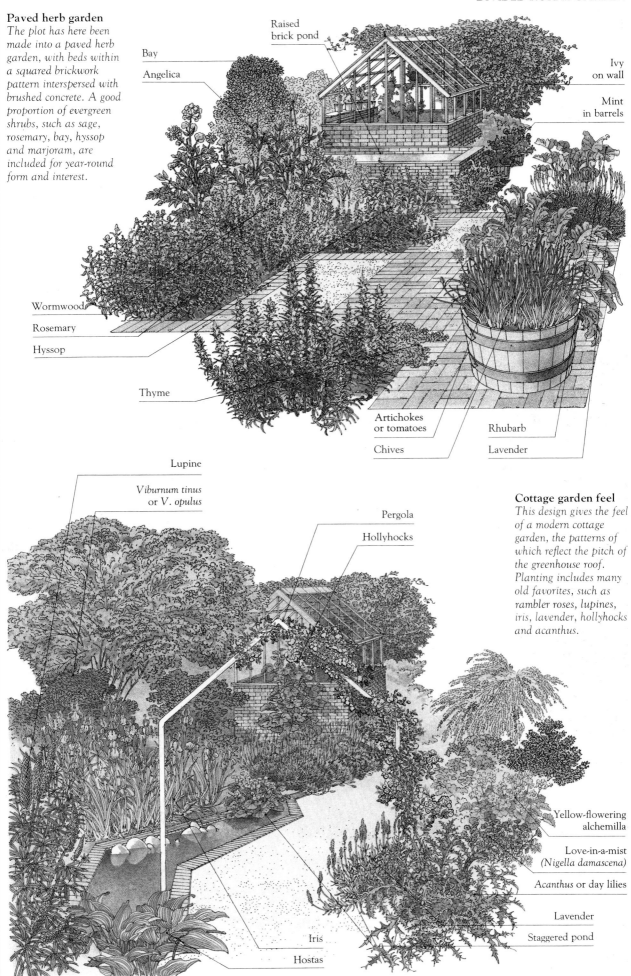

Paved herb garden
The plot has here been made into a paved herb garden, with beds within a squared brickwork pattern interspersed with brushed concrete. A good proportion of evergreen shrubs, such as sage, rosemary, bay, hyssop and marjoram, are included for year-round form and interest.

Bay

Angelica

Raised
brick pond

Ivy
on wall

Mint
in barrels

Wormwood

Rosemary

Hyssop

Thyme

Artichokes
or tomatoes

Chives

Rhubarb

Lavender

Lupine

Viburnum tinus
or *V. opulus*

Pergola

Hollyhocks

Cottage garden feel
This design gives the feel of a modern cottage garden, the patterns of which reflect the pitch of the greenhouse roof. Planting includes many old favorites, such as rambler roses, lupines, iris, lavender, hollyhocks and acanthus.

Yellow-flowering
alchemilla

Love-in-a-mist
(*Nigella damascena*)

Acanthus or day lilies

Lavender

Staggered pond

Iris

Hostas

Sheltered corner

This small segment of a garden adjoining a house is enclosed and south facing, forming an attractive, sheltered corner. The area appears sunken as there is a surrounding retaining wall that creates an L-shaped raised bed to enclose the pool and waterfall. The scheme works well by combining a private section of garden with an area that also gives views to the garden and countryside beyond.

The proposals opposite completely separate the corner from its surroundings, to create an outside room screened for shelter and privacy. Both proposals retain the raised bed of the original to preserve the feeling of enclosure. The retaining wall is built of abutting U-shaped pre-cast concrete units, laid on their sides so that a shelf is provided for casual seating. In the example, top, similar concrete units have been used to provide an occasional table, and wooden screening in the mood of the existing structure baffles the view to provide extra seclusion.

The lower design makes more of the seating area with the addition of a wooden pergola, cantilevered from the existing timber surround to provide a canopy that hosts climbing plants

Major elements of the existing planting have been retained, but the top design has a simpler overall plan while in the lower suggestion the area is enclosed with dense evergreen planting to give additional shelter and a greater feeling of privacy.

Strong three-dimensional shape, *below. This sunken, sheltered corner adjoining a house is largely taken up with a pool and its waterfall inlet. An intermediate level has been created as a seating area. Structural elements and planting combine to provide a wealth of visual interest.*

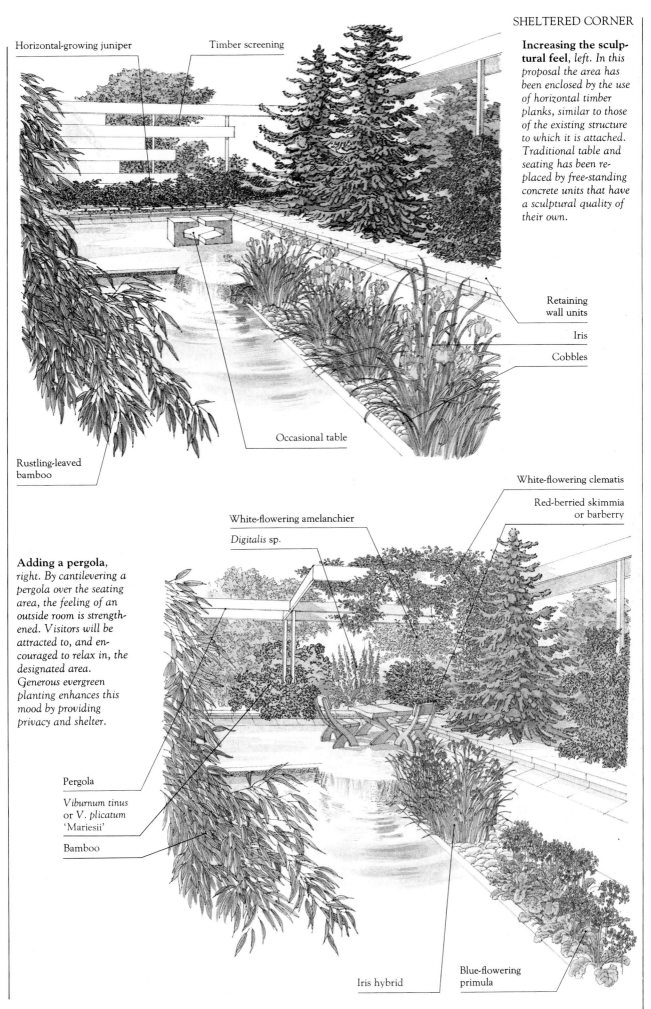

Horizontal-growing juniper

Timber screening

Increasing the sculptural feel, *left. In this proposal the area has been enclosed by the use of horizontal timber planks, similar to those of the existing structure to which it is attached. Traditional table and seating has been replaced by free-standing concrete units that have a sculptural quality of their own.*

Retaining wall units

Iris

Cobbles

Occasional table

Rustling-leaved bamboo

White-flowering clematis

Red-berried skimmia or barberry

White-flowering amelanchier

Digitalis sp.

Adding a pergola, *right. By cantilevering a pergola over the seating area, the feeling of an outside room is strengthened. Visitors will be attracted to, and encouraged to relax in, the designated area. Generous evergreen planting enhances this mood by providing privacy and shelter.*

Pergola

Viburnum tinus or *V. plicatum* 'Mariesii'

Bamboo

Iris hybrid

Blue-flowering primula

71

An unusual frontage

A small area of planting to offset the public façade of your house, and to lead to an entrance, is often a tricky one to design and plant, for the result must be satisfying the whole year round. If there is a gateway its appearance introduces another problem.

The existing frontage, below, has a garden area a little more than a meter wide. The gateway and fencing which back it are both as simple as possible in stained timber – a treatment in total sympathy with the uncompromising house façade. Planting is subordinate to the strength of the structures although the plant forms are helped by a "mulch" of large cobbles and pebbles. Name plate and latch are admirably clear and are illuminated at night by the well-positioned lighting pillar.

Any alternative treatments for this situation must also work in sympathy with the house frontage, perhaps softening it, but certainly not starkly contrasting with it. They should be eye-catching and strong in form,

utilizing plants that will stand the wear-and-tear of a situation alongside a busy path.

The two alternatives shown opposite both have strong visual elements close to the gate. The top version incorporates a small area of water, while below, the attraction is a sculptural grouping in timber, including a squared lighting pillar. In both examples, planting has been kept largely maintenance-free. The rising line of the planting towards the façade is also a constant factor. In this way the strong horizontal line of the house balcony is broken, when viewed at eye level, by the taller planting.

A modern front approach, *below. This front garden has simple fencing and paving to match the strong lines and tones of the house façade. The planting is lightweight by comparison.*

Introducing water, *right. Here the fencing is retained but the timber extended in simple trip rails to prevent people from walking into the small formal pool. The linear paving is also retained with the inclusion of a strip of cobbles which further protects the water. Planting between the water and the house has strong form and color, the leaves of stag's horn sumach (Rhus typhina) contrasting with a horizontal juniper (Juniperus sabina tamarscifolia) and the shrubby willow.*

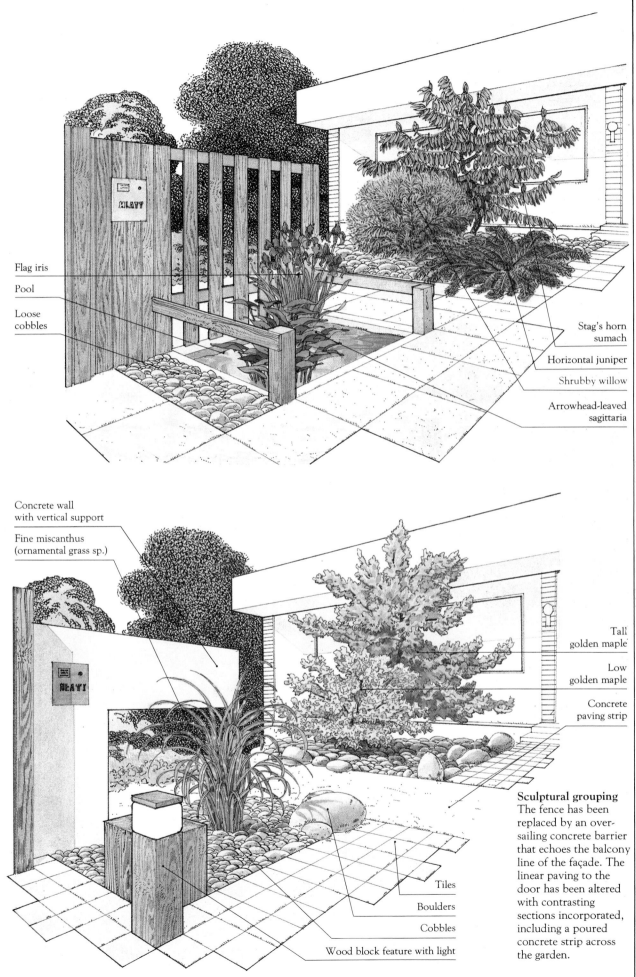

Flag iris

Pool

Loose
cobbles

Stag's horn
sumach

Horizontal juniper

Shrubby willow

Arrowhead-leaved
sagittaria

Concrete wall
with vertical support

Fine miscanthus
(ornamental grass sp.)

Tall
golden maple

Low
golden maple

Concrete
paving strip

Tiles

Boulders

Cobbles

Wood block feature with light

Sculptural grouping
The fence has been
replaced by an over-
sailing concrete barrier
that echoes the balcony
line of the façade. The
linear paving to the
door has been altered
with contrasting
sections incorporated,
including a poured
concrete strip across
the garden.

73

Garden with a view

The garden with an imposing view has its own set of design problems. The example below highlights some of them. A pool has been chosen as the link between the garden and the country beyond and the result is dramatic. The far banking of the pool forms an invisible boundary. A small sculpture of a hawk, a bird of the countryside beyond, placed centrally on the far edge of the pool, further links garden and countryside. In such a situation the gardener has to decide on the balance between the attraction of the foreground garden planting and the attraction of the view beyond. This balance is altered by revealing more or less of the view and by altering the strength of the pool composition in relation to the whole.

The two proposals opposite show alternative arrangements. In the top example, the foreground detail has been cleared so that the far bank line has much of the feel of the hills beyond. The sculpture is now set higher and to one side so that it counterpoises the prospect against planting that complements the view without detracting from it.

The lower proposal reduces the width of the view. Larger planting on the left has been designed to create a feeling of the country encroaching into the garden. This planting is of garden forms of indigenous genera, such as shrub roses. In the left foreground, the stag's horn sumach (*Rhus typhina*) is a good compromise between rural and "domestic" plants and acts as a foil to a simple fountain.

The existing pool
Water can make an attractive transition between garden and countryside. Here the detailing of the pond is natural, with boulders used to make an informal surround.

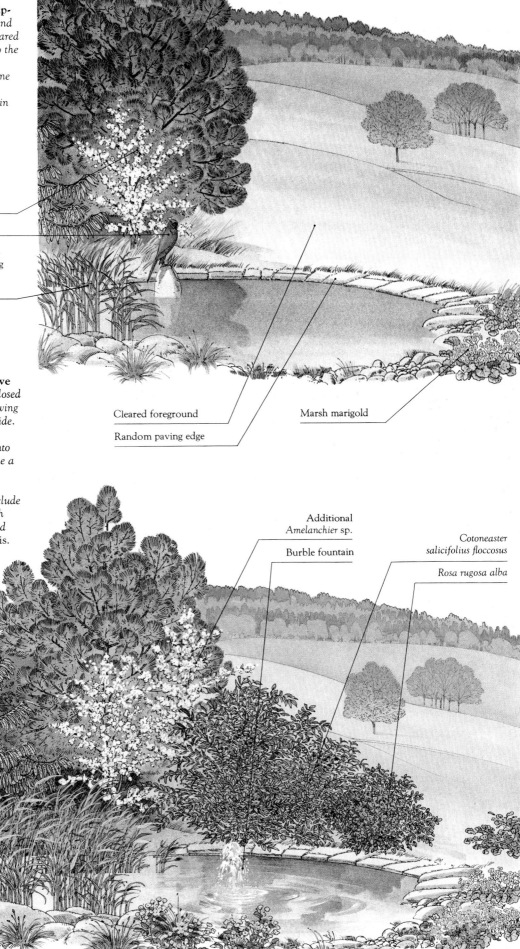

Counterposed sculpture, *right. Foreground details have been cleared to open the garden to the view, with the bird sculpture placed to one side to balance it. Planting remains as in the original.*

Existing white-flowering *Amelanchier* sp.

Bird sculpture

Existing summer-flowering rush (*Butomus umbellatus*)

Fountain alternative
The view has been closed on the left, thus drawing the eye to the other side. Planting has been allowed to intrude into the garden and frame a simple fountain. In addition to Rhus typhina, *subjects include* Helleborus *sp., with* Amelanchier *sp. and* Arundinaria sinensis.

Cleared foreground

Random paving edge

Marsh marigold

Rhus typhina

Additional *Amelanchier* sp.

Burble fountain

Cotoneaster salicifolius floccosus

Rosa rugosa alba

75

Flight of steps

Steps are expensive to build but, when well sited and well finished, give a garden added interest. All too often, however, gardeners economize, making steps too narrow and too steep. A flight should be a sculptural feature, leading you from one area to another or welcoming you and your guests when used as a house access.

The view below is of a meandering flight of steps, surfaced with cut granite and with a wood retainer forming the riser. The strong horizontal line of the steps contrasts well with the vertical shapes of the grasses and plants on either side. A light fitting has been added as an incidental feature that leads you on while providing nightime illumination.

An alternative treatment, top right, has gravel on the step treads and allows planting to flow into the landings, with boulder groups making the finished result more sculptural. The design center right is suitable for the entrance to a house, incorporating name plate and lighting. By turning some of the steps, added interest is given to the arrangement. The shallow retaining wall provides a casual seat and offers a measure of privacy to the garden beyond.

The steps in the example bottom right are more ornamental and incorporate a waterfall feature, which can be easily worked from a small, submersible pump located in a reservoir at the foot of the flight.

Random steps *These steps are well proportioned, being neither too long nor too steep. The textured surface, retained by timber verticals, makes them safe in all weathers and additionally the flight is lit for night use. Vertical plant forms have been chosen to complement the horizontal lines of the steps.*

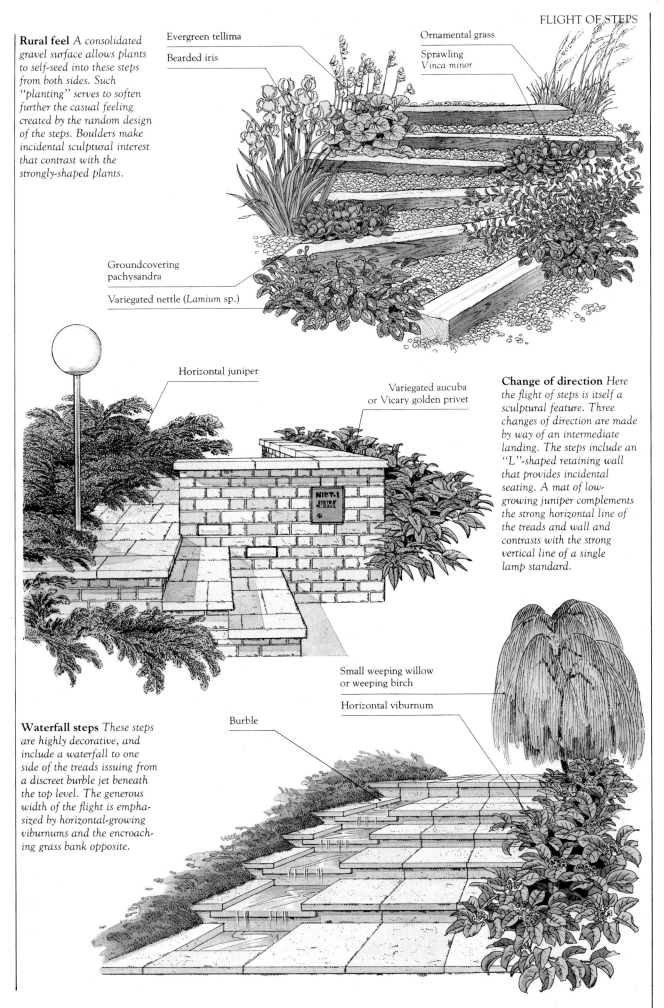

Rural feel *A consolidated gravel surface allows plants to self-seed into these steps from both sides. Such "planting" serves to soften further the casual feeling created by the random design of the steps. Boulders make incidental sculptural interest that contrast with the strongly-shaped plants.*

Evergreen tellima

Bearded iris

Ornamental grass

Sprawling *Vinca minor*

Groundcovering pachysandra

Variegated nettle (*Lamium* sp.)

Horizontal juniper

Variegated aucuba or Vicary golden privet

Change of direction *Here the flight of steps is itself a sculptural feature. Three changes of direction are made by way of an intermediate landing. The steps include an "L"-shaped retaining wall that provides incidental seating. A mat of low-growing juniper complements the strong horizontal line of the treads and wall and contrasts with the strong vertical line of a single lamp standard.*

Small weeping willow or weeping birch

Horizontal viburnum

Burble

Waterfall steps *These steps are highly decorative, and include a waterfall to one side of the treads issuing from a discreet burble jet beneath the top level. The generous width of the flight is emphasized by horizontal-growing viburnums and the encroaching grass bank opposite.*

77

Garden with a barn

An old barn is a great asset in a garden, not only for storage but to provide a feature in its own right. Too often a barn's potential is not fully realized, however, for some garden plans underplay this useful, and often attractive, addition. The solution is to fashion the surrounding garden to suit whatever function you want the barn to perform. In the photograph below, the garden's main feature is a barn with a corrugated iron roof. The barn is used as a retreat and as a place for storage. Whatever the original function of the barn, it is now very much part of the garden plan.

My two alternative designs, opposite, are aimed at strengthening the link between the barn and the rest of the garden. The top design uses the barn as a shelter and background to a swimming-pool. Barns and swimming-pools belong to different eras and careful planning is necessary if they are to tie together satisfactorily. The barn structure has been given greater emphasis by adding an ornamental turret. The roof has been tiled and the walls are now in brick. This material is used again in the square patterning of the terrace which surrounds the swimming-pool and which is then infilled with concrete poured *in situ* and finally given a brushed surface finish.

The lower proposal retains a rural feel and the planting is larger to create a sheltered corner in which to sit or sunbathe. Older-style plants with gentle forms and shapes enhance this mood. Both proposed designs have strong ground patterns that are evident through the plantings and features. These patterns emanate from a regular grid based on the spacing of the piers or walls of the barn so both layouts are bound to link garden and barn strongly. In the pool-house variations I have gone so far as to leave the grid complete as a ground pattern in paving brick.

An integrated rural feature *An old barn, such as this with a corrugated iron roof painted black, can either be a handsome addition or an eyesore in a garden. To combine the two successfully, ensure that your planting harmonizes with the structure.*

Pool-house variation, *right. In this rather extravagant proposal, the barn has become a pool-house. This new function is at odds with the character of the building but some restyling makes it work in harmony with the swimming-pool. Planting, which includes cypresses, phormiums and pelargoniums, strengthens the link.*

Cypress or juniper 'Skyrocket'

White-flowering
rambler rose

Spiky phormium
or yucca

White-flowering buddleia

Plumbago capensis
or Jackman clematis

Red-hot pokers

Yellow-flowering
koelreuteria

In situ concrete

Paving brick

Swimming-pool

Scarlet-flowering
pelargoniums

Enhancing the rural mood, *below.*
Planting in this example, which in-
cludes pyracanthas, lilacs and irises,
dominates the structure to enhance the
rural mood and provide a sheltered area
for sitting or sunbathing.

Red-berried pyracantha

Verbascum olympicum
or day-lilies

Mulberry

Blue-flowering
wisteria

Brick edge

Euphorbia wulfenii
or *E. epithymoides*

White-flowering shrub rose

Lemon-flowering potentilla

Iris

White-flowering
lilac

Yellow-flowering
alchemilla

Walled side-garden

One of the less pleasant aspects of many town gardens is the narrow section of ground at the side of the house which provides a link between front and rear. It is invariably a wind tunnel and mostly in the shade. Often the area is used to store rubbish and sometimes fuel, such as logs. Whether to incorporate the area decoratively into the rest of the garden is a difficult decision depending on the width of the passage way and the sort of view into the rear garden that is possible. If the passage is narrow, you might block direct access with a gate to give security to the rear of the house and to conceal household storage. If, as below, the side area is wider

there is an opportunity to create an enclosed area with its own character, or to incorporate the area into the rear garden.

The existing side-garden has been roofed over with a pergola in stained softwood. The paving is of granite blocks laid in a brick pattern. The house wall, to the left, projects to a timber extension about which the rear garden space turns to the left out of view. The side garden we see is passage-like since it is not specifically tied to the rear garden. In both the alternative treatments for the space, illustrated opposite, the side-garden has been considered as part of the rear garden, so apparently opening out the space available.

Enclosed walkway
Closely-spaced pergola beams and plant-supporting wall battens, stained to match, increase the feeling of enclosure in the existing side-garden. Yellow rudbeckia and incidental color in containers combines with sprawling planting to block the view to the rear wall of the garden.

Radiating pattern *A small planting area at the base of the vertical support for the rear roof canopy has been used as the center of a radiating pattern which extends into the side-garden. Spiky phormiums punctuate the center of the pattern and, from this, brick paviers have been laid in straight courses that diverge with distance. The resulting gaps have been infilled with random-size cobbles to match the cobble infill adjacent to the house wall. The angles of the pergola horizontals above echo the radiating pattern below. A paved space has been allowed for dustbins. Planting augments the strong ground patterning with a pampas grass (Cortaderia selloana) featured among the cobbles.*

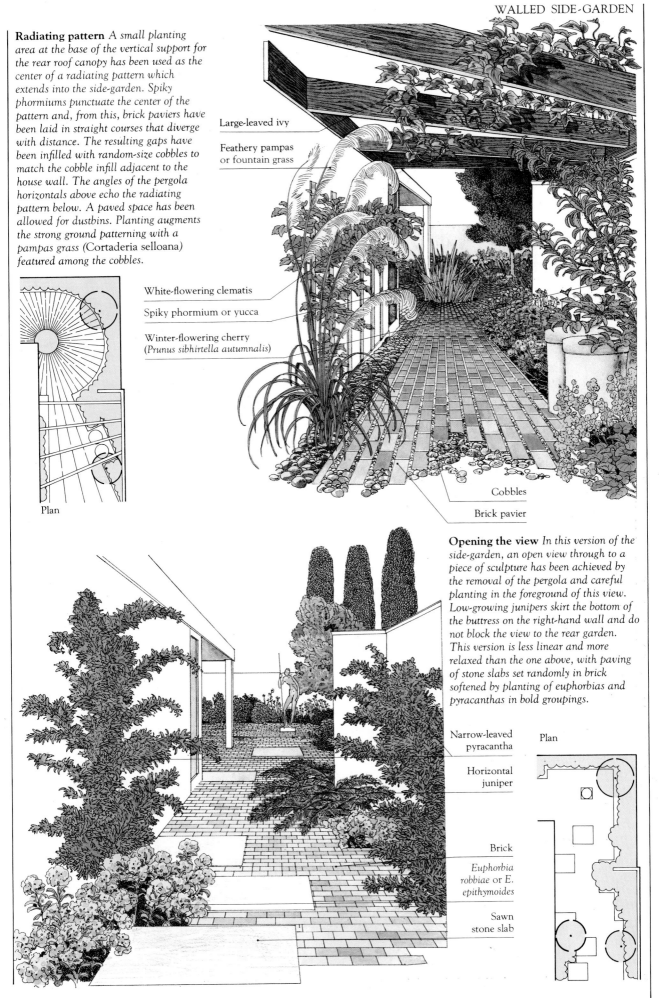

Large-leaved ivy

Feathery pampas or fountain grass

White-flowering clematis

Spiky phormium or yucca

Winter-flowering cherry (*Prunus sibhirtella autumnalis*)

Plan

Cobbles

Brick pavier

Opening the view *In this version of the side-garden, an open view through to a piece of sculpture has been achieved by the removal of the pergola and careful planting in the foreground of this view. Low-growing junipers skirt the bottom of the buttress on the right-hand wall and do not block the view to the rear garden. This version is less linear and more relaxed than the one above, with paving of stone slabs set randomly in brick softened by planting of euphorbias and pyracanthas in bold groupings.*

Narrow-leaved pyracantha

Horizontal juniper

Plan

Brick

Euphorbia robbiae or *E. epithymoides*

Sawn stone slab

81

Square garden

A square garden, such as the one shown below, presents itself to the viewer in one go and so a bold and simple design is particularly important. The existing garden is well-used with features made of the terrace and a small raised pond. The terrace commands a view of the pretty, old-fashioned planting that surrounds areas of lawn.

I have tried to draw the layout together in the two proposals opposite. The top design is dominated by curves. A radiating brick pattern in front of the raised pool and a curved sweep of lawn tie the new terrace to the existing one, where brick is now used to form a step. Strong, curving shapes need equally bold clumps of planting.

If you do not like curves or if you want a more architectural shape to your garden, the second idea may provide the solution. This comprises a series of interlocking squares, culminating at the raised pool. Use a gravelled surface instead of grass if you are anxious to avoid heavy gardening, and then allow certain plants, such as hosta, day-lily, bergenia and ornamental grasses, to soften the effect by growing through it to make generous clumps.

Piecemeal charm, *left. This is a garden that has developed over a long time. Its original planting is now a foil to new features, such as the foreground terrace and a pond that is similarly raised, but within a brick surround.*

Interlocking squares, *right. Here, an overall effect is achieved by using brick squares. Gravel rather than grass forms the surface, in which plants can be allowed to seed themselves. Planting is full, with this mid-summer view showing the successful use of bulbs and annuals within a framework of perennials. Interest and form throughout the year are provided by the two Prunus subhirtella autumnalis, Viburnum plicatum, and the evergreen planting.*

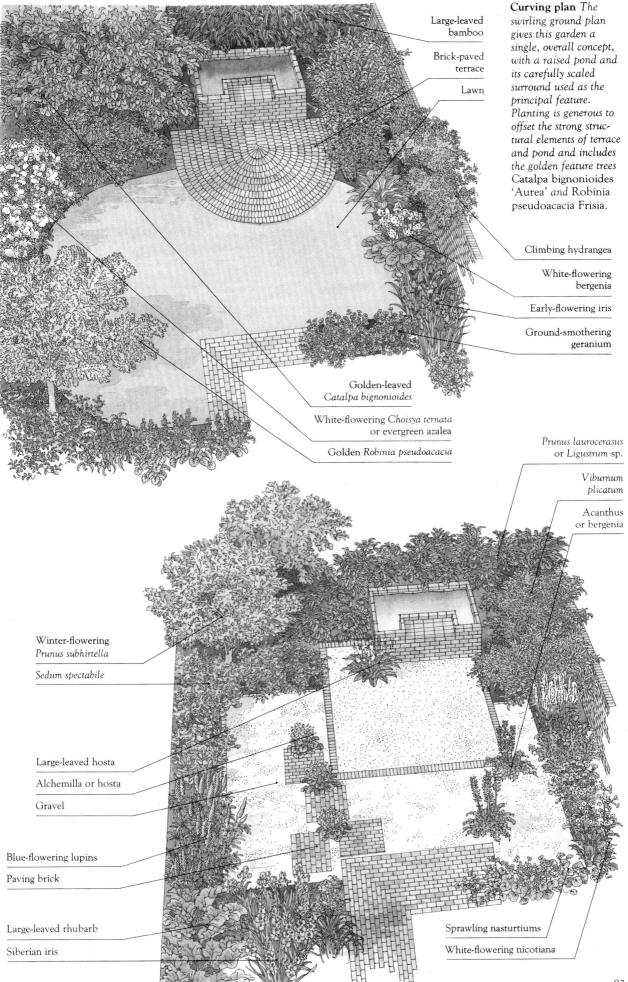

Curving plan *The swirling ground plan gives this garden a single, overall concept, with a raised pond and its carefully scaled surround used as the principal feature. Planting is generous to offset the strong structural elements of terrace and pond and includes the golden feature trees* Catalpa bignonioides *'Aurea' and* Robinia pseudoacacia Frisia.

Large-leaved bamboo

Brick-paved terrace

Lawn

Climbing hydrangea

White-flowering bergenia

Early-flowering iris

Ground-smothering geranium

Golden-leaved *Catalpa bignonioides*

White-flowering *Choisya ternata* or evergreen azalea

Golden *Robinia pseudoacacia*

Prunus laurocerasus or *Ligustrum* sp.

Viburnum plicatum

Acanthus or bergenia

Winter-flowering *Prunus subhirtella*

Sedum spectabile

Large-leaved hosta

Alchemilla or hosta

Gravel

Blue-flowering lupins

Paving brick

Large-leaved rhubarb

Siberian iris

Sprawling nasturtiums

White-flowering nicotiana

Terraced garden

The architect of this modern house excavated an area outside, both to form a garden and to provide light for the lower rooms. Surrounding the chief dug-out area, terraced steps have been constructed and retained by vertical timber posts sunk into the ground. The planting is of ericaceous species that have their own charm, with various conifers that punctuate different levels of the garden.

The garden design at the top of the opposite page tries to bridge the visual gap and provide a plant scheme matching the excitement of the house. For example, Italian cypresses (*Cupressus sempervirens*) have been used to give height to the planting. Bolder areas of growth, with open areas of gravel,

are in harmony with the modern style of the angular concrete and glass building.

The lower proposal is simpler. The individual plants chosen are small but the areas of planting are generous, alternating with open spaces. This design includes patches of annual color as well as roses.

An alternative means of changing the garden completely would be to re-shape the terracing. My suggestions for the steeply rising site are shown below right.

Existing amphitheatre *The unusual terracing of the site links the striking building with its garden strongly and provides rank upon rank of interesting planting areas.*

Alternative terracing schemes, *below. This series of diagrams shows the existing terracing scheme and two proposals that would alter the feel of this rather unusual garden.*

1 Existing terracing
2 Abstracted pattern
3 Graded top level with a sunbathing "room".

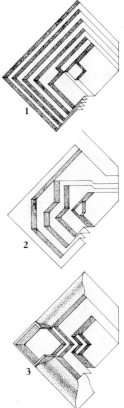

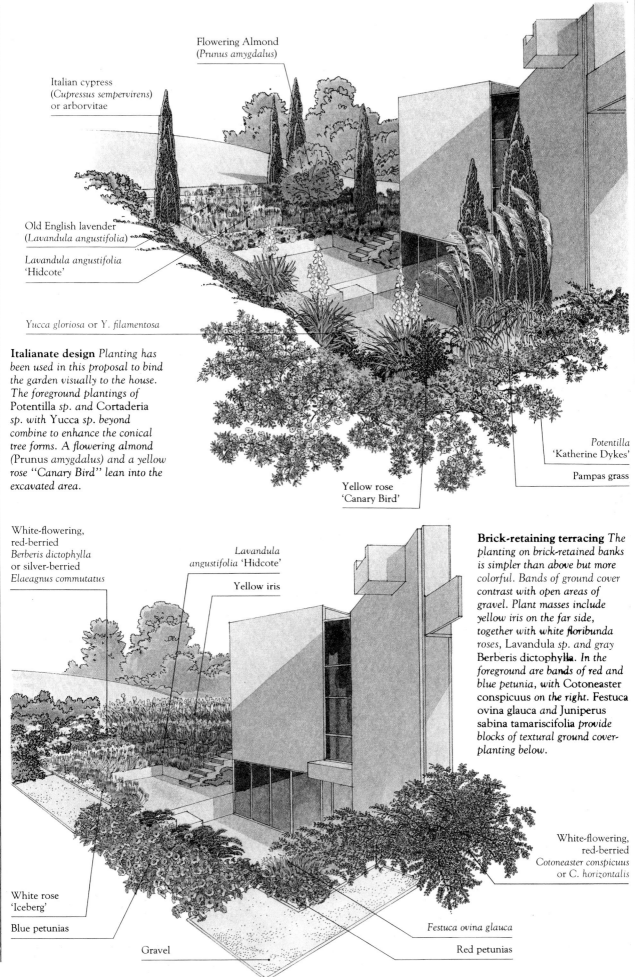

Flowering Almond
(*Prunus amygdalus*)

Italian cypress
(*Cupressus sempervirens*)
or arborvitae

Old English lavender
(*Lavandula angustifolia*)

Lavandula angustifolia
'Hidcote'

Yucca gloriosa or *Y. filamentosa*

Italianate design *Planting has
been used in this proposal to bind
the garden visually to the house.
The foreground plantings of
Potentilla sp. and Cortaderia
sp. with Yucca sp. beyond
combine to enhance the conical
tree forms. A flowering almond
(Prunus amygdalus) and a yellow
rose "Canary Bird" lean into the
excavated area.*

Potentilla
'Katherine Dykes'

Pampas grass

Yellow rose
'Canary Bird'

White-flowering,
red-berried
Berberis dictophylla
or silver-berried
Elaeagnus commutatus

*Lavandula
angustifolia* 'Hidcote'

Yellow iris

Brick-retaining terracing *The
planting on brick-retained banks
is simpler than above but more
colorful. Bands of ground cover
contrast with open areas of
gravel. Plant masses include
yellow iris on the far side,
together with white floribunda
roses, Lavandula sp. and gray
Berberis dictophylla. In the
foreground are bands of red and
blue petunia, with Cotoneaster
conspicuus on the right. Festuca
ovina glauca and Juniperus
sabina tamariscifolia provide
blocks of textural ground cover-
planting below.*

White-flowering,
red-berried
Cotoneaster conspicuus
or *C. horizontalis*

White rose
'Iceberg'

Blue petunias

Gravel

Festuca ovina glauca

Red petunias

85

Suburban garden

The design below is an effective treatment for the side of a garden and, when seen from ground level and from the house, works as a visual progression down the length of the site. Interesting and detailed paving makes the junction between the lawn and the detail on the right. Some good planting in the foreground screens an informal pool in the Japanese manner.

The top example, opposite, provides more interest at the terrace end of the garden by means of a piece of sculpture, with descending areas of water beneath it. The concept is crisper than the original, with the strong form of both the pools and the sculpture softened by bold planting. The bamboo clump remains but it is now backed by a mass of yellow-flowering *Ligularia* sp., beyond which is a group of the horizontally layered foliage of *Viburnum plicatum* 'Mariesii'. Low junipers reach down to the water beneath the sculpture and these are backed by autumn flowering *Anemone japonica alba*. A formal, clipped hedge completes the progression, from behind which the paving emerges to provide a balance to the sculpture.

The bottom idea makes more of a feature of the terrace that ends the garden, extending it back towards the house in an abstract concept of interlocking squares at different levels. These are tied together by a small, circular pool with *Sagittaria* sp. making strong foliage planting within it. Planting in this design is subordinate to the structural concept, with bamboo retained to sit among a low planting of *Hypericum calycinum*.

Formal approach, *right. This is a more formal approach to the use of water, with the flow allowed to descend at intervals and provide foreground interest to the concrete sculpture. The top, paved terrace now acts as a counter-balance to this feature. Planting complements the sculpture and bamboo is included for its bold leaf shapes, mixed with flower color.*

Finely-detailed flank *Attractive paving leads the eye down this half of a garden. Half-way is an informal Japanese pool, screened by a large bamboo. Seen straight on, this feature is well organized and handsomely displayed against a bold lattice fence with* Clematis montana *growing through it.*

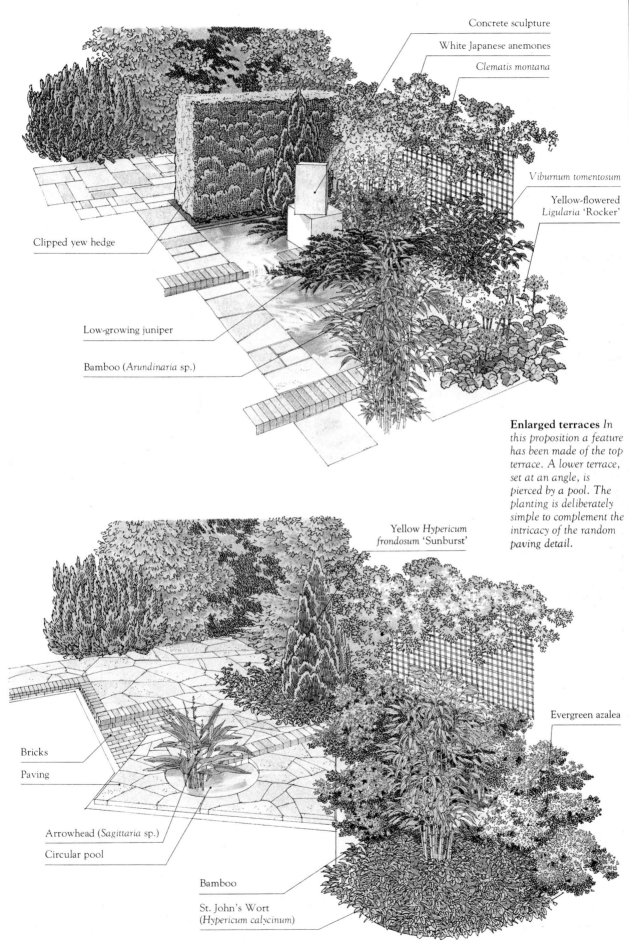

Concrete sculpture

White Japanese anemones

Clematis montana

Viburnum tomentosum

Yellow-flowered
Ligularia 'Rocker'

Clipped yew hedge

Low-growing juniper

Bamboo (*Arundinaria* sp.)

Enlarged terraces *In
this proposition a feature
has been made of the top
terrace. A lower terrace,
set at an angle, is
pierced by a pool. The
planting is deliberately
simple to complement the
intricacy of the random
paving detail.*

Yellow *Hypericum
frondosum* 'Sunburst'

Evergreen azalea

Bricks

Paving

Arrowhead (*Sagittaria* sp.)

Circular pool

Bamboo

St. John's Wort
(*Hypericum calycinum*)

87

Ground pattern garden

The layout of this garden makes a strong ground pattern to be looked down upon from the terrace that surrounds the house. The pattern is picked out in granite setts, mostly across lawn, and consists of pathways connecting circular islands. Granite blocks are laid below the level of the grass so that mowing is not impeded and so care of the complex lawn shapes is easy.

The treatment in the top example, opposite, is dramatic, for the centers of the setted circles have become simple pools of water, each with a small fountain jet. Surrounding these are swirling masses of ground cover planting of *Juniperus sabina tamariscifolia* and *Stachys lanata*, interspersed with yellow or white floribunda roses, colors that should not be mixed. The taller planting on the left is of *Cotoneaster salicifolius floccosus*, with evergreen or deciduous viburnums on the right.

Another way of changing the three-dimensional shape of the garden would be to use the existing ground pattern as the basis for a rose garden, an example of which is shown in the diagram right.

The lower treatment opposite overlays these existing features with an even stronger ground pattern, some of which remains grass while the rest is planted. This gives the garden more of a traditional feeling. Sculptural features have been made of the circles, which now include topiary plants from the range hornbeam (*Carpinus* sp.), privet (*Ligustrum* sp.) or bay (*Laurus nobilis*). In place of bay, which is not winter-hardy in cold regions, use yew (*Taxus* sp.).

Paving pattern, *below. The existing garden, with its pattern of interconnecting decorative paths linking all corners of the area, has been designed to be effective when viewed from the terrace.*

Rose garden alternative *In the plan below, I have superimposed a curving pattern over the design. The central swathe is of grass and the surrounding areas planted with floribunda roses. Grade the rose colors gently.*

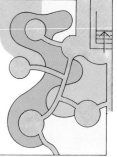

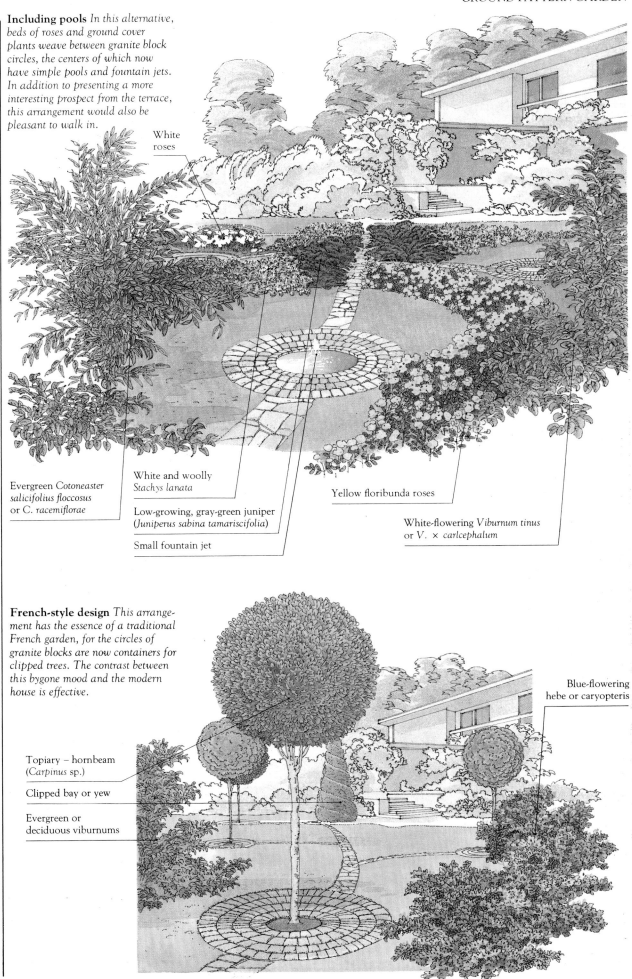

Including pools *In this alternative, beds of roses and ground cover plants weave between granite block circles, the centers of which now have simple pools and fountain jets. In addition to presenting a more interesting prospect from the terrace, this arrangement would also be pleasant to walk in.*

White roses

Evergreen *Cotoneaster salicifolius floccosus* or *C. racemiflorae*

White and woolly *Stachys lanata*

Low-growing, gray-green juniper (*Juniperus sabina tamariscifolia*)

Small fountain jet

Yellow floribunda roses

White-flowering *Viburnum tinus* or *V. × carlcephalum*

French-style design *This arrangement has the essence of a traditional French garden, for the circles of granite blocks are now containers for clipped trees. The contrast between this bygone mood and the modern house is effective.*

Blue-flowering hebe or caryopteris

Topiary – hornbeam (*Carpinus* sp.)

Clipped bay or yew

Evergreen or deciduous viburnums

89

Rural entrance

The stepped entrance to this house was designed at the same time as the building (or at the same time as extensive re-building) for the proportions and detailing are harmonious with the house. The combined structure of house and garden is successful as it seems to blend into the surround of natural woodland. An assortment of pots and planting on the stepped levels is centered on the stump of an old pine tree that must have once been a prime feature of the site. The steps themselves are set at wide intervals to create a relaxed approach to the house entrance.

In the first proposal opposite I have suggested clearing the levels of decoration completely and replacing the dead trunk with a young pine, similar to those behind the house. In the second proposal, I have chosen to strengthen the strong natural character of the environment by using groups of boulders on the stepped levels.

In both alternatives I have suggested planting low masses of the shrubby *Pinus mugo* to link the garden with the natural woodland beyond. To add color, one might include "wild" plant forms such as the foxglove (*Digitalis* sp.) and spectacular giant cow-parsley (*Heracleum mantegazzianum*) with its large, handsome divided leaves and white flower heads up to three metre (9 ft) high.

Combining good looks with utility *This is a well-designed entrance that looks attractive while providing such useful features as a log store. The steps leading to the building are broad for a relaxed effect, with brick-on-edge risers and pre-cast paving stone treads.*

Strengthening the rural feel, *right. The design is made simpler and more sympathetic with the surrounding woodland by clearing the levels. The central, dead pine trunk, around which the existing scheme was designed, has been replaced by a young pine that becomes a prime feature. The scale of all new planting complements the long horizontal lines of the stepped levels.*

Young Scots pine
(*Pinus sylvestris*)

Existing
Rhododendron sp.

Existing
Cotoneaster sp.

Shrubby *Pinus mugo*

Dramatic boulder groupings, *below. A more
individual effect has been achieved here with
massive rock groupings and giant cow-parsley. The
strength of this design results from the contrast
between the rounded forms of the boulders and the
horizontal lines of the step treads.*

Giant cow-parsley

Boulder grouping

Pinus mugo

Cobble bed

91

A rock garden

The rock garden below is a successful feature. The "outcrops" of rock of which it is made look natural, resembling strata exposed by the elements. Much of the planting appears to be shaped by its site so that rocks and plants complement one another.

In each of the two alternative designs, opposite, a specific weathering process has been simulated. In the top example, the rocks are part of a composition that includes water—the "worn" rock faces looking in towards the water. A still sheet of water will reflect a rocky landscape and provide an area of calm that will balance the drama of rock and plants.

In the lower design, rock faces have been supposedly exposed by weathering from the right of the illustration. The rock group is split by a gravel path. In both alternative designs the plants used are mostly ground-hugging, with *Saxifraga* sp. and *Sempervivum* sp. used to simulate the hardy primary growth of exposed sites.

When planting a rock garden, think carefully about the natural form you are copying. An alpine bluff has characteristics that the gardener should note. An exposed rock face will produce a crumble of rock particles, or scree, at its base in which only hardy, tufted plants could find a home. Larger, less hardy plants only survive in the areas sheltered by the rock formation away from the exposed face. It is in such areas that any fastigiate plant must be sited. A well-sited vertically growing plant will relieve the otherwise horizontal forms that go to make a rock garden.

Rockery feature *In this garden, the rockery is a separate feature divided by paths from the rest of the garden. Lines of rock strata are discernible, giving the rockery island a feel of authenticity. Planting includes attractive, low-growing species in the foreground and shrubby masses behind the main rock grouping.*

Introducing water, *right. This alternative combines water with rocks, including a modest waterfall with its resulting pool. The fastigiate conifer, placed centrally, echoes the vertical line of the waterfall. The pool is made to look completely natural with no visible surround. Planting follows the plan for the original rockery except for a horizontal-growing juniper and low, pool-side planting of sedums and primulas.*

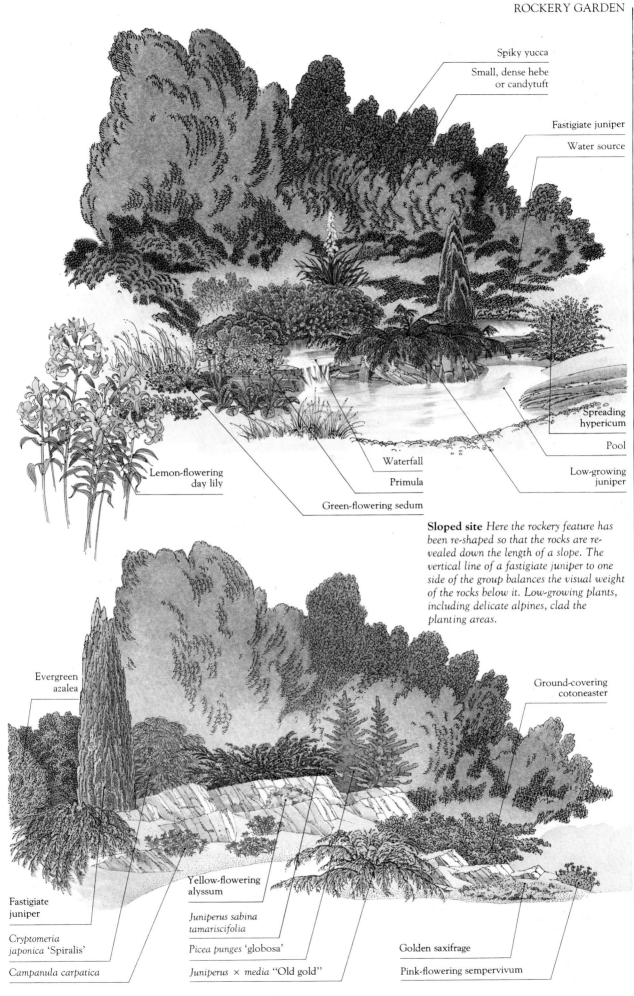

Spiky yucca

Small, dense hebe
or candytuft

Fastigiate juniper

Water source

Spreading
hypericum

Pool

Low-growing
juniper

Lemon-flowering
day lily

Waterfall

Primula

Green-flowering sedum

Sloped site *Here the rockery feature has
been re-shaped so that the rocks are re-
vealed down the length of a slope. The
vertical line of a fastigiate juniper to one
side of the group balances the visual weight
of the rocks below it. Low-growing plants,
including delicate alpines, clad the
planting areas.*

Evergreen
azalea

Ground-covering
cotoneaster

Fastigiate
juniper

*Cryptomeria
japonica* 'Spiralis'

Campanula carpatica

Yellow-flowering
alyssum

*Juniperus sabina
tamariscifolia*

Picea punges 'globosa'

Juniperus × media "Old gold"

Golden saxifrage

Pink-flowering sempervivum

93

Small urban garden

This small, colorful area is typical of many urban gardens, both in size and content. It is well designed and executed, with paving and raised borders in the same brick. The pattern is staggered to allow a screen for rear access to the parking space beyond but the chief concern has been to provide a pleasant space for family use.

The proposals suggested opposite are for an identical space, but that above is sheltered by a neighboring tree. A shaded garden is never as colorful as one in sun, but its mass of greenery can be cool and inviting in the summer. Winter interest is provided by broad-leaved evergreens such as rhododendrons and azaleas, leucothoe, pieris and hollies. One of the hardier hollies, inkberry (*Ilex glabra*), survives well in an urban environment. In those regions where winters are too

harsh for broad-leaved evergreens, rely on tall-growing yews (*Taxus*) and hemlock (*Tsuga canadensis*) for background and screening. Fill in with small deciduous trees and shrubs such as amelanchier, redbud and winged euonymus for all-year, texture effects.

Grasses, as in the proposal, opposite, below, grow best in light, open gardens and will survive in dry ground. The diversity of leaf forms and height is considerable. Foliage color is also wide ranging and includes green, gold, blue, grey and purple and many of these colors are spotted and striped.

Bright enclosed space *This well-designed, small European garden is seen here at its most colorful in early summer. Planting includes roses, yellow Achillea sp. and, in the foreground, delphiniums and a small maple.*

Dry soil alternative, *right. In this alternative design I have imagined the garden to be over-shadowed by a neighboring tree, which will make the soil dry. The plants used are less colorful than in the existing garden but greener and fuller. Emphasis is now on shape and much of the planting is evergreen to last the year through. Bulbs, hosta and foxgloves provide spring and summer interest.*

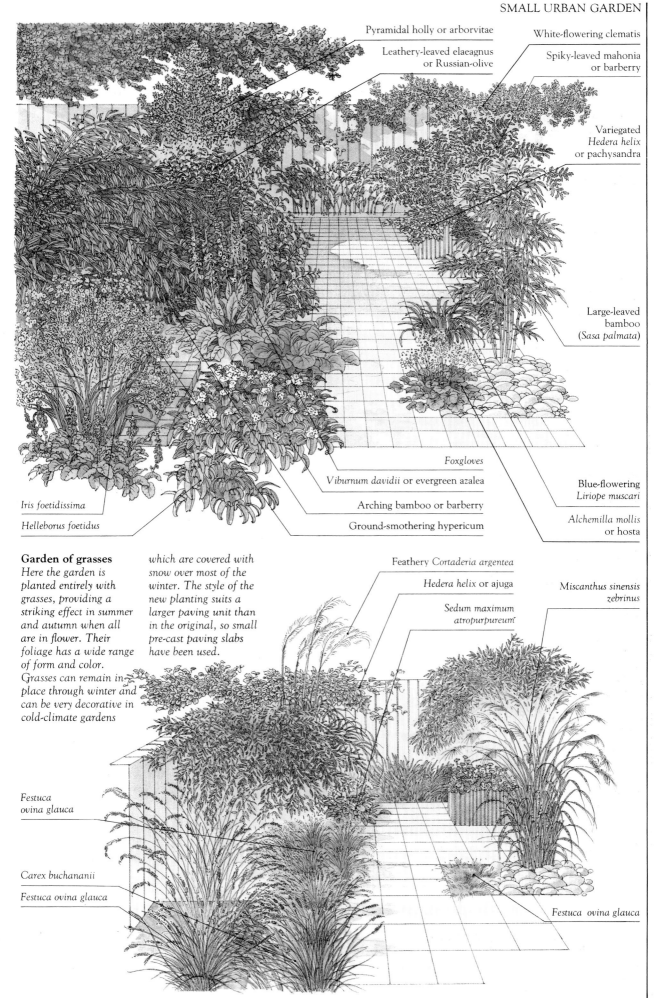

Pyramidal holly or arborvitae

Leathery-leaved elaeagnus
or Russian-olive

White-flowering clematis

Spiky-leaved mahonia
or barberry

Variegated
Hedera helix
or pachysandra

Large-leaved
bamboo
(*Sasa palmata*)

Foxgloves

Viburnum davidii or evergreen azalea

Arching bamboo or barberry

Ground-smothering hypericum

Blue-flowering
Liriope muscari

Alchemilla mollis
or hosta

Iris foetidissima

Helleborus foetidus

Garden of grasses
Here the garden is
planted entirely with
grasses, providing a
striking effect in summer
and autumn when all
are in flower. Their
foliage has a wide range
of form and color.
Grasses can remain in
place through winter and
can be very decorative in
cold-climate gardens

which are covered with
snow over most of the
winter. The style of the
new planting suits a
larger paving unit than
in the original, so small
pre-cast paving slabs
have been used.

Feathery *Cortaderia argentea*

Hedera helix or ajuga

*Sedum maximum
atropurpureum*

*Miscanthus sinensis
zebrinus*

*Festuca
ovina glauca*

Carex buchananii

Festuca ovina glauca

Festuca ovina glauca

Southern frontage

The front of this handsome Southern house has an "L"-shaped covered way which provides shade from the sun as well as shelter from the rain. Beyond the covered way is a large cedar while, within the square formed by the path, there is a beautiful, established golden maple (*Acer japonica* 'Aureum').

A front garden is the setting for a house and, as the scene for coming and going, it should provide a balancing, tranquil and static appearance. The existing design of this garden consists of a long curving border surrounding a simple circular pond. The border divides the house from the garden and, having separated the two, the eye is then held by the fountain.

The first proposed design, opposite above, uses a simple gravel surfacing to bind together the disparate elements of the garden. Since the attraction of the existing house and trees is essentially one of form, the theme is continued with clumps of bamboo and masses of low-growing *Juniperus sabina tamariscifolia* complementing the pool,

which now has a small vertical fountain splash. A low azalea mound beneath the existing maple brings the eye down to ground level again. Gravel used in this way should be laid in quite a thin layer, rolled and consolidated into another layer of binding gravel (see p. 131).

Gravel is used again in the checkered pattern of the second layout, opposite below. Squares of gravel alternate with masses of boxwood in a more formal and architectural garden. Each square is edged in brick to match the surfacing of the entrance path. Other plants could be used instead, depending on soil, climate and the desired effect. Lavender, for instance, would provide a woolier look, though it should be clipped after flowering. Planting must be evergreen, however, in order to maintain the pattern throughout the seasons. It would be possible, though, by raising each planting area by even only a brick's height, to use either roses or a single color of annual bedding plants and still hold the pattern through the year.

Curved front garden
A front garden design, bordered by covered walks and dominated by fine trees, should essentially be a simple pattern offsetting the house beyond. A strong serpentine line divides lawn from planting and outlines the static shape of the well-proportioned circular pool.

Gravelled landscape *The anchor of this proposal is the use of one ground medium – gravel – in which new plants are set to complement those already present. They include bamboo (Arundinaria sp.), masses of low Juniperus sp., and a mound of azalea beneath the existing Acer japonica 'Aureum'. The fountain jet has become a single vertical, giving a restful effect.*

Cedar (*Cedrus atlantica*)

Covered way

Golden maple (*Acer japonica 'Aureum'*)

Covered way

Bamboo

Gravel

Low-growing juniper

Fountain

Slab edging

Azalea

Cedar

Golden maple

Checkerboard effect *This design is architectural and works by focusing attention on the covered ways. The pattern is created in brickwork. Squares filled with gravel alternate with masses of low, clipped boxwood (Buxus sp.). Such a solution makes features of the two fine existing trees, a golden maple and a cedar, complementing the simple formality of the house as well.*

Covered way

Gravelled squares

Low-clipped box

97

Narrow walled garden

It is in the walled urban garden that one can most safely be bold in design, for what is within the walls need relate to little else. Any garden pattern within the uncompromising lines of surrounding brick walls has to be strong and heavily planted to create a balance between greenery and the structure of the garden. The narrow, walled garden below is dominated by a large tree, so small-scale planting would anyway be inappropriate.

The present design is one of contrast. The crisp, hard lines of the brick-paved terrace are divided by a pool, which runs the width of the garden beyond. Beyond the pool a sense of mystery prevails, with a woodland-style path and fuzzy planting to soften the effects of the surrounding walls while under-lining the seclusion the boundary offers.

I have suggested two abstract designs, both of which have strong patterns when seen from the house. The first proposal, opposite above, comprises a series of interlocking planting and gravel areas, separated by brick-on-edge. The simple planting scheme consists only of ferns, for these are ideal for a shaded, town situation.

The lower proposal is more formal and emphasizes the existing pond. Large masses of planting contrast with areas of brick paving, the whole culminating in a simple structure of a tiled roof on four verticals over the rear entrance.

Mixing two styles *It is difficult to combine two styles in a small garden but here it is achieved in dramatic style in a very narrow garden. Being totally enclosed, the garden's surroundings have been ignored and a place of mystery created inside. Brick has been chosen to match the walls for the terrace and pool details.*

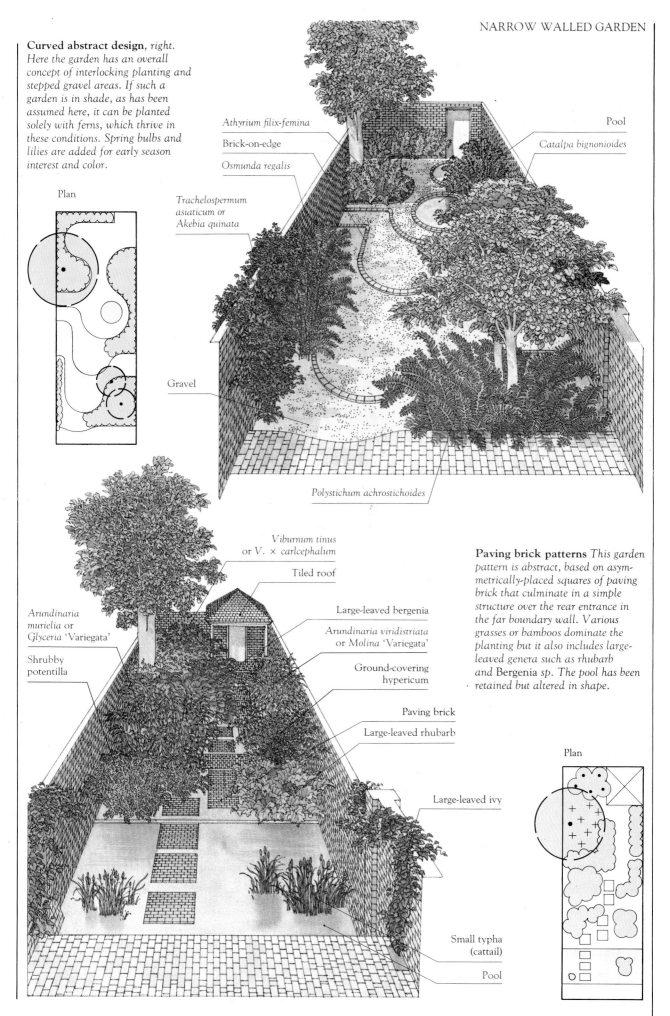

Curved abstract design, *right.*
Here the garden has an overall
concept of interlocking planting and
stepped gravel areas. If such a
garden is in shade, as has been
assumed here, it can be planted
solely with ferns, which thrive in
these conditions. Spring bulbs and
lilies are added for early season
interest and color.

Plan

Athyrium filix-femina

Brick-on-edge

Osmunda regalis

Trachelospermum
asiaticum or
Akebia quinata

Gravel

Pool

Catalpa bignonioides

Polystichum achrostichoides

Arundinaria
murielia or
Glyceria 'Variegata'

Shrubby
potentilla

Viburnum tinus
or V. × carlcephalum

Tiled roof

Large-leaved bergenia

Arundinaria viridistriata
or Molina 'Variegata'

Ground-covering
hypericum

Paving brick

Large-leaved rhubarb

Large-leaved ivy

Small typha
(cattail)

Pool

Paving brick patterns *This garden*
pattern is abstract, based on asym-
metrically-placed squares of paving
brick that culminate in a simple
structure over the rear entrance in
the far boundary wall. Various
grasses or bamboos dominate the
planting but it also includes large-
leaved genera such as rhubarb
and Bergenia sp. The pool has been
retained but altered in shape.

Plan

Balcony garden

This attractive balcony is obviously a source of great pleasure. The large opening doorway gives easy access to the outside space, extending the room in summer months and allowing an unrestricted view to greenery in winter.

The chief feature of my alternative suggestion is a metal or wooden box (which could be watered automatically), planted with box wood (*Buxus* sp.) and trimmed to the same shape as the valance. Annuals planted in spherical containers reflect the bobble edging of the valance. These planting spheres are constructed in metal mesh on the principle of the hanging basket, welded to a metal vertical set into the planting box below. They are lined with moss and filled with compost. Annuals such as lobelia and impatiens are planted through the moss. They will need daily watering from above.

The existing flooring of the balcony is of lightweight tiles with asbestos content. Red or brown quarry tiles are an alternative or, where there is no hazard of frost, colored ceramic tiles.

Summertime balcony, *right. The collection of potted plants helps this balcony to become an interesting and colorful extension of the room it adjoins. The floor covering and plant containers are plain to offset strongly-colored blooms.*

All year alternative *In this substitute treatment, the balcony becomes a place with strong form that continues to give pleasure and protection through the winter months. The evergreen box hedge provides much of this form. In summer, the balcony is enlivened with spheres of color provided by annual planting in containers, such as that far right.*

Box hedging clipped to echo the pelmet frill shape

White-painted wooden planting boxes

Blue-flowering lobelia mixed with pink impatiens or petunias

Lightweight colored tiles

Planting sphere, *below. A spherical mesh container, such as that shown here, is easy to construct with wire netting, or even by connecting two hemispherical hanging baskets. In my alternative design, such spheres are welded to verticals.*

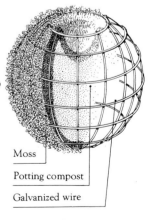

Moss

Potting compost

Galvanized wire

CONSTRUCTING YOUR GARDEN

Drainage, irrigation and electricity

Selecting and making boundaries, screens, levels and surfaces

Introducing features and structures

Preliminaries

By now you should have a clear idea of the pattern and form you are planning for your future garden. The time has come to create it in hard materials, such as walls and paving, which you will later infill with shrubs, mixed planting, and grass or other ground cover. Built features, such as garden sheds, must also be considered so that they can be integrated into the plan rather than merely added later.

It is at this stage that you decide on the materials that you will use: consider what is available locally, what would look appropriate for your area and what the cost of different materials is. In a traditional setting, stone looks well either for walls or paving. The smaller elements of brick or granite blocks are also suitable and, being crisp in outline, are equally suitable in a modern setting. Much depends on the way you use the materials to infill your pattern. Broadly, the smaller the element the more the details will be noticed. For this reason, brick paths are less dynamic than those made of concrete slabs that merge and lead the eye to the path's termination. Pre-cast concrete slabs tend to be modern in feeling and, although many are modified with rusticated finishes, this will not deceive anyone into thinking they are real stone. Concrete in its many forms is a universal material and, laid *in situ* for paving, one not to be despised. Combinations of materials can be used to break up a large hard area, though the detailing should never become fussy.

The suitability of wood for garden use also depends on your location and what is available at a reasonable price. Cedarwood, for instance, is found throughout the United States, though it is no longer cheap. Other softwood can also be used and it is available in most areas of Europe. In the United Kingdom, softwood is widely available but unfortunately the climate does not lend itself to its use for outside flooring or decking since the long, damp winters make it wet and slippery no matter how well treated. Railway and the smaller landscape ties are excellent for garden use and are heavily impregnated with preservative. Their proportions are generous and they therefore take many years to decompose.

The pattern you have on paper, albeit a working drawing, is still only two-dimensional. By incorporating wall and step heights, depths of ponds and so on, you make the plan three-dimensional. Remember that it is the different levels, the feeling of enclosure given by planting, and also the areas of void contrasted with the mass and height of solids, that makes a garden such a pleasant place in which to be. It is a fallacy to suppose that the abundance and brilliance of flower color in a garden affects this basic feeling in any way at all.

Before pegging out the design which you have evolved on paper to see whether it will be satisfactory, you will probably have to clear the site. If you are starting from scratch in a new garden, it may be builders' rubble that will have to go. Older gardens may need someone else's unsuitable planting removed. Nevertheless, think hard before removing any major item, such as a tree, an area of paving or a line of hedge, for it might be possible for you to incorporate them into your new plan. Trees can be thinned and branches removed or braced to make a new shape, although this is work best done by a qualified tree surgeon. Hedges, if overgrown, can also be cut back.

Clear all weeds from the site, either by using a herbicide (being sure to keep pets and children away when newly applied) or renting a sickle bar mower or even resorting to bulldozing.

The plan so far If you have worked your way through the section on planning your garden and have perhaps been inspired by the gardens illustrated in the Garden-by-garden guide, your own garden plan should look something like this. You should have resolved the positions of surfaces, boundaries, features and the areas for planting, although as yet there will be no detail about the materials to be used.

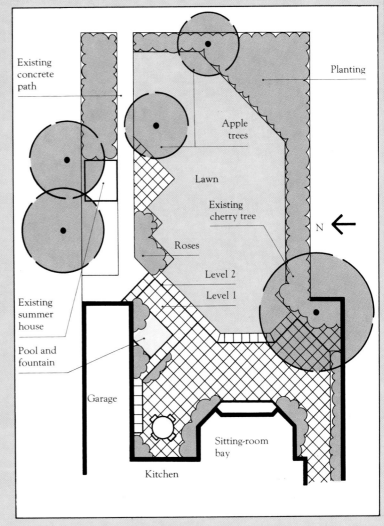

Existing concrete path

Planting

Apple trees

Lawn

Existing cherry tree

Roses

N

Level 2

Level 1

Existing summer house

Pool and fountain

Garage

Sitting-room bay

Kitchen

Marking out the design on the site

You can now translate your plan into reality outside, using white string and pegs, to see if your ideas really work. At this stage you will be rewarded for keeping to a grid system in your design for it will be easy to line up your shapes with the buildings which you used to evolve it, and any unpleasant little corners will now become apparent.

Having pegged out the straight runs, tackle the circles (easy to deduce if you have worked to a scale plan) by using a central peg and string attached to it. Scrape out the necessary arcs in the earth with a nail or stick and peg these lines out too.

Once you have described all your patterns with pegs, join them with string. This will enable you to read the overall layout when you stand back from the garden. Look at the pattern from several vantage points – from an upstairs window, from ground level and from outside the site. Then walk on the pathways you have outlined, ensuring that there is room for a wheelbarrow or a mower and that you can easily get round corners. If there is an access path to the front door, make sure that there is a comparatively straight way down the middle, even if the outline twists, for otherwise visitors will cut unnecessary corners. If you have marked out a terraced area that is supposed to be in sunshine, estimate the course of the sun in summer and ensure that there is no unexpected area of cast shadow.

If you are planning a drive, ensure that it is wide enough for you to get out of a car on either side and that there is room to turn it, if needs be. In short, check that your planning ideas are practical as well as visually satisfying from all angles.

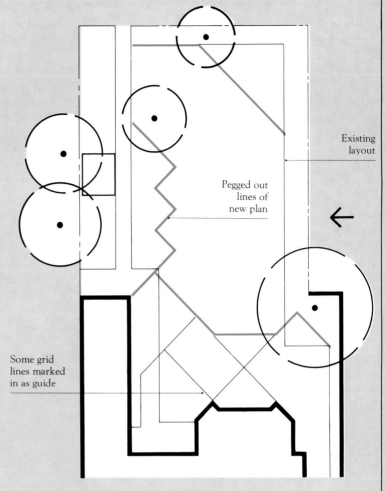

Existing layout

Pegged out lines of new plan

Some grid lines marked in as guide

Pegging out, *above. Having evolved your plan on paper, peg out the outlines on the ground using stakes and string. If you have worked to the correct scale, from an accurate outline survey, your measurements will translate to the real garden. Adjust your outlines to delete any awkward corners and angles that you notice.*

Assessing the layout, *right. Before you start digging or building, go indoors and study the pegged out pattern from all the windows that look on to the garden, imagining steps and changes of level where necessary. You might see aspects of the plan that require slight modification to make all views from the house satisfying. The view from upstairs windows is particularly useful and can provide the mind's eye with a clear impression of the future garden.*

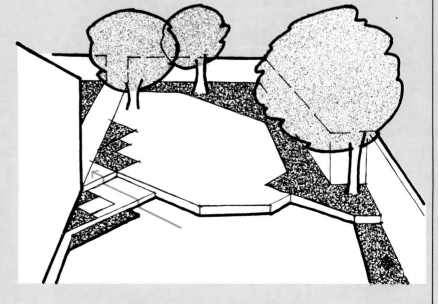

Drainage

Few small gardens need a full drainage system but where drainage is necessary it will be obvious, for the garden, or parts of it, will be wet underfoot for long periods. It is possible, however, that your site is on low-lying ground and, while dry in summer, the water-table will rise in winter to make the area wet again. The natural vegetation will indicate this – rushy grasses and little else.

By far the most likely cause of dampness, especially in a new garden, is a layer of clay from excavations that has been dumped and spread on site by the house builder. Often he disguises this with a thin layer of topsoil but the clay soon becomes an impervious layer that prevents drainage. Break this layer and the water will disperse.

Dig an inspection hole, a meter square and a meter deep, if you are in any doubt about the need to drain a particular area. In this way you will be able to see the soil profile and know how much topsoil and subsoil there is. After rain, you will also see how quickly water drains away. It is possible that your hole will fill with water when it is not raining, indicating that you have reached the water table. However, if you do at so shallow a depth your house will have needed special foundations and you are probably aware of this from a surveyor's report.

If the site is on natural clay, you have no alternative but to replace it with fertile top-soil. However, a soil with a proportion of clay may have become consolidated by heavy machinery working on it. Often this can be greatly improved by cultivating the surface to break-up the clay deposits that have been consolidated.

If your site really does need draining, you will have to install an underground system with pipes of either clay or flexible plastic. These are laid to a pattern according to the site, with feeder runs to the main outlet pipe running to a neighboring ditch or to the surface water drainage system of the house. Never connect a garden drainage system to the mains drainage system. In the United Kingdom this, in fact, is illegal.

The depth of the drainage runs, and their proximity to each other, will depend on the consistency and composition of the soil. It is important to realize that to overdrain a site is as pointless as trying to garden on one that is wet, for you are facilitating the rapid escape of all the essential minerals which are held in soluble form and feed the plants' roots.

The kind of drainage that a garden is much more likely to need deals with only a small area, which, for a number of reasons, may have standing water on it after rain. To drain this may only need a simple pipe run to a soakaway or dry well. It is a hole, a meter square (3 ft³) and at least a meter (3 ft) deep, which is filled with rubble. It will act as a reservoir to hold drainage water, allowing it to disperse gradually. Such a soakaway should be sited under areas that will later be planted and at a distance from the house. The lifespan of a soakaway may only be five years or so, but this again will depend on the soil.

Soakaways can also drain areas at the base of contoured mounds or be sited along the edge of an area of paving, which has been laid to fall to it.

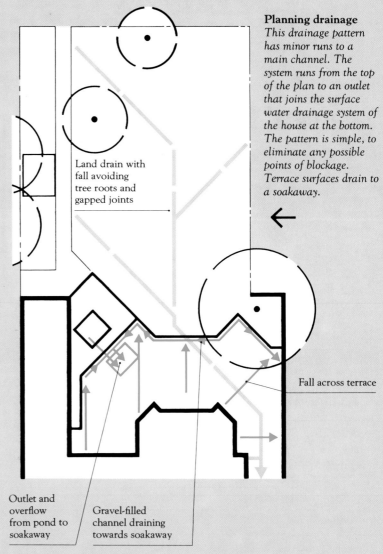

Land drain with fall avoiding tree roots and gapped joints

Fall across terrace

Outlet and overflow from pond to soakaway

Gravel-filled channel draining towards soakaway

Planning drainage
This drainage pattern has minor runs to a main channel. The system runs from the top of the plan to an outlet that joins the surface water drainage system of the house at the bottom. The pattern is simple, to eliminate any possible points of blockage. Terrace surfaces drain to a soakaway.

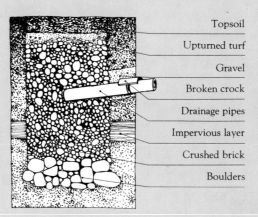

Topsoil

Upturned turf

Gravel

Broken crock

Drainage pipes

Impervious layer

Crushed brick

Boulders

Soakaway or dry well
A soakaway might well be all the extra drainage you require. An ideal example penetrates any impervious layers in the soil and so allows any water draining in to pass down quickly through the layers of gravel and crushed brick to soil that is less likely to become saturated.

Irrigation

Watering a garden, no matter what its size, is traditionally done by a hand-held can or hose. This is time-consuming and laborious, however, and other methods are readily available today.

The simplest, non-manual irrigation system is a perforated hose, passing across a planted area or over pots on a roof, which when turned on produces a gentle trickle of water. A hose can, of course, be laid when a garden has been fully constructed.

At the other end of the scale, there is a sophisticated grid system of pipes that can be sunk just below ground surface at an early stage of garden planning. This has counter-sunk nozzles, with a metal recess above each at ground level. When the system is switched on, the pressure of water pushes the nozzles just above ground level to release a spray, the coverage from one nozzle reaching that of the next to soak the whole area equally. On switching off, the nozzles sink down – a facility that is particularly useful on a lawn since it allows even mowing of the area. These systems can be timed to switch on and off automatically, much as a central heating system does.

Between these two extremes of irrigation system are oscillators which sweep water to-and-fro across an area to a distance determined by the pressure which drives them.

Electricity

It is usually necessary to bury cables for outside lighting under, or possibly around, structural elements before the garden plan is completed to avoid subsequent disruption.

Gardens need electricity for lighting, and to power equipment such as a fountain or a swimming-pool filtration plant. Power is also needed in the greenhouse, for an electric saw in the workshop and, if you have an electric mower, an outside socket is useful at a distance from the house to avoid an inconvenient length of cable.

All cables should be located along the bottom of a wall, or be contained within protective piping and buried at a level below that likely to be pierced by cultivation tools. Cables need full external-type insulation, with outlet sockets having screw caps and sited above the height at which a small child could reach them, as shown right.

When planning cables and lighting points to entrance paths, ensure that you have places for low lights at any changes of level you are likely to use at night.

It is worth investing some time and money to achieve really effective lighting, for not only does it allow you to enjoy a view of your garden from inside during winter evenings but it is also a worthwhile burglar deterrent. See an electrician for intricate systems.

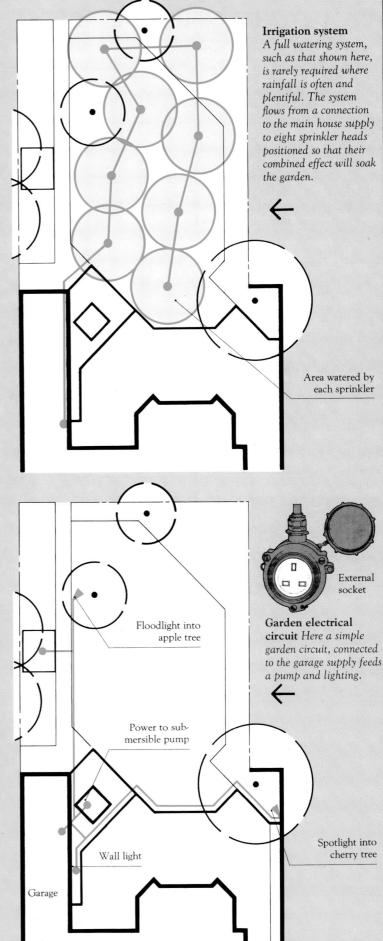

Irrigation system
A full watering system, such as that shown here, is rarely required where rainfall is often and plentiful. The system flows from a connection to the main house supply to eight sprinkler heads positioned so that their combined effect will soak the garden.

Area watered by each sprinkler

External socket

Garden electrical circuit *Here a simple garden circuit, connected to the garage supply feeds a pump and lighting.*

Floodlight into apple tree

Power to submersible pump

Spotlight into cherry tree

Wall light

Garage

Boundaries and enclosures

While boundaries delineate the perimeter of a site, a garden might be divided up internally with more decorative screens. Many people inherit a boundary fence or wall with their property, but as with every other feature in the garden the particular type of boundary and the degree of enclosure which it offers must depend on location.

The shapes of gardens tend to be regular, especially with newer properties, and the mistake is often made of surrounding the site with some standard form of structure that only emphasizes the regularity. The simplest way to relieve this monotony and to break the confines of a boundary visually is to vary the material of which it is made. Use brick or stone adjacent to the house or terrace, and perhaps timber for the rest, or build a boundary of the same material throughout, but vary the height to work with your overall pattern. More interesting still is to allow the line of the boundary to break into the site itself as part of your design so that the layout appears to flow round corners, making your garden appear larger.

Your choice of boundary construction should not ignore security or the need for privacy, a necessity to keep your children or dog in, or other people's out. But these considerations should not inhibit your attempts to mold a more interesting space.

Walls

Walls can be built of brick, stone, of concrete blocks, or of concrete poured *in situ*, though this latter method is usually reserved for retaining walls within the garden as it is stronger. Different wall materials (see p. 109) are used in different ways, the thickness of the structure depending on its height. Thickness will also influence the frequency with which piers or buttresses are used to support the wall. You can get away without these supports by staggering the wall in zig-zag fashion, or by simply stepping the line of the wall forwards and backwards by the thickness of a brick. Curving or serpentine walls will also support themselves, although they require much more space.

The elements of a stone wall are usually thick enough to support themselves without buttressing. Concrete blocks are now available in a variety of acceptable and attractive finishes and sizes and the larger ones do not require buttressing.

The way in which you finish, or cap, your wall can make an enormous difference to its final appearance. Stone walls have traditional cappings in various areas, such as a course of slate. The capping of a brick wall will depend on its thickness, but a course of bricks on edge is the usual finish. Concrete block walls can be finished with concrete slabs (to match a neighboring terrace perhaps), or brick can be used. Tile, slate or metal cappings might also be considered for a crisp, architectural appearance to the retaining wall.

Before embarking on a major fence or wall project along a boundary, check with your building inspector to be sure you are not violating any local ordinances.

Wall strength

Below are some of the ways of building a strong and stable wall without the need for piers. The one-brick-thick wall takes its strength from overlapping at intervals of not more than 2.5 m (8 ft) no more than 1.75 m (5½ ft) high. The zig-zag and crinkle-crankle walls take strength from their deviations.

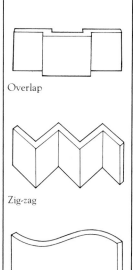

Overlap

Zig-zag

Crinkle-crankle

Stone

Almost any kind of stone can be used for wall construction – granite, limestone, slate or sandstone. The two main types of wall stones are known as ashlar and rubble stones, of which the latter comprises three groups. Random rubble, which is of uncut stone, is laid coursed or uncoursed. Squared rubble, which is of roughly dressed stone, is laid regularly coursed, irregularly coursed, or uncoursed. Miscellaneous rubble walls use traditional materials and construction methods.

Most stone walls are built in random rubble. No cutting is done to fit the stone together and they are so placed within the wall that there is an adequate distribution of pressure over a maximum area, with no continuous vertical joints. To stabilize the wall, header stones are used every square metre (1.19 yd²) and should ideally run right through the wall. Whether this type of wall is coursed or uncoursed, all joints should be well-filled and flushed with mortar. A decorative variation can be achieved by filling some of the joints with soil and growing alpines in them. To construct a wall in stone of which one side only is to be seen, you can erect a concrete block wall first and face this with stone, tying the two with galvanized cleats.

Traditional stone wall *No mortar has been used to joint the miscellaneous rubble of this wall, just patience to ensure vertical joints do not coincide.*

Brick

Brick is the most commonly used material for building walls. There are three types that are suitable for external use. Commons, which are made for general purpose building, are the cheapest. They have no finish and are particularly subject to weathering. Facings, used where appearance is of prime importance, have either a hand finish or a wire-cut weather resistant finish on the side facings only. And lastly, engineering bricks, which are the hardest and most impervious bricks.

Bricks which are laid horizontally in the direction of the wall are known as stretchers, while those laid end-on, across the direction of the wall, are known as headers. The arrangement of bricks within a wall is known as the bond. The virtues of different bonds are mainly aesthetic. Bonds do have marginally differing strengths, so the bond will, to some extent, depend on the thickness of the wall.

For a wall one brick thick, the bond is usually of stretchers alone. Such a wall should not be much higher than one meter (3 ft). In construction of higher walls, use a Flemish or English bond, both of which have headers periodically binding the double thickness of brick. A more decorative bonding can be used on the facing side of a 300-mm (1 ft) wall.

A suitable mortar mix for most exterior walls, subject to normal exposure, is of cement:lime:sand, in the proportions 1:1:8–9. Brickwork which is liable to water saturation, or which is subject to severe exposure and freezing temperatures, might have a mix of 1:1:5–6.

Mellowed brickwork, *right. Walls mellow with age and will become the home of ivy and lichens. However, ivy will eventually damage brick walls.*

Building with used bricks, *below. Different types of old brick have been used here for a multi-colored effect. Now clean of old mortar, they make an open-work wall.*

Brick bonding

The four standard types of brickwork bonding, shown right, are generally used in wall construction, although they might equally be used as a paving pattern (see p. 129). The crispness of the bond is either emphasized or subdued by the style of pointing (the method of trowelling the joints) and the color of the mortar you use.

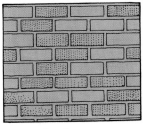
Running bond

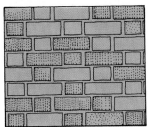
Flemish bond

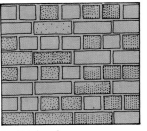
English bond

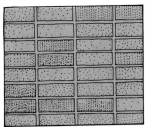
Stack bond

Brick wall construction

A wall must be built on stable and adequate foundations to eliminate any risk of subsequent movement. It is not possible to make exact rules as to the dimensions of foundations for various types of walls, since the bearing capacity of soils vary, particularly those with a high moisture content, such as many of the clays.

The depth of foundations depends on the level at which frost or the movement of ground moisture occurs. In most cases, a depth of 450 to 600 mm (1½–2 ft) is sufficient. Unless there are difficult site conditions, such as poor drainage (when you will need to take expert advice), a concrete mix of 1:2:4–6, cement:sharp sand:aggregate, is correct for normal wall foundation work.

The brick courses are built up from the foundation with great care taken to keep the wall square, both horizontally and vertically, and the amount of mortar used consistent.

English bond brick wall *This brick wall is the usual two-brick thickness (300 mm) (1 ft) and is being laid in English bond, with one course of headers and the next of stretchers.*

Stretcher course

Header course

Concrete foundation

Cappings

It is usually necessary to put a protective capping, or coping, along the top of a wall since most bricks are only weatherproof on the finished face. Below are two standard cappings. On the left is the traditional method known as brick-on-edge. On the right, paving slabs have been used with an overhang proportionate to their thickness.

Brick-on-edge

Concrete slab

Concrete block

Standard concrete or reconstituted stone blocks are available, which have been molded to look like worked stone. These are perfectly sound for wall construction, but personally I do not like one material made to look like another. Most materials are quite valid in their own right and concrete is no exception. Plain concrete blocks are hard to beat for their strength, economy and speed of construction and they are now available in a variety of colors and finishes. There is a far wider range of finishes available than the crude, gray aggregate finish of the early material. Colors vary to match local brick or stone, these materials sometimes being crushed and used as a part of the aggregate of the block. The blocks may be utilized in a variety of ways to produce either a decorative finish or a perfectly simple one. Concrete blocks can be colored after construction. Concrete blocks are available in a standard exterior heavyweight grade, or as lightweights which are composed of lightweight aggregate in a more porous texture. The latter may have to be rendered for outside use but are ideal for roof garden construction where weight is a problem (see p. 160).

Enlivening concrete with colour *This concrete block wall is of the course aggregate type and is used as a retaining wall with a paving slab finish. The wall is coloured to brighten a dull section of rear garden.*

Concrete block wall-construction

Concrete blocks are considerably larger than bricks, so building a wall in this material is much faster and, therefore, far cheaper. The large size of cavity wall blocks makes piers unnecessary for a standard wall, although such blocks are usually reserved for retaining walls (see p. 120). Solid concrete wall blocks are half the thickness and will require the support of piers used with the same frequency as for brick walls (see p. 107). A similar concrete foundation is also required.

Cappings *As with bricks, the block wall should have a protective capping. Pre-cast paving slabs lend themselves to this function well.*

Concrete foundation

Slab and wooden cappings

Wall designs

Some ideas for using solid boundaries to break up your site are shown below. Using your own invention for the boundary of a site is an important step towards creating interesting shapes within it. Plan the boundary in conjunction with your two-dimensional plan, and relate it, as far as possible, to the scale of your house and the scale of your garden.

Interrupted boundary

Walls to direct a view

Wall at an angle

Walls to create interest

Curving walls

Wall materials

There is a vast range of wall materials in brick, stone and concrete but their suitability will depend on your location. Using local materials is often the right decision and it also makes sense economically to use what is to hand. The scale of each component you use is important and must be sympathetic to the scale of other materials already present. You might consciously contrast the scale, using smooth runs of concrete with random stone, large concrete blocks with small bricks, or just different sizes and types of brick. With this last method you will also need to consider differences of texture.

Pre-cast concrete units

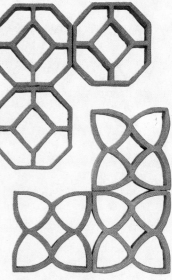

Terracotta units

Brick

The textural and color differences of the brick samples below are obvious. The engineering brick, top, is hardest. It is therefore the most resistant to damp. Below this are three types of "infill brick", which are the cheapest, and facing bricks.

Reconstituted stone

Different areas produce different rock, which can be crushed and used as the aggregate in the composition of reconstituted stone blocks. Reconstituted stone block is easier to transport and lay than natural stone.

Open screen wall units

Scale, texture and pattern will help you decide the type of open screen unit you need. An open screen is generally more successful when used sparingly, only piercing a solid wall, for example, as a decorative element, since any great area becomes boring. The finer elements in terracotta, being lighter, may be used on roof terraces as wind baffles, rather than barriers that cause turbulence.

Concrete block

The concrete block is a much maligned element for garden construction work. It is comparatively cheap, easy to erect and is an honest contemporary material. Hollow blocks or cavity blocks are approximately 300 mm (1 ft) deep, while solid blocks are about half that. Finishes vary from coarse to smooth and glazed.

17 Cavity block
18 Smooth solid
19 Rock-faced solid

1 Engineering brick
2–4 Flettons
5–10 Facing bricks

11–14 Split aggregate blocks
15–16 Pre-cast blocks

Stone

Where suitable, the scale and texture of various stones cannot be bettered and will usually mix well with other hard materials. However, the cost of labor, cartage, and handling difficulties often make its use prohibitive.

20 Sandstone
21 Granite
22–23 Limestones

Fencing

A fence serves the same function as a wall, although its construction need not be so massive or its form solid. Like a wall, its type and height should be dictated by situation and location – urban or rural. Strict attention should be paid to the siting of a fence which is set up along the line of demarcation between two properties to ensure that no encroachment is made on either side. It is usual practice to face the best side of the fence outwards from your site with the supports on the inside.

The materials most used for constructing fences are wood, metal and concrete. Concrete is usually reserved as a supporting material while there is an infinite variety of combinations of materials for possible infills, see-through or solid, which you can either design yourself or buy ready-made. Some types of prefabricated, fixed length panel are widely available. Local types of panel are made on the spot and are easily adapted to non-standard intervals.

A fence is no stronger than its weakest part, so the detailing of a fence to make sure that it has no weaknesses is important. A well-detailed fence will not only be more resilient but it will also last longer. Consider both the types of infill and support, the way in which you intend to fix the supports in the ground and, with wooden fences, the way in which you can further protect against rot with cappings and gravel boards.

The type of wood used in fence construction will considerably alter its lifespan. The principal European woods used for fencing are oak (English and European), larch, western red cedar and sweet chestnut, although other woods may be used when suitable, such as Douglas fir, Scots pine, ash, elm or beech. Redwood or cedar are used in the United States, split redwood being referred to as grapestalk since it is used traditionally to support grapevines.

Bark must be stripped from wood to prevent premature decaying of the wood, and the exposed grain must be treated with a preservative or sealed and painted. After using a creosote preservative on wood it cannot then be painted. Plants will not grow against it for a season, as newly applied, creosote gives off fumes which burn vegetation. Exposed metal components liable to rust, should be galvanized, zinc-coated or painted. Use screws rather than nails for fixings for a longer lasting finish.

When using poured concrete as a supporting material to fix fence posts, there are two alternative methods. The posts can be positioned independently, with careful measurement, and left standing until the concrete sets before the infills are attached. If there is a necessity for a completed boundary in one step, the posts and infills can be constructed at the same time if you make sure to support the posts with temporary wooden stays until the post foundations have set. The fence will need supporting for at least two days.

Novel urban fencing
Espalier fruit trees have been trained against latticework attached to the front boundary wall of this residence. The effect is crisp and urban.

Picket or palisade

Picket fencing is a see-through, decorative version of close board fencing which can have either a cottage or urban feel. It has a similar construction with post and arris rails, but its height is considerably less and the verticals, or pales, are spaced battens with rounded or pointed tops. To achieve a crisp, New England look, this type of fence should be painted white.

For an individual finish you can design your own end decoration for the palings of a picket fence. Six ideas for decorative palings are shown below, from a simple curve to complicated sawn shapes.

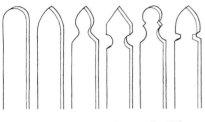

Traditional rural fencing, *right. White-painted picket, or palisade, fencing continues the cottage garden feel of the planting beyond in this garden. Such a fence needs annual maintenance if it is not to look shabby.*

Post and rail

Post and rail describes the simplest way of fencing with wood, or wood and metal, with one, two or three horizontal rails, between regularly spaced posts. There are a number of different construction methods with the rails either nailed to the posts or mortised into them. In the former, the verticals should be 1.8 m (6 ft) apart, while the latter method allows a greater spacing of 2.8 m (9 ft). The horizontal rails can be infilled decoratively as below.

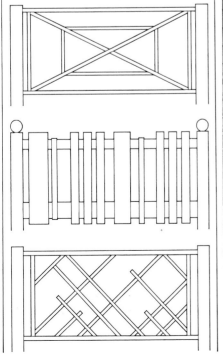

Ranch style

Known as baffle fencing in the United States, ranch fencing is made up of horizontal boards, spaced at regular intervals and secured to posts set not more than 2.75 m (9 ft) apart. Height of the fence should be between 1.35 and 1.85 m (4½–6 ft) high.

Board on board fencing is a variation of the ranch style fence, where the horizontals are secured alternately to each side of the verticals, providing a fence which looks equally good on both sides. Ranch style boarding can also be attached vertically to arris rails (the horizontal rails which are usually associated with close board fencing, as described on p. 112) to produce a totally different effect. Ranch fencing is either painted or treated with a wood preservative.

Shared boundary fencing *Open ranch-style fencing, which looks equally good from either side, is ideal as a boundary demarcation between properties. Whether open or close board (as in the diagram below), this fencing is an ideal plant support.*

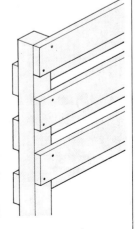

Close board

This type of fence will give privacy and shelter, and is available in pre-fabricated panels but is usually built on site. It is built of overlapping, feather-edged boards, between stout timber or concrete posts about 2.75 m (9 ft) apart, nailed to two or three horizontal arris rails which slot into mortises cut into the posts. Fitting a gravel board between the posts and just clear of the ground will protect the light feather-edged timber from wet rot. A capping strip along the top of the fence will prevent weathering of the end grain from above. This type of fence is suitable for most locations, rural or urban.

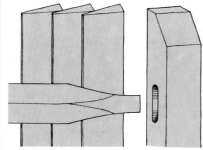

Close board construction *Arris rails slot into mortises cut into the posts to form the support for the overlapping verticals.*

Woven panel

Various weaves and sizes of pre-fabricated wooden slat fence panel are available. The life span of this type of fencing depends on the quality of the wood used for making the slats. Oak and cedar need little maintenance and are best, while soft-woods require regular treatment with a preservative. Use stout concrete or wood posts to support the fence panels and wood string cappings and gravel board to counter rot.

Fence and wall combination *Tough woven panels of cedar make up this fence which sits on a low brick wall.*

Bamboo

Bamboo makes an ideal screening panel which can be used on a boundary, particularly as a backing for growing bamboo or any plant of strong "architectural" shape. Make up panels of bamboo, lashing the stems, or culms, to cross members of a heavier wood with wire or heavy cord. Bamboo should not be nailed as it will split. When trimming the culms, they should be cut just above a joint to prevent moisture collecting in the hollow stems. Ensure too that the bases of the culms do not come in contact with the ground, as they will rot. It is also possible to buy rolls of split bamboo (the type used for shading) which can be attached with wire to any openwork fencing, like chain link, in order to provide instant privacy or shelter. The lifespan of such temporary fencing, however, is limited.

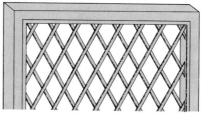

Traditional use of bamboo *A section of the bamboo fencing used in the gardens of the Katsura Palace, Kyoto. The vertical stems, or culms, are lashed to a horizontal, as below.*

Wooden trellis

In Europe, trellis work is relatively simple, being of diamond or square patterns in light softwood and made into panels about 1.8 m (2 yd) square. Folding trellis should be set within a rigid frame to give it stability. Much of this prefabricated material is lightweight and rots quickly, if the plants which it supports do not break it first.

The American market offers a far larger range of trellis work much of which is suitable for overhead shading as well as see-through fencing. French provincial, Spanish and Chinese-style patterns are available. The more ornate the infill to your framework, the more important the siting of it. If a particular pattern works with your house frontage, trellis work can provide a handsome boundary, but if isolated from the house, trellis is probably best used as a screening material (see p. 118).

Framing trellis *To extend the life of trellis it should be fitted into a timber surround, and held by a timber fillet.*

Hurdling and snow fencing

In England, you can buy 1.8 m (6 ft) panels of hurdling in either willow or hazel. These vary in height up to 1.8 m. The traditional use of hurdling is to provide a temporary shelter for sheep during lambing, but it also makes excellent garden screening. In California an unusual low rustic fence can be made from grape stakes. Snow fencing – wire-bound pickets in redwood stain or white – is widely available and sturdy and attractive if properly installed.

Plastic

There are various types of plastic fencing system available which imitate painted post and rail, post and chain or palisade-style fencing. These can be used to mark boundaries and need little maintenance but they are lightweight in structure and are not tough enough for general garden use. Plastic posts are usually hollow and should be filled with aggregate for better anchorage. Plastic is better considered as a material to be used in conjunction with others, such as wood or metal. Various types of rigid plastic sheeting infill might be used in the same way as the corrugated fiberglass sheet is used opposite.

Metal

There are two common groups of metal fencing. One, for urban use, is the painted iron railing which is made up of vertical bars and often finished with a spike or dart to provide a substantial see-through barrier. This is the type of fence that fronts many late eighteenth- and early nineteenth-century town houses throughout Europe. The other group comprises line wire, wire mesh and chain link (sometimes plastic coated), all of which are strained between concrete, metal or timber verticals, the end posts taking most of the strain. Such fencing is manufactured by the roll so the distance which you set the posts apart is a matter of choice. It provides the minimum in privacy when used as a boundary, but can provide a worthwhile measure of security if well constructed. Wire mesh is a good support for light climbing plants.

Less common fencing materials

Panels of sheet fiberglass can be used to make light and decorative fencing panels if incorporated within a wooden frame, as below, within the fence verticals. Varying degrees of opacity and a variety of colored finishes are available. Corrugated panels are also available. Exterior plywood can also be used as a fencing element.

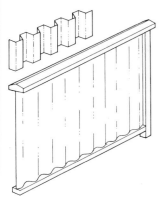

Fence post construction

It is essential to have sound verticals to hold your fence.

Timber posts should always be treated with preservative. But no matter how well protected, wooden posts set directly into earth will rot relatively quickly, and wooden posts set directly into concrete will also rot, if after a longer period. Where you can, fix the post at ground level to a metal plate or proprietary metal fixing, and then set that into concrete. Alternatively, you can use a concrete spur set in concrete to bolt the post to.

If you must set wood directly into earth or concrete prevent the wood from decaying for as long as possible. Where the soil is stable, place a large stone at the bottom of each post hole, to preserve the wood end grain, and backfill a little at a time with earth keeping the post absolutely vertical and tamping the earth in around the post. The odd piece of stone wedged hard against the post will help to keep the post firm. When locating posts in lighter, sandy soil, where less stability is possible, you must backfill with wet concrete. Do not set the end of the post directly into concrete, which might hold water, but again set the post on a large stone. Backfill for 100 mm

or so with gravelly soil before pouring concrete mix around the post. A standard mix for concrete used for post fixing is 1:3:5, cement:sand:aggregate. To cut down on the amount of concrete needed, bed the odd stone around the post as well.

Where heavy frost is likely it might bring with it the problems of cracking concrete and heaving of the earth. To minimize the damage caused by heaving, dig the post holes 300 mm (1 ft) below depth that frost can penetrate in your area, and shovel in a little gravel for drainage. Drive galvanized nails part way into the sides at the foot of each post, then position each post into the gravel before pouring the concrete around the nailed sections. Complete the backfill using gravel or gravelly soil.

To prevent the concrete collars around posts from cracking when wet posts freeze and expand, cut wooden wedges to the width of the posts, oil them, and place them alongside each post before you pour in the concrete. When the concrete has set, remove the wedges and fill the cavities with tar or sand.

If you are using concrete or metal fence posts, these are best set directly in concrete.

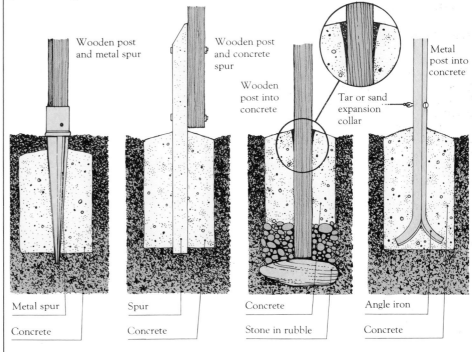

Wooden post and metal spur

Wooden post and concrete spur

Wooden post into concrete

Tar or sand expansion collar

Metal post into concrete

Metal spur

Concrete

Spur

Concrete

Concrete

Stone in rubble

Angle iron

Concrete

Post cappings

Hardwood fence post tops can be simply shaped to repel rain water. The life of softwood posts is considerably lengthened by fitting caps to prevent water from permeating the exposed end grain. These can be made of wood or non-corrosive metal sheet.

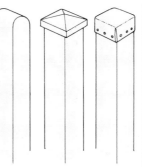

Post hole borer
A very useful tool to buy or borrow when constructing a fence, is a post hole borer. It allows you to remove the minimum of earth when digging post holes.

113

Fencing materials

Ready-made fencing panels available on the market are fairly standard; the major types are illustrated here. The purpose of the fence and its location will help you decide on the type you need. Plastic is obviously slick and urban, wattle fencing rural in feel, and the range available between these extremes is large. It is generally a false economy to invest in too cheap a fence, made of inferior material that will deteriorate quickly.

If you choose wooden fencing, ensure that it is well impregnated with preservative, either dipped in it or treated under pressure. Fit it with a protective capping and a gravel board beneath the lowest panel which can be renewed on its own, for the lowest area of the panel will always rot first. None of these maintenance points will be of any use, however, if the verticals which hold the fence are not of the soundest material and well pinioned into the ground.

Plastic fences

Maintenance will be reduced to a minimum if you select a plastic fence, and it will not rot either. Visually, such a crisp fence is attractive but physically it can be weak and unable, for example, to support the weight of children playing on it. Plastic fence is useful to define boundary divisions in an urban situation rather than to give privacy.

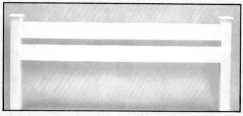

Ranch

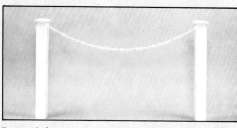

Post and chain

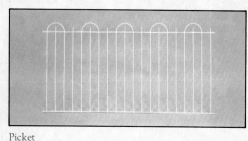

Picket

Panel fencing

Illustrated below are three standard types of wooden fence, of which there are many permutations according to the size and weave of the wood used in their construction. Most are made of soft wood. Larchlap fencing cannot be seen through, while inter-woven panels may be. Trellis fencing is ideal for plant support, the combination of wood and greenery providing a pleasant see-through background. This can be enhanced by an evergreen planting of shrubs in front.

Larchlap

Inter-woven

Trellis

Picket and hurdle

Picket fencing, when painted, has an urban feel about it, and when stained makes an admirable boundary and looks well in most other situations too. Its height can vary according to its function. Such a fence should be set at least 75 mm (3 in) above ground, if the base of the verticals are not to rot.

Wattle fencing is not built to last; traditionally it provides seasonal shelter during lambing. Its lifespan can be up to five years, however, and as a temporary measure, until planting has grown, or as a wind shelter to protect young or tender planting, it cannot be beaten.

Netting

Use netting fencing over large boundary runs where wood is too expensive, or where you want to define your site but retain any view from within it. Verticals can be wood but concrete is better, since they must support stressing wires along the top and bottom of the mesh. Chain link fencing, which is wire, or wire covered with colored plastic is the strongest mesh. Plastic chicken wire is less tensile than chain link but is ideal for more general garden use, for infilling decorative panels and to support rampant climbers such as pole beans and sweetpeas. Plastic-coated wire picket is usually used as a temporary measure and needs strong support at close intervals.

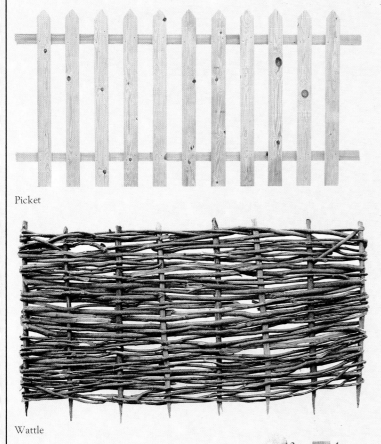

Picket

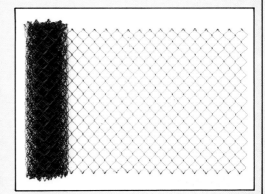

Plastic-coated chain link

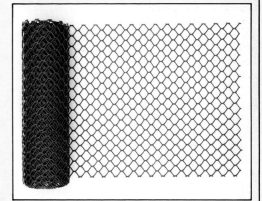

Plastic-coated chicken wire

Wattle

Posts

Whatever your particular fencing infill, it is the strength of its supports that will make the structure work. Concrete posts set into concrete below ground undoubtedly provide the most solid support, and when well matched with the infill look perfectly acceptable. In wet ground, or when stock might rub or brush the fence, concrete is wise. For a more sympathetic feeling, wood to match the infill panel is often necessary. The verticals may be sawn or left natural. All bark, however, must be removed, since it harbors pests and encourages rot.

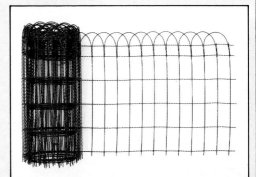

Plastic-coated wire picket

1 Concrete spur
2 Metal foot
3 Concrete post
4 Softwood post
5 Larch post

Gates

Why have the same front gate as your neighbor? Try to design your own gate so that the entrance to your garden is special and avoid the standard catalogue approach of cheap, overdecorative ironwork.

First decide exactly what you want of your gate. If it is a gate on to a public thoroughfare, should it stop people from looking in, or give them a glimpse of your garden? Is it just to keep children or pets in, or should it be a security gate? Is the gate to be decorative, or a utilitarian entrance and exit for pedestrians and/or cars? Answer these questions and you should be able to decide on dimensions and whether the gate should be a solid one, or openwork. Then decide on style, considering the style of your house (against which the gate is often seen) and the type of boundary it will pierce. If a wooden gate is to pierce an existing wooden fence, vary its construction or the gate will be lost when closed.

Consider the mechanics of your gate well – there is nothing more irritating if it fails. The piers on either side must be sturdy enough to support the gate and the hinges should be strong enough to prevent it from sagging. Always use three hinges in preference to two, and ensure that the lock or latch is durable and childproof as well as easy to see. If your gate carries your name or the house number, fit a spring to close the gate so the information can be seen at all times.

An entrance of character *A beautifully detailed, white-painted wooden gate, which is wholly in character with the house to which it leads as well as being decorative in its own right.*

Construction

Build your gate to last, for it will take heavy wear from undiscerning visitors. The construction details, right, are for a wooden picket gate which has both horizontal and cross braces to support the verticals. The horizontals are mortised into the hanging and closing stiles, and these are glued and secured with wooden dowels so that any rusting of screws is avoided.

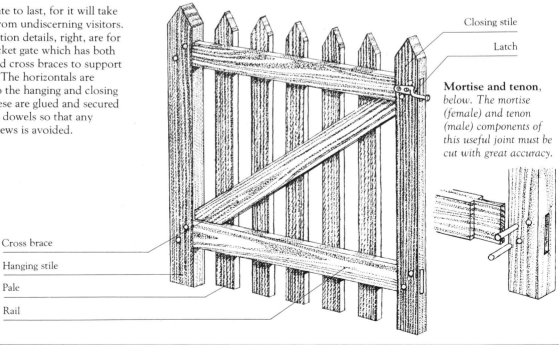

Closing stile

Latch

Mortise and tenon, *below. The mortise (female) and tenon (male) components of this useful joint must be cut with great accuracy.*

Cross brace

Hanging stile

Pale

Rail

Traditional oak gate *left. The stout supports, which balance the heavy detail of this gate, are in dressed stone. Also note the tough-looking latch which has been chosen to match the style.*

Gates with style *below. This beautiful white-painted wooden gate with a lattice top, pierces an old stone wall. Bottom, one half of a pair of sunray entrance gates in white-painted wood. The supporting wood pier is massive, but in scale.*

Matching gate to boundary

Below are four examples of gates set into a variety of boundary types. The secret of their success lies in the relationship between the proportions of fence or wall to gate. The character of the gates also reflects or offsets the character of the boundary they pierce.

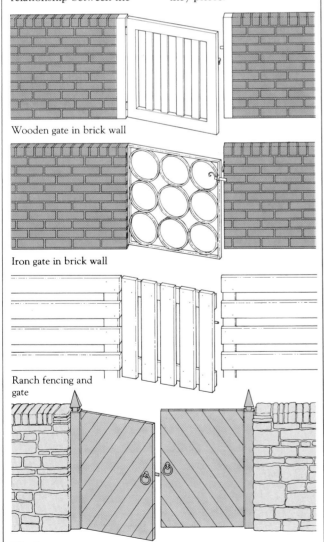

Wooden gate in brick wall

Iron gate in brick wall

Ranch fencing and gate

Wooden gate in stone

Internal walls and screens

You saw on page 106 how a boundary can be used to break up a site without necessarily dividing it up completely, like commas in a sentence. The use of screens within the garden, whether walls, fencing or hedges (see p. 196), goes one step further in the molding of space. As with boundaries, any internal screen should work within the original framework and pattern of your plan as described in Planning Your Garden.

A screen might be used to shelter a sitting area, or to partially hide a gas tank, the area for hanging washing, the rubbish dump, or even the vegetable patch if it cannot be well integrated. The density of such a screen can be less than for a boundary as no security measure is necessary, but to be effective it should provide screening throughout the year. A framework which supports a deciduous climbing plant will not be an efficient screen in the winter.

Various openwork concrete or terracotta building units are available which can provide an admirable screen. The simpler their pattern the more effective they are as a backdrop to any plants grown in conjunction with them. An openwork brick wall will perform a similar function.

Many forms of wooden fencing can be adapted to accept patterned infills within a simple surrounding frame, as shown right. Screens for special purposes, such as to shelter a swimming pool, may be see-through and constructed of more unusual screening materials. Heavy, expensive sheet material, however, such as glass, requires professional advice and specialist construction.

Open block screens

Screen blocks are of Middle Eastern origin, and intended to baffle a view while allowing a cooling breeze. Used incorrectly, they have the reverse effect of drawing the eye and, in northern climates, allowing a draft! Use the screening block sparingly therefore, and contrast its bold shape with large-leafed evergreen plants, as in the photograph, right.

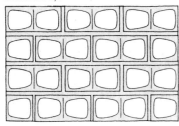

Hollow blocks used sideways

Making your own screens

On the right are some ideas for screens to be used within the garden in conjunction with planting.

1 *This idea uses driftwood within a framework, although any bough might be incorporated, provided that you remove its bark and treat it with preservative.*

2 *Here the frame has a simple infill of bamboo verticals which would look particularly well if bamboo were planted on either side.*

3 *Chain link fencing, or plastic-coated netting, can also be used as an infill material. Grow large-leafed vines, climbing beans or ivy through the link to thicken the screen through the year.*

4 *Rope, threaded through a surrounding frame, and finally knotted, will give a nautical flavor to a swimming-pool surround screen. The rope can be natural hemp, or a colored man-made type.*

5 *The louvred screen is a good way to direct a view, while blocking it from straight on.*

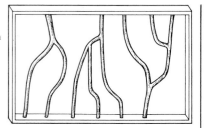
1

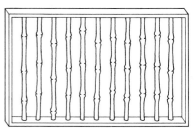
2

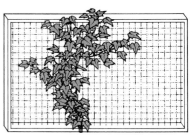
3

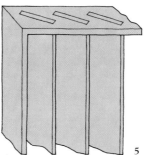

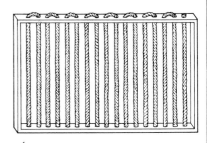
5   4

Changing levels

It is easy to end up with an ideal residence set in a garden of totally unmanageable levels. A solution to the difficulties of a sloping site where space is limited, is to build retaining walls to hold the earth back. A retaining wall will provide a strong, structural change of level and is the most suitable method of changing levels in a built-up area. However, a more economic solution is to grade out the site in banks or contoured mounds. This requires more space but can result in a pleasant rolling effect, perhaps backing up rocky outcrops, or a more carved and chiselled effect.

However you decide to change levels, the major practical consideration is the stabilizing of soil on your banks to stop loose soil from washing downhill in heavy rain. Pegged turf will stabilize a bank immediately (see p. 198), but the gradient which you grass should be gentle in section so that your mowing machine, of whatever type, can operate. Planting of a decorative ground cover (see p. 200) will also stabilize a bank, but make sure to use bold masses of individual types so as not to disrupt the flow of your ground shaping.

A gradient of 30 degrees to the horizontal is considered a reasonable gradient for a cylinder mowing machine. A gradient of 45 degrees can be managed by a rotary type of mower and is just practicable as a planted bank once the subjects are established. When planting a bank like this, it is advisable to plant through a coarse netting which is pegged into the earth and will retain it until roots establish themselves.

Importing earth to create garden banks can be an expensive business when you consider that shrubs require a minimum depth of 450 mm (18 in) of topsoil (grass can do with as little as 75 mm (3 in) however). But an advantage of molded banks is that you can hide any unwanted rubble or surplus spoil from building operations, or the excavations from a pool, beneath them.

Any ground shaping which you intend to appear natural should not look like a man-made dump on the top of natural earth. Always remember to clear topsoil to one side before building the bank or mound, then rake the topsoil back over it. If the spoil which you want to hide is not consolidated enough it will be liable to sinkage. Another pitfall to beware is that consolidated builders' rubble will provide such an excellent drainage system that topsoil over a mound will drain and become impoverished more quickly than other areas of the garden. In addition, surplus rainwater will tend to collect in puddles at the bottom of your banks, unless you provide for this with a drain run or soak away (see p. 103).

Gentle ground shaping *Gentle ground shaping has been used in this garden to encompass a swimming pool and to give it shelter. The material used to make the mounds was probably the excavation from the pool.*

Banks and steps

Various ways of creating banks, and so shaping your site, are shown in the series of sketches, right. The effect might be chiselled (1), or rolling (2). To achieve a complete undulating landscape, however small, requires space (4) unless you fake half of the roll with a retaining wall(3). To create ground interest with a slight change of level in a site, excavate a shallow step on the cut-and-fill principle (5). Always remember to remove topsoil before starting land shaping so that it can be replaced to form the new surface for planting.

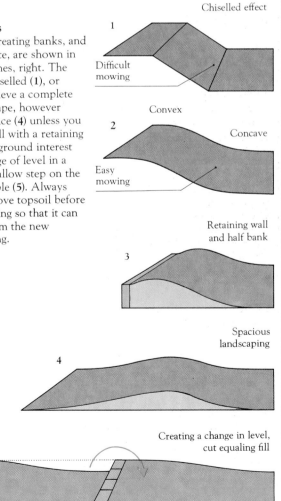

Chiselled effect

1

Difficult mowing

Convex

2

Concave

Easy mowing

Retaining wall and half bank

3

Spacious landscaping

4

Creating a change in level, cut equaling fill

5

Retaining walls

The construction of a retaining wall more than 750 mm (30 in) high is a project that should not be undertaken lightly, particularly if the soil which you are to retain, and into which you must dig, is heavy and needs draining. Any retaining structure will have to fight against the full, wet weight of earth behind it since you are creating a barrier to the natural drainage flow downhill. Provision for drainage is essential if your structure is to be sound and lasting. Do not take any chances where the proposed retaining wall is near a building. Seek expert advice, epecially where the slope to be altered is steep.

It is often not necessary to build a retaining wall at all if you grade out the bank in a series of "cut and fill" exercises, that you then turf or plant to retain. If you do decide to use retaining structures to support a particularly steep bank, you can use a similarly piecemeal approach, choosing a series of small walls.

The strongest type of retaining wall is one of concrete poured *in situ*, reinforced with metal rods or welded wire mesh – a specialist engineering job. Hollow concrete blocks, which have been reinforced with metal rods and then filled with poured concrete (see Appendix for the mix to use) will also make a solid retaining wall. Brick has less strength, being a smaller element, and when used for retaining walls should not be built more than a meter (3 ft) high unless as a fascia for reinforced concrete backing. Natural stone which has been cut on one side, or roughly dressed, makes a good solid retaining wall, particularly if it is built on the batter (sloped into the earth which it is to retain). A dry-stone wall with provision for planting within its structure, gives a charming rustic effect where it is desirable. However, stone is neither available, nor suitable, everywhere.

Wood may be used as a retaining material either in the form of railway line ties, or of logs, set into the ground vertically. Planks can be used horizontally, but with this method the vertical supports for the planks must be tied back into the bank with, for example, metal rods set into buried concrete and bolted to the supports. Depending on its imperviousness, wood will rot comparatively quickly, however.

To eliminate the build up of water behind your retaining wall, it is essential that it is pierced regularly by weep holes. These can either take the form of a gap in the jointing, or preferably a drain pipe set through the wall, angled downwards to a flush finish on the wall's face 150 mm (6 in) above ground level. Direct the water behind the wall to the weep hole by backfilling against it with a thickness of ash or rubble. A land drain at the base of the retaining wall may be required to take surplus drain-off. You will extend the life of a retaining wall by incorporating a damp-proof course and backing the wall with a waterproofing agent as well.

Retained banks *Massive lumps of stone have been beautifully ground to form this random retainer to a garden bank. Steps traverse the gradient, with a sculptural stone grouping beyond.*

Retaining-wall designs

Four designs for retaining walls are shown below. The top example uses concrete building blocks stepped back into the bank, and the one below it is constructed with pre-shaped concrete units. The poured concrete retainer has an angled shape for added strength. Such a wall should not normally be built higher than one metre. For higher construction you should seek specialist building advice.

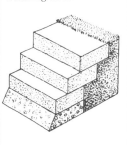

Building blocks

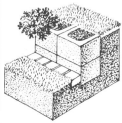

Pre-cast units

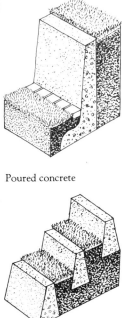

Poured concrete

Poured concrete units

Retained lawn *Stepped retaining walls in stone, with planting between each, retain this lawn area. Across the wall is a random run of steps.*

Construction

It is essential that a retaining wall is strong, as the weight of wet earth it holds is very heavy. The higher the wall, the stronger it has to be. In general, the larger the individual elements of the construction, the stronger the retaining wall will be. Water build up behind the wall must be allowed to escape through weep holes at the base. An infill of ash or clinker behind the wall will direct water to the drainage area and the weep holes. Whether the wall is damp-proofed or not will depend on its location and the type of wall, and whether you want plants in it, or only over it. It is not possible to damp-proof a wall partially filled with earth and plants.

A brick or concrete retaining wall will obviously last longer if it does not absorb water from the earth which it retains. To achieve this you must put a waterproof layer (of which there are many proprietary varieties available) behind the wall and the earth behind.

Concrete block *This is a solid concrete block wall built on a concrete foundation, with a paving stone coping along the top. Weep holes are vertical un-mortared joints. An edge of brick or concrete strip at the base of the wall makes mowing easier. Hollow concrete blocks can be used to construct a stronger wall, pierced by reinforcement rods, as above. The hollows are finally filled with wet concrete before capping.*

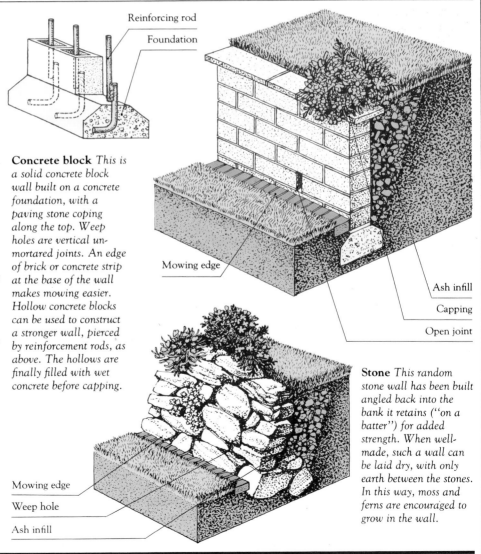

Reinforcing rod

Foundation

Mowing edge

Ash infill

Capping

Open joint

Mowing edge

Weep hole

Ash infill

Stone *This random stone wall has been built angled back into the bank it retains ("on a batter") for added strength. When well-made, such a wall can be laid dry, with only earth between the stones. In this way, moss and ferns are encouraged to grow in the wall.*

Steps and ramps

Few people can afford sculpture for their garden, but a good run of steps – not necessarily a huge flight – well-sited and interestingly composed, can more than compensate for its lack. Steps used in the rhythm of the garden can become not only a focal point, but an interesting and useful feature. They can provide a feature, a vantage point and a temporary perch.

Steps must be gentle, low and wide. Too steep a flight will quicken the pace unnecessarily. Making the steps as wide as you can will have the effect of making them look as gracious and inviting as possible. Plan your steps as a means of getting from level A to level B, but not necessarily in the shortest time. Consider them as part of the patchwork of materials which make up your garden pattern.

The materials you use for constructing the steps will dictate their form to a certain extent. In addition, the paving materials you intend to use at the top and bottom of the steps, or for any retaining walls nearby will also affect your choice.

After making a flight of equally-spaced steps fit into a bank, you will often be left with an awkward cut or fill area on each side of the flight. The treatment of this area can be a problem. If it is grassed, it can be difficult to mow. Sometimes a retaining wall holding the steps on either side is the neatest solution.

There is often no necessity to run your steps straight up and down the slope. If space allows, the run might go left or right for a period, with a landing on the turn. In this way, flights of steps can become more sculptural. For a similarly dramatic effect, you might decide on a more unusual construction still, such as steps cantilevered from a solid retaining wall.

There are flat gardens that can be considerably improved by simply constructing the occasional step right across the site. Such steps should articulate the garden plan, providing ground interest and encouraging the eye to remain within the site.

Gardens constructed on different levels with steps between them, will present a problem when it comes to using wheelbarrows or lawn mowers. These tools can be given a ramped route of their own if the area is large enough, or failing this, you might run a ramp at the side of any steps. If the ascent is gentle enough, it is possible to have ramped sections between two or three steps. Whatever the solution, such a garden will not be an easy one to work.

The consideration of safety must be a priority when building steps. Treads which are too smooth, or will wear quickly to an unstable surface, are equally dangerous. Treads set absolutely level will not shed rainwater quickly so presenting a hazard which is increased in icy weather when any standing water will freeze.

Shallow steps *This romantic flight of steps sweeps up a gentle incline under an overhanging wisteria. The retaining wall which edges the flight, would be more successful if it encouraged the eye to move with the curve of the steps, but the overall effect is inviting and altogether grand.*

Turfed steps *In this example, bricks have been used on end to form the risers to a turfed flight of steps. While appearing pleasantly rural, this method of construction will be difficult to maintain, since mowing will be difficult and edging of the grass necessary against the riser. The coping to the retaining wall which edges the flight has been specially shaped to match.*

Construction

Step construction is similar to paving (see p. 126), and building retaining walls (see p. 121), for each step riser (the vertical component) is a miniature retaining wall. You must pay particular attention, however, to the treads (the horizontal components). Each must be well set in concrete, with allowance for water runoff to left and right. Whether the edges of the treads meet with the edges of the risers to make right angles, or whether you make the treads overhang the risers, depends on the effect you want. The former is crisp and architectural, while the latter method creates a shadow line along each riser which makes each tread appear to float. The height of each riser should be approximately 150 mm (6 in), with the treads about 380 mm (15 in) wide. To decide on the number of steps that you require, first measure the change of level across the slope (see p. 31) and then divide it by the riser height. It is often necessary either to cut into the bank, or to build it up, at top or bottom, to make the slope fit the steps.

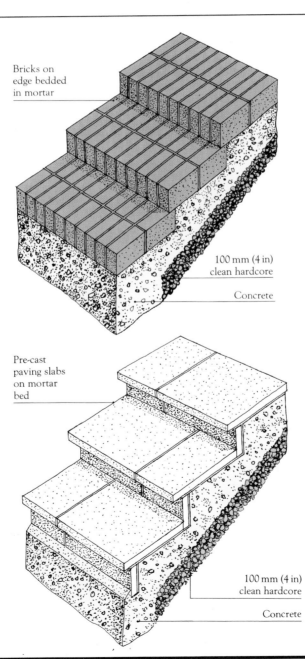

Bricks on edge bedded in mortar

100 mm (4 in) clean hardcore

Concrete

Pre-cast paving slabs on mortar bed

100 mm (4 in) clean hardcore

Concrete

Ramps

A ramp is cheaper to construct than steps and is easier to negotiate, especially with machinery. The surface should be of a rough, gripping material, such as brushed concrete or gravel. With a stepped ramp, shown below, the ramped sections should have a gradient no steeper than 1 in 12, with steps not exceeding 115 mm (4½ in). For approaches to garages, or over areas needing a more refined surface, use paving or brick, but with the individual elements haunched for grip.

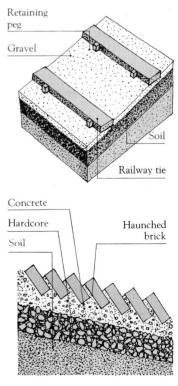

Retaining peg

Gravel

Soil

Railway tie

Concrete

Hardcore

Soil

Haunched brick

Using different materials

Most types of paving material may also be used for steps, and it makes sense to connect paths at the top and bottom of steps by using the same material between. Architects have particular rules for step heights and tread widths which conform to various building regulations. But in the garden, the general rule is the gentler the flight of good wide treads, the more pleasant the steps. However, be ruled by the appearance of the materials you use. The tree trunk slices, bottom, for example, make attractive "stepping-stone" treads.

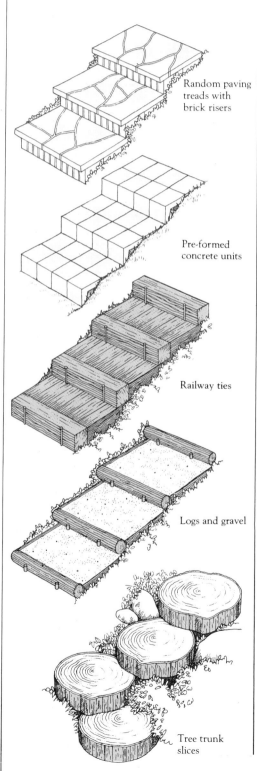

Random paving treads with brick risers

Pre-formed concrete units

Railway ties

Logs and gravel

Tree trunk slices

Random steps *A flight of stone steps, such as that above, is suitable for crossing a rockery or rough bank where it will complement a rural feel.* *It would be totally unsuitable, however, in a more formal setting, such as the approach to a house.*

Cantilevered treads

When space is limited, steps should be tucked into a corner, as in the photograph right. The structure is of stained softwood, supported on a central wooden rib which is let into the wall beneath a landing. Alternatively, treads may be cantilevered from a wall as in the diagram, below.

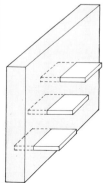

Step designs

We tend to be too rigid in our ideas for steps, making simple flights that run straight up and down. With a little ingenuity, the direction of the flight may be altered so that the finished effect is more casual and more of a sculptured feature in the garden. If your garden plan lends itself to it, you can incorporate a landing in the flight of steps, changing the course through 90 degrees, or even 180 degrees if there is room for two landings.

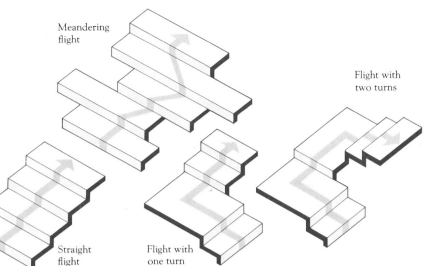

Meandering flight

Flight with two turns

Straight flight

Flight with one turn

Sympathetic planting for steps

The plants that you choose to flank or cover steps are important if the flight is to be properly integrated into the garden. A "weedy" look can create a magical effect. To achieve the feeling of longstanding random growth, leave planting pockets at the sides of the flight, or leave jointing open for planting. Select species that will not become too rampant, and that can take a certain amount of wear. Herbs are ideal as they will smell when brushed. Try chamomile (*Chamaemelum nobile*), catmint (*Nepeta* × *faassenii*), or mixed-colored, low-growing thymes (*Thymus* sp.).

The way in which you plant the areas bordering a flight of steps can change the character of the steps completely. A straight flight can be made to appear curved or staggered from side to side, by letting plants encroach on to the sides of the flight in a planned fashion. Starkness can be softened, or purely functional steps given a lift with strong "architectural" planting.

Soft planting, *above. Woodland strawberry (Fragaria vesca) covers the risers of these stone steps and gives a pretty, edible result. The flight has been further softened with planting at the sides of the steps.*

Abundant planting, *left. The effect of the herbaceous planting on either side of this straight flight of steps is to give it a meandering line. This is an example of excellent grouping of plants to complement a structural feature.*

Surfaces

Now that you have shaped up the garden, with all its walls, changes of level and steps positioned and built, you are ready to get down to filling the areas of ground pattern with planting, lawn, water or a hard surfacing medium of some kind. Whatever medium you choose from those shown on the next pages, hard surfacing should provide the stepping off point to enjoy the garden as well as providing a link between buildings and the soft, planted areas of the garden.

Paving

In the gardens of northern Europe and much of the United States, paving is the principal surfacing medium. The choice of paving you make will depend on the character of your site and the materials you have chosen to use so far, but more significantly on the price of different pavings. With a limited budget the choice must be between having a larger paved area in a cheaper medium, or a smaller area in a more expensive one.

Decide on the feeling of the paving you need. If it is to be the base of an outside room, that is a terrace next to the house, or in a sunny location elsewhere in the garden, it will provide a full stop in the garden plan and must therefore be strongly detailed. If it is simply to be a hard surface connecting point A with point B, it need not be decorative. I prefer simple paving patterns that provide a background to any elements placed on, or planted around, the surface. Remember that paving near the house has the additional purpose of setting off the building.

When paving is being laid adjoining a building, it should only butt the wall if 150 mm (6 in) below the damp proof course. Where this is impossible, allow for a gap of about 75 mm (3 in) between the edge of the paving and the wall of the building, and fill it with clean pea gravel.

All paving should be laid with a slight fall across its surface (away from the house in adjacent paving) of about 50 mm (2 in) in two metres (6½ ft). Over a small area, drain off into neighboring planting or to a lawn if your soil drains well. For larger areas, lay a drain run at the edge of the paved area, linked to a soakaway (see p. 103). Where this is not possible, as in an enclosed yard, lay the paving to fall to a central gully, which might link to a soakaway, or to surface water drainage from the house.

Whatever paving you choose, try to avoid having to cut too many elements. Keep the outlines of paved areas simple and consider the possibility of working out the framework grid for your garden design (see p. 38) to fit multiples of the paving unit dimensions.

Pre-cast paving slabs

Most pavings for family pedestrian use will need to have a hard-core base of 100 mm (4 in), according to the soil conditions (on clay you might manage with a little less). Over this, the slabs should be laid in 50 mm (2 in) of builder's sand, if each slab is heavy, or sand and cement if the slabs are smaller and require firmer support. Considering the thickness of the slabs themselves, say another 50 mm (2 in), it will be necessary to dig to a depth of at least 200 mm (8 in) if the finished paving surface is to be flush with surrounding levels. Brush sand or sand and cement (depending on your chosen bedding materials) dry into joints.

Slab path, *above. Pre-cast paving slabs in a simple walling bond pattern.*

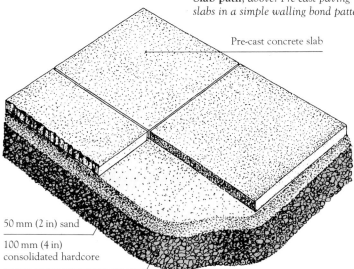

Pre-cast concrete slab

50 mm (2 in) sand

100 mm (4 in) consolidated hardcore

Poured concrete

Concrete laid *in situ* should only be used on perfectly stable soils which are not liable to frost upheaval, or where the water table is high. It is one of the cheapest methods of laying a large area of hard surfacing. You pour newly mixed concrete, on the spot, into a frame of your own construction. The frame need only be temporary, but might be formed by other surfacing, such as brick or paving stone. Make a temporary frame from 25 mm by 75 mm (1 × 3 in) planks held rigid and level allowing for the necessary fall) by stout pegs, over a well-consolidated 75-mm (3-in) base of either fine hardcore or binding gravel. Temperature changes will make a poured concrete surface crack if you make its area too large for its thickness. A good thickness in the garden is 100 mm (4 in) and you should keep sections of *in situ* concrete to 4 m by 4 m (13 × 13 ft). Divide larger areas with wooden expansion joints. Lay concrete paths in 4-m (13-ft) sections.

100 mm (4 in) concrete (see Appendix for mix)

Temporary wooden shuttering

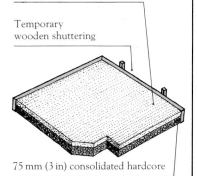

75 mm (3 in) consolidated hardcore

Stone

Quarried stone may be split and given a sawn or rubbed face for use as paving. The choice of a particular stone will depend on several factors. These include its durability and whether its surface will become smooth and slippery, particularly when wet, or fracture in the frost. The stone thickness will vary from 50 to 75 mm (2 to 3 in) depending on the size of the flags.

On normal soils (light or sandy clays, fine sands, sand and gravel, or gravel), lay the stone flags on a 75-mm (3-in) layer of clean hardcore, or similar granular base material, blinded over with sand. If large and heavy enough, the flags may be laid directly on to the sand. Spot bedding, where a dot of mortar is put at each corner and in the center of the underside of each flag, will assist the levelling process. Allow for a cross fall of 1:32 across the paved area. Brush in a dry 1:1 sand and cement mix to seal the joints.

Random paving

Random paving (where each unit is of nondescript shape) should be laid on exactly the same foundation as pre-cast paving slabs. When laid badly, this type of paving is known as "crazy", which rather speaks for itself. It soon becomes weed infested and uneven. Laid well, the sizeable individual elements should be tailored to fit each other so that the joints are no wider than those of regular forms of paving, and the overall area is level. The jointing should be as for pre-cast slabs.

Bold use of stone, *above. Stone paving should be laid in simple, bold areas, as in this stepped terrace.*

Traditional paving, *below. This traditional stone paving shows how each slab must be laid with accuracy.*

Paving patterns

A heavy paving pattern is only attractive when it is used to fulfil a particular function, such as to draw attention to a particular area. It is preferable not to mix colored slabs in your pattern but simply to use designs as below.

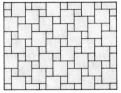

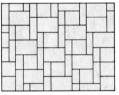

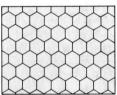

Paving and plants

The inclusion of plants amongst paving can create a very pretty effect as in these two photographs. The effect is strongest if only one type of plant is used but it is only possible with large, stable paving elements.

Combining paving and plants, however, will restrict the usage of the paved area. Plan open joints for planting carefully so that the character of the paving is enhanced rather than obliterated.

Small unit paving

Paving with small units, such as those shown on the next pages, and including brick and granite blocks, gives easier paving of awkward shapes in the garden and provides a richer surface texture. However, small-unit paving is usually more expensive than putting down larger units, such as pre-cast concrete slabs. It is not always the material itself which is more expensive, but the cost of having a mass of small elements, such as bricks, laid. And to try to save on laying small-unit paving well by cutting cost on the base materials, or how the jointing is finished, is a false economy. You will only end up with a weed-infested, uneven and probably dangerous, surface. Well-laid and finished, small-unit paving can be very impressive over relatively small areas. It will attract the eye and will be a feature in its own right.

Plain coursing *In this European garden, bricks have been laid in straight courses to give an architectural feel to the path. The walls and steps are built of a standard concrete unit, with large cobbles laid loose to fill the beds at the base of the walls.*

Construction

Any small paving unit (whether it be brick, patio blocks, or any of the proprietary paviers now available) is prone to shift after laying because of its relative light weight and small surface area. To prevent this, and for normal wear, each element needs to be buried in a 25-mm (1-in) mortar base, over a 75-mm (3-in) solid hardcore base. When the area is complete, simply brush a dry mix of sand and cement (4:1) between the joints. This mixture will gradually take up moisture from the ground and slowly set. In places where small unit paving is to take heavy wear, it should be laid on a concrete base over a consolidated sub-base as explained for *in situ* concrete on page 126.

However, you can use a less durable concrete mix of 1:1:6, cement, sand and aggregate for this purpose, making the base about 100 mm (4 in) thick. When the concrete has set, the paving units can be laid on top, pointing them with mortar as if you were building a horizontal wall. When nearly dry, the mortar should be rubbed back.
Before fixing a single element, make sure that your pattern will work by laying out the paving loose. Some intricately shaped paviers are now available which interlock to form a predetermined pattern. You will find that there are alternative ways of interlocking the elements, however, to alter slightly the overall effect of the paving.

Jointing *After brushing dry mortar between the joints of small-unit paving, wait for it to absorb some moisture and start to dry. Before it dries completely, run the rounded end of a stick along the joints to produce a neat concave finish between each unit.*

Small-unit edging

The usual method of supporting edges is an outside row of bricks edge-on. The edging row can be laid to give a zig-zag effect or, to give a raised edge. Alternatively, you can use a reinforced concrete edging strip.

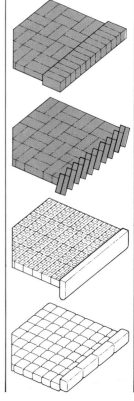

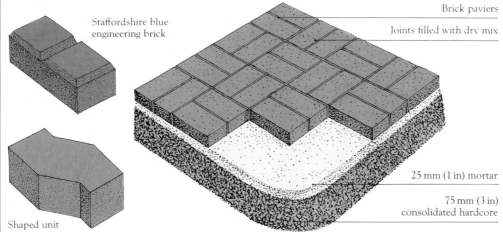

Staffordshire blue engineering brick

Shaped unit

Brick paviers

Joints filled with dry mix

25 mm (1 in) mortar

75 mm (3 in) consolidated hardcore

Brick paving

More houses are constructed of brick than of any other material, and a similar brick used to pave garden areas adjoining the house is a sure way of achieving integration of building and site. This will create a pleasant wrap-around feel.

When considering walls in the section on boundaries and enclosures (see p. 106), you will have seen the variety of facing bricks which are available for building and you might be able to match the brick of the facing walls of your house. But although facing bricks are made for exterior walls, they are not specifically recommended for exterior paving. Used for paving they will sooner or later flake and become uneven

through the action of frost. This effect can be desirable, particularly in a period setting. For a crisper, longer lasting brick surface, use brick paviers. These have been fired to become harder than wall bricks, and although they are more expensive they are easier to lay because they are thinner, slightly wider and longer. Another alternative is to use engineering bricks which, although the same size as facing bricks, are, like brick paviers, much more durable. Take care not to lay too large an area of brick paving in too fancy a pattern, for the mix soon becomes too rich. There is something special about good brick paving, but too much of it becomes indigestible.

Patterns in brick

Brick (or brick pavier) is an adaptable paving medium. It can be laid face down to present the bottom, or bedding face of the brick, or laid on edge to present a side, or stretcher face. You can interlock bricks in a variety of ways and bricks can be cut. These variables give you a great variety of possible paving patterns, five of which are shown below. Over larger areas, the richness of color and the quantity of elements required should encourage you to choose a simple ground pattern. Such patterns include all-aligning coursing and simple wall bonding patterns.

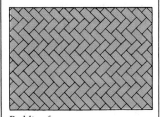

Bedding faces

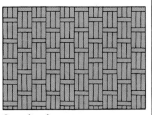

Bedding faces using halves

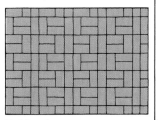

Bedding faces

Stretcher faces

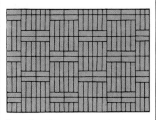

Stretcher faces

Recessed pointing, *above. This terrace has a surface of broken courses of brickwork. The pointing of the bricks has been recessed so that each element is clearly defined.*

Stepped terrace, *left. External building bricks have been used to create a crisp step in a terrace which is surfaced in alternating courses of paving bricks, and paving bricks on edge.*

Granite or Belgian blocks

Blocks are a hard, quarried stone surfacing material. They are gray and either roughly brick shaped, or half this size and roughly cubic. They were used originally as an extremely durable road surfacing material, close-packed in sand. Where old road surfaces are being removed it is sometimes possible to obtain used blocks from your local supply outlet. New blocks are mostly imported and are therefore an expensive medium to use. However, granite is a material which is alien to many situations so consider its use carefully. Granite blocks are laid in a 50-mm (2-in) bed of sand and cement (3:1), close-packed, over a 100-mm (4-in) solid hardcore base. More of the sand and cement mix should be brushed between the blocks where possible before lightly watering the surface and allowing the mortar to harden.

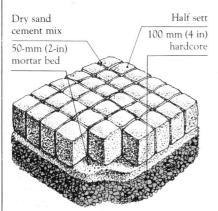

Dry sand cement mix
Half sett
100 mm (4 in) hardcore
50-mm (2-in) mortar bed

Squared granite blocks, *above. The feeling of granite blocks is hard and urban. Here they have been used as both a retaining curb to a planted area and as a surfacing material.*

Concrete paving blocks, *right. These are blocks made of concrete, giving a more refined finish than granite.*

Cobbles

Cobbles are rounded stones which have been formed by glacial action or by the action of the sea. They are graded and sold in various sizes for use in the garden. Laid loose and in contrast with bold foliage plants, they create a Japanese effect. Cobbles are difficult to walk on and they may be used as a deterrent, infilling corners which would otherwise be trodden on.

For an altogether crisper effect, cobbles may be laid on end, tight-packed together like eggs in a carton. Such paving makes an admirable infilling when creating a paving pattern. When using cobbles in this way they will need to be retained by a curb of some type, such as brick-on-edge, granite blocks or concrete. The cobbles are laid in 35 mm (1½ in) of dry sand and cement (3:1) over a 75-mm (3-in) layer of consolidated hardcore or hoggin. Brush a little of the dry mix through the cobbles when the laying is complete and then water them. The finished result should show little mortar.

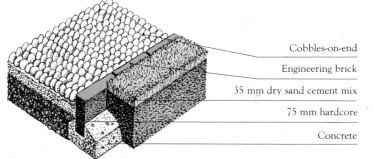

Cobbles-on-end
Engineering brick
35 mm dry sand cement mix
75 mm hardcore
Concrete

Cobbles for paving *These cobbles, laid in a random pattern on their sides, with a flattish side uppermost, are obviously for walking on. Usually cobbles are laid end on to discourage pedestrians.*

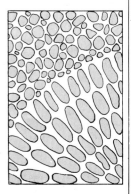

Inventive use of cobbles, *above. Different patterns are possible using cobbles of varying sizes and thicknesses.*

Soft surfacing

Between the extremes of hard paved surfacing and soft ground cover planting or lawn, there is the technique of "soft" surfacing. It is more relaxed in feel than the former and needs less maintenance than the latter, and being cheap has great potential for the small garden. The usual soft surfacing media are various sizes of gravel and stone. Also used are wood and bark chips, materials which are often used as a mulch spread over planted areas to reduce evaporation. Used as a soft surfacing material, bark looks best in a woodland setting.

Soft surfacings are an ideal alternative for small areas or for people who want a restricted amount of planting that will always look crisp and clean in its surround. They are equally usable in country courtyards, suburban front areas or tight urban gardens.

A retaining edge is important for all soft surfacing materials as without one they tend to spread. Within this retaining edge soft surfacings only require periodic maintenance as described in the chapter on care and maintenance. Weeds in gravel or crushed stone can be hoed or hand pulled after rain with ease. But the finished effect should be random and casual, with plants allowed to self-seed, so a weed-free approach is not always essential.

Pea gravel and gravel

Pea shingle is small chippings of stone which have been smoothed by the action of water. It is dredged from low-lying, inland pits or taken from the beach. It is the smallest sized gravel and requires raking periodically to maintain a neat appearance. Other gravel grades consist of the sharp chippings of natural rock obtained from a quarry. Both gravel and crushed rock have marked regional differences depending on the type of rock from which they originated. The traditional use of rock or gravel is for surfacing drives or roadways, where it is rolled into a bituminous preparation. It can also be laid loose, but consolidated, as a cheap garden surfacing. The material should be retained by a curb and 20 mm ($\frac{3}{4}$ in) should be rolled into a 75-mm ($\frac{3}{4}$-in) hard, gravelly base, otherwise it becomes difficult to walk through. The surfacing layer needs replenishing each summer to retain its crisp effect. Increasingly, stone and gravel are being used as media in which to plant. The preparation of the ground beneath depends on soil type. If limestone or gravelly roll the 20-mm ($\frac{3}{4}$-in) surfacing layer on to the soil and plant through it. Where the soil is sandy or clayey, you need to hold the gravel by spreading it over a 75-mm (3-in) base. Pockets will have to be made through both layers for the roots of plants to penetrate to the soil below. After some time, however, there is a build up of soil within the layers and you will be able to plant directly into the gravel.

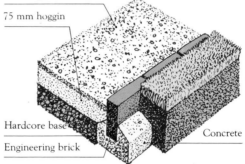

20 mm gravel
75 mm hoggin
Hardcore base
Engineering brick
Concrete

Planting in gravel, *below. Random planting in consolidated gravel is possible, as shown here in my own garden. Bold clumps of* Verbascum bombyciferum *feature in the foreground with masses of* Alchemilla mollis *and* Limnanthes *sp. beyond.*

Paving materials

There is a bewildering selection of types of paving though most people settle for concrete in one form or another since it is the cheapest and most universally available material. But it is all too easy to be conditioned by what your local supplier holds. So remember that the range is varied and shop around. Do not be afraid of mixing materials, though be sure in your mind of the finished result you seek.

Textured paving

In selecting your paving, first choose a color to blend with your house. Wet an area of the slab to see what it looks like. Then determine the size of each slab, to fit with your ground pattern or grid and to avoid too much cutting. Where you need to cut and tailor the slabs (usually a sign of your ground pattern not working) use a good quality slab since cheaper ones tend to crumble. Lastly, select for texture, bearing in mind the function of the paved area.

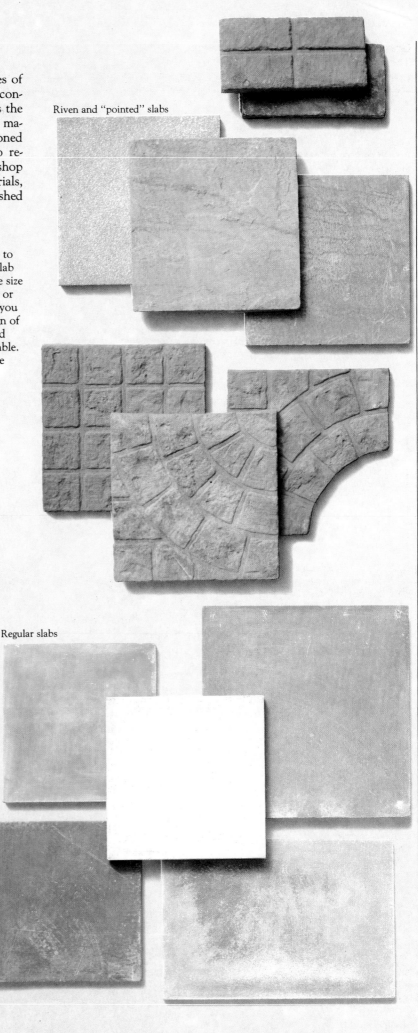

Riven and "pointed" slabs

Shaped slabs

Regular slabs

Smooth paving

If you want to stand chairs and a table on your paving, choose a smooth finish. When introducing a pattern into a large area of smooth paving, make sure that the outline of the overall plan and the pattern of the infill do not fight each other. As for textured paving, choose the color of smooth paving to match your house and wet the slabs before making your final choice to test change in color and slip-resistance.

Gravels

There are as many gravel types as there are stone types, for one is a chip off the other. The chipping sizes vary as well, so there is considerable variety in color and texture, as shown below.

Pea gravel

This is excavated from saline or fresh-water pits and does not have any sharp edges.

Stone paving

There is a timeless, massive quality about stone paving that seems correct in almost any situation. However, its variable thickness makes it difficult to lay. Old York stone, used for English interior flooring and for street pavements, is very handsome although its availability is decreasing.

Small unit paving

It is the correct use of the smaller units of paving that often sets the style of your garden, roof terrace or conservatory. Broadly, the more sophisticated the mood you seek the finer the finish should be. Granite blocks and paviers are for heavy wear, but are unsurpassed when well finished. Finer brick and tile finishes are excellent for interconnecting use, joining indoors and outside. The new concrete interlocking pavier supports vehicles yet is refined enough for domestic use. Too large a laid area of the more refined small units can create a back-yard feeling.

1 Granite blocks
2 Granite paviers
3 Brick pavier
4 Stable tile
5 Brick paviers
6 Interlocking paviers
7 Quarry tiles

Cobbles

When a sea-washed pebble is large enough to make a usable element on its own, it is known as a cobble. Laid close together, they make a simple but positive finish.

8–9 Sawn sandstone
10–11 Dressed sandstone
12 Random sandstone
13–14 Random limestone
15 Random ironstone
16 Random slate

133

Mixing materials

The dividing line between a successful mix of paving materials and an unrestful muddle of them, is very thin. So when you find yourself with a few slabs or bricks left over from this or that job and want to combine them in a random way, the rules for success are to keep the areas of each material as large as possible and to interlock the materials so that the transition from one to another is smooth.

Various types of paving can be mixed to produce a more calculated pattern. The stronger the pattern, the larger the area should be. The decision to lay a particular combination of paving materials is generally dictated by economics. A large area of brick might be too expensive, for example, but a brick pattern infilled with concrete or gravel, will make the project considerably cheaper.

Be very careful about introducing a mix of colors into your paving design. Remember that too rich a mix is likely to produce paving that vies with any planting or other feature that abuts it. Some of the paving colors manufactured clash violently with foliage.

Stone mix *The transition in surfacing from granite blocks, through cobbles, to random stone and then back to blocks, has been handled with sensitivity. The stone trough is related in size and texture to the stone slabs of the paving.*

Wood in gravel, *left. These slices of tree trunk have been used as stepping "stones" through coarse gravel. During the winter, the wooden areas can become slippery unless wire-brushed.*

Slabs in cobbles, *right. Here, hexagonal pre-cast concrete slabs are laid in pebbles. The bevelled edge of the slabs will prevent them breaking.*

Ties and cobbles
Old railway ties are here set to radiate round a gentle curve. Loose cobbles are used to infill the joints and will provide a better grip in winter. The scale of the cobbles offsets that of the ties well.

A complete mix, *right. This consciously designed mix of paving materials dominates the flower beds piercing it and the furniture set upon it. Pre-cast concrete slabs form a grid that has a wooden infill. In the foreground, coloured bricks have been used.*

Mixing brick and slabs
When mixing materials, be positive about your plan. On the right are three ways of paving a small terrace. Assume that it adjoins the house on one side, so that brick is a linking material between house and garden. The top terrace is entirely in brick with an area left open for random planting. It is important to leave enough uninterrupted space for table and chairs if they are required. The middle terrace has an equal amount of brick and slab that has been laid in a conscious pattern. The last version uses the slabs predominantly, with a random infill of brick, to give what is perhaps the most satisfying effect.

The inclusion of larger paving units, such as pre-cast concrete slabs, will cost less than paving entirely with small units. Be careful, however, to compare the dimensions of the larger and smaller units so that your pattern allows for the least possible amount of cutting.

Cesspool covers
Irritatingly, a cesspool cover is often sited in the area that you have designated for a terrace, and at the wrong angle compared with the planned direction of your paving units. You can deal with this problem in a number of different ways. Whichever you choose you must be positive about the solution or you will end up making a feature of the cover rather than hiding it. You can buy replacement covers which have an inverted metal tray into which you cut and fit a section of the surrounding surfacing material. However, these lids are too shallow to take earth for plants or lawn. Or you can plan for the inspection cover to sit within a cobbled or gravelled area that is strong enough to dominate. An adjacent shrubby crawler, such as a cotoneaster, will screen the cover. Failing all else, pave or grass the surrounding area and paint the cover black. You will soon forget the cover if you do not draw the eye to it by doing anything such as placing a planted tub on top.

Decking

Decking (areas of wooden planking) is not an English form of surfacing but it is often used on the Continent and in the United States. Climatic factors are the prime reason. Long, moist winters in the British Isles make wood slippery and unattractive while more extreme climates with longer, hotter and drier summers are appropriate for decking even though decks may be snow-covered in winter. Such a climate makes for extended periods of outside summer living when the wooden deck can be put to many uses.

Cost is another factor which controls the use of decking in the garden. In areas where wood is relatively cheap, decking becomes an attractive method of surfacing. Where wood is plentiful decking will provide a sympathetic link between garden and surrounding countryside.

There are three types of decking. The simplest type is low level and provides an alternative to terracing. It is usually supported by concrete piers or short timber or metal posts. In towns, such decks are often useful as a transition between a turn-of-the-century house and its garden. These often have basements and a well-sited deck can be a useful bridge between the garden level and the ground floor.

Hillside decks provide a method of creating level space where none exists. Correctly sited, they can provide a platform for spectacular views. This type of deck is costly to construct and might require the expertise of an architect, especially if the deck adjoins the house. An architect will also be aware of any local building regulations with which you must comply.

The third type of wood decking is used to provide a surface for a roof garden where the original roofing material was unsuitable for pedestrians and garden elements. Where any major construction is envisaged to convert a roof space for use as a garden, you should take the advice of an architect or a structural engineer so that the load the roof can bear is established. Plant containers alone can be extremely heavy.

A successful deck depends on the quality of the wood you use and its maintenance. It is obviously necessary to choose a wood with high resistance to decay, splintering and warping. Redwood is the ideal decking wood, and is only available in the United States. It does not require treatment with preservative. Red cedar is similarly durable and available on a wider scale. Pines, larches and spruces also provide wood that is usable for decking but all require preservative treatment. It is important that the wood you use can be sawn without splintering and will accept nails readily. The number of fixings required in deck construction necessitates the use of galvanized nails rather than screws.

Construction

Low level decking is relatively easy to construct once you have made your choice of wood. The deck depends on firm, poured concrete footings (foundations) below ground level. Dig out holes for these beneath the final positions of the piers of the proposed deck, and use temporary wooden formers to establish a substantial slab of concrete. You can buy proprietary pre-cast concrete piers which sit on the footings and provide the bases for the wooden posts which will take the wooden frame of the deck. The wooden posts must be cut to allow for any changes in ground level so the 100 × 100 mm (4 in) beams that form the basis of the deck structure are indeed level. These beams support 100 × 50 mm 4 × 2 in) joists which support the decking planks. The structure is nailed together, the wooden posts being nailed to nailing blocks let into the wet concrete of the footings. Where decking is used at low level, make sure that weed growth is suppressed beneath the deck. One method is to spread black plastic sheeting between the deck supporting posts. The visible sections of sheeting can then be covered with pebbles or gravel.

Deck

Joist

Beam

Post

Pier

Footing

Stepped terrace *This timber deck is well-detailed and extensive, with full-width steps between two levels. The timber used for the decking matches that of the house façade and is simply laid.*

Decking patterns

The simpler the pattern of wood you devise for your deck, the simpler the supporting structure need be. Less wood and construction time are other advantages. If you want a fancy pattern, however, relate it to the patterns of neighboring wooden structures, such as fencing.

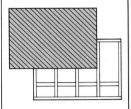

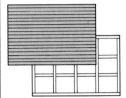

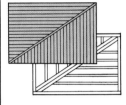

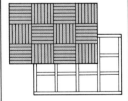

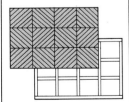

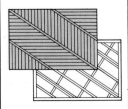

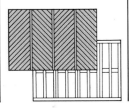

Linked decking, *above. In this example, bold decking steps have been used in conjunction with retaining walls constructed of railway ties. These elements have a solid feel and* *this characteristic is emphasized by intermediate concrete block steps. The staining of the wood used in the construction, and its proportion, marry with the wooden house fascia.*

Deck design

The design for a wooden deck, shown in the diagram, right, provides useful terrace space which might adjoin any house. In place of a handrail or balustrading, the edges of the deck have been built up to surround the area and to provide casual bench seating. A further raised section, doubling as a table, lifts to provide useful storage space, possibly for cushions or garden equipment.

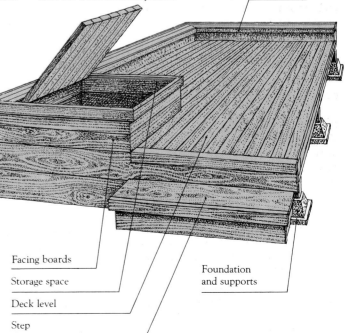

Seating

Facing boards

Storage space

Deck level

Step

Foundation and supports

Features

Having established the basic layout and working areas of your garden, you can now start indulging in flights of fancy and think about realizing any eye-catching features that you want to incorporate, such as raised beds, rockeries or water areas in their various forms, including streams and channels.

Nowadays, few gardens are large enough to include many features and, in a small area, you should make your special interest set the character for the whole garden. Avoid at all costs a series of unrelated eye-catchers, divided by grass or planting, making the garden a collection of oddments. The most common cause of such a state is misjudgment of scale. The rockery, for instance (that peculiarly English garden feature), can all too easily become a pimple in your layout. To have any measure of success, a rockery must look natural, as though it were an escarpment of natural rock exposed through the action of wind and rain. It is this outcrop which is planted about with alpine plants. Water is often incorporated with rock outcrops in the garden, either as a pool or as a stream. Both can look charming but can also easily become pretentious unless you keep the concept bold and simple.

Rockeries and raised beds

Making a rock grouping look natural is not only the result of placing the rock in strata but also in the selection of a rock indigenous to your area, if indeed there is one. You must also make sure that the build-up of land to the outcrop looks natural. On flat land the build-up should be gradual and so considerable space is required, as shown in the diagram opposite.

If you do not have room for natural groupings of rock, there is no reason why you should not grow alpines in contrived changes of level which create various raised beds. Such beds are effective and far more at home than a rockery in an urban setting. Given that many alpines are small plants, it makes sense to grow them in raised beds where their often exquisite forms can be better appreciated. The raised bed can also provide the well-drained, open situation that alpines thrive in. In the wild, many alpines root in scree or shale, which can be substituted by gravel or pebbles in the garden. You might consider incorporating raised beds in a terrace to provide shelter from drafts and screening.

Natural rock groupings *In these two groupings, stone is well-integrated into the garden surround. Notice how, in both cases, the stone sits in a bank, looking as though weather has exposed it. The stratification, or graining, of the rock runs in the same direction as it would if occurring naturally. The rocks used do not look like currants stuck in a cake.*

Rockery construction

You do not need a mountain of earth to make a realistic rock outcrop. You can utilize any gentle gradient in the garden; otherwise you will have to change levels (see p. 119), either creating a simple mound or by constructing a retaining wall. You will see from the diagram below, however, that the mound should not be too high, nor too cramped. Try to use slabs of rock to let into the bank so that you can create the impression of naturally occurring strata. Much of the rock will be covered by backfilling with earth and a substitute for scree, such as gravel (see the scree bed, below). The backfill should be

well-drained – a prerequisite for all alpine plants – but it does not need to be rich. Soil accompanying granite or ironstone tends to be acid, while soil accompanying limestone is alkaline so you should recreate this and choose your plants accordingly (see pp. 16–17). If you do not have enough room for both sides of the mound, the lower diagram shows how you might fake the mounded effect with a low retaining wall. This construction is particularly useful for siting a rockery at the edge of your site. In this case, however, do not allow the retaining wall to be seen or you will spoil the effect.

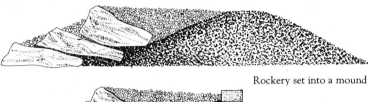

Rockery set into a mound

Rockery set into a bank
held by a retaining wall

The realistic rock garden *This example shows how much space can be required to harmonize the scale of outcrops with the environment.*

Scree bed construction

In a natural situation, a bed of scree is composed of chippings of the parent rock. It is not only uncomfortable to walk on, but also dangerous, since it is liable to slip. It is naturally well-drained and so dries out quickly. Plants growing in scree tend to be in semi-shade in the lee of larger rocks and this is a situation which you might seek to recreate in your garden, building up the bed as shown right.
You can site a scree bed in a similar position to a rockery, you can

combine the two or you can raise the scree bed within retaining walls of brick (as below), stone or railway ties to show off small alpine plants to best effect. Below is a series of brick retaining walls which might be backfilled with scree beds to support a selection of alpine plants which will crawl through the gravel finish and cascade over the low walls. Brick steps have been incorporated to negotiate the bank which sweeps into the structure on the right.

Section through a scree bed in the garden

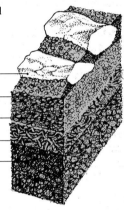

Rock bedded in gravel

Ground level

Gravel

Rough peat

Hardcore

Scree beds in retaining walls *This corner idea combines steps and retaining walls to provide raised beds for alpines. Anyone using the stepped route across the beds will be encouraged to stop and study the plant groups.*

Water

Water has an attraction which will draw the eye more than any other feature in the garden. It has almost the strength of a building in a garden layout, while having the unique attribute of reflecting light. It is a feature which, if well-integrated into a garden, can be an enormous addition, but if used badly, will spoil any progress you have made, becoming an irritation and rivalling other features of far gentler attraction. To avoid such problems, water should be used with discretion and as part of the structure of your garden design. In small gardens, it is probably best to use water in a formal way, in conjunction with the building or as a sculptural feature, such as a water container of some sort, or a fountain. The informal use of water (that is water in free-form shapes that imitate naturally occurring ponds) calls for greater space than the small garden allows, unless the whole garden is given over to congruous informal styling.

It is necessary to be absolutely clear about which category of water you want to include in your garden, then to decide whether it is to be flowing or still, and lastly, to ensure that it will be safe for children using the garden. There is little sense in planning a magnificent decorative pool, only to have to cage it for safety. Many suburban gardeners have to wire over their pools to prevent birds from stealing their fish and to prevent falling leaves from contaminating the water.

Decide on the depth of the pool according to its purpose. Shallow pools of about 300 mm (1 ft) depth appear deeper if sides are painted black, using a waterproof paint. A greater depth is necessary if you want pond life. Fish must be able to get under ice if the pond freezes in winter.

Whatever the type of water you want to include in your layout, whether formal or informal, it must always be clear and sparkling. To achieve this, water must either be running, using a pumped recycling system, or you need to establish a balance of pond life which includes oxygenating plants (at least ten per square metre (10.76 ft²) of water surface), snails and fish. A balance creates a food chain which excludes the green algae that stain surfaces and cloud water. Small water containers should be drained and refilled regularly.

Finely-detailed pool *Sympathetic planting and detailing masks the rigid outline of this beautiful pool. There is a fine balance between water, planting and hard surfacing.*

Types of pool

First consider the shape of pool you want, for this will determine how well-integrated it will look in your garden. Below are designs based on circles. While a plain circle is formal, pool shapes devised from interconnecting circles (as in the bottom two examples) can be treated formally or informally.

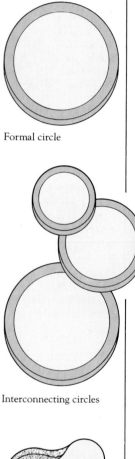

Formal circle

Interconnecting circles

Shape devised from intersecting circles with graded beaches

Formal use of water

"Formal" use of water in the garden refers to strictly geometric-shaped containers, pools or channels. Crisp detailing of edging and of any steps which might run through such elements is vital. Edgings should usually overhang the water by at least 50 mm (2 in) so any variance in the height of the water due to evaporation is hidden in the shadow of the overhang. Without the overhang you will also see the green line which stains the rim of any pool. Stepping stones through the water should be detailed in the same way so that they appear to float on the surface.

Formal pools are often constructed in waterproofed and reinforced concrete or are of concrete block or brick, rendered with a waterproof facing. The former method is stronger. Fiberglass pre-molded pools are also available up to a considerable size in formal shapes but they do not have outlet or overflow facilities. A formal pool can be still and reflective, its surface broken only by the occasional iris or rush clump or it may be agitated by a fountain. Avoid too great a fountain display for the area of water. The height of a fountain jet should not be more than the distance from the source of the jet to the edge of the pool.

Formally contained water can be most attractive when it is raised rather than sunken. There is a great charm associated with sitting on the edge of a raised pool and it is safer if children use the garden regularly.

Formal pool, informal planting, *above. The outline of this pool is "L"-shaped, although the wooden tie surround has been extended laterally to form an adjacent step. Informal planting softens the rigid shapes.*

Hexagonal raised pool *The strictly formal lines of this hexagonal pool in brickwork are broken by a solitary clump of irises.*

Construction

Small pools should be constructed in waterproof concrete (see Appendix for a suitable mix), allowing you to incorporate in the construction both an outlet to a dry well, for occasional cleaning, and, more important, an overflow to prevent flooding in heavy rain. Where frost is likely, the concrete should be reinforced and the pool made with sloping sides to allow the ice to expand upwards as it freezes. Failing this precaution, a softwood plank can be floated in the pool, which will allow the ice to expand into it.

You may also build into the pool a shelf recess for marsh-type plants. Allow all edgings to overhang vertical faces by 50 mm (2 in) to conceal any variance in water height due to evaporation. This will also hide the inevitable green scum line of algae at the edge of the surface of the water.

To plant in the water you will need special containers which are designed to hold a rooting medium and the root systems of water plants (see p. 214).

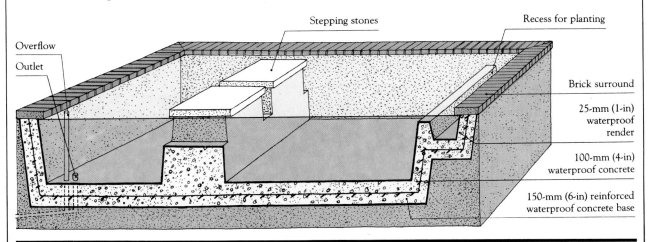

Stepping stones

Recess for planting

Overflow

Outlet

Brick surround

25-mm (1-in) waterproof render

100-mm (4-in) waterproof concrete

150-mm (6-in) reinforced waterproof concrete base

Informal use of water

Water used informally needs space to be successful, for you are trying to simulate a natural pool with eddies and bays of planting running into the water and contrasting with beaches of pebbles. To sustain this effect convincingly, the whole of a small garden needs to be planted and designed informally. Alternatively, a more contrived, Japanese, informal boulder pool is possible, backed with bamboos. Anything between these extremes is too demanding of a pool in a small area.

A plain, planted circle of water in an informal setting can be attractive, where you are creating a contrast of form. On a small scale, however, the dribbling stream and informal pool emanating from a rockery always looks contrived. Informal pools can be constructed in concrete, though the edging seldom looks convincing, and small, concrete-lined streams tend to crack. The most successful pools today are constructed by excavating a hole, adding a layer of sand, and then lining it with a

strong gauge plastic or butyl rubber sheet, preferably black. The edges should be held down and screened with a cobble or gravel beach. Planting, however, is difficult if it is to be convincing and hide the very edge of the sheet. The bottom of the pool can be lined with rounded pebbles and planted, the plants being held in purpose-made underwater containers. Care must be taken not to perforate the sheet lining since a small leak is practically impossible to locate.

Japanese effect The boundaries of this informal pool, in the Japanese manner, are carefully screened by boulders and planting. The effect is enhanced by the sharp contrast of the simple wooden bridges that cross it.

Construction

The area of an informal pool must be larger than that of a formal one if the effect is not to be pretentious. Plastic or butyl rubber sheeting makes an ideal lining for these larger amorphous shapes. The drawback to such a lining, however, is the need to hide the edge of the plastic carefully, together with any folds. Two ways of edging such a pool, when the sheeting has been laid on a 75-mm (3-in) sand layer, are illustrated

On the left is the informal beach effect, in which the gradient is shallow enough to hold the boulders laid over the sheet, and to prevent them from slipping to the bottom of the pool. An alternative is to lay the sheet over preformed steps, cut into the earth, to hold the beach. On the right, a straight edging is achieved by wrapping the sheet over a block retaining wall and laying a brick or stone coping over it.

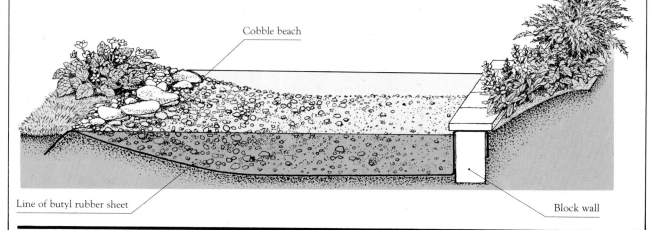

Cobble beach

Line of butyl rubber sheet

Block wall

Waterfalls

The gentle ripple of falling water has a more subtle attraction than the play of a fountain, but falling water needs bright sunlight to enliven it. Some of the most successful small waterfalls are those between level changes of small, formal pools, for as a design element they provide a strong vertical connection between sheets of water. Technically, one should not seek too large an over-flow or the amount of water to be pumped back will demand a huge pump. The amount of water that a gentle overflow uses can easily be returned by a submersible pump. When constructing an overflow, the design of the lip over which the water passes is crucial if the water is not to cling to it and then dribble down the face beneath. A flat stone that projects 50 mm (2 in) at the overflow might reject the flow of water; failing this, use a tile or piece of slate with a groove cut near its edge, along the underside, to break the water flow.
For pumping larger heads of water, the pump should be located "onshore" just outside the pool area, at the lowest level and be placed in a waterproof brick box with a slab over it. Whether you require a submersible pump or an onshore version, pumps require an electrical supply (see p. 105).

A waterfall effect, *right. Each of the lipped saucers in this arrangement over-flows into the saucer below and finally into a simple, concrete, circular pool.*

Stepside waterfall, *above. The idea of water running at the side of steps or a path originates in the Middle East, where running water is used to cool the air. Here it is used as a decorative device.*

Simulated mountain stream *Rocks and water are used here to simulate a mountain stream. The water needs only to trickle gently to create the desired effect. A simple submersible pump maintains the supply.*

Fountains

Wind can play havoc with fountains, quickly emptying the pool if the jet of water is too high. The height of the fountain should therefore be no more than that of the dis-tance from its source to the pool surround. In a domestic setting, keep the jet simple. It should either be placed centrally or allowed to play diagonally.

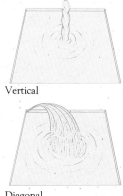

Vertical

Diagonal

Swimming-pools

Nothing is so demanding in a garden as a swimming-pool. Size can be played down by reducing the intensity of color of its lining and by altering the edging to it, but such an area of water will always dominate its surroundings. For this reason, its shape should fit carefully into the overall garden plan to minimize its bulk. It is a fallacy to suppose that the more bizarre the swimming-pool's shape, the more it integrates itself into a site. In fact, the simpler the pool's shape and that of the terrace which surrounds it (for pool and surround should be considered as one), the easier it is to fit a garden plan. Remember that you can use the shape of the swimming-pool terrace to adjust the shape of the pool slightly, so that the combination of pool and terrace better fits the site. However, it is best to tailor the shape of your pool to your garden plan from the outset, keeping it as simple as possible. Simple shapes are also more practical, since they are easier to heat, cover and swim in. Remember that, unlike a hotel swimming pool, the pool at home in a small garden has to be lived with throughout the year. Nothing is more depressing than a summer blue pool under leaden winter skies and to cover it with stretched canvas is unsightly, so consider a darker color.

The site for a swimming-pool must be open, sunny and away from deciduous trees to prevent fallen leaves from littering the water and poolside. It should not be constructed where the water table is too near the surface, or the whole structure will be subject to movement. There should be easy access to the site for digging machinery and a use to which the excavated soil can be put (see p. 119) as cartage is expensive. With the completed pool you will need storage space for maintenance gear, a site for the filtration plant and ideally a place for changing.

The actual structural work of building a pool should be undertaken by specialists who will advise you, but it is as well to know the questions to ask.

Pool types vary. When constructed of concrete they are either built and reinforced *in situ* or wet concrete is sprayed on to concrete block walls. Alternatively, they may be of cast fiberglass, or polythene or butyl rubber sheet within a metal casing or frame. The framed varieties are usually not built into the ground and, though cheaper, are not particularly attractive. However, with a decking surround, they can be successfully integrated into their site. They have some advantages. They can be moved at the end of the season and, being shallow and above ground, warm up quickly. Those contemplating a heated pool might consider using solar energy, but the panels have to be correctly sited to catch the sun.

The epitome of summer *A well-sited pool in the garden epitomizes the essence of summer – hot days and lazy lounging. The fixtures at this pool side (see p. 233), as well as the pool itself, combine to make the ideal setting.*

Pool shapes

The shape of a swimming-pool should be dictated by site, use (for play or for serious swimming too) and, of course, cost. A one-off shape will be more expensive than a standard-shaped model and may well need more heating, for warm, underwater convection currents tend not to permeate tight angles. Below are some simple pool shapes.

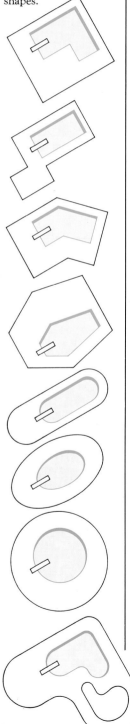

Pool edging

A swimming-pool's edging provides the trim to the pool as braiding completes a cushion. Above all it should not be slippery. Lighting and a scum trap can be well-integrated into proprietary moldings, which are pre-formed. Example (1) has a recessed scum trap below the level of the edging. Example (2) allows the raised pool surface to overflow into a surrounding scum trap. The two lower examples, (3) and (4), play down the fact that the pool is for swimming because they could surround an ornamental pool being in concrete slab, quarry tile or brick. Such edgings do not complement bright blue pool linings, but rather gray or black linings.

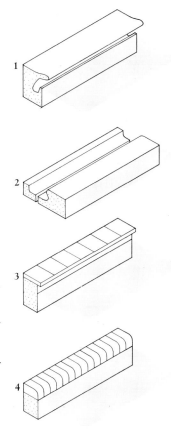

Successful integration *The decking for sunbathing and the tailoring of this poolside to a garden setting, make this example so attractive. Simple planting provides a useful partial screen between terrace and pool.*

Successful pools

The successful swimming-pool fits the garden design rather than dominating it. It should be a useful feature that serves its purpose – both for swimming and poolside relaxation. Ideally, it should also be a feature of beauty which has some of the attributes of a formal ornamental pool.

A feature of beauty, *below. Few have such a dramatic location for their swimming-pool. But this free-shaped pool above an Italian lake exemplifies how successful the swimming pool can be as a water feature.*

Divided functions, *above. This pool has been wisely divided to provide a shallow pool area for young children's play away from the deeper swimming area. Children are at constant risk by a swimming-pool and, unless they can swim well, should always wear a life jacket for safety.*

Plants near a pool

The obvious hazard when planting too near a pool is that leaves from deciduous species will drop into it; evergreens, too, will shed some leaves. Plants that are spiky or poisonous should also be avoided, especially if children use the swimming-pool.

Plants too close to a pool can suffer from the effects of chlorine, though this depends on how the chlorine is administered. Seek the advice of a pool purification expert as to the suitability of the system that is installed.

Despite the problems, planting is often necessary to shelter a pool from drafts and to relieve and soften large areas of paving with which pools are usually surrounded. Where grass is used as an alternative surface, care must of course be taken to ensure that cuttings do not get into the pool. You might consider using plants in portable containers as temporary decoration when the pool is not in use.

Recreational areas

The term "recreational area" is here used to mean those parts of a garden that are reserved for special activities – play areas, for example, or the barbecue corner.

Children can be very destructive within a garden if it is not designed to accommodate their play. Since the garden is often the only safe area for their games, it is sensible to orientate it to them, for balls and bicycles will otherwise inevitably end up among growing things. However, a child's play facilities will have to be changed as it grows older. Toddlers need a small grassed area, within sight of the house but well away from water or steps, and they appreciate bold splashes of color at this stage. When they are a few years older, they enjoy simple changes of level, for example grass steps or a gentle bank to roll down.

A sandpit is always popular. Where possible, make it large enough for the children to get in it, so that it can become a house or a desert island for them – fantasy is a major part of their play. Allow for a flat space within the sandpit on which they can make sand pies or castles, for otherwise this will be done on the surround of the sandpit, with an unsightly result.

Very shallow water for splashing in is usually greatly enjoyed, but keep it well away from the sand or the result will be mud everywhere. Shallow water raised to a toddler's eye height is safer and can be used for sailing boats. Both sandpit and pool can ultimately be adapted to become decorative garden pools.

As children get older, they will want more space for their activities – a route for bicycles, somewhere to kick a ball, to play with a tennis racquet and so on. Some hard surfacing will allow for table tennis outside. Often, space is needed for tinkering with machines and a corner for pets. Most of these areas will, however, inevitably be at the expense of more pleasant landscape amenities.

The major purpose of the recreational area of a garden, as far as children are concerned, is to have fun. Children must be allowed to run about, kick a ball, cycle and climb without being inhibited. If you incorporate a climbing toy, site it on grass or within an area surfaced in a soft medium, such as pulverized bark. This will make falls a little less dangerous for children.

Fun in the garden *If the garden is a place to be used for recreation, especially by children, careful planning will make playtime more* *enjoyable, safer and less of a strain on the fabric of the garden. Use durable materials and planting where they are necessary.*

Sandpits

It is essential that a sandpit is large enough to play in, is well-drained and is filled with the correct sand. A depth of roughly 300 mm (1 ft) of sand (not builders') is needed. The sand should be contained within a concrete, brick or wooden structure and be laid on paving slabs, which are themselves laid over a layer of fine hardcore or ash. To allow for drainage, the slabs should not be jointed.
In towns, the perennial hazard of a sandpit is of cats using them. Construct a simple lid, with a wooden surround and infilled with netting of some sort. This can be put on when the sandpit is not being used.

Pre-cast slabs

Pre-cast slabs with joints left open for drainage

Sharp sand

Ash or hardcore

Brick

Climbing frames

Most proprietary climbing frames quickly become defunct as children develop. Try to build your own adaptable climbing frame from an old tree trunk that will provide a point of minor sculptural interest, and can eventually be sawn for logs. remove rough bark and splinters by wirebrushing.

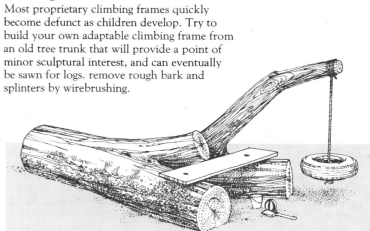

Barbecues

An adults' recreation area needs as much careful consideration as children's play elements in the garden. The barbecue area can become the centerpiece of a terrace garden in summer, but to be really useful it has to be designed and built to work as smoothly as the stove in your kitchen. There must also be adequate and convenient storage space for cooking implements and charcoal. Various forms of mobile barbecue are on the market but it is fairly easy to construct your own in brick. You can also build-in lighting and a worktop, which the movable barbecue always lacks.

Such a structure can be designed into a terrace layout and will still be attractive when not being used. Care must be taken, however, to ensure that prevailing winds will not blow smoke from the barbecue towards the house, your neighbors, or where people are likely to sit. When the barbecue is not sited directly within a line of vision, it may be used as a place for burning garden waste in winter, if locally allowed. Allow for plenty of space surrounding the structure, both for the cook and for guests. On a chilly summer evening, hot charcoal is compelling and will attract a crowd when the barbecue is over. Flat raised surfaces to the sides of the barbecue structure are necessary for serving, depositing plates, for relishes, glasses and bottles. After a summer party, it is very annoying to have to retrieve empty glasses and cups from planted areas.

Construction

If you are likely to have a number of people to serve from the barbecue, the cooking grill should be about 1 m by 500 mm (3 ft × 2 ft) in size. A smaller size will guarantee that some of your guests will have to sit waiting for their food while others eat. The cooking grill can be held neatly in the coursing of a well-built brick structure, such as that shown below. The charcoal tray slots below the grill and is similarly removable. Allow at least a square meter (10 ft²) to the right and left of the cooking area for preparation and serving food.

Make sure that the overall height of the barbecue unit is convenient for your height, comparing it with the height of your kitchen worktops. You can build in cupboards, as shown, beneath the worktops, ensuring that the doors are waterproof. Electricity supply from the house to a sealable socket will allow you to install a portable spotlight or standard lamp (see p. 105).

The barbecue structure will sit directly on a well-constructed terrace or on its own concrete foundation (see p. 126). A poured concrete infill beneath the grill is a useful protection.

Grill over charcoal tray

Quarry tile worktop

Sand and cement screed over concrete lintel

Concrete lintel to support worktop

Cupboard for barbecue tools and crockery

Concrete base above ground level

Charcoal store

An outdoor kitchen
A well-designed area for preparing and serving food can be the perfect complement to an area for outdoor entertaining. This integrated food preparation area, with its wealth of storage space and worktops, is possible in a hot, dry, predictable climate.

Structures

No matter how well you planned your garden, it is often necessary, after a number of years, to add structures within it, as a new hobby is taken up, you buy an additional car and garden tools proliferate. The available range of pre-constructed buildings is considerable, as is the selection of materials of which they are made. You must make a firm policy, however, to choose the same materials or from one manufacturer's range, to prevent the new buildings appearing haphazard. Manufactured structures are usually modern and crisp in line, so if your house is of another period you will have to screen your new buildings from view.

Price will affect the buildings you buy but, as a general rule, the larger the building the easier it is to integrate into a garden, for it is the difference in scale between house and new structure that is difficult to reconcile. With the smaller pre-constructed buildings there is also the problem that their height is often out of scale to their ground plan.

Unity can be achieved by grouping your structures – a shed, a greenhouse, frame, compost area and possibly gas tank – so they can be served by one path. Another method is to employ a windowless wall to support lean-to structures. The rule is to build-in your new structures rather than merely add them.

Conservatories and garden rooms

Conservatories and garden rooms are often listed together but their function is quite different. A garden room is an extension to a house, while a conservatory, although attached to a house, is part of the garden. The emphasis in a conservatory is on growing decorative plants under glass. Its furnishing and flooring will therefore have to sustain frequent watering and general plant husbandry. The garden room, on the other hand, is furnished as part of the house and is merely decorated with plants.

A garden room can be used as a summer sitting-room, but since large areas of glass are essential it will become too cold in winter and too hot in summer without double glazing. Windows can be opened, of course, but drafts become a problem. Unless well controlled, therefore, the uses to which a garden room can be put are limited by temperature. Nevertheless, it makes an excellent work space or a games room for children.

There is an increasing range of conservatories on the market, from traditional Gothic to modern styles. Most conservatories are constructed of softwood and then painted white, but this treatment demands regular maintenance and re-painting. Plants may be sited in beds or in pots on the ground or raised on shelving. Considerable care and maintenance of plants is required, however, unless you invest in an automatic watering device, since in warm weather plants may need watering twice a day.

But a conservatory amply repays all the work entailed, for it will provide you with a growing garden through the long dark days of winter, with hyacinths and narcissus, cascading mimosa or a Banksian rose, as early as January. In summer, a conservatory makes an ideal area for evening entertaining.

For the best effect, keep your planting and furnishing to a particular style and on no account let your conservatory degenerate into a collection of potted oddments. Make it tropical with large-leaved plants, or light and pretty within a particular color range, but at all costs be positive in your approach.

Purpose-built unit *A loggia-type conservatory, this was purpose made to connect two buildings, to accommodate a limited number of plants and provide an entrance to the garden. The construction is made into an attractive feature in a garden area that would otherwise be both drafty and perhaps uninteresting.*

The plantsman's conservatory *This conservatory has been designed more for growing plants than for family use, but space has been found for some incidental seating within a bower of planting in the 19th-century manner.*

Occasional dining-room, *below. In this example, the conservatory has been made into a handsome dining-room for summer use. The floor is tiled, both to facilitate maintenance of the plants and to provide a practical medium on which to stand furniture. The blinds, which are adjustable, keep the conservatory cool throughout the summer.*

Making use of the conservatory

A corner of your conservatory can be used as a small greenhouse, but you must first build staging at a convenient height (see p. 151). On this you can divide, pot up and pot on your plants, along with propagating from your existing stock or striking cuttings collected along the way. Propagating the sort of exotic plant that makes a conservatory particularly special can become a passion. Illustrated below are two types of propagator for the enthusiast. Both have electrically heated wires running through gravel. The top unit is enclosed for greater humidity.

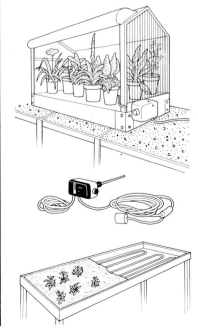

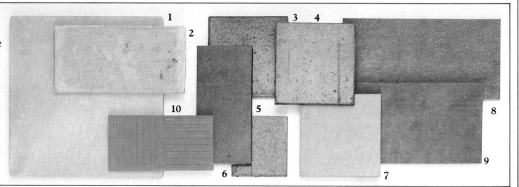

Conservatory pavings Tiles of natural materials – brick, stone and slate – come in many subtle colors and are hard-wearing, making ideal flooring for a conservatory.

1, 2 Sawn stone
3–7 Quarry tiles
8, 9 Slate tiles
10 Non-slip terracotta

Period home extension, *left. This conservatory, a home extension for year-round use, provides ample space for both plants and a dining area. The mood is predominantly of the Edwardian period, characterized by the tiled flooring and the basket-work seating.*

Modern garden room, *right. The feeling of this glazed extension, which forms a garden room, is modern. There is plenty of space for family use, punctuated by bold masses of foliage and color. Potted plants can be moved about to adjust the room for different numbers and uses.*

Alternative types of staging

Standard, commercially-produced staging systems are often more decorative than purpose-built structures but will not necessarily fit into awkward spaces. Moreover, some types of bought staging are little more than shelves, which soon become dirty from drainage. The top example illustrated below is of simple metal shelving. Below this is a metal framework containing deep trays for gravel, a useful way of keeping pots moist during absences from home. The third system is another example of stepped metal shelving. The two bottom systems have a metal frame with a wooden duck-board infill. However, these horizontals are subject to rotting.

Staging construction

Your staging must be of stout construction to support the considerable weight of gravel and of pots when filled and watered. Use 50 mm (2 in) angle-iron for legs, which should be set in concrete, and the tray, which must be welded to the legs and hold corrugated asbestos sheeting. Braces are needed under the sheeting and at the angle between the legs and the horizontal tray. At this point, paint the iron to prevent rust. Then cover the corrugated sheet with a layer of fine, washed gravel into which pots can be set. The gravel will both soak up surplus drainage moisture and at the same time help maintain moisture in the pots, which will soak up water by capillary action.

Brace

Gravel or pebbles

Angle iron

Corrugated asbestos sheet

Splay feet in concrete

Storage structures

Where to put garden tools, outdoor furniture in winter, bicycles, toys and the many other items that are used periodically in the garden is a common problem. Storage for these items seems to be totally overlooked by modern architects. As a family grows older the problem increases with discarded toys and leisure equipment accumulating. Apart from the obvious bulky items, such as a lawn mower, gardeners often collect a wealth of fertilizers and pesticides. Many of these are highly poisonous and should be kept in a waterproof place at a height beyond the reach of children. Then there are growing media: for seeds, mixes for cuttings and perhaps mixes for house plants. Add your gardening boots to the list and you end up with quite a storage problem.

Where possible, make a virtue out of necessity and use an out-building, where available, or consider building a new one that fits your garden plan, perhaps adjacent to an existing wall or fence. Failing this, you might consider a storage shed, but before constructing one it is advisable to consult your local bye-laws as some are quite strict about where you can build and to what dimensions. Choose a simple structure that fits your plan and you will be surprised how inconspicuous a utilitarian building can be. If you do want advice on screening, however, see page 118.

On the public side of the house there is often a need to place dustbins or to enclose gas or electricity meters. Simple units that conceal these items are played down when they, too, support your overall garden plan.

Traditional garden potting-shed *The diversity of well-used tools in this storage area and potting-shed indicates the sort of storage problem a keen gardener can have. Most people are unlikely to need such a large storage space but a smaller potting-shed can have similar character.*

Purpose-built storage structures
Specific storage problems can sometimes be solved with a purpose-built structure to suit the dimensions of the items that need storage. Such units are successful if they harmonize with the construction of your garden. Wooden structures, for example, might match the style of fencing.

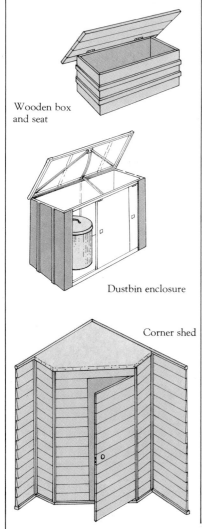

Wooden box and seat

Dustbin enclosure

Corner shed

Garden sheds

The structures illustrated below give an impression of the range available. The size of unit you choose must be influenced by the size of your garden, but it is often easier to integrate a larger unit into your layout than a smaller one. If you already have another free-standing structure sited in the garden, such as a garage or a greenhouse, consider siting your shed next to it to avoid too many service paths and too much hard surfacing.

Wide-doored shed in metal and plastic

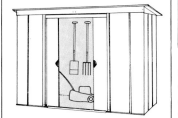

Simple wooden shed

Metal section shed with sliding doors

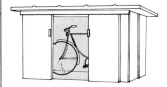

Half-sized shed in metal

Shade house, *above. A shade house, such as this lattice-framed example, is used for storing house plants that like cool conditions and some shade.*

Simple storage structure, *below. This structure is built of concrete block. The roof is of hardboard with a felt covering, and the doors are wooden.*

Foundations

Solid foundations are essential for any structure. The recommended foundation for a substantial garden storage structure is a poured concrete float at least 150 mm (6 in) thick (see Appendix for a suitable mix), over a consolidated hardcore base. Alternatively, you can use any well-laid hard surfacing which matches other areas in your garden layout. Wooden sheds are usually bought with a wooden floor which sits on joists to allow ventilation under the structure.

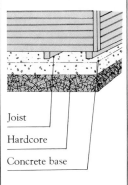

Joist

Hardcore

Concrete base

Storing tools

Garden tools should always be put away clean. Oil the tines and blades of steel tools and periodically oil any untreated wooden handles. It is very disheartening to work with ill-kept, rusty equipment. Many of the new garden tool "systems" have plastic-coated handles that accept a range of attachments. These might save space. Whether you have new-design or traditional tools, it is a good idea to hang as many of them on the walls of your storage area as you can. This will keep the tools in good condition and leave vital floor space free for bulky equipment. A racking system, such as that shown right, grips handles neatly and provides hooks, all on an adjustable base.

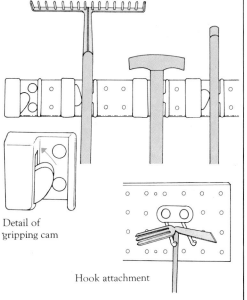

Detail of gripping cam

Hook attachment

153

Greenhouses and frames

Many specialist books have been written on the siting and structure of these useful additions to the garden but our primary concern here is with their appearance. Appearance, however, has to be tempered with practicality, for some of the greenhouse models on the market are too small and contrived in shape to be of much use. The "plantsman" will first decide on the greenhouse that is suitable for his growing needs, considering its appearance second. The determining factors will be the type of crop he wishes to grow and how much time he can spare on the maintenance of the greenhouse.

The siting, as well as the function of the greenhouse, will to an extent determine the type you need. The materials of which it is constructed can be painted or stained softwood, cedar or metal. The shape may be of the ridge type, the lean-to, the hexagonal or many sided, which themselves might be ridged, or it can be dome-shaped.

Greenhouses can now be fully automatic, in watering, ventilation and shading, but such sophistication becomes practicable only when there is a reasonably large area of glass. Most people settle for a greenhouse which they use for over-wintering, and then for seed sowing in spring and the propagation of cuttings for later summer use. Tomatoes and peppers can be grown throughout the summer, but without automatic equipment their watering can become a chore. The smaller the greenhouse the more difficult it is to control the temperature, and therefore the watering. A frame with underground heating would provide most people with all the glass they really need. The range of frame types is limited. It is reasonably easy to build your own of brick or, less permanently, of wood, with a simple lift-up framed glass top. If frames are not heated with underground wires, they can still be used to harden plants which have been raised from seed.

Both frames and greenhouses will need to be sited where sunshine is plentiful and therefore free from the overhang of trees. You must remember that in winter, snow is liable to build up on a greenhouse roof and must be cleared regularly. Overhanging trees will deposit collected snow with what might be disastrous results.

Frames and greenhouses should be serviced by hard, dry paths, wide enough for a wheelbarrow. Allow plenty of space around them for standing pots and boxes. Treated as small, efficient working units, frames and greenhouses can make handsome features on their own and need little screening.

Greenhouse as a feature In this Dutch garden, the greenhouse has been treated as a prime feature of the layout and partially screened by decorative planting. The surround to the wooden-framed house has been hard-surfaced.

Greenhouse types

The basic types of greenhouse for small gardens are shown below. They are constructed in metal or cedar (both needing little protection) or in softwood (requiring regular painting). Whether you choose free-standing or lean-to, glass-to-the-ground or half-bricked, is a matter of personal taste.

Wooden-walled

Wooden-walled span roof

Metal frame, glass-to-floor

Lean-to on brick base

Metal-framed dome

Siting the greenhouse

Make sure that your greenhouse gets adequate sunlight away from the shade of trees and buildings. Ideally, the longest axis of a free-standing greenhouse should be positioned north/south, so that the sun crosses it during the course of the day, giving equal shares of direct sunlight to both sides. However, the final siting of your greenhouse must be dictated by your overall garden plan which should provide water and electricity (see pp. 104–105).

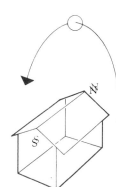

Colorful lean-to, *left. A lean-to timber greenhouse is often easier to site in a small garden than a free-standing model, as you can utilize any sunny wall. Here, use of colour increases the feel of summer.*

Window-sill greenhouse, *above. A south-facing, window-sill greenhouse is a neat solution to the problem of siting a full-size greenhouse in a small garden or where there is none at all.*

Cold frame construction

A simple cold frame, used to harden off plants in transition from a greenhouse to open ground or to germinate annual or vegetable seeds, can be easily constructed. A wooden, sloping-sided box should be made (about 1.2 m square/1.4 yd²) to fit the size of glazed panel available for the lid of the frame. This panel can either be purpose built, or you might use an old window frame. The lid to the frame illustrated simply rests against the low side of the construction. It can be lifted, slid and propped at the back of the frame. If your frame is to last you will need to treat the unprotected wood with preservative. Creosote fumes will kill seedlings so make sure that you use one of the "safe" wood preservatives on the market and give the frame plenty of time to dry. Alternatively, paint the frame, perhaps to match the white of a painted greenhouse. If the frame is used for growing plants in containers it can be positioned on hard surfacing where rot is less of a problem than if the frame stands on soil.

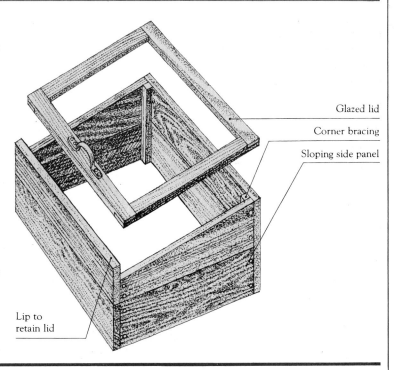

Glazed lid

Corner bracing

Sloping side panel

Lip to retain lid

Pergolas

In climates sunnier than that of northern Europe, the pergola is traditionally used to shade a path. In the British Isles it is more usefully employed as a roof transition from inside the house to the garden; alternatively, it can act solely as a support for ramblers or climbing plants. In urban areas, where gardens are overlooked, the pergola gives some measure of privacy to anyone sitting beneath it and, provided that you consider which way to run the horizontals of your structure, it need not inhibit sunlight. The pergola structure over a terrace area is one of the ways of creating an outside room, a place in which, rather than on which, to be. When a pergola abuts the house, it controls the view from inside, framing a portion of the garden while at the same time extending the proportion of the room from inside.

The detailing of the pergola must match the period of your home, for it will be seen both against your house and from within it. The proportions of the various parts of a pergola must balance. All too often the verticals that hold the pergola's horizontals are disproportionately large. The scale of the wooden horizontals (and wood is the material most suitable for this bridge on a domestic scale) must depend on the length it has to span between supports, and this too will depend on the sort of wood, hard- or softwood, that you propose using. The scale suitable for most terraces ought not to require a span of much more than 3–3.5 m ($11\frac{1}{2}$ ft), for if the wood is too large it is oppressive and if too narrow it warps. Traditional wooden horizontals in the British Isles are of massive oak spars, though in Mediterranean areas unsawn softwood was, and is, used. In the United States, red-wood is the first choice. Cypress and cedar are also durable but any good wood can be used if treated with a preservative, being kept stained or painted as necessary.

The verticals for a pergola of appropriate period might be columns of stone or of a reconstituted substitute. Alternatively, they can be of timber or metal. Unless the situation demands something different, the detailing of the material should be as simple as possible. The structure has a function to perform, that of supporting plants, so let them be the featured item rather than the clever detail of your structure. When a pergola adjoins masonry, it can either be let into the structure or, more easily, it can sit into an L-shaped metal shoe plugged to the wall.

If wood is too heavy a material for the horizontals of your particular situation, you might consider using strained wire, either over a roof garden or from wall to wall in a town garden. Trained vines or hops along these wires give shade in summer and let light through in winter.

Although the pergola is a simple and very effective way of linking inside and outside when constructed as an extension to a house wall, it can also be used to establish an enclosed space away from the house. Where two walls meet at right angles in the far corner of a larger garden, for example, a pergola can create a secluded seating area of great charm. In this case the style of the pergola is not so dependent on the style of the house, allowing you more freedom in the choice of materials.

Pergola for strong sunlight *This beautifully detailed pergola makes the area it encloses an extension of the house from which it leads. Such clean lines complement bright sunshine as the shadows from the pergola create linear patterns on walls and floor. The steps leading to the terrace area are of concrete poured in situ. The paving also has a consistent linear pattern.*

Traditional pergola
This covered walkway designed by the British architect, Lutyens, is built in traditional materials – oak and stone. Gertrude Jekyll, the English horti-culturist, planted the "room" through which the path leads.

Sheltered rural corner, *right. Lightweight softwood has been used to give a rustic, restful feel to a cottage terrace pergola.*

Pergola construction

Stained softwood beams and scaffolding poles can be used to make a simple pergola, as shown right. The beams sit in proprietary metal joist shoes where they meet the support-ing wall. At the opposite end of each beam, scaffolding poles have been let into the wood for half the thickness of the beam. These poles must be firmly bedded in concrete foundations beneath the surface they pierce. The run of beams is braced laterally with a metal tie. Plant support wires should be fixed along the underside of the beams and climbing plants (see p. 212) trained along them. Terrace paving units should be spaced so that pergola verticals coincide with a joint if possible.

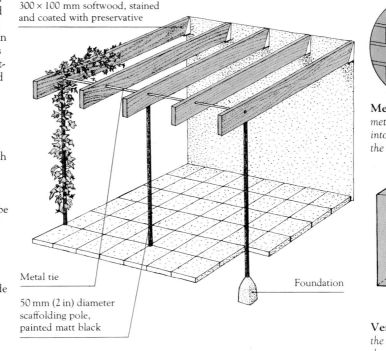

300 × 100 mm softwood, stained and coated with preservative

Metal tie

50 mm (2 in) diameter scaffolding pole, painted matt black

Foundation

Metal shoe fixing *This metal joist shoe is let into the wall and fixed to the mortar.*

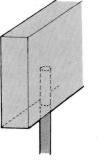

Vertical housing *Drill the horizontal to accept the upright.*

Structures for shade and decoration

The garden structures in this category include shelters, sunrooms, gazeboes and arbor supports. Such structures should provide shade from the sun and shelter from the wind while also giving a feeling of protection, for it is easier to relax comfortably outside with your chair or lounger against or near a structure than in an open position.

There are many different sizes and styles of prefabricated structures available. They are mostly of wood, either painted or treated with a preservative. If the shelter is close to your house or other structures, it should match or complement them. However, the charm of such structures is that they are usually secluded in larger gardens and can therefore create their own style.

I think it is important, when constructing a sunroom, that there is adequate ventilation to prevent overheating.

A simple, roofed shelter providing shade is a structure which lends itself to your own design. It does not need to have a waterproof roof but one that merely shades the sun's rays. Where there are existing walls or fences you might be able to use them partially to support a canopy. Corners formed by walls are particularly useful in this respect as very simple techniques can be employed to join wood or a metal frame to fill the corner.

Simple frameworks make ideal supports for climbing plants that will help to provide shade. Purpose-built plant supports in painted iron are a traditional feature that could suit the style of your garden, providing a crisp outline to an arbor. They can be combined with climbing plants or pleached trees to form an enclosed space.

Ideas for summerhouses

All the structures illustrated below could be sited as garden features to punctuate the rhythm of your plan. They can also be used for numerous practical purposes, such as providing a shaded seating area, a space for children to play or for storage of garden seating and equipment.

Brick-built sunroom, *right. This purpose-built garden structure has a sliding glass door, making it ideal for outside entertaining in summer. With the doors closed, the room is still useful in cool weather.*

Arbor support, *below. An open metal structure such as this can be used either unadorned as a decorative focal point or as a support for climbing plants, making a shaded garden room.*

Bamboo canopy

Slat-roofed "A" frame

Tiled canopy

Octagonal gazebo

Carports and garages

As with all ancillary structures, try to incorporate a carport or garage within the overall design of your house, but if the building must be separate, the use of similar materials to those of the house will provide a visual link, as will repeating the roof pitch of the house. If you are constructing a flat roof make the line of the fascia of the garage extend some building line of the house. When there is a path between the house and the new structure, design gates or fencing to unite the buildings across the gap.

Here and in England, the garage is often the first thing you see as you turn into the drive. The detailing of a garage frontage, including the doors, is therefore important, as is the hard-surfaced area leading to it. The approach should be wide enough for easy access and egress from the car on both sides; it should also be provided with suitable drainage so that it can be used as a car washing area. Remember that driveways and the bases for carports and garages have to be specially constructed to take the weight of vehicular traffic. This involves thicker-than-normal layers of consolidated hardcore and surfacing. Take professional advice about the exact dimensions, depending on the surface material you choose and your soil type.

When constructing a new carport or a second garage adjacent to an existing one, consider turning it at 90 degrees to the other, to produce a courtyard feel, but ensure that you provide adequate turning space for cars.

Incorporating a garage

When building a garage try to incorporate it into the overall house design. Here this has been achieved by fitting it into a corner and using the same materials, roof angles and window and door sizes as those of the house.

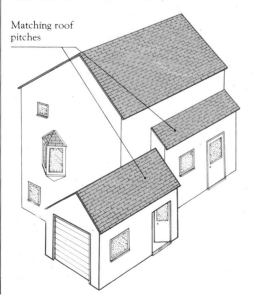

Matching roof pitches

Carport designs

A carport is a significantly large structure in the garden and deserves thoughtful planning. Consider the range of materials available to you and use the open-sided nature of the structure as an advantage to allow easy access to and from your car. The two examples, right, include space for useful storage at one end. One example is constructed in wood, the other in exterior grade concrete building block.

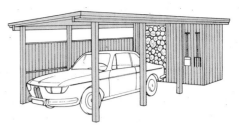

All-wood construction

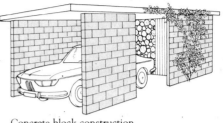

Concrete block construction

Successful carport, *above. A wood carport extended to provide a covered way to the house entrance, tying the two structures together.*

Hiding a garage, *below. If you have an unattractive garage, disguise it with planting. Here pyracantha has been clipped to garage shape.*

Roof gardens

To turn part of a domestic roof area into a garden is only possible if the roof was specifically designed to be load bearing. The overall weight of wet earth is enormous and considerable depth of earth is needed to grow anything other than shallow-rooted plants.

When starting a roof garden, it is essential that you determine what weight your roof will bear and to do this accurately you will need the advice of an architect or structural engineer. You may also need the permission of your ground landlord and, should you propose any structural alterations, planning permission too. Some authorities will not even permit any screening structure round the roof which is visible from the street below. Remember that structural additions must be tough to withstand winter buffeting by wind and rain. The combination of wind and intense sun makes watering a major undertaking through the year. Moreover, we tend to think of a roof garden only in summer, but the pots, plants and structures need tending the whole time.

Having done your preliminary homework, draw up the dimensions of your roof area and proceed to plan the space as if it were a living-room, orientating your seating to the sun and attractive views, much as you would to the fire or television set inside. When you have estimated the working areas, consider screening from neighbors as well as wind. In such cases you may need top screening in addition to that at the sides. When planning allows, an overhead pergola, from which panels can be hung, gives this facility.

Decide whether any planting you contemplate is to be contained within permanent structures or within movable pots. If the former, and the roof structure allows, build up your containers in as light a material as possible, allowing for drainage and adequate root space for the mature plants of your choice. 500 mm (20 in) depth of soil on drainage, is the minimum quantity for most planting. Trees need almost double this amount of earth.

After the planting positions, the next point to consider is surfacing. Weight again is important: thin tiles are ideal, in terracotta or even glazed flooring tiles; paving brick is good and slate should be considered. Marble, too, might be used, for it remains cool underfoot in summer. Wooden decking is the ideal flooring over an existing bitumen roof surface.

As with every garden setting, style your arrangement to produce a dramatic effect. Your plants will then become features within the outside room. Ensure that any pots are deep enough and constructed in fiberglass or plastic for lightness. All containers should be filled with a specially prepared lightweight mixture, over adequate drainage material. These lightweight soilless mixes contain little, if any, fertilizer, which must be compensated for by regular feedings.

Watering will be much easier if you install an irrigation system by threading a hose through your planting, regularly punctured with holes and fed from a gently trickling tap.

The plants which you select for your roof should be tough and able to withstand wind. For this reason, keep the planting low. Go for quantity which will screen and couch you in greenery, rather than delicate quality.

A garden on a roof is an expensive indulgence in materials, plants and their maintenance, but most of all in its installation for, unless the materials can be manhandled through your house, they must be winched or otherwise lifted up the outside of the house. Despite this, a private roof garden in town is a marvellous addition to any home.

Roof terrace planting containers
Architects designing roof terraces often build-in large planting containers, such as that below.

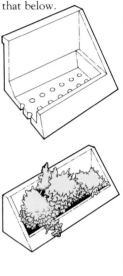

Screening

One of the hazards of roof gardening is the wind, which can whip the area throughout most of the year. Wind not only flattens plants but dries them out, particularly when combined with strong sun. A high, solid barrier protects only those plants directly in its lee, causing turbulence elsewhere. Better is a slatted wooden boundary, or even a mesh of some sort, to filter the full force of the wind.

The other reason for a screen boundary, of course, is to achieve privacy. If tall boundary screens are not possible, try to establish inner partitions of planting, and possibly a light pergola structure to provide screening.

Wooden screen, *left. This cedar-wood screen not only looks decorative but would be an extremely effective wind filter on a roof.*

Vine support, *above. Light metal supports are here threaded with wires to support vines. When mature, vines provide an ideal protection from sun.*

Construction idea

When weight allows, build areas for planting using hollowed bricks, and try to establish a lush growth. In this way, you shelter the roof space and provide yourself with corners around which chairs can be moved as the prevailing wind or draft dictates. Allow for adequate drainage and use a growing mix with a high proportion of lightweight fill. Plants will root into this but will need plenty of feeding, preferably with liquid fertilizer. It is worth considering some form of automatic watering to save labor. In order to provide storage space for tools, pots and feeds, consider using built-in seats, as illustrated, with lift-up lids. They may not be the most comfortable of seats but they are ideal for parties.

Large scale roof garden *A roof garden can serve the rooms which surround it. This example has permanent, built-in seating and broad islands of quarry tiling. Bold masses of evergreen planting divide the view when seen from the different overlooking rooms.*

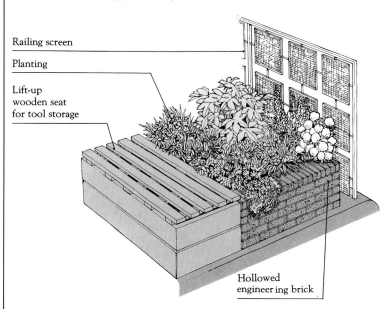

Railing screen

Planting

Lift-up wooden seat for tool storage

Hollowed engineering brick

Balconies

Many of the rules for roof gardening are applicable to the balcony, although the styling of the finish should be in character with the room it adjoins as opposed to the fantasy world one can create on a roof. The balcony, however, is usually more sheltered than the roof, often being covered by another balcony above, which will not allow rain water to reach your plants.

Decide exactly what it is you want from your balcony. There is inevitably a feeling of vulnerability when standing on it and this has to be overcome by screening if it is to become a place on which to sit and take the sun. Glass panels, if not structurally part of the building, can be fitted within an existing metal railing to provide this, without detracting from the building's façade. Few planning authorities will allow anything more. Screening, of course, should not impede the view; neither should planting, particularly when seen from inside the house.

Weight will always be a problem on balconies and before making any radical changes, or even introducing a single tub, check whether it will be safe. Where applicable, you should also check the strength of any structure above your balcony, since hanging containers can make a pleasant alternative treatment, as can a light, removable screen of zig-zag yachting rope.

One of the hazards of many balcony gardens, unless designed with containers built-in, is that water can drip on your neighbors beneath when pots are watered. If you are not using self-watering containers, therefore,

ensure that you have trays under pots to take surplus moisture once it has passed through the compost and drainage materials.

The type of plants you select should be tough, like those for a roof garden, but make sure they are in accord with the building. You might also consider using herbs in containers, for they will grow well in these situations and are, of course, useful too.

Many balconies are not suitable for greenery or, receiving no sun, are rarely used as a seating area. In such cases you might consider siting a piece of statuary or sculpture on the balcony (in fiberglass for lightness), set in an area of cobbles for textural variation if the structure will tolerate the additional weight.

It is important to think about what your terrace or balcony will look like from within the house, for it is from there that it will most often be seen. Consider lighting it to make a feature of the space and station plants within it accordingly. Then try to connect the two areas, inside and outside, with fabrics, such as awnings and internal curtains. You can further enhance this interconnecting feel by using the same flooring, since quarry tiles, slate and brick are all suitable for both inside and outside use.

Tented enclosure *An awning covers this balcony, turning it into an attractive tented enclosure for outside summer living. Surrounding greenery increases the privacy.*

Balcony ideas
Below are some different possibilities where space is at a premium and the balcony is overshadowed from above. Any fixtures are best built-in to save space.

For wind shelter or privacy, fix a stout wooden roller blind to the balcony above.

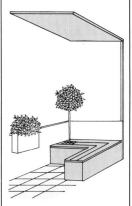

Build a small bench seat with a lifting lid for storage of cushions in summer months.

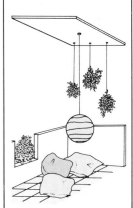

Leave the floor clear by hanging baskets for annuals from above, with a light fixture.

Outward-looking arrangement *A magnificent view dictates an outward-looking style for this balcony, as opposed to the inward-looking balcony on the opposite page. The boldly-shaped furniture and railing surround suggest the scale of a ground level garden.*

View from above, *below. The appearance of a balcony as seen from above is often important in towns. In this case a balcony has been entirely furnished with plants in containers to a design best seen from above. There is a glass infill to the metal balcony surround for draft protection.*

Self-watering pots

Self-watering pots have a reservoir of water which is drawn into the growing medium by a wick. They overcome the daily chore of watering required on windy and sunny roofs and balconies.

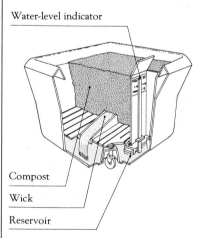

Water-level indicator

Compost

Wick

Reservoir

The balcony from inside

A balcony is more often looked at through windows and doors than walked on. Some balconies are not for walking on at all, being too noisy or shaded. If this is the case, plant the balcony or use it in a way which benefits the room which looks on to it. Make a composition of the balcony wall, the access and the balcony beyond.

Crisp styling *The windows are connected internally by the curtain track and pelmet. The curtain material blends with the canopy over the balcony.*

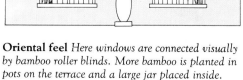

Oriental feel *Here windows are connected visually by bamboo roller blinds. More bamboo is planted in pots on the terrace and a large jar placed inside.*

Using plants on balconies

The key to the selection of plants for the
balcony container must be to select those species
that can withstand a certain amount of draught
and wind. There must, of course, be easy access
to the plants for watering and dead heading.
Remember that the arrangement that you
establish in the first flush of enthusiasm in early
summer has to be maintained throughout the
season, including any holiday period, so do not
overreach yourself. It is far better to have a fine
display of something quite simple than an
unsatisfactory showing of rare or bizarre plants.
Conversely, you might consider a permanent
planting of perennials and small shrubs, in
which case you will need only incidental spots of
colourful annual plants on the balcony.

Spectacular display,
*above. This planting
style is for the balcony
enthusiast, providing
total summer privacy.
The selection is mainly
of geraniums in differing
tones of pink, but with
some petunia and
convolvulus distributed
throughout. Plants are
hung individually in pots
on a wooden frame.*

Color and form, *left.
A small Italian roof
terrace is bright with
yellow daisies and the
bold form of agave.
Color planting gives
instant impact and
character. The display is
enhanced even by the
inclusion of a caged
canary, a feature which
is hardly to be recom-
mended, however.*

Stackable pots

Various units and containers are on
the market that can be stacked against
a support to produce an interesting
textured surface in themselves and
which, when planted, can create a
waterfall of colour.
Each terracotta unit, right, needs only
one retaining fixer to hold it, for the
weight of the earth stabilizes individual
units. On the far right are concrete
units that can be used for planting
against a wall, although some form of
waterproofing is necessary if damp is
not to penetrate the wall. Plants in
units such as these require regular
watering in the growing season.

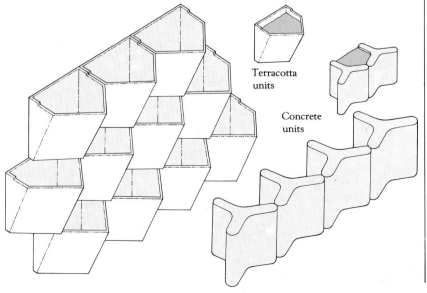

Terracotta
units

Concrete
units

Window-boxes

For many an urban dweller the window-box is his only contribution to landscape, but a row of houses ablaze with window-box color is an enormous pleasure in a town. Plants most often grown are geraniums and begonias, but you may wish for a greater variety of plant material in your box. Before considering what it might contain, however, you must select the container itself.

The type of window-box you need will depend very much on your window and how it opens, and whether, indeed, you will site your box outside. It is possible to have one for herbs, for instance, along the inside of the kitchen window. If your windows open outwards, your window-boxes will need to be suspended on strong metal brackets below the window so that any growth within them does not impede the opening. European windows tend to open inwards and old houses have sash windows that make the fixing, planting and subsequent attention of your box a far easier task. Sometimes "window"-boxes are sited around a low retaining wall, on a roof or balcony. Wherever the box and whatever its material, it must be securely fixed.

Window-boxes at one time were always constructed of wood; later they were of metal and today the most favored material is plastic. Many are often too shallow for a plant to be healthy throughout the whole season. The best boxes are still made of wood, but with a lift-out metal lining for easier planting. This gives the plants' roots insulation from what can be the lethal intensity of sunshine. A thin layer of lining plastic is not sufficient to protect them.

The compost for a window-box should be rich in organic material or peat to retain moisture, but plants will still need regular feeding with a proprietary liquid fertilizer since frequent watering will leach out minerals fairly quickly. Drainage should obviously be good. A reasonable drainage layer – say 50 mm (2 in) of broken terracotta pot – should line the base of the window-box, which must have drainage holes through the base to allow for the escape of surplus water. Standing water in an undrained container will cause roots to rot, which will ultimately kill the plant. Over the broken crock, put coarse organic matter to stop the soil from percolating into the drainage. Allow a 50-mm (2-in) space to the rim of the box when you have consolidated the soil for watering. The choice of plants for the window-box has traditionally been among bulbs for springs, then impatiens, geraniums, begonias, ageratum and petunias. All these provide spring to summer color in sunny situations.

Conventional display *This is a conventional, but nonetheless attractive, window-box planting of evergreens and conifers, together with begonias.*

Attaching boxes

It is essential that your windox-box is securely fixed, especially when it overhangs a public way. Boxes on ledges with inward opening European or sash-windows may have a brace on either side, attached to the window surround. Boxes beneath an outward opening window should be held within an angled bracket, securely fixed to the wall or window.

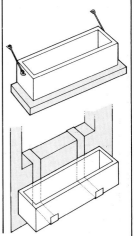

Window-box construction

There are many types of planting box on the market, and in a wide range of materials, but it is still sometimes necessary to construct your own to a particular size. Where possible use hardwood, for it will last much longer. Failing this, a serviceable container can be made using wood that has been seasoned and treated with preservative under pressure, then allowed to stand for several weeks. Use zinc-coated screws, counter sunk in the construction. Ensure that there is adequate drainage, using plastic inserts through the drainage holes so that the damp does not seep into the end grain of the wood. Make the structure stout for, when filled with wet earth, there is considerable outward pressure. Ideally, you should line the container with a metal tray, which can be easily removed for replanting.

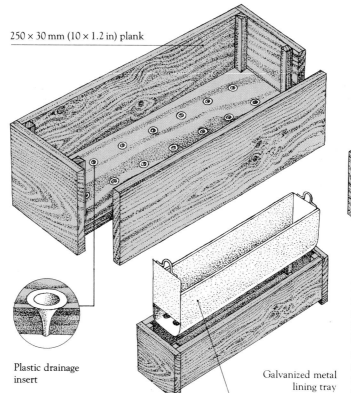

250 × 30 mm (10 × 1.2 in) plank

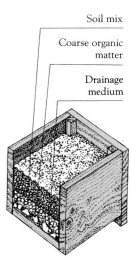

Soil mix

Coarse organic matter

Drainage medium

Plastic drainage insert

Galvanized metal lining tray

Filling the box *Line the bottom of the box with 50 mm (2 in) of broken pot, ensuring that large pieces cover the drainage holes. Then add coarse organic materials before filling with growing medium.*

City window-box, *above. The simplicity of this window and window-box is an entirely satisfactory treatment in town – red geraniums in an asbestos box. The wooden wedges level the box and facilitate drainage, but when watering care must be taken to prevent the excess falling onto balconies beneath.*

Blending window boxes and façade
Use your plants dramatically to work with your house. Here geraniums and petunias suit the wall color. The shrubs on either side of the darker coloured doors are evergreen Choisya ternata.

CHOOSING AND USING PLANTS

Scale, form, shape and color

Selecting, positioning and combining plants, from
trees to ground cover

Planting the garden

Having completed most of the aspects of a garden's plan, plants, the life-giving element in any garden, can finally be considered.

Older, larger gardens were cut out of existing woodland or enclosed from surrounding countryside by clipped hedges. The modern, invariably smaller garden is now more likely to be formed by the surrounding walls of neighboring houses, fences and garage walls. The problem is no longer that of creating a growing frame of trees and hedges and using plants to decorate it inside, but rather that of using plants to soften and punctuate the space defined around your house following a consciously designed plan.

It is probable that you will be working with a relatively small area so the range of plants that you can use will be limited by their ultimate size. Your choice must support the scale of your garden space. You will have scaled your garden plan to the house (see page 38) and now the planting must be scaled to match the plan.

The range of plants from which to choose is further limited to those with strong shape, form, texture or smell, if you want to create or support a sense of character in the garden, all the year round. How they are grouped and in what numbers is also vital. A strong garden plan will always be weakened by the liquorice-allsorts effect caused by the one-of-this-and-one-of-that type of planting.

In choosing plants it helps to be aware of the period in which plants were introduced to particular locations. By choosing plants that are suitable for a specific situation according to their origin and to the period of their introduction a planting plan is strengthened. Cedar of Lebanon (*Cedrus libani*), for example, epitomizes 18th-century style, while the monkey puzzle tree (*Araucaria auracana*) is redolent of Victorian villa gardens. Both would seem incorrect – though they might well grow (where winter hardy) – in each other's location.

Some plants look well in a rural setting but are not usually acceptable in towns. The birch (*Betula* sp.) is an example of this, as is alder (*Alnus* sp.). Conversely, decoratively hybridized trees look out of scale and out of tune with indigenous rural planting. Japanese cherries (*Prunus* sp.), eucalyptus and the increasingly ubiquitous golden *Cupressocyparis leylandii* are amongst them.

Groups of plants have a particular character, according to their native location. And the cultivated forms of a native range of plants can usually make the bones of your garden selection. Some groups are modified by soil type. Rhododendrons and azaleas, for

Cottage garden-style planting *The selection of shrubs and herbaceous plants shown here is full and flowing, complying with the cottage garden tradition of relaxed planting.*

Structured planting, *right. Compared with the loose planting style above, here planting is tightly structured. Clipped masses contrast with freer plant shapes to make sculptural plant groups.*

example, like acid soil, while delphinium and lilacs respond to limestone. Then there are the ranges of plants growing naturally that are characteristic of certain climates, as for example the herbs and shrubs with resinous stems from hot Mediterranean regions. Rosemary, cistus, lavender, sage and the semi-desert types of plant, such as yucca, are other examples. Some plants prefer light, cool woodland shade, while the vast range of annuals and biennials are happier in open meadowland. Anyone who has climbed a mountain above its lower reaches will know that as the climate becomes colder the range of plants, and indeed their size, is rapidly reduced, until only tiny alpenrose or eidelweiss cling in the lee of rocks at the tops of mountains. Another obvious range of plant material, having its own peculiar style, is that suitable for moist locations, though within this there are sub-divisions of plants which need just damp soil, through moist to wet.

I emphasize the natural locations of plants because though the cultivated forms of wild plants will grow in alien sites and conditions, they must be mixed within the garden carefully. A yucca will probably grow quite well next to a fern, but you should not site them in that way for their original locations were totally different and they will not look "natural" together. However, this is a difficult area in which to be specific, for it concerns the individual's personal response to plants in the light of his own experience.

All of the plants we have discussed have their own particular shape, leaf characteristics and flower color because they have adapted themselves to their location. Plants with large leaves, for example, tend to originate in shady areas, for the size of the leaves is designed to catch the maximum amount of light. Plants from desert areas often have fleshy, sword-shaped leaves, adapted to conserve moisture and deflect sunlight. When

European style, *left.*
The planting here relies on form and shape rather than colour. Plants combine with rock groupings and the water feature to present a complete composition. The plants used are hardy enough to withstand cold winter temperatures.

English style, *right.*
This full English planting places great emphasis on flower colour and diverse foliage forms. There is little conscious structure in the arrangement of plant groupings but their effect is romantic and grand. A classical pedestal and planted bowl provides a focal point. In winter the impact of the planting will be much reduced.

mixing garden plants, it is these characteristics of shape with which you should juggle for they remain constant throughout the year whereas flower color is transitory. Only when you have built up the outline character of the planting of your site, and styled it according to its location, should you consider plant color.

Planting is fraught with hazards but these can be identified and, once a plant's suitability to a particular situation is established, you can begin to think of the plant's uses in building up your composition. There is a definite order in which this should be done.

You should seek to develop an everchanging plant arrangement to make up your garden mass, remembering that ultimately you will see little earth. This is a basic theory of planting design. Your aim in choosing and using plants is to achieve a recognizable overall form and to fulfill your garden plan.

Plant classification

Whereas common names of plants vary widely from area to area, use of the scientific name allows you to be certain of a specific plant.

The first word in a plant's classification is the genus name, for example *Acer*, *Berberis* or *Cotoneaster*. There are, however, approximately seventy sorts of cotoneaster, of which half are generally available. Some are 30 mm (1.2 in) high while others become trees. The second name identifies the species of a genus (for example, *Cotoneaster horizontalis*) and it often describes the character of the plant in question. You might see *Cotoneaster* sp. written. This is the accepted abbreviation of

Cotoneaster species and refers to all the species of the genus *Cotoneaster* or, alternatively, one of the species of the genus *Cotoneaster* without specifying which. If there is more than one natural variety of the same species there will be a third Latin name to identify each. If a variety has been produced by human intervention it is known as a cultivated variety or cultivar (usually abbreviated to cv.). In this case the third name will be in a modern language, and may be something like 'Crimson Rose'. Sometimes two genera or two species are crossed (hybridized). A hybrid is usually denoted by a × (multiplication) sign before the species name.

Principles of planting

When a garden has been built it remains incomplete until it is planted. How many and which plants you choose and how you group them depends on many factors. Planting can simply answer a specific requirement, such as to disguise an unsightly view, to give shade, to provide food, to appeal to the sense of smell or to fill a damp and shady corner. But more often, plants make the green bulky infill of the framework to extend the design while giving pleasure throughout the year with seasonal changes of color and texture in foliage, stems, berries, fruits and flowers.

You should also remember that the garden, if not a conscious duplication of natural vegetation, as in the ecologist's wild garden, often contains features that imitate nature. Pools, rockeries and stream beds depend on plants and groupings that interpret the sort of planting that occurs naturally, no matter how stylized to suit your garden. There are, of course, other lessons to learn from nature's distribution. An area of natural vegetation is often dominated by one or two species with only the occasional intrusion of others. This fact gives an area its feel, whether it be pine woodland or heather moor. It is to the landscape of such areas that we retreat to relax on holiday, and it is a similarly simple and discreet planting scheme that will provide a place of enjoyment in the garden. It is not necessary to fill every corner with a different species of plant. True, a garden is a contrived place and many (including the horticulturist) see merit in the range of plants that it is possible to include, but my interest lies between the contrived flower borders in many gardens and the gentle spontaneity of natural plant grouping.

These days many people have neither the time nor the inclination to garden intensively, so the obvious answer is to settle for relaxed planting that allows nature to influence the result, perhaps letting wild plants remain alongside their hybridized relatives.

Contiguous to these reasons for choosing plants is the desire to make plant groupings that satisfy personal taste in form, shape and color. Successful groupings will strengthen a ground pattern, contrast with background planting or support a certain color scheme. Your increasing knowledge of plants, experience in the garden and, I hope, the examples in this book, will help you to make successful groups of plants that work on all scales from trees down to the smallest ground cover subjects.

Planting for year-round interest

The series of three pictures, below, show the same garden in (from top to bottom) spring, mid and late summer. All three examples show how plants have been grouped to provide handsome ground cover throughout the year. In spring, narcissus, planted between emergent perennials, are in flower as the young needles begin to sprout on the foreground larch (*Larix* sp.).

Then, in summer, bold masses of *Sedum spectabile* with *Gypsophylla* sp. provide ground interest for the two bold clumps of *Lasiagrostis* sp. There is yellow *Sedum spathulifolium* in the foreground, with invasive *Polygonum* sp. on the right. By the end of summer the grasses have died down but the massed sedums look spectacular.

Imitating nature

Nature's vegetation has always been an inspiration for garden planting where the gardener seeks to create his own section of the countryside. Natural features have their own characteristic vegetation and can only be successfully included in the garden if you first analyze the natural form carefully, as I have done with a stream bed, below. You will then be able to establish planting areas in the correct positions and choose plants of a scale and form that suit.

Garden as an extension of the countryside, *above. The foreground planting in this damp location is domestic, but it reflects its location for over the mown path wild planting folds naturally into the background of trees, with incidental sculptural elements on the left, such as the fern.*

Natural forms translated for the garden, *below. A stream bed has been recreated here through a dry swath of boulders that make a shoreline effect formed by a larger river. Such a treatment demands riverbank planting like the willows in this example.*

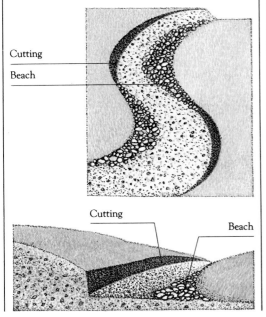

Cutting

Beach

Cutting

Beach

Considering shape, form and color

Once you have decided on the sort of planting you want, and the scale of plants needed to achieve it, you can consider other plant characteristics. For example, is a suitable plant deciduous, evergreen or even semi-evergreen; what is its flower color and the duration of its flowering period in relation to that of other plants in the grouping? Then consider leaf color, being sure to consider the entire year since some plants begin with pale green or gold leaves which become green by summer, while others are first green and then take on glowing autumn colors.

Stem color can also be extremely exciting in winter, when, for example, thickets of pollarded *Cornus* and *Salix* sp. may range in color from chrome yellow, through orange and red to dull burgundy.

After the color of flowers, you should consider fruit and berry color for autumn and early winter interest. Lastly, think about texture, both of leaf and stem. The textural differences of one leaf from another are the result of their adaptation to their original habitats. Many of the hairy gray leaves, which are invaluable for mixed borders, are from the southern hemisphere and have strong visual and tactile qualities. One of the most appealing is the silky gray leaf of *Convolvulus cneorum*. Other textures, like that of the holly (*Ilex* sp.) leaf, are smooth and glossy, while many of the Mediterranean herb plants have crisp leaves of culinary value. Do not overlook the texture of stems, for they may be smooth and glossy or soft and scaled, like some conifers.

These are the qualities with which you compose your plant groupings. The more diverse the shapes, colors and textures, the stronger the grouping will be.

Planting for foliage, left. All these leaves are small and create a light, feathery feeling of gray foliage. The groupings include *Anaphalis*, *Artemisia*, *Stachys* and *Rosmarinus* sp.

Planting for color, right. These strong colors suit bright sunshine. Pelargoniums and darker sweet peas (*Lathyrus odoratus*) are mixed beneath a fig and a vine.

Planting for form, below. Here the dominating feature is form. The leaves of *Hosta sieboldiana* and *Crocosmia* sp. are enclosed by yellow *Lysimachia thyrsiflora*.

Planning and planting a bed

You can compose your plants on site for small areas but you will find it is impossible to visualize a whole border, juggling with all the plant characteristics you want. It is far better to get an outline down on paper first.

Using your final garden layout as an underlay, trace off the areas to be planted and start working to scale on them. First list your priorities, starting with special feature trees or shrubs, which should emphasize or balance a design feature; then background skeleton or screening trees and shrubs.

According to the scale of your site, use a number of particular plants together, perhaps three of some and five of another. Plant through these if you like with a standard tree or two for increased height and density, though you must remember that ultimately the shrubs beneath them will be in shade. Use plenty of evergreen so that the plan will work throughout winter.

Your catalogue will provide you with ultimate heights and spreads, which in turn will give you a clue to planting distances. Tall shrubs can be two meters (6½ ft) apart, medium shrubs 1.5 metres (5 ft) and so on (see p. 187). The earth between the plants will soon be covered over as the plants grow, but if you wish you can temporarily brighten gaps with sunflowers or nicotiana.

After your screen shrubs, start composing decorative species in front of them. Think

---

Putting your planting plan on paper

The garden plan that you decided on by the end of the chapter on Planning your garden left blank spaces for planting areas. When visualizing the plan you will have imagined the planting areas in three dimensions but the details of which plants you locate where can only be settled when you have some knowledge and experience of plants. Look at the examples of planting shown in this chapter for inspiration.

You will, by now, be used to drawing to scale. Taking dimensions from your plan, draw each planting area to a size that is useful, considering the detail that you need to include. Although you will be separating each bed from the overall plan, you must keep its location in the garden in mind. Decide on a system of symbols to denote the types of plants on your plan, remembering that every plant must have its exact planting position marked clearly. It is also important to show the amount of space you are leaving for the spread of plants. The best method of doing this is to draw center circles to represent the spread of each plant, again using scale measurements. Then use dots and crosses for smaller plants. A climbing plant can be indicated by a triangular symbol drawn with its flat side against the proposed support for the plant.

Stage 1 Select a feature tree that will either become the focal point of the planting area, or at least counteract another strong feature, such as the house itself or a view. In this example, two *Phormium tenax* have been chosen as a balancing feature within the same bed for the feature tree, *Acer negundo* 'Variegatum'.

Stage 2 Add evergreen peripheral planting of shrubs and climbers that will contain the site, giving privacy and shelter and making the green walls against which decorative planting is seen. This "skeleton" principle should also apply to smaller plants, including ground cover material. Here, hellebores, bergenia and an iris have been included as a framework.

Stage 3 Fill in with decorative shrubs of a smaller scale, considering color harmony and contrast, height, shape contrasts (winter and summer), leaf shapes, textures and stem qualities. Work down in scale, adding decorative herbaceous material (not included in this scheme) and finally ground cover.

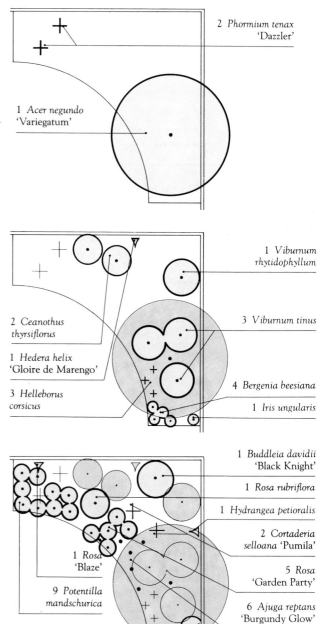

2 *Phormium tenax* 'Dazzler'

1 *Acer negundo* 'Variegatum'

1 *Viburnum rhytidophyllum*

3 *Viburnum tinus*

4 *Bergenia beesiana*

1 *Iris ungularis*

2 *Ceanothus thyrsiflorus*

1 *Hedera helix* 'Gloire de Marengo'

3 *Helleborus corsicus*

1 *Buddleia davidii* 'Black Knight'

1 *Rosa rubriflora*

1 *Hydrangea petioralis*

2 *Cortaderia selloana* 'Pumila'

5 *Rosa* 'Garden Party'

6 *Ajuga reptans* 'Burgundy Glow'

1 *Solanum crispum*

1 *Rosa* 'Blaze'

9 *Potentilla mandschurica*

first about strong architectural forms (*Phormium* and *Yucca* sp., for example) for the sunny parts, and the bold-leaved hostas and bergenias for the shadier areas. Contrast these strong shapes with softer, fluffier plants flowing around them. At this stage color as well as form must come into your thinking. Try to compose in ranges of color, a method which will also make your selecting process easier. Match the color of a wall, for example, or perhaps the color of your carpet in the room overlooking the planting. You might combine soft pinks and grays with a touch of purple and some white, for instance; or bright orange, yellow and red, lightened by gray and so on. Your colors help to set the mood of your garden, and this in turn should be suggested by your house and its location. Consider the same principles of form and color when deciding on

herbaceous planting, not necessarily using it in specific borders but perhaps mixing tall delphiniums with later-flowering summer shrubs, which will prop up the delphiniums and screen their dying tops. Then consider bulbs, not simply those for spring but lilies for summer, autumn crocus and so on. Site a rose or two against an old tree or some other suitable vertical support.

Put all this down on paper, ensuring that you have included all your favorite species. You must now be ruthless and eliminate about half the number you have selected. The most common mistake of the inexperienced is to plant too much.

If you have clearly defined each plant you want to include in your plan and indicated where each is to be sited, you can use this as a reference sheet and begin your planting in the garden with confidence.

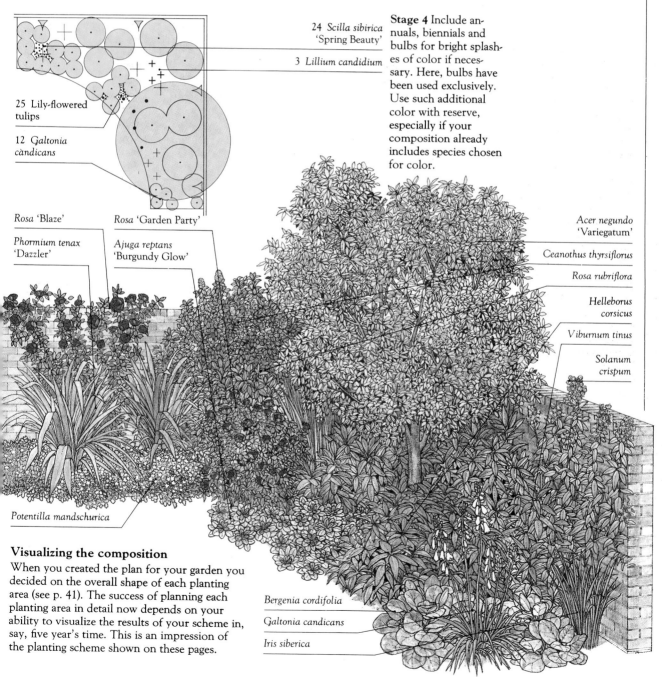

24 *Scilla sibirica* 'Spring Beauty'

3 *Lillium candidium*

25 Lily-flowered tulips

12 *Galtonia candicans*

Rosa 'Blaze'

Rosa 'Garden Party'

Phormium tenax 'Dazzler'

Ajuga reptans 'Burgundy Glow'

Potentilla mandschurica

Stage 4 Include annuals, biennials and bulbs for bright splashes of color if necessary. Here, bulbs have been used exclusively. Use such additional color with reserve, especially if your composition already includes species chosen for color.

Acer negundo 'Variegatum'

Ceanothus thyrsiflorus

Rosa rubriflora

Helleborus corsicus

Viburnum tinus

Solanum crispum

Bergenia cordifolia

Galtonia candicans

Iris siberica

Visualizing the composition

When you created the plan for your garden you decided on the overall shape of each planting area (see p. 41). The success of planning each planting area in detail now depends on your ability to visualize the results of your scheme in, say, five year's time. This is an impression of the planting scheme shown on these pages.

Trees

Whatever a tree's attributes, it will be the shape, both in summer and winter, that will be its abiding characteristic and the one that will influence the selection of other plants nearby. Trees will ultimately be the largest element in a garden and, when planting, one needs to think ahead since they grow quite quickly, not only upwards but outwards, when well maintained. So when making your selection be clear about the tree's eventual shape, size and color.

Broadly, tree shapes can be categorized as follows: fastigiate or columnar; pyramidal or conical; broadly columnar; broad-headed or round-topped, and pendulous or weeping. Within that grouping, the head of the tree may be thick, allowing little light through its foliage to plants beneath, sometimes inhibiting growth altogether, or light and fluffy, giving a dappled shade to growth below.

Although we see only the part of a tree that is above ground, the section below ground must not be forgotten. This is the feeding and anchorage system, not quite as large as the visible part but not far short of it in certain cases and in certain soils. As a general rule, the thinner the foliage the lighter the root run, since a heavy anchorage is not then necessary. Remember, therefore, that when planting in the region of existing trees, or adding new ones to an area of established planting, any nutrient held in solution in the ground will be absorbed by their rooting systems, to the deprivation of all else.

Contrasting foliage
Here the gray foliage of a mature eucalyptus and shrubby Atriplex halimus *is contrasted against the dark mass of a large clipped yew hedge (*Taxus *sp.). A willow-leaved pear (*Pyrus salicifolia*) backs the eucalyptus.*

Foliage backdrop, *above. The light foliage of an* Acer negundo *shades a seating area in this garden. To the right of the lawn is a whitebeam*

(Sorbus aria 'Lutetiana') *grouped with the handsome red boughs of the evergreen* Arbutus unedo.

Root systems

It is as well to realize that some species of tree and shrub have almost as much root below ground level as they have branches above, especially when they are growing in good loamy soil. Much of such a root system consists of minute feeder roots that penetrate the film of water that surrounds each individual granule of soil. Wherever there is a water source, roots will grow towards it so large trees should not be planted too close to any drainage runs.

You must remember the extent of roots when you are caring for established plants and introducing new ones. Consider the vast network of roots beneath a mature tree, a clipped hedge or a number of pruned shrubs. Not only will these roots require such a vast amount of feeding that they will impoverish soil in their locality but they also present a barrier for new planting.

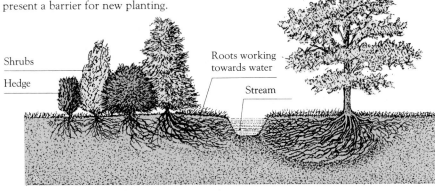

Shrubs

Hedge

Roots working towards water

Stream

The scale of the background trees that you propose planting should be carefully considered before you decide on their siting within the overall layout. Few small gardens can accommodate a forest tree – a beech (*Fagus* sp.), for instance, or an ash (*Fraxinus* sp.) or indeed any of the large conifers. Poplars (*Populus* sp.), which are often planted as screen trees, may be categorised as medium-sized trees, although they can grow to great heights. Even the notorious *Cupressocyparis leylandii* reaches 10–15 meters (33–50 ft) in height – and quickly. So have a care before planting and consult your catalogue to be sure of a tree's potential; then think carefully where to site it so that it will not block out the sun, infringe on a neighbor's garden or undermine your house with its invasive root run. Tree roots can be particularly damaging in areas with wet clay soils where coarse feeders will take up the available moisture through a dry period, and so cause cracking of the medium surrounding their roots – including the foundations of your house, if they are anywhere nearby.

Hotter climates call for the use of taller trees near the house to shade it. Select trees with less dense foliage, to allow some light through. Such types invariably have shallow roots – as, for example, the false acacia (*Robinia pseudoacacia*).

Trees that are selected to provide a screen to a bad view may be more profitably sited closer to the house rather than at the garden's perimeter. Not only are more trees needed when planted along the edge, but they can all too easily draw the eyes to the precise point that you are trying to disguise.

Tree shapes

The basic characteristic tree shapes are shown below. These shapes relate to any size of tree, from forest species to small decorative hybrids. Some shapes, such as horizontal, suggest movement, while others, such as fastigiate, create static points in the garden that arrest the eye.

Fastigiate Conical

Weeping

Round

Flat-topped

Horizontal

Woodland grouping *This grouping of trees resembles light woodland in a naturally occurring situation. Good groupings of trees always look attractive but especially so when bathed in autumn sunlight as here. In the foreground are species of white-barked birch.*

179

Small trees

The range of trees most suited to the smaller garden is extensive. While suitable when placed against existing, larger trees, they can equally well be grouped to provide either a screen within your garden or to become a decorative element in themselves. The life span of the smaller tree tends to be shorter than that of the forest tree, but maturity is reached more quickly. Smaller trees grow naturally on higher ground, where wind and cold inhibits taller growth, and this is worth remembering when selecting species for roof garden planting.

The type of small tree you might use can be divided into two categories: those that are decorative and those that may be used to infill and build up your screen planting. But here personal taste is involved, for what I consider decorative you may not.

It is generally agreed that the genera *Prunus* (cherry and plum), *Malus* (crab apple) and *Crataegus* (thorn), will fit into the decorative list, since they all flower, fruit and have a degree of autumn color. None, however, has any sculptural quality and you will look at a bare tree for half the year. Conifers, on the other hand, have their full shape the whole year round, but when used *en masse* provide a shape which is too demanding to fit most planting plans and too boring to view.

For me, the smaller variety of silver birch or the thin weeping head of the willow-leaved pear (*Pyrus salicifolia*) are preferable substitutes to conifers. I also admire gnarled old apple trees, dead or alive. More exotic, good value small trees are many of the maples (*Acer* sp.), admired not only for their leaves but for their branches and autumn color. They are not grown for flower, but magnolias are and the adult tree has a good shape. The golden catalpa (*Catalpa bignonioides*), growing 5 m (16 ft) in height, is spectacular when in flower, but it is most memorable for its huge heart-shaped leaves. The showering sprays of golden *Genista aethnensis*, and the midsummer gold of *Koelreuteria paniculata* followed by bronze bladder fruits, are also attractive. Golden robinia (R. pseudoacacia 'Frisia') develops into a pretty tree too. *Amelanchier canadensis*, the shadblow, is a charming white-blossomed spring alternative to the cherry that has distinctive sculptural qualities.

For autumn color you might consider *Cercidiphyllum japonicum*, the Katsura tree, for a lime-free soil. The leaves turn smokey pink, red or gold, and foliage is similar to the eastern redbud (*Cercis canadensis*) with its purple, rose-type flowers in early May forming on its bare branches.

In the wild garden, I enjoy the spring leaves of whitebeam (*Sorbus aria* 'Lutescens') and the autumn fruits of rowan (*Sorbus aucuparia*), but these are probably better used as infill between "feature" trees. This category also includes alders (*Alnus* sp.), hornbeam (*Carpinus* sp.) and hazels (*Corylus* sp.). A small tree for "feature" and "infill" is *Oxydendrum arboreum* with drooping flowers in summer and red foliage in autumn.

All these personal preferences have to be tempered with sound reason, however. Different locations at the same latitude might not support the same tree because of contrasted altitudes, for example. Climatic variations will also affect your choice of tree. The long cold winters and hot summers that occur in much of North America do not support the same trees as the less extreme conditions of the British Isles.

My personal dislikes within this category include trees with purple foliage, which I find too eye-catching and generally heavy and leaden within a composition. I hate deep pink-blossomed cherries, whose flowers

Dominating maple
The golden foliage of a Japanese maple (Acer japonicum 'Aureum') dominates this garden. Both this maple and the Acer palmatum dissectum 'Atropurpureum' in the left foreground, are often listed as shrubs but will become small, eye-catching trees.

Distinctive tree shapes *These four examples show the variety of tree shapes available. Right is a young* Cornus florida *with its layered branches. Far right is a round-headed Japanese cherry. Below is the characteristic leaning form of an old apple tree, while below right is the drooping form of an aged pine.*

clash horribly with bright spring grass and deep yellow daffodils. I also shun laburnums, for while being spectacular when well-placed, finding the right place is very difficult.

My personal antipathy towards conifers stems from an upbringing in northern England where acre upon acre of once-open moorland has been struck ecologically dead by too rigid and too similar conifer afforestation patterns. This state of affairs is now tempered by contour planting and some inclusion of hardwoods, but my prejudice remains and it is not removed by the rows of bizarre coniferous subjects on display in any garden center. They epitomize the lengths to which our horticultural industry will go to achieve another sale at the expense of more natural plants and planting. However, certain conifers have a place within the garden's layout when carefully used, for their strong forms – whether prostrate, conical or horizontal – can be an asset to emphasize a point. Their strong coloring must be considered carefully though, for one glaucous blue spruce (*Picea pungens* 'Glauca'), for example, will, in maturity, dominate all around it.

Many of the dark, matt green conifers make admirable background and shelter.

Using trees within a garden presents a problem of scale unless you have acres of space. It is better to choose bold groupings if you can and to plant three or more of your chosen trees together. Parallel flowering can often be a problem, for in spring there is a flush of color, then a gap, then early summer color, and then another gap before the autumn crescendo. So try to choose your trees and plant them to provide a continuity of visual interest throughout the year.

Buying small trees
Small trees available commercially are categorized according to size and form (below). You should be very careful to establish the adult form of the tree you are buying, choosing specimens with healthy stems and shoots.

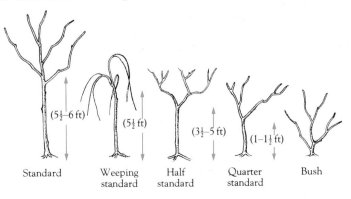

Standard	Weeping standard	Half standard	Quarter standard	Bush
(5½–6 ft)	(5½ ft)	(3½–5 ft)	(1–1½ ft)	

Planting a tree

For generations it was normal practice to plant most saplings in autumn, when trees are dormant, because all stock was sold bare-rooted. Today, however, it is possible to buy container-grown trees and shrubs so that they can be planted without disturbing roots more or less throughout the year, always provided there is not frost in the ground.

The hole in which the tree is to be planted should be excavated to about 1 m (3 ft) square. Fork over the ground at the base of the hole before putting in well-rotted compost, leafmold, peat moss and farmyard manure or the like to a depth of 200 mm (8 in). Then fork this in to the bottom layer of earth. Next, put the tree, which should have been well-watered, in the base of the hole, slit down the side of the container and gently remove it so as not to disturb the roots. You must clear the underside of the root ball, however, if the tree was potted in the traditional way with

a drainage medium in the base of the container. Ensure that the finished earth line will not be above that of the tree in its pot when you have planted it in your garden. If it is, lift the tree and add more earth and manure to the bottom of the hole. Before backfilling the hole, knock in a sound stake at the side of the root ball. In this way you will avoid driving the stake through the tree's young roots. Backfill the hole with as organic a topsoil as you can, gently shaking the stem up and down to ensure that soil settles between the roots, and firming the soil round the root ball as you go with your heel. You must be certain to examine the tree frequently as it will need regular, sometimes daily, watering during dry spells. This is especially important if the tree was planted out of its dormant period.

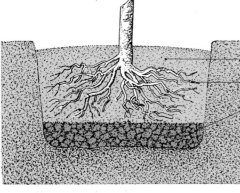

Topsoil with organic
materials incorporated

Damaged roots pruned

Forked soil

Staking and tying

Tie a newly planted tree to a stake with plastic cord. It is important, if you are planting a tree during the growing season, to keep it adequately watered, almost daily in most cases. This will encourage the roots to grow out of the tight ball that results from containerized growth into your prepared earth, quickly allowing them both to feed and support the tree. Trees planted in an exposed position must be provided with a stake set at an angle to the wind while those with particularly heavy heads may need additional staking and ties.

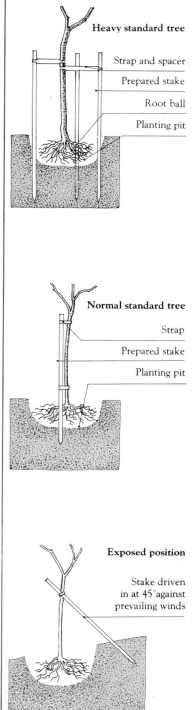

Heavy standard tree

Strap and spacer

Prepared stake

Root ball

Planting pit

Normal standard tree

Strap

Prepared stake

Planting pit

Exposed position

Stake driven
in at 45°against
prevailing winds

Planting for contrast, *above. The handsome light gold foliage of* Robinia pseudoacacia 'Frisia' *stands out against a matt-green hedge.*

Highlit apple tree, *left. Many trees can be enhanced with lighting, but the source must be low for complete cover.*

Training trees

Early medieval gardeners were enthusiastic shapers of plants for they needed to restrain and control their plants to achieve the formal symmetry of the patterned *parterres* so popular at the time. Successive moods of Romanticism encouraged a greater freedom and looseness in planting, even the copying of natural planting patterns, but today a greater awareness of form in the garden has renewed interest in tree shaping and encouraged the contrast of loose, natural plant shapes with trained plant forms. And together with topiary (the art of clipping) the training of trees is popular as a cheap alternative to sculpture in the garden.

Pleaching is the training of deciduous (sometimes flowering) trees upon a frame so that their branches entwine to form a green wall or canopy. An extension of this type of training is the topworking of fruit trees in the 17th-century French tradition. The shapes across the middle of this page show some examples of espalier and cordon forms trained against wires. The maintenance of shaped trees is outlined on page 251.

Pleaching laburnum and wisteria, *right.*
Laburnum trained over a metal frame gives the effect of a golden tunnel. Wisteria is interspersed to create a similar, purplish effect a little later.

1 Fan
2 Feather
3 Single oblique cordon
4 Double cordon
5 Five grid
6 Single "U"
7 Double "U"
8 Espalier

Pleached Hornbeam
Carpinus betulus *has been pleached to give a tunnel effect, leading the eye to a white bench seat. Clumps of blue-gray rue (*Ruta graveolens) *are planted at the base of each tree to increase the feeling of enclosure at ground level.*

Hedges

The plants most commonly clipped are those that make garden hedges. These are of three types: the loose form, which needs little restraining and includes genera such as *Berberis, Escallonia* and *Pyracantha*; species that need pruning rather than clipping, such as laurel (*Prunus laurocerasus*), and, finally, hedges that should be kept tight and compact by clipping, including *Buxus* sp., *Carpinus* sp., *Cupressocyparis leylandii, Fagus* sp., *Ilex* sp., *Ligustrum* sp., *Lonicera nitida* and *Taxus* sp..

The type of hedge that you select will depend on its location, the character of the site and what you want the hedge to do. Location will dictate species to some extent, particularly with regard to the amount of snow that falls, for in areas of heavy snowfall the clipped hedge can be crushed unless snow is shaken off regularly. Shaping the hedge to a point can help but that may not be the shape you require.

A common mistake is to plant the components of a hedge far too close together in order to achieve a thick screen quickly. Few people then either water or feed the hedge, with the result that on, reaching maturity individual plants within the hedge die down. So be sure to plant at recommended distances – and be patient. Remember, too, when selecting your species, that the quick growers do not miraculously stop their rapid growth when they have reached the height you want.

Clipped peacocks, *right. Topiary is part of the cottage garden tradition but its origins stem from the formal 17th-century garden.*

Traditional archway, *above. Yew (Taxus baccata) is here clipped to form an archway, with other clipped pyramidal forms of yew beyond. The architectural potential of this form of plant training is enormous, for it can be traditional, as here, or modern.*

Hedge designs

If you have the time, hedge plants give you great scope for designing in three-dimensions. This terrace is planted with hedge subjects, in a design containing contrasts of form, color and texture. The planting formation for a boundary hedge, below, should be combined with the planting distances shown right.

Ilex aquifolium

Buxus sempervirens 'Suffruticosa'

Taxus baccata 'Aurea'

Buxus sempervirens 'Handsworthiensis'

Plant spacing (mm, ins)

Buxus sempervirens 'Handsworthiensis'	450, 18
Carpinus betulus	450, 18
Cupressocyparis leylandii	750, 30
Fagus sylvatica	475, 19
Ilex aquifolium	500, 20
Ligustrum sp.	450, 18
Lonicera nitida	275, 11
Prunus laurocerasus	700, 28
Taxus baccata	500, 20
Berberis thunbergii	300, 12
Bucus sempervirens 'Suffruticosa'	300, 12
Lavandula angustifolia	300, 12
Aantolina chamaecyparissus	250, 10

Shrubs

When first looking at a garden it is often the brightest color or the most curiously shaped plant that catches the eye. However, the impact of these plants depends on their setting – the setting largely created by background planting. It is the background shrubs that do all the hard work, for it is against them that everything else is seen. They will also give the garden winter form, foliage for cutting and provide food and shelter for wild life if you are concerned about conservation.

The scale of this sort of planting will depend on the size of your garden, but as a general rule groupings of shrubs should be bold and simple.

Evergreens come into their own here, for they do the job the year round. Unfortunately the majority of broad-leaved evergreens lack winter hardiness and are limited to the South and West Coast. If you live here, consider evergreen forms of such genera as *Cotoneaster*, *Viburnum* and *Pyracantha*. You will see the diversity of sizes, forms and colors available. Next look at bamboos (*Arundinaria* sp.), the privets (*Ligustrum* sp., not to be despised), the laurels (especially *Prunus laurocerasus* and *Prunus lusitanica*), *Berberis*, *Mahonia*, *Elaeagnus*, *Escallonia* and

Enonymus sp., yew (*Taxus* sp.), box (*Buxus* sp.) and bay (*Laurus nobilis*), ascertaining which are suitable for your soil, location and climate. Camellias are hardy to Washington, D.C. and grow in like climates. Where the planting is to be exposed to wind or sea spray, select hardy shrubs for they must provide a good line of resistance.

Rhododendrons are a special case since they will only thrive on an acid soil. Although

Shrubs for foliage color, *below. This mixed grouping of deciduous and evergreen shrubs, with small trees and some perennials, has foliage that is mostly gold in color. Compositions are often strengthened by selecting a single color range.*

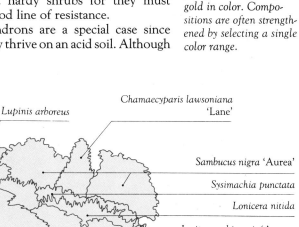

Lupinis arboreus

Chamaecyparis lawsoniana 'Lane'

Sambucus nigra 'Aurea'

Sysimachia punctata

Lonicera nitida

Juniperus chinensis 'Aureopfitzerana'

Alchemilla mollis

Ulex sp.

they (along with their near relatives *Pieris* sp., *Kalmia* sp., *Leucothoe* sp.) are more winter hardy than the previous evergreens, their culture is still restricted to the Pacific Northwest, Upper South and Northeast.

Amongst and in front of this evergreen background you can now start to choose and place your larger deciduous shrubs.

Azaleas must be first choice for late spring scent and flower. Others, just as useful, are winter-hazel (*Corylopsis*) for a wild effect, or gray-foliage sea buckthorn (*Hippophae rhamnoides*); buddleia and the spring-flowering spireas are quick growing, good flowering but short-lived shrubs, ideal for interplanting with slower evergreens and which can then be cut out in about five years' time. *Chaenomeles* sp. might be included in the list for both early season and autumnal interest, with species of the genus *Cornus* for their foliage, stem color or flowers. The flowering currants (*Ribes* sp.) also make useful infill, if you can stand their smell. Korean abelialeaf (*Abeliophyllum distichum*) has pretty white flowers that resemble those of forsythia but appear earlier. Late freezes can kill the emerging buds.

Some forms of forsythia have a strong yellow flower and an ugly upright stance. Much more attractive is the lemon, flaccid-growing *Forsythia suspensa* 'Atrocarpa' which flower arrangers love. For later flowering

Hydrangea combination, *above. A beautiful late-summer flowering grouping of* Hydrangea involucrata, *with its purplish flowers and large, sterile white ray florets, contrasted with the more usual mophead* Hydrangea macrophylla 'Ami Pasquier'. *A proprietary hydrangea colorant is necessary in alkaline soils to retain blue flower shades, if this is wanted.*

Acid soil shrubs, *left.* Heaths (Erica *sp.*) *thrive in an acid soil. In the foreground of this view of a large garden, they are grown with low-growing, partially evergreen hybrid azaleas. The background is made up of species of deciduous Japanese maple.*

grow philadelphus for its delicious, evocative scent, the cream forms of which are particularly beautiful. The larger and more rampant forms of shrub rose make excellent background material where space is ample. The Japanese snowball (*Viburnum plicatum* 'Mariesii') is ideal for mid-to-late spring blooms, but none of the deciduous viburnums nor lilac (*Syringa* sp.) in its various forms should be overlooked.

Most of the shrubs mentioned so far are spring flowering. The later, summer-flowering shrubs – such as *Clethra alnifolia*, *Abelia grandiflora*, rose-of-Sharon, hydrangeas, vitex may need a more prominent siting. Where summer-flowering shrubs are to be spot planted (that is individually, perhaps in grass), the technique is the same as for container grown trees (see p. 182). Usually, however, shrubs will be planted in a prepared bed as part of your ground pattern.

Ideally, such an area should be hand dug. In the past, planting areas and vegetable gardens were "double dug", that is the earth was turned over, with organic manure incorporated and weeds removed, to two spits (spade depths) deep, provided that the depth of topsoil allowed for this treatment. Working in this way with earth, you increase topsoil fertility quite quickly. Nowadays gardens tend, if hand dug at all, to be turned to one spit deep only, with the incorporation of organic matter, but even this process can be expensive. But as you may get only one chance of cultivating a bed before planting a new garden, it is money well spent for it will create a good foundation for later growth. Machine cultivation of the earth, even with organic matter added, tends to be an altogether shallower process but can be satisfactory if done slowly.

A more up-to-date method of creating a bed is to "weed kill" a grass area to your bed's pattern. After a month or so, plant your shrubs directly into the brown mass of dead grass, then mulch over the surface with rotted manure or compost. This, however, should be done in autumn so that the organic material will be taken down by worms through winter and spring. A summer mulch of rotted manure tends to dry out and form hard little clumps, which are difficult to disperse and which will be constantly raked over by birds.

As with trees, if you are planting stock that is not bare rooted (that is, pre-grown in a container), you may plant throughout the season, although you must water well. Autumn, or spring for less hardy subjects (the time to plant bare-rooted stock), is still the best time for planting when the work is on a considerable scale.

Planting distances for shrubs

It is difficult to be specific about the spacing between shrubs for it depends on how quickly you want to achieve an interlocking mass of plants. You must also consider the rates of growth of different plants. Some rhododendrons grow to 5 m across, but slowly, so I would plant them 2 m apart. Five years is the maximum time you should have to wait for the desired result, given that in this time some shrubs will need to be cut right back or thinned drastically.

At the foot of this page there is a simple guide to the ultimate sizes of some commonly-used shrubs. Of these, I recommend that the large, tall shrubs should be planted 2 m apart, medium-sized ones 1.5 m apart and small shrubs only 1 m. For other species, check ultimate sizes and then place them in one of the size categories for yourself. Generally, the beginner plants his material too close together, worrying that his newly-bought bundles of winter twigs will never burgeon out in spring. Until they knit together, you might want to cultivate the ground between shrubs. Cover it with a mulch or plant perennial bulbs or annuals. Try sunflowers (*Helianthus* sp. or *Nicotania* sp.) in tall shrub areas for bulk during the first few years.

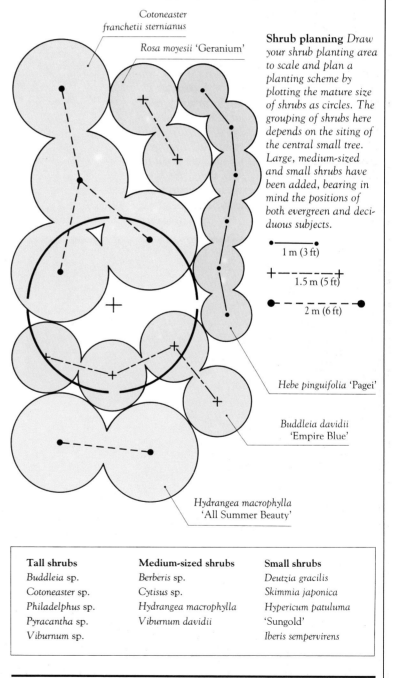

Cotoneaster franchetii sternianus

Rosa moyesii 'Geranium'

Hebe pinguifolia 'Pagei'

Buddleia davidii 'Empire Blue'

Hydrangea macrophylla 'All Summer Beauty'

Shrub planning *Draw your shrub planting area to scale and plan a planting scheme by plotting the mature size of shrubs as circles. The grouping of shrubs here depends on the siting of the central small tree. Large, medium-sized and small shrubs have been added, bearing in mind the positions of both evergreen and deciduous subjects.*

1 m (3 ft)

1.5 m (5 ft)

2 m (6 ft)

Tall shrubs	Medium-sized shrubs	Small shrubs
Buddleia sp.	*Berberis* sp.	*Deutzia gracilis*
Cotoneaster sp.	*Cytisus* sp.	*Skimmia japonica*
Philadelphus sp.	*Hydrangea macrophylla*	*Hypericum patuluma* 'Sungold'
Pyracantha sp.	*Viburnum davidii*	*Iberis sempervirens*
Viburnum sp.		

Feature shrubs

Plant selection has so far been for its service-ability and its bulk. It is against this mass that you should now start to arrange your decorative plants, your star items, to maintain sculptural and color interest throughout the year. Much of your selection will, of course, depend on your location (whether hot or cold), on your garden's position (whether sunny or in shade), and on your soil (whether dry or damp). But there is a range of quite tough plants that seems to survive fairly well in most conditions, and which can provide the structural element of your decorative shrubs. For want of a better term, this range may be called one of "architectural" interest. In the same way as we placed "special" trees before considering infill between them, so one might work with architectural shrubs. No matter how brilliant your colour selection (if that is your aim), some element of form within the concept will help shape its appearance throughout the year.

Start with those plants that, if left unchecked, would become trees. Examples include *Aralia elata*, which if pruned back each autumn develop huge pinnate leaves a meter in length, and *Eucalyptus gunnii* which, if kept cut down, has beautiful, fine gray leaves that make a good foil to many colors. Spikey cordylines will also articulate your border, though they should have their heads tied up through cold winters. The suckering sumach (*Rhus typhina*, or its cut-leaved

form), makes a beautiful architectural addition to your garden, with brilliant autumn colours and a lovely skeletal shape in winter. Californians will know *Fatsia japonica* for its handsome, evergreen, fig-like leaves, and *Fatshedera lizei*, a more sprawling relative, crossed with ivy, that grows well in shade. Then consider *Magnolia grandiflora*, a magnificent free-standing tree in sheltered areas but a background wall shrub in more exposed ones, and the fig (*Ficus carica*), although it is not evergreen.

Tree peonies (*Paeonia delavayi*) have a statuesque quality, with ravishing flowers in spring, as has *Viburnum rhytidophyllum*, with lax ribbed leaves 75 mm (3 in) long. *Arundinaria palmata*, a bamboo, is not for mixing with smaller species since it is too rampant, but it also has vivid ribbed leaves.

Shrubs to establish character *Below, the grasses and bamboos of this garden are largely responsible for its character. All are evergreen and hardy. Bottom, in this mixed border the backing shrub rose is* Rosa moyesii, *with the strong horizontal form of* Juniperus chinensis *in front of it. These shrubs provide a foil to the vertical spires of foxglove (*Digitalis *sp.) and the spikes of perennial* Salvia superba.

Curving border

This example of planting relies heavily on feature shrubs and is shown above in the spring and in plan, right. The border combines shape, texture and leaf form and deciduous and evergreen species are well-balanced. While the color combinations are particularly attractive in spring, summer interest will be provided by white floribunda roses, by the magenta flowers of *Stachys lanata* and the cream flowering spikes of *Yucca filamentosa*.

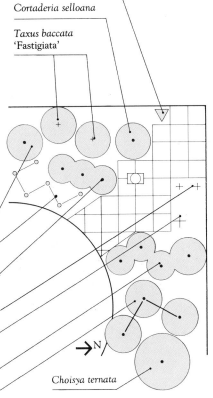

Clematis montana 'Alba'

Cortaderia selloana

Taxus baccata 'Fastigiata'

Rosmarinus officinalis 'Miss Jessup's upright'

Stachys lanata

Yucca filamentosa

Iris × gernabuca 'Jane Philips'

Ceanothus thyrsiflorus

Potentilla fruticosa 'Katherine Dykes'

Rosa floribunda 'Iceberg'

Choisya ternata

→N

Bold grouping *Although the foreground hosta (Hosta plantaginea 'Royal Standard') is a plant of distinctive form it is made more dramatic by the background of Phormium tenax and Lonicera nitida 'Baggesen's Gold'.*

189

It will always provide an instant Japanese effect. Coming down in size, use handsome yuccas grouped together in your composition, and New Zealand flax (*Phormium* sp.) if you garden in Florida or California. Consider the small *Viburnum davidii* (though it becomes 2 m (6 ft) tall), *Skimmia* sp., and *Choisya ternata*, the Mexican orange blossom, an evergreen with fleshy, pinnate leaves, for mild winter climates only.

Between these judiciously placed architectural species, start to blend and contrast in simple groupings the other decorative shrubs of your choice, keeping the interest dispersed throughout the season. Try to achieve a positive arrangement rather than a jumble of plants, using two, three or four individual plants from the larger scale species and eight or nine from the smaller.

My particular favorites include many of the genus *Berberis*, for smaller subjects mix well with them; broom (*Cytisus* sp.) and *Ceratostigma* sp. for late-season blue, all the sweet-smelling species of *Cistus* for hot, dry places, and *Cotinus* sp. for purple foliage.

Herbs have summer flowering value and some, like the little herb *Ruta* sp., have the added attraction of being evergreen (gray). Hydrangeas, too, make summer color. I prefer the lacecaps to the more blatant blue or pink mop-headed *Hydrangea macrophylla* Much neglected are tree lupins (*Lupinus*

Shrub planting for scent

Although many scented shrubs bloom early in the year, their flowers are not spectacular and the plants seldom possess architectural form. Some of them, such as *Sarcococca* sp., *Mahonia japonica* (one of the few with a shape of character), *Choisya ternata* and forms of daphne, are not particular about their site so they can be put in a corner near a door or a window so that their perfume will waft indoors in the summer. But to make a visually satisfying border with shrubs of strong scent, you need to include plants with stronger shapes, forms or colors.

In this example, a corner bed is "pinioned" by two clipped, pyramidal *Carpinus betulus*. Around this point of emphasis are grouped shrubs that combine in form and color as well as providing a variety of scents throughout the season.

Sarcococca humilis

Elaeagnus commutata

Rosa rubrifolia

Berberis stenophylla

Carpinus betulus 'Pyramidalis'

Syringa chinensis

Myrtus communis

Chimonanthus fragrans

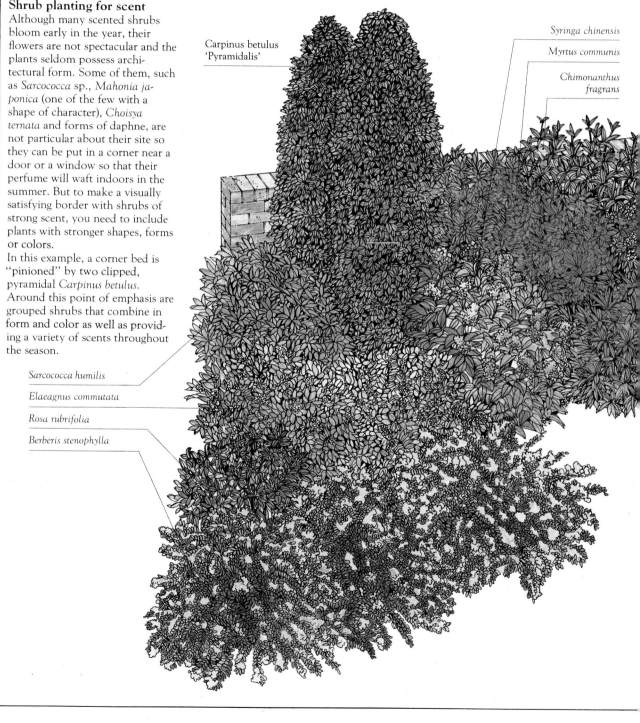

arboreus), which are easy to grow but are limited to their native California. Having more or less the same range of brightness, but being smaller in scale, is the ever increasing range of potentilla cultivars, which flower throughout the season until the frost. *Romneya coulteri*, the white Californian tree poppy, is exquisite but difficult to establish.

Many of the smaller, old fashioned roses are good all-rounders. For its foliage and hips, *Rosa rubrifolia* is splendid – indeed, all the *Rosa rugosa* cultivars, together with *Rosa moyesii*, have good autumn hips. I love the tight cabbage flowers of the Bourbon roses (*Rosa borboniana*), 'Madame Isaac Pereire' and 'Madame Pierre Oger'.

Certain floribunda roses will mix well with decorative shrubs, too; try mixing them with lavender and sage for a charming effect. Indeed, many of the shrubby herbs can be used decoratively in a border, but they are discussed separately (see p.217).

There is a wide range of shrubs which I have not included: those with gray foliage, *Artemisia arborescens* for example, will lighten the tone of any border. Although quite hardy in the British Isles, I have found many gray foliage shrubs almost impossible to obtain as little as 20 miles across the Channel, where they will not stand the winter's increased severity. Most need a good, open, warm and sheltered site.

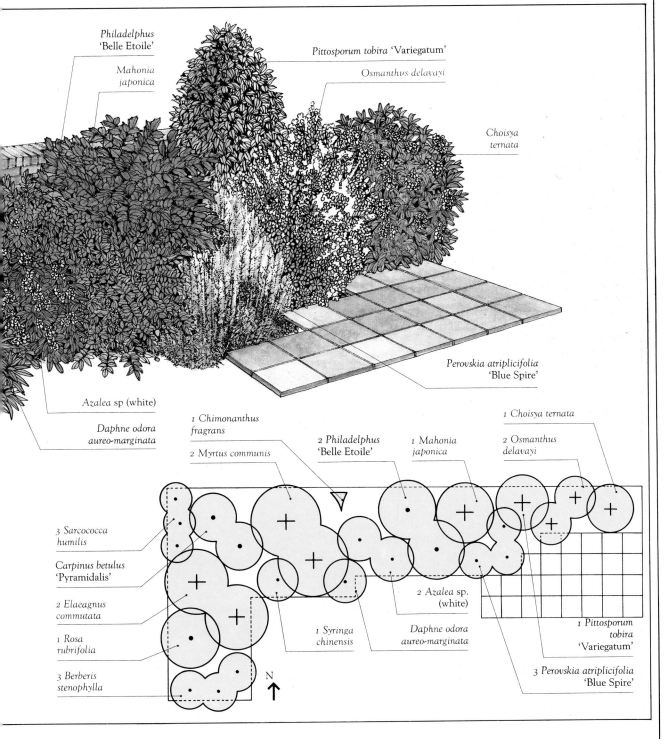

191

Perennials

Perennials are the group of plants whose flowers give permanent summer color. Few are evergreen but most are fairly easy to grow. There are types of perennials suitable for every location and condition. The clue to their needs is often found in the soil types and climate of the country from which they first came. Many of the gray-foliaged perennials, for instance, originated in New Zealand, while many of the plants with brilliantly colored daisy-type flowers came from South Africa. Perennial plants that are indigenous to northern Europe tend to be those with flowers of softer hue, even though *en masse* they will provide a vivid spectacle, as is proven by successful "herbaceous" and "mixed" borders.

The difference between a pure herbaceous border and a mixed one is that the mixed border includes shrubs as well as perennials, which not only lengthen the period of attraction but physically support the arrangement. A mixed border is easier to maintain, for much free-standing, perennial material needs staking to support it throughout summer. This, I suspect, is because the earth we provide for them is over-rich. In the high desert areas of Iran many of the parents of our hybrid garden subjects survive in the most arid conditions, though perennials in the main prefer a moist, slightly acid soil.

When making your selection choose a suitable shape and size of plant before considering color, for these characteristics will last at least all summer while the flower may be present for as little as a week. Peonies, for instance, are in perfect bloom for only a few days, since it is usually too hot or too wet for their delicate flowers to survive. In a capricious way, however, it is precisely this fleeting quality we seek to capture. So it is vital that your peonies are sited in front of a bold and later flowering plant to make a virtue of their persistent foliage.

Within the range of plants I call architectural, high on my list of favourites are euphorbias for their year-round interest. They are closely followed by different species of hellebore. Grey verbascum, with its towering lemon spikes, improves any border, as do the huge leaves of the globe artichoke (*Cynara scolymus*). *Macleaya cordata* is equally handsome but needs space, as it spreads rapidly. The useful day lilies (*Hemerocallis*) sp. have an exceptional colour range and are extremely adaptable. Sedums are useful, too, for their late summer interest; the purple forms are particularly handsome, especially

Summer-flowering perennial planting
This is a fine selection of early summer-flowering perennials, including bulbous plants, with delphiniums dominating the scene, tall Eremurus sp. and then foxgloves behind. In the foreground are iris and large, leathery bergenia leaves, with the blue globe thistle heads of Echinops ritro.

when mixed with Japanese anemone (*Anemone × hybrida* 'Alba'). The humble bergenia is ideal for front row, evergreen interest, as is the high summer sprawl of *Alchemilla mollis*. Some of the cranesbills (*Geranium* sp.) are easy to grow and have dense foliage of character. They are also useful as ground-cover plants (see p. 201). Grasses are often worth including among these striking perennials that will form the skeleton of a planting area. They form a plant group in their own right from 2 m-high (6 ft) beauties, which rustle in the breeze, to minute, soft cushions of bright blue, gray or green foliage. Most grasses are hardy but can become invasive and need frequent dividing.

Incorporate into this framework your other perennial favorites of less imposing form, using their color to compose your picture. A genus that flowers very early each spring is *Doronicum*, soon followed by the myriad colors of iris. Behind their stands of sword-like leaves, the cool spires of delphinium soon rise and, later, campanulas of similar shades. As summer progresses, the colors of flowering perennials are warmer. Sun roses (*Helianthemum* sp.) range from pink to orange and yellow. *Helenium* and *Helianthus* sp. provide the hot colors, oranges and browns. Phlox can be used to follow these plants (use plenty of white forms to cool your planting) and then, for

Planting distances for perennials

It is impossible to be precise about planting distances for perennials, for some, such as globe artichokes (*Cynara scolymus*), grow to about a meter (3 ft) across while others are a few centimeters (3–7 in). As a general guideline to the number you need in a border, however, allow five to every square meter (10 ft²) (see diagram). Make your selection by shape as well as color. Here are tall blue lupines grouped with the blue heads of *Erigeron* sp. in front.

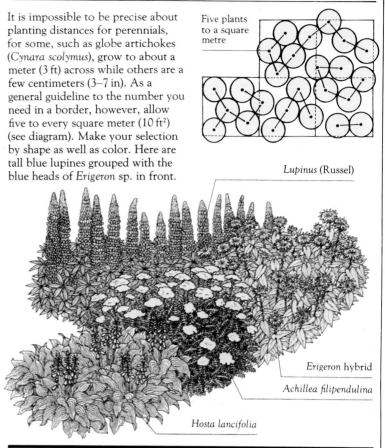

Five plants to a square metre

Lupinus (Russel)

Erigeron hybrid

Achillea filipendulina

Hosta lancifolia

Orange border *The perennials in this yellow and orange border include* Campanula *sp., with half-hardy* Gazania *sp., lemon* Antirrhinum *and gray foliaged* Helichrysum *sp. In the foreground are annual pot marigolds (*Calendula officinalis*).*

flowering into autumn, there are chrysan-themums and asters.

The colors of these summer flowers are bewildering in their variety, but one way to master this abundance is to plan your border and make your selection in a particular color range. Alternatively, stick to grasses in one area and plants with daisy flowers in another. Try to eliminate too many varieties and do not accept from friends snippets of those plants that you do not really want.

When you have made your selection, plant in bold clumps and drift one mass into another. If you are buying from a garden center, you will often find that one good young plant can be separated into two or three and, while the group will be thin in its first year, perennials grow rapidly.

Once established, some will need to be divided nearly every year. This is especially so of grasses. Perennials grow out from the center and eventually leave a hole in the middle of the plant. This dividing of plants is usually spring work (as described in Care and maintenance, see p. 255), so you must re-member which plant is which for in early spring you may not recognize them. Label each carefully in autumn so that you will know what is where when you come to deal with them in the new year.

Random spring planting, left. A mixed and random spring planting in an English garden of foreground Alchemilla mollis backed by Euphorbia wulfunii. Over to the right are Spanish iris and Primula sp., with angelica (Angelica archangelica) behind.

Mixed grasses, right. The grass species in this example of perennial planting are clustered beneath an ailanthus tree at the front of an American house. Attractive, feathery seed heads indicate Lasiogrostis splendens and Pennisetum orientale.

An evergreen perennial planting design

The range of perennial plants that will grow in light shade is more extensive than is usually supposed and it is this tolerance that is the common factor between the plants chosen for this scheme. The species included have adapted to their situation by modifying their leaf forms, making them particu-larly attractive. This, however, has been at the expense of bright flower color, for plants in shade usually have flowers of muted white, pink or blue.

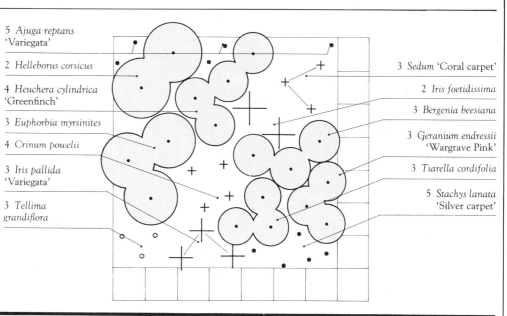

5 *Ajuga reptans* 'Variegata'

2 *Helleborus corsicus*

4 *Heuchera cylindrica* 'Greenfinch'

3 *Euphorbia myrsinites*

4 *Crinum powelii*

3 *Iris pallida* 'Variegata'

3 *Tellima grandiflora*

3 *Sedum* 'Coral carpet'

2 *Iris foetidissima*

3 *Bergenia beesiana*

3 *Geranium endressii* 'Wargrave Pink'

3 *Tiarella cordifolia*

5 *Stachys lanata* 'Silver carpet'

A mixed border planting design

This mixed border, shown as it would appear in mid summer, largely comprises evergreen subjects for year-round interest. At the back are the dense foliage shapes of *Cotoneaster wardii*, *Lonicera nitida* and *Stephanandra tanakae*. These not only form a screen against which smaller plants can be placed but provide a support for them, obviating the need to stake and tie. Plants in the middle distance include *Mentha rotundifolia variegata*, a spreading, decorative mint with attractive green and white leaves, *Anthemis* *tinctoria*, which produces bright yellow, daisy-like flowers in mid summer, and *Allium flavum*, an ornamental onion with bright yellow flowers. Foreground material is mostly ground cover and includes *Salvia officinalis* 'Purpurea', a spreading purple sage with attractive foliage color, and *Limnanthes douglasii*, a California native which has profuse white flowers. The plants were chosen not only for their size and shape, but for colors – principally yellows, blues and white – that work harmoniously together.

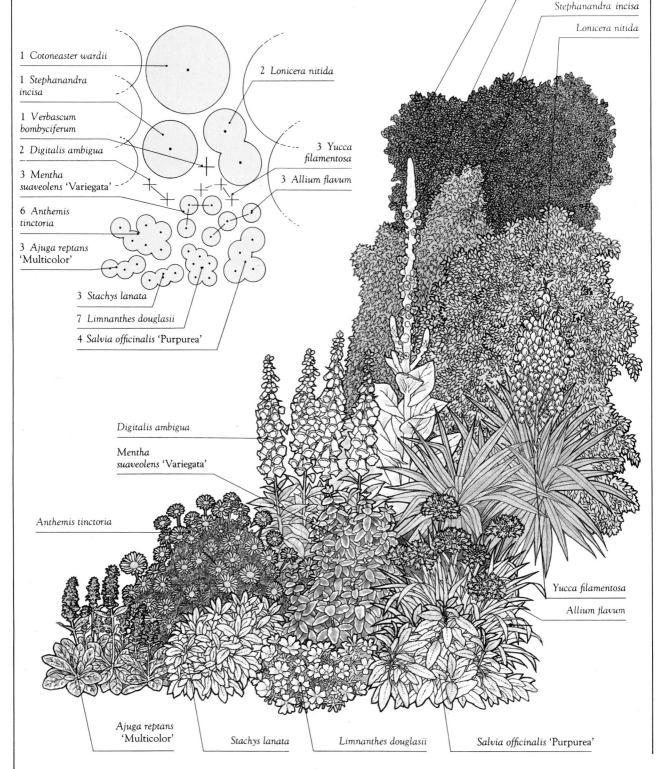

1 *Cotoneaster wardii*

1 *Stephanandra incisa*

1 *Verbascum bombyciferum*

2 *Digitalis ambigua*

3 *Mentha suaveolens* 'Variegata'

6 *Anthemis tinctoria*

3 *Ajuga reptans* 'Multicolor'

3 *Stachys lanata*

7 *Limnanthes douglasii*

4 *Salvia officinalis* 'Purpurea'

2 *Lonicera nitida*

3 *Yucca filamentosa*

3 *Allium flavum*

Cotoneaster wardii

Verbascum bombyciferum

Stephanandra incisa

Lonicera nitida

Digitalis ambigua

Mentha suaveolens 'Variegata'

Anthemis tinctoria

Yucca filamentosa

Allium flavum

Ajuga reptans 'Multicolor'

Stachys lanata

Limnanthes douglasii

Salvia officinalis 'Purpurea'

Annuals

Annual plants that develop from seed, flower, produce seeds and then die in one year. Many of their flowers are extremely bright and, in the main, they provide the colorful splashes in the garden, on the roof garden or in the window-box. With few exceptions, the flowering period of annuals is extremely short, so successive sowing of seeds or planting of seedlings is often necessary to maintain the display. There are some annuals, however, that self-seed and will continue to come up year after year in a random way, appearing in the most unexpected places. Among these are marigolds (*Tagetes*), the tobacco plant (*Nicotiana*), nasturtiums (*Tropaeolum*) and sweet-alyssum (*Lobularia maritima*).

Until a few years ago, gardeners prepared bedding schemes for annuals as the main feature of their gardens. Island beds would be prepared and filled with maturing plants that would be replaced *en masse* with later-flowering kinds at the first signs of fading. This sort of annual extravaganza is now restricted to public spaces since the labour costs and price of oil for heating greenhouses in which annual seedlings are nurtured has become extremely expensive.

Annuals differ somewhat in their hardiness and this can affect their propagation. The directions on most seed packets can aid you in determining when and how to sow. In general, the hardiest annuals can be sown in the open ground in early spring, even before the soil seems workable and before frosts have stopped.

Among my favorites in this category are sweet-alyssum (*Lobularia maritima*), pot-marigold (*Calendula officinalis*), larkspur (*Consolida ambigua*) and California-poppy (*Eschscholtzia californica*) and true annual poppies.

Less hardy and requiring a longer growing period before flowering size is reached are ageratum, the invaluable many varieties of *Impatiens*, *Lobelia erinus* and marigolds (*Tagetes*). Start their seeds indoors, either in a sunny window or under flourescent lights.

Annuals are today used to thicken out young shrub planting schemes and give quick height (cleome is ideal for this) or to enliven the front of a mixed planting scheme.

Use annual color in big bold splashes or intermingle colors to give the alpine meadow, cottage garden feel, depending on the effect you seek. Remember that taller species may need staking.

As soon as your annuals have died down, be decisive and either cut them back, when you will get another flowering if the season is young, or take them out and seed a quickly maturing alternative.

Informal annual color *This example shows zinnias and bedding dahlias growing beneath fruit trees. Dahlias can be grown from seed but it is customary to propagate by splitting tubers. Zinnia seed can be sown directly in the open ground after the soil warms. Or seeds can be started indoors.*

Using yellow, orange and red

Annual flower color in summer is predominantly yellow, orange and red in the northern hemisphere. These colors can be harsh and strident and must therefore be carefully sited, for they will inevitably dominate the surroundings, particularly in a natural, rural garden. To accommodate them best, plant these brightly-colored annuals either in the foreground or to one side of a main view. Avoid siting them at the far end of your garden, for this will have the effect of making the intervening space seem less, foreshortening the prospect. Used sensitively, however, yellows, oranges and reds can be extremely effective, particularly when muted by lighter flower color among them. Lemon and strong pink, for example, will dilute brighter colors when mixed with them; white, too, has the same effect and its addition brings instant sharpness to any color combination. Purple is another useful color when seeking to tone down these bright colors.

Warm color mix with white, *left.* Nemesia strumosa *is a plant whose mixed colors embody the essence of summer. Here, paler shades offset the hot colors.*

Undiluted yellow, *below. Antirrhinums can be mixed with perennials or sited in front of shrubs but are most effective when planted in drifts.*

1 *Thunbergia alata*

2 *Zinnia* 'Old Mexico'

3 *Antirrhinum* 'Topper'

4 *Gazania* 'Sunshine'

5 *Tagetes* sp.

6 *Helianthus* sp.

7 *Calendula* 'Pacific Beauty'

8 *Gaillardia* 'Gaity'

9 *Nemesia strumosa*

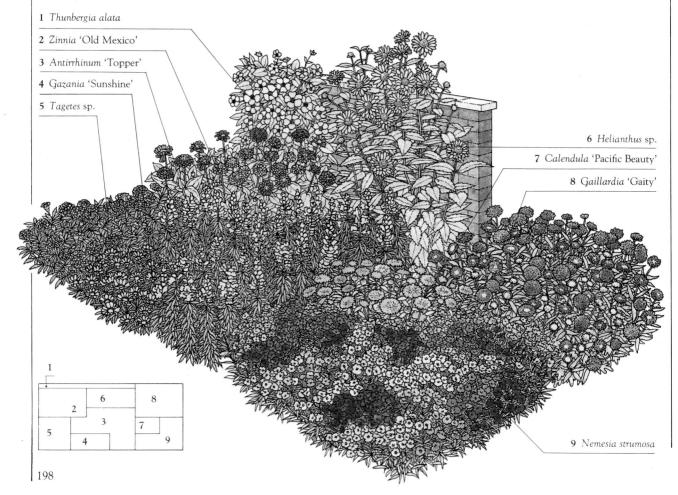

Using white and cream

White flowers mixed with other flower colors will always lighten the effect; when used entirely on their own, however, they will probably look cold, for white needs plenty of green to enrich it. Selectors and hybridizers of annuals have produced white plants that are so covered in flowers that their vital green foliage is masked.

White annuals look superb, however, when mixed with herbaceous plant material and while the justly-famed white gardens of England rely on perennials to create this effect, they are always supported by annual planting. Solid white planting in window-boxes over a whole façade also looks crisp, sharp and sometimes spectacular.

Cream should never be used as a substitute for white, for it has a warmth and quality of its own. As with lemon, use cream to soften strong, hot colors, or with green or gold flowers or foliage. Cream also looks well in conjunction with the vivid green of a well-kept lawn.

Cream contrast, *above.* *Soft and cream-colored* Mesembryanthemum criniflorum *flowers are especially effective when mixed with deep pink. The white* Arabis albida *strikes a harsh note, however, in the composition.*

Pure white, *left. White petunias have a striking purity about them and make some of the finest annual bedding material. They will only thrive, however, if they receive plenty of sun.*

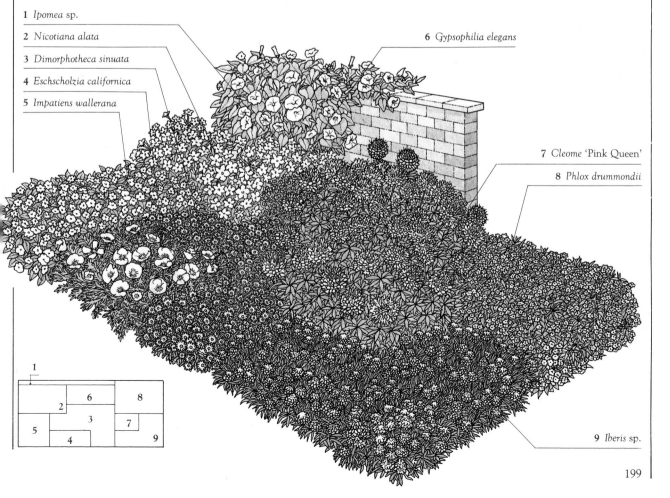

1 *Ipomea* sp.

2 *Nicotiana alata*

3 *Dimorphotheca sinuata*

4 *Eschscholzia californica*

5 *Impatiens wallerana*

6 *Gypsophilia elegans*

7 *Cleome* 'Pink Queen'

8 *Phlox drummondii*

9 *Iberis* sp.

Using blue

Blue is a very strong color and should therefore be used with care in a garden. Too much will look brash, too little merely irritates. Siting is all important. Be guided by nature, for it is a color that occurs naturally in light shade or diffused through meadow grass.

Rich blue coloring is at its best when there is a cloudless sky and bright sun, for then it reflects the canopy. These conditions seldom obtain in the British Isles, for instance, and without them I personally find blue too demanding a color, unless carefully softened with pinks, grays and perhaps a touch of purple.

Blue is naturally a spring and early summer flower color, but I find blue crocus difficult to fit into a plan in spring and blue asters depressing later in the year. The rule is to be careful where you site blue annuals if you are seeking a natural effect. If, however, you want a grand, dominating sweep of color in your garden, this color cannot be bettered.

True blue clusters, *above. The Californian bluebell,* Phacelia campanularia, *produces the purest blue, bee-attracting flowers amongst a carpet of bushy, soft leaves.*

Evocative morning glory, *left. Nothing is as evocative of hot summer mornings as the purple-blue of morning glory* (Ipomoea tricolor). *This is an annual climber that will reach 6–7 m (19–22 ft) in height in full sunlight.*

1 *Ipomoea tricolor*

2 *Salpiglossis sinuata*

3 *Heliotropium arborescens*

4 *Callistephus chinensis*

5 *Ageratum houstonianum*

6 *Consolida ambigua*

7 *Nigella damascena*

8 *Campanula medium*

9 *Petunia* hybrid

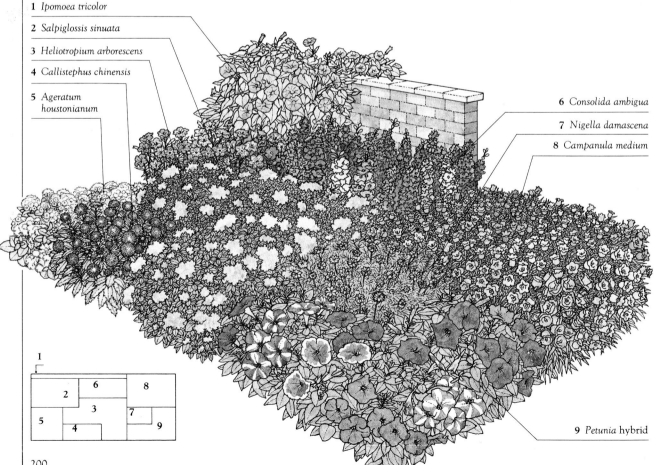

Lawns and ground cover

We are fortunate in northern Europe that grass, the primary natural ground covering mixed with herbs, grows so easily. Indeed, in the British Isles we carve out many of our gardens from this greensward, but there are few other parts of the world where grass will grow with ease.

Lawns take many forms. Real lawn enthusiasts treat their grass as though it were a bowling green, maintaining a weed-free, lurid emerald carpet of fine grass throughout the year, even during a drought, by mowing twice a week. This is both costly in time and finance, for this type of lawn must be fed and dressed regularly. And it will certainly not be the sort of place where children and pets can play. For normal family use, a coarse grade lawn is quite adequate and I do not mind seeing the odd weed within it.

The alternative to a closely mown lawn is one that is rough cut. By allowing the grass to grow longer, and mowing only a path or paths through it, you will cut down on the area which needs weekly care and you will also encourage flowers to grow within the rough area. Such treatment suggests a rural feel and can look charming with fruit trees grown in the longer grass. By leaving grass uncut for periods, you can successfully hide the inevitable raggy look of bulbs dying down after spring flowering in a mown lawn.

The establishment of wild flowers in a lawn is not as easy as one might suppose for, if you sow seeds, grass will inevitably swamp the tiny seedlings. So plant young plants by hand through the grass in drifts to establish a good coverage of wild flowers. The timing of your mowing will, of course, be dependent on the wild flowers that you establish and the length to which you allow the grass to grow.

To create a real flowery mead or alpine meadow, you should cultivate your ground freshly and sow a flower seed/grass mix suitable for your area. The grass seed must include a slow-growing type, with whose competition the emergent flower seedlings can cope. Coarse grasses will quickly swamp flowering plants and ruin the effect.

Large scale ground cover Epimedium *sp. has been used in this Dutch garden as ground cover between bold, brick stepping stones beside an attractive pool. The stone circles have been repeated in shape but on a larger scale in the paved area beyond to extend the overall garden design.*

Lawn variations

Lawn types vary enormously, from the emerald, weed-free suburban plot to the wild flower meadow. The type you make will depend on your taste, the lawn's function and the character of the garden of which it is part. It is therefore necessary to be clear about what you want the lawn for.

Is it simply to be looked at, or will your lawn be a place for playing and lounging upon?

Once your decision is made, you can buy the appropriate seed, for today there is a great variety. There are fine grass seed mixes available that will produce a lawn beautiful to look at but difficult to maintain and easily damaged. Or there are coarse grass seed mixes that will develop into a hard-wearing lawn. (See p. 280.)

Wild garden meadow, *right. A handsome example of dog- or ox-eye daisy* (Chrysanthemum leucanthemum), *growing in rough grass. This grass is roughly mown, as if mowing hay, after the daisies have flowered in July.*

Grass of different lengths, *below. This garden has a mixture of mown and rough grass, with some color provided by clover* (Trifolium *sp.*). *While a fine, mown lawn suffers from drought in high summer, longer grass, and particularly clover, remains green.*

Mowing edges *When you are laying grass, either turf or seed, against a wall or at the bottom of steps, make a mowing edge along the base of the structure, just below grass level, so that you can cut over the edge and reach all the grass. Without this, you will either have to hand cut the grass at the edges or leave a permanent tuft.*

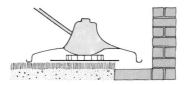

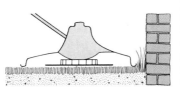

A useful lawn, *above. This "family" lawn is finely mown and carefully tended but composed of coarse grass to withstand hard wear.*

Plan for a mowing pattern, *right. You can mow patterns within a rough grass area, in this case between fruit and flowering trees. Within the rough grass plant a variety of bulbs.*

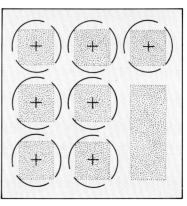

The establishment and proper maintenance of an all-grass lawn is a discipline of its own (see p. 256). You have the choice of using seed (see p. 280), which is relatively cheap to buy but costly in time while the seed is first growing, or turf, which is relatively expensive but fast to turn into a lawn.

Those with a small area to be covered, who do not want the chore of regular maintenance, the elderly or handicapped for example, and those without children, should consider other forms of ground cover planting. You will have seen in the section on establishing soft surfacing (see p. 131) how successful random planting in gravel can be. You can use the same technique of random planting within a growing framework. A beautiful clump of grass within a surround of low *Cotoneaster dammeri*, through which spring and autumn bulbs emerge, flower and then die down, can be very attractive. The natural form of this type of planting is the ivy (*Hedera* sp.) covering of a woodland floor, or the heath (*Erica* sp.) covering of heaths and moorlands. The technique can be used to plant decorative borders as well. The virtue of using either taller shrubs that sweep to the ground, like *Viburnum tinus* or *Hydrangea*

sp., or specific ground cover plants, is that they eliminate weeds, provided that you have first established the ground cover in clean ground. Weeds growing through ground cover are very difficult to remove.

Between the extremes of the lawn and informal ground cover planting, there are intermediate types of ground cover that can be walked upon occasionally. These include aromatic herbs that will release characteristic perfumes. Where climate permits, chamomile (*Anthemis* sp.) has been used as a ground cover planting since the Middle Ages. It was often employed to cover raised seating areas in traditional herb gardens and still can be in a full sun position. But chamomile tends to look bedraggled in winter and, while it can stand some frost, does not like being covered in snow for any length of time.

Mixed low-growing thymes are hardier and can create a rugged, aromatic ground cover, having waves of flower through it according to the species used. Both these ground coverings, however, need an open sunny position.

The various forms of *Ajuga* sp., though not traffic-proof, will grow easily anywhere and make excellent low ground cover. All

Roof garden treatment *Ground cover planting needs little thickness of soil, since sustenance usually comes to the plant through the multiple rootings of its runners. This makes them ideal for roof gardens, where weight is a critical factor. In this pattern English ivy* (Hedera helix) *is kept clipped to retain the plan's outline.* Rhododendron *sp. are planted through the ivy to provide color.* Pleached Platanus orientalis *surround two sides of the area.*

their leaves are purple or purple streaked. *Alchemilla mollis* becomes a wonderful summer carpet of green flowers with umbrella-shaped leaves that hold every drop of moisture. *Armeria maritima*, or thrift, is an alpine but makes dense evergreen cushions of foliage with rosy pink flowers in May and June. Various species of the genus *Berberis* have attractive flowers, foliage and berries, a good example being *Berberis thumbergii* 'Atropurpurea'. Within the wide range of cotoneasters, many are rampant and therefore useful as ground cover. Many will hang over a wall in a picturesque way. One of my favorite species is *Cotoneaster dammeri*, more particularly the cultivar 'Skogholm'. Cotoneasters will all grow under trees or shrubs or in the open.

Use *Dianthus* sp. to underplant roses, but remember that they prefer a sunny position in a well-drained soil. The prettily leaved genus *Epimedium* will grow in most situations and has divided, evergreen glossy leaves. Heaths (*Erica* sp.) can be grown on their own in a special area of the garden; they are better shown with other heaths than grouped with ground cover plants. They prefer full sun and nearly all hate lime, so are characteristic of a particular soil.

For a sunny bank, try the low-growing forms of the genus *Genista*, most of which are covered in bright broom-like yellow flowers in early summer. While usually used in the front line of the mixed border, cranesbill (*Geranium* sp.) makes an excellent and colorful ground cover, with pretty leaves in sun or light shade.

All the ivies are excellent ground cover plants in any situation. Once established, however, they can swamp everything else. The same can be said of the ground covering species of *Hypericum*, but both are useful for that corner in which nothing else will grow.

Horizontal-growing coniferous juniper makes good ground cover and grows remarkably fast. So does *Lamium maculatum*, a nettle, which not only romps sideways but will also work its way into shrubs. In hot places such as the southern States of the USA, *Liriope muscari*, with foliage like a rush and grape hyacinth-type flowers, can be used to cover large flat areas to make striking, but not walkable, lawns.

Lonicera pileata is a favorite evergreen plant of mine, having a pleasant spraying shape though no flowers that you would recognize as being from the genus. *Pachysandra terminalis* (Japanese spurge) is an almost prostrate evergreen carpeter and is a classic ground cover plant. For the wild area of your garden, the golden star (*Chrysoganum virginianum*) covers the ground, its bright green leaves dotted with yellow daisies from spring to late summer. It does well in any ordinary soil, including wet land. For a very shady situation, consider *Sarcococca*

humilis, which is dull, shrubby and evergreen but has the most delightfully scented white flowers in spring. Sweet woodruff (*Galium odoratum*) forms low clumps of greenery with distinctive whorled leaves.

I personally find the much favoured *Vinca* genus invasive and ugly as ground cover, though there is no denying the beauty of its blue periwinkle flowers. Avoid *Vinca major* at all costs as it is just too smothering; *Vinca minor* is tolerable if you cut it back in spring after flowering to encourage bushiness.

Useful ground cover, *right. This ground cover planting within a scree or alpine garden has Erica sp. in the left foreground and a low Euonymus fortunei beyond. The central gold mass is of creeping Jenny (Lysimachia sp.), beyond which are marjoram and a low juniper. Low blue gentians appear at random.*
Far right, Hypericum calycinum makes striking ground cover on a bank retaining a flight of stone steps.

A ground cover planting design

This plan and projection is for a south facing courtyard, enclosed within three walls. "Spot planting" of feature shrubs punctuate the garden but most of the planting is ground cover. This provides year round interest with flower colour but more especially with texture and leaf shape. A design such as this needs careful maintenance to ensure that the plant masses remain separated and in the forms that the designer intended. A pattern of stepping stones helps to divide up the planted areas.

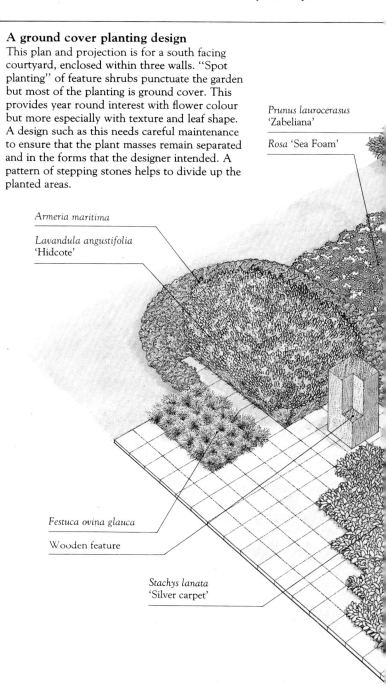

Prunus laurocerasus 'Zabeliana'

Rosa 'Sea Foam'

Armeria maritima

Lavandula angustifolia 'Hidcote'

Festuca ovina glauca

Wooden feature

Stachys lanata 'Silver carpet'

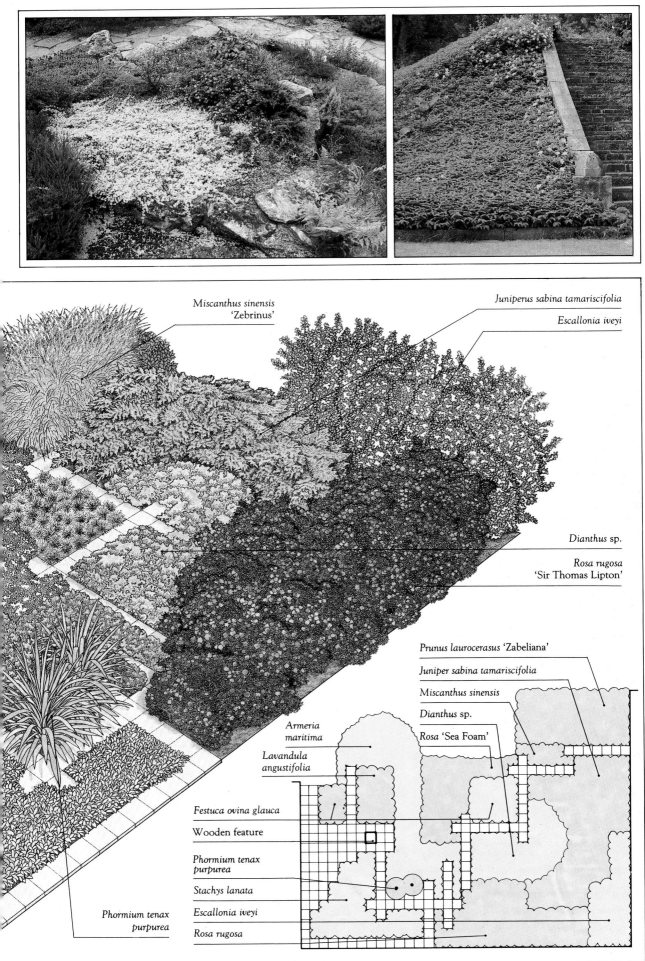

Miscanthus sinensis
'Zebrinus'

Juniperus sabina tamariscifolia

Escallonia iveyi

Dianthus sp.

Rosa rugosa
'Sir Thomas Lipton'

Prunus laurocerasus 'Zabeliana'

Juniper sabina tamariscifolia

Miscanthus sinensis

Dianthus sp.

Rosa 'Sea Foam'

Armeria
maritima

Lavandula
angustifolia

Festuca ovina glauca

Wooden feature

Phormium tenax
purpurea

Stachys lanata

Escallonia iveyi

Rosa rugosa

Phormium tenax
purpurea

205

Plants for shade

It is often thought that shade is one of the greatest problems of urban gardening for in cities and towns plants must often grow under overhanging trees or within the shadow of buildings and walls. In fact, there is quite a range of plants that have adapted to shade by developing larger leaves (often at the expense of brilliant flower color) and it is this characteristic that can be used to make strong planting designs.

There are two sorts of shady garden area, determined by location: those that are damp, perhaps getting no sun at all and subject to drip from overhead trees; and dry areas, which, due to dense overhanging plants that do not allow drips through, are sheltered from rain.

Most of the maples (*Acer* sp.) do exceptionally well in moist, shady conditions; use the snake bark forms for winter interest in addition to the usual Japanese type. Alder (*Alnus* sp.) does well, as do all forms of thorn (*Crataegus* sp.), poplars (*Populus* sp.) and willows (*Salix* sp.). The bird cherry (*Prunus*

Shaded urban garden, *left. An overhanging laurel* (Prunus laurocerasus) *shades this urban garden so a bold-leaved* Fatsia japonica *has been grouped with ferns against a small-leaved bamboo. The ferns are* Athyrium filix-femina *with the far smaller-leaved* Polystichum setiferum *'Divisilobum'.*

Damp shade *Far left,* Anemone japonica *and the tender* Aspidistra elatior *make up a summer grouping with a stone birdbath against a background of* Hedera *sp. The green ground cover plant is* Helxine *sp., which not only tolerates but requires dampness.*
Left, massed Hosta undulata *'Variegata' make a striking composition with osmunda fern beneath* Fatsia japonica. *The plant to the left, at the base of the archway, is* Helleborus corsicus.

Shade planting with a Japanese flavor *The planting plan of this small rear garden reflects the shaded conditions and makes a virtue of them. Bamboo, Japanese maple and ferns create a leafy scene beyond the simple sliding glass doors with a distinct Japanese flavor. The simple wooden decking and the sand bed add to the effect. The encroaching bamboo is desirable but it will have to be restrained to prevent it overwhelming everything else, which it will do quickly.*

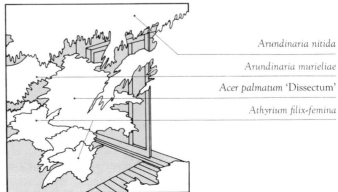

Arundinaria nitida

Arundinaria murieliae

Acer palmatum 'Dissectum'

Athyrium filix-femina

padus) flourishes, and so does *Cercidyphyllum japonicum*, a beautiful spring and autumn foliage tree.

On a smaller scale, from among shrubby subjects, goat's beard (*Aruncus sylvester*) will thrive and put on a huge show of creamy yellow flowers each summer. In a sheltered location, camellias thrive in moist shade and in mild winter climates are rewarding in both leaf and flower. They prefer neutral through to acid soils. Try *Clethra* sp. for white flowers with a seductive scent.

A hardy stand-by for damp shade conditions is the whole range of *Cornus* sp., which are good in leaf and retain attractive colored stems throughout winter. The large-leaved *Fatsia japonica*, for mild winter regions only, thrives in moist shade, putting on a mass of green flowers in late summer. For late winter flowers that stud their bare stems, consider witch-hazel (*Hamamelis* sp.), whose scented, twisted flower heads are long-lasting and immune to frost. Hydrangeas are essential for late summer interest in shade. Plant the gentle flowered lacecap varieties rather than the more common full-headed types.

Privet (*Ligustrum* sp.) should not be overlooked. There are many attractive large-leaved forms, and even the golden form of the common *Ligustrum ovalifolium*, when left untrimmed, is spectacularly bright throughout winter. Another often-despised plant, but which comes into its own in shade, is cherry laurel (*Prunus laurocerasus*).

Among the perennials, my favorites for shade include *Helleborus* sp. for early spring flowering, *Hosta* sp. and the dramatic leaves of *Rheum palmatum* 'Rubrum', a sort of decorative rhubarb.

Commonly-used ground cover plants for damp shade include *Hedera hibernica*, *Pachysandra* and *Vinca* sp. Many of the bamboos, being hardy and lovers of moisture, are excellent for this type of shade and will even succeed in very chalky soils. While one of the joys of bamboo is the sound of wind rustling through its fronds, it does not, in fact, like an open, windy situation. Once established, however, bamboos are some of the most beautiful and elegant of all evergreens and their height and forms vary considerably. Make your selection from the large genera of *Arundinaria* or *Phyllostachys*.

There is increasing interest in the hardy ferns – and with good reason, for most are easy to grow, are not fussy about soil, and prefer the cool, light-shaded, moist conditions on the north side of many gardens.

The range of plants suitable for a dry, shady location is smaller but, among trees, you can choose from the genera *Caragana*, *Gleditsia* and *Robinia* if you avoid the golden forms. Among shrubs are *Amelanchia laevis* for spring and summer interest and

many forms of *Berberis*. Sea buckthorn (*Hippophae rhamnoides*) grows fast and has striking gray foliage. Flowering currants (*Ribes* sp.) flourish in light, dry shade, as do elders (*Sambucus* sp.).

Ground cover plants for dry shade include many of the large-leaved *Bergenia* sp. and perennial blue *Brunnera macrophylla* that flower at about the same time. *Lamium* sp., though rampant, make excellent cover, as does *Lonicera pileata*, which is shrubby.

Many grasses grow well in dry shade. Most are easy to cultivate and many are evergreen. Pampas grass (*Cortaderia selloana*) is a standard favorite and thrives in dry shade, as do forms of *Festuca* and *Luzula* sp.

Grass and bamboos
Top, Cortaderia solloana, *a popular pampas grass. A much more compact form*, Cortaderia pumila, *is ideal for the smaller gardens.*
Above, Arundinaria viridistriata, *an unusual bamboo with rich yellow and green variegated leaves borne on erect, purplish canes. This plant can reach 2 m but shade stunts its growth.*

A planting design for dry shade

Plants suitable for dry shade are less numerous than those which prefer moisture; selecting species is therefore more a question of finding what will tolerate the conditions rather than what will flourish in it. The scheme planned on the right is for a corner of a house beneath an old pear or apple tree. To enliven what might be a dull area, plants have been selected for their gold leaves or flowers, with other foliage to complement them. A dark corner such as this will benefit from regular applications of organic compost, which will help to hold moisture in the dry soil. Otherwise, the pear tree will tend to extract much of the moisture and nutrients from the soil, leaving it impoverished.

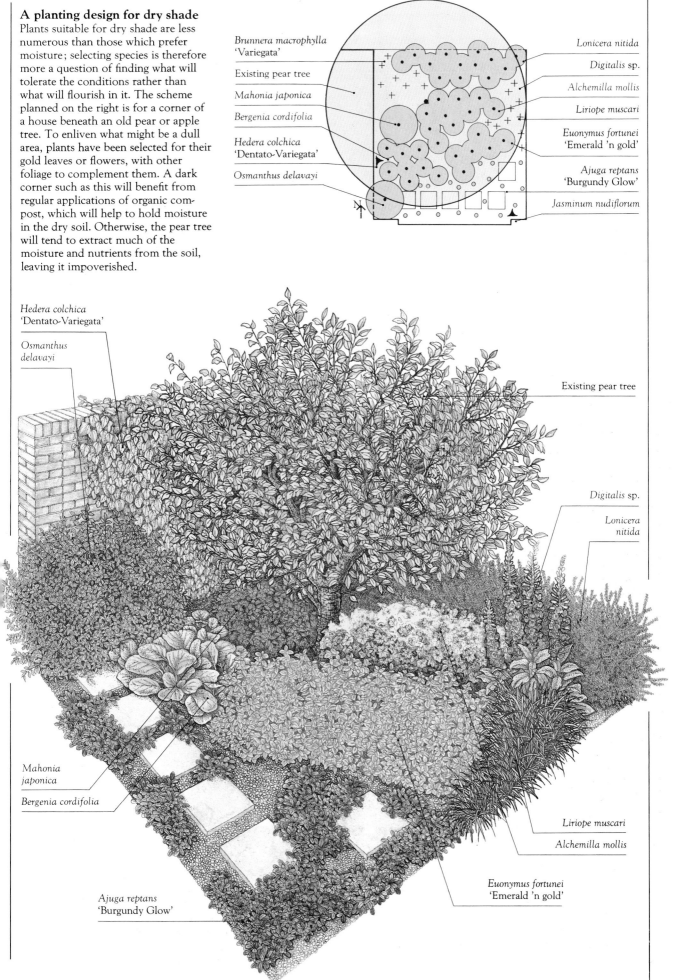

Brunnera macrophylla 'Variegata'

Existing pear tree

Mahonia japonica

Bergenia cordifolia

Hedera colchica 'Dentato-Variegata'

Osmanthus delavayi

Lonicera nitida

Digitalis sp.

Alchemilla mollis

Liriope muscari

Euonymus fortunei 'Emerald 'n gold'

Ajuga reptans 'Burgundy Glow'

Jasminum nudiflorum

Hedera colchica 'Dentato-Variegata'

Osmanthus delavayi

Existing pear tree

Digitalis sp.

Lonicera nitida

Mahonia japonica

Bergenia cordifolia

Liriope muscari

Alchemilla mollis

Euonymus fortunei 'Emerald 'n gold'

Ajuga reptans 'Burgundy Glow'

Bulbs

All too often we think of bulbs (a term I use to include corms, tubers and rhizomes) as spring features only, but in fact it is possible to have them in bloom throughout the year.

Plant bulbs either "naturally", that is as if scattered in drifts in grass, or incorporate them with mixed planting, where their dying leaves will not be so obvious. The secret to their correct use depends on their natural habitat, how they grow there and on their shape. Some, such as hyacinths and *Galtonia* sp., have a formality that needs to be offset by other plants, while others, such as *Narcissus* sp. and snowdrop (*Galanthus* sp.), are never successful within a border and need to be planted in a more natural way.

Winter and spring-flowing bulbs dominate planting areas during their flowering season, when they announce the demise of winter. In the British Isles, for example, the winter aconite (*Eranthis hyemalis*) and snowdrop appear as early as December. These are followed by crocus, then early narcissus such as the cultivar 'February Gold'. Anemones begin to show soon afterwards and are followed by other daffodils, *Chionodoxa luciliae* and grape hyacinths (*Muscari* sp.). Hyacinths are well-suited to tubs and formal beds, as are tulips. I love the lily-flowered types of tulip for their flopping informality and some of the parrot tulips for their bizarre colors. In early summer come the bright-colored forms of Dutch iris, followed by the architectural forms of *Allium* sp. and *Ixia* sp. from South Africa. Majestic crown imperials (*Fritillaria imperialis*) are also magnificent.

In high summer there are the white hyacinths (*Galtonia candicans*), all the lilies and the simple butterfly gladioli. Forms of autumn crocus then brighten the dying garden.

If you want bulbs to emerge through low shrubs in planted areas, place them in casual groups rather than regular, circular patches; they look more natural this way.

To plant bulbs in natural-looking drifts in lawn, scatter them casually across the growing area, as shown opposite, and then plant them where they land. Plant to the correct depth, of course, but do not space the bulbs out or you will lose the random effect. The late daffodils will not have finished flowering when you start to mow your lawn and will need a further six weeks after flowering to allow their foliage to die down before you cut the grass over them, for until their leaves have dried out bulbs are making their growth for the next year. You will therefore have an area of longer, rougher grass containing dying leaves within your lawn. It is important that the outline of this longer grass is part of the overall pattern of your garden.

Bulbs in containers, *above. Bulbous plants grouped in pots can make a bright splash of spring colour. This grouping includes narcissus and iris.*

Massed bulbs, *below. Mixed daffodils have been "naturalized" in grass in this English garden. Such profusion takes a number of years.*

Scatter planting

Within a prescribed outline, distribute your bulbs casually and then plant them where they have fallen. In this way you will achieve a pleasantly natural effect when they appear and later flower. Plant bulbs to the correct depth either with a special bulb planter or with a spade. Dig the spade in, lever up a section of turf while you put in the bulb and then firm down the earth.

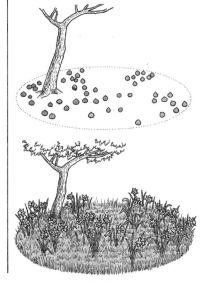

Unusual bulbs *All too often gardeners regard bulbs solely as spring plants, overlooking the contribution they can make to a garden through the year. Non-spring flowering examples include Allium sp., right, and Lilium odysseum, below. Some lilies require special treatment but others are easy to grow and will make an attractive, scented addition to your garden.*

Patterns with bulbs

To alleviate the untidy tufted appearance of dying bulbous-plant leaves on a lawn, plant your bulbs within carefully planned areas that can be left as long grass. About six weeks after the flowers have withered, the leaves will die down. You will then be able to mow that part of your lawn as well as the unplanted areas if desired, or maintain different grass lengths. After grass has been allowed to grow and seed, do not try to cut it close in one operation. Gradually reduce the height of cut.

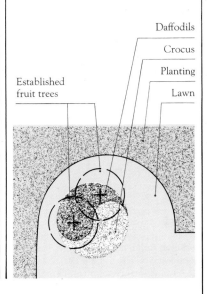

Established fruit trees

Daffodils

Crocus

Planting

Lawn

211

Climbing plants

Plants "climb" in one of several ways. Some have aerial roots which adhere to a structure, like ivies (*Hedera*) and the climbing hydrangea (*Hydrangea anomala petiolaris*). Others cling by tendrils, a well-known example being the grape (*Vitis*). Other vines that climb by tendrils are Virginia creeper (*Parthenocissus quinquefolia*), clematis (leaf stalks become tendrils) and passion-flower (*Passiflora caerulea*). Boston-ivy (*Parthenocissus tricuspidata*) clings by means of rootlets attached to tendrils. Many vines, like the honeysuckles (*Lonicera*), wisteria, silver lace vine (*Polygonum aubertii*), fiveleaf akebia (*A. quinata*) and the rampant kudzu vine (*Pueraria lobata*), are twiners. Climbing and rambler roses can only support themselves by pushing their long branches in among a host plant or through a trellis.

Another category of "climbers" includes pyracantha and California-lilac (*Ceanothus* sp.) that like the shelter of a wall or fence and can be trained to grow against either support and become sturdy.

A few climbers are evergreen and these are ideal where screening is needed. For the South and other mild climate regions, there is trumpet vine (*Bignonia capreolata*), madeira vine (*Boussingaultia baselloides*) and Armand clematis (*Clematis armandii*). In the north there are varieties of winter-creeper (*Euonymus fortunei*) and ivy (*Hedera helix*). Hall's honeysuckle (*Lonicera japonica* 'Halliana') has evergreen or semi-evergreen foliage and *L. japonica* 'Aureo-reticulata' has yellow-veined leaves.

Remember that once vines have covered your fence, they will not necessarily stop growing. One of the fastest growing is silver lace vine which grows as much as 6–9 m (20–30 ft) in a season, quickly smothering its support with a froth of green-white flowers. A personal favorite is the non-fruiting *Vitis coignetiae*, another fast grower with huge leaves that change color in autumn to brilliant orange and crimson shades.

Discreet support, *below. The profusion of planting in this small town garden is dominated by a climbing rose. Climbing roses must be supported, although supports can be easily camouflaged. In this example, the support is detachable so that the wall behind can be painted easily.*

Versatile ivies, *above. This photograph shows the adaptability of ivy. In one case it has been allowed to ramble through a juniper tree, while in another it can be seen clinging to a wall. The varieties are* Hedera helix *'Buttercup' and 'Caenwoodiana'.*

Climbers on frontages

The supports that you choose for climbers on a house front should not dominate or be at odds with the symmetry of your frontage. Also match the scale of the support to the scale of the climber – a bold support needs bold foliage, while a fine tracery of leaves needs a fine support. Against masonry walls, consider running wires, supported on "vine eyes", parallel with the mortar courses. A wooden lattice should coincide with the proportions of windows and door-frames.

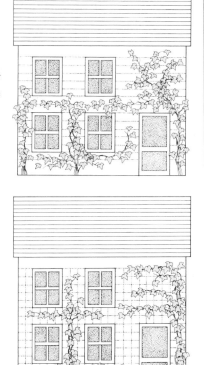

Above right, horizontal wires on "vine eyes". Below right, squared trellis is spaced to match windows and door.

Wall adornment, *above. Much of the charm of the old brick walls, above, is created by their climbing plants – in the top example, a climbing rose and a honeysuckle (Lonicera sp.) on the wall above. Both are attached to imperceptible wires that run parallel with the courses of the wall. The climbing rose will be detached from its support for reshaping (see p. 258) while the new shoots of honeysuckle are tucked under the wires as they grow.*

Climbers at night *The three-dimensional shapes of established climbing plants make them particularly good subjects for artificial lighting. Here, a variety of climbers combine with a house and make the floral walls of an enchanting seating area.*

213

Water plants

Water plants, like plants growing in normal ground, have characteristics that reflect their location and specific needs. The amount of moisture they require, for example, will vary, some liking only damp roots, others, such as certain reeds and rushes, grow in 500 mm (20 in) of water. There are also aquatic plants that are mostly submerged, allowing only their leaves to float on the surface of the water. Water lilies are typical of this group. Still others are fully submerged and act as oxygenators in water.

The condition that most affects aquatic plants is whether the water is running or still. Soil content is not of such vital importance as the depth at which the rooting medium is set to hold the plant roots. These two categories – nature of water and depth of planting – divide the range of water plants into two groups.

Because aquatics are not subject to the same needs as plants on dry land, many feeding from the water itself, they have adapted their form of growth; thus, they often have large leaves (as do those of plants living in shade) and it is this characteristic that makes them so attractive in planting compositions. There are many that grow horizontally, like water lilies; others have huge rhubarb-type leaves, such as *Rheum* sp., the decorative form of rhubarb, and the larger *Gunnera* sp. (suitable for mild areas). In contrast, some aquatics have leaves that are vertical and spiky. It is the contrast of vertical with horizontal that can make water planting so dramatic – consider, for example, the simple arrangement of a weeping willow over a sheet of still water.

The most effective groupings in water tend to be sparse and composed of two or three types of plant only. Look at natural water planting, and this point will become immediately obvious. Bold drifts of one subject against a mass of another, with areas of clear water between, offset each other. This is normal planting design procedure, but gardeners are often disconcerted by the presence of water.

Before choosing your plant material for use with water, decide where the plant is to grow and the depth of soil and water you are allowing it. You may have to build a ledge of

Complementing a basin feature *Water is recycled by a submerged pump into the stone basin and then the pond. Plants include arrowhead* Sagittaria lancifolia, *water lilies* (Nymphaea sp.) *and* Potamogeton densus, *notable for its elongated and close-packed leaves.*

specific height to suit some marginal plants. You can, of course, alter the height of plants in water when they have been planted in plastic containers by raising or lowering the container on bricks. These containers are specially made, with open lattice sides, and dark-colored so that they will not be seen when submerged. Larger, boggy areas should be planted to look natural, but remember to stick to simple groupings.

You must decide whether you want a truly natural look for your water planting or not, for decorative plants and ducks do not go together. Remember, too, that some weeds and floating plants become invasive in certain areas, so study local conditions when making planting decisions. The correct time of year for planting most aquatic plants is in April, May or June, as plant life is just starting to grow vigorously. By the following winter your water plants will have established good enough root anchorage to survive cold weather except for tropical water lilies.

Water lilies will make a great deal of growth in the course of one season if planted in good garden soil. Without this, the leaves will be stunted and plants will not flower. Ideally, the mix should be made up of six parts of good loam well mixed with one part of cow manure or coarse bonemeal. When the roots have been planted in loam and manure within containers, spread a layer of pure loam over it, then a layer of gravel to anchor the fine content when it is sunk into water. This ensures that the cow manure will not rise to the surface to decompose, foul the water and poison the fish.

Submerged oxygenators can be planted in pure loam, free of manure. Do not use dredgings from the pool, for this has little

Mature planting, *above. The planting in this attractive pond includes water lilies and reed mace (*Typha latifolia), *with* Iris × germanica, *which flowers in June, in the foreground.*

Early bloom, *left. These yellow-flowering marsh marigolds (*Caltha palustris) *brighten the side of the pond early in the year and often blossom again in the autumn. The variegated leaves are those of* Iris sibirica *'Variegata.'*

Water planting methods

Different types of water plant (see p. 278) require different planting techniques so that they are set at the right depth. A built-in shelf at the side of a pool is an ideal site for marginal plants. In a pool with a well-balanced habitat for pond life, you can plant in soil established beneath sand and cobbles on the pool floor. Planting in a proprietary basket (as shown on p. 216) is more convenient. You can use blocks to adjust the height of the planting baskets.

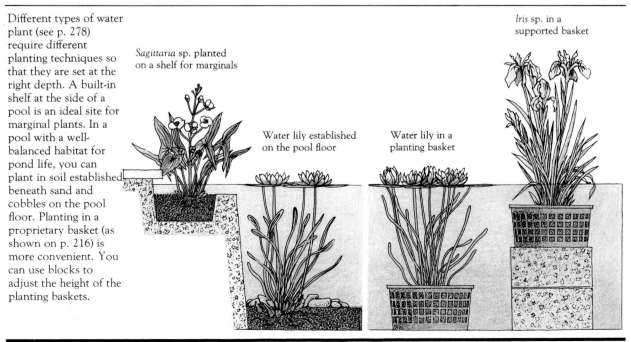

Iris sp. in a supported basket

Sagittaria sp. planted on a shelf for marginals

Water lily established on the pool floor

Water lily in a planting basket

food value and not even a weed will grow on it, as witness the heaps of uncultivated mud often seen by the banks of ditches and canals.

On receiving a new consignment of plants, remove any dead or broken foliage and lightly trim the roots. Often the remaining leaves will die off but new ones will appear in a few days.

When planting is completed, patience is needed filling the pool; it must be done gradually. The shock of cold water to plants that have already suffered from being moved during their growing period can prove fatal. To minimize the risk, fill the pool slowly and at first leave the water level only deep enough to cover the plant crowns. Then leave the pool for a few days before adding more water. To avoid disturbing dirt or mud, fill the pool by directing the flow from a hose into a plant pot set on the bottom. Do not run the water too quickly. When you are introducing plants into a full pool, lower them to their final position, if it is to be deep, over a period of days by altering brick heights standing beneath their containers.

New ponds and pools inevitably take time to clear, for you have to wait until the correct balance of plant life to fish, snails and the volume of water is achieved. This may take as long as a full season. Do not keep emptying your pool to clean it, since on refilling the whole cycle has to start again.

Water planter *Water lily ready to be introduced into the pond.*

Gravel

Rich compost

Hessian lining

Marginal planting *The bold leaves of Rodgersia sp. make a background to this boggy planting that includes Primula japonica in the foreground, Astilbe sp. on the left, and a form of Polygonum.*

Pondside grouping *Bamboos and grasses are not dependent on a boggy site but their vertical shapes can be very effective when planted in association with water, as in this example. Rushes (Butomus sp.) and Scirpus sp. – true water plants – complete the pondside grouping.*

Herbs

Herbs, whether shrubby or perennial, are useful decorative additions to a mixed planting in a garden. Certain herbs may also be included in your list of decorative trees, for bay (*Laurus nobilis*), myrtle (*Myrtus communis*) and witch-hazel (*Hamamelis* sp.) will reach such proportions. There are also good arguments for having a herb garden on its own. For anyone with a small area in an open and sunny position, herbs are ideal: they are not over fussy as to soil quality, they have decorative foliage and are more or less fragrant. Those that are not hardy can be grown as summer additions, if planted annually in the spring.

Perhaps more important than their decorative value are the culinary properties of herbs. Their value as an additive is being increasingly appreciated in times of tasteless packaged food. Certain herbs, of course, are classic additions to certain foods in different parts of the world: rosemary in Provence, sweet basil in Italy, marjoram in Greece and cumin in Persia.

In the East, spices are widely used for their medicinal properties. Even in the West, the use of herbs as medicine is becoming more widespread with the renewed interest in homeopathy as an alternative to the use of synthetic drugs and surgery. Herbs may be used in tissanes which can be sleep-inducive, tranquilizing, painkilling or purgative.

Herbs may also be used dried in *pot pourri* to scent your house in a natural way. The essential oils of many herbs can be extracted and compounded to produce scents and body oils, using the crushed root of orris (*Iris × germanica florentina*) as a stabilizing agent.

Herbs are a vital component in the increasingly popular treatment known as aromatherapy.

With all these healing and restorative properties, it is not surprising that over the centuries herbs have gathered a certain amount of myth, with extravagant claims made on their behalf. However, modern scientific methods of analysis are indicating that these claims are not entirely groundless and they are being newly quantified.

Many of the plants we commonly include in mixed planting are, in fact, herbs, including specimens for most types of location, such as *Gaultheria procumbens*, St John's wort (*Hypericum perforatum*), *Rosa damascena*, *Rosa gallica*, hollyhock (*Alcea rosea*), sunflower (*Helianthus annuus*), juniper (*Juniperus communis*) and one of the brooms (*Cytisus scoparius*).

Most herbs prefer an open, sunny position in which to grow, with moderately good, neutral soil. Mint, chives and parsley, however, will grow perfectly well in part shade.

In lighter, dappled shade you can grow angelica, celery (*Apium graveolens dulce*) and chervil (*Anthriscus cerefolium*). All these herbs are for use in the kitchen.

Many herbal books suggest that you grow your herbs within strict, formalized patterns edged with box, as was the practice in medieval times. Anyone who has grown herbs, however, will realize how invasive they can be, and it seems a waste of effort to be constantly restraining them to conform to a rigid design. The glory of a herb garden is its profusion, alive with the hum of bees on a hot summer day. Therefore build up your herb garden planting plan much along the lines of your general garden planting. Firstly, consider which herbs are deciduous and which evergreen; then ascertain their ultimate heights, color of foliage and form of

Herb border *A large box (Buxus sp.) backs this arrangement of herbs, which includes the gray-leaved curry plant (Helichrysum angustifolium), sage (Salvia officinalis), thyme (Thymus sp.), winter savory (Satureia montana) and a large purple plantain (Plantago sp.). Herbs will provide neat clumps of plant material, as in this example, provided that you have managed their autumnal trim and thin.*

growth. Consider their flowers but remember that while many herbs become laden with flowers, these are transitory and their other attributes will be dominant.

Eye-catching features can be useful foils in a herb garden. In the design below, changes of level are used, comprising a raised bed and a step. Another focal point is a simple pot feature. This might as easily be a piece of sculpture, or even an attractive bee-hive in which you could in fact keep bees.

You will need hard-surfaced access to your herbs as they need clipping, dividing and picking regularly. This surfacing can, however, be interspersed or bordered with low-growing thymes or chamomile to scent your way. An alternative is to devote a narrow border to herbs so that you have access along its length.

I do not include mints (*Mentha* sp.), horse radish (*Armoracia rusticana*) and comfrey (*Symphytum officinale*) among general herb

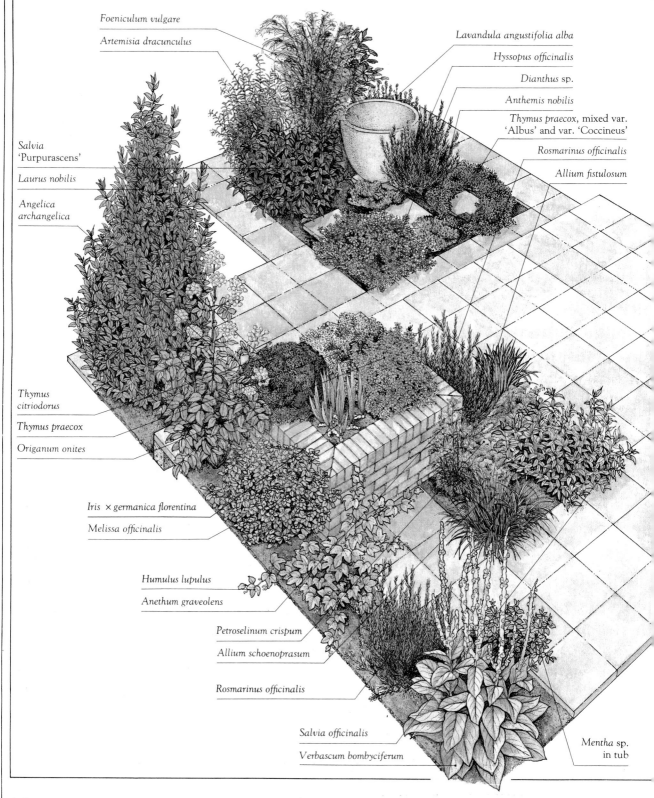

Foeniculum vulgare

Artemisia dracunculus

Lavandula angustifolia alba

Hyssopus officinalis

Dianthus sp.

Anthemis nobilis

Thymus praecox, mixed var. 'Albus' and var. 'Coccineus'

Rosmarinus officinalis

Allium fistulosum

Salvia 'Purpurascens'

Laurus nobilis

Angelica archangelica

Thymus citriodorus

Thymus praecox

Origanum onites

Iris × germanica florentina

Melissa officinalis

Humulus lupulus

Anethum graveolens

Petroselinum crispum

Allium schoenoprasum

Rosmarinus officinalis

Salvia officinalis

Verbascum bombyciferum

Mentha sp. in tub

planting because they are so invasive. For these herbs, make a separate collection in individual tubs. Their foliage and flower colors are well worthwhile. Apple and Egyptian mint (*Mentha suaveolens*) are particularly handsome. I also keep the 'Dark Opal' form of sweet basil (*Ocimum basilicum*) in a separate pot as it likes a very hot position, is annual and can be kept quite dry.

Your herb garden will need regular attention, particularly the cutting back of dead flowers. Plants such as chives need to be divided and replanted on a regular basis (see p. 259) to retain shape and vigor.

Garden designs are often successful because they have a single underlying theme. Herbs can provide such a theme while offering a range of plant material that is interesting and useful.

A herb garden design

The herbal planting illustrated here would fit into any open garden, either as an item on its own or merging into the general garden planting around it. Alternatively, it might form a terrace, facing south if possible so as to be in full sun. The pattern is made up of three small beds, each between 2 and 3 m (6–10 ft) square. One bed is raised 450 mm (18 in) within a brick wall. Overall pattern is dominated by eight woody herbs: two *Rosmarinus officinalis* and a bay tree (*Laurus nobilis*, not hardy in cold climates) and sages

(*Salvia* sp.), for all these are evergreen. In the growing season the planting is backed by the tall spikes of, first, the stately, yellow-green-flowering Angelica (*Angelica archangelica*) and, later, by lemon-flowering gray mullein (*Verbascum bombiciferum*).

An eye-catching herb is the Welsh onion (*Allium fistulosum*), whose spikey shape is repeated at a lower level by chives (*Allium schoenoprasum*). These are contrasted with clumps of parsley (*Petroselinum crispum*) and annual dill (*Anethum graveolens*). In the raised bed,

the composition is of shrubby thyme species with orris (*Iris × germanica florentina*), bushy pot marjoram (*Origanum onites*) and low, golden forms of thyme.

The largest bed, on the lower level of the garden, has stepping stones within it to match the main paving. These support an attractive pot with a bold, simple form that contrasts with the tall lovage (*Levisticum officinale*) behind, the adjacent feathery leaves of fennel (*Foeniculum vulgare*) and intense blue flowers of hyssop (*Hyssopus officinalis*).

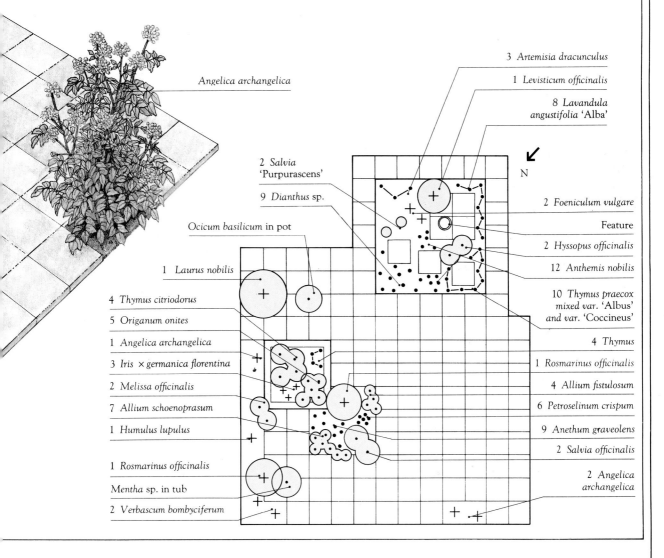

Angelica archangelica

3 Artemisia dracunculus
1 Levisticum officinalis
8 Lavandula angustifolia 'Alba'

2 Salvia 'Purpurascens'

9 Dianthus sp.

N

2 Foeniculum vulgare
Feature
2 Hyssopus officinalis
12 Anthemis nobilis

Ocicum basilicum in pot

1 Laurus nobilis

4 Thymus citriodorus
5 Origanum onites
1 Angelica archangelica
3 Iris × germanica florentina
2 Melissa officinalis
7 Allium schoenoprasum
1 Humulus lupulus

1 Rosmarinus officinalis
Mentha sp. in tub
2 Verbascum bombyciferum

10 Thymus praecox mixed var. 'Albus' and var. 'Coccineus'
4 Thymus
1 Rosmarinus officinalis
4 Allium fistulosum
6 Petroselinum crispum
9 Anethum graveolens
2 Salvia officinalis
2 Angelica archangelica

Vegetables

Most people hide the vegetable garden as far from the house as possible because they do not think it decorative. I disagree. Vegetables may not be flowery but well-organized rows looking healthy and green can make a fine display. To have the vegetable patch adjacent to the kitchen door is also extremely convenient, provided there is an open, sunny space for it.

However, urban dwellers, if they have gardens at all, have little space for vegetables, so a rented allotment at the edge of the town may be the next best thing. In the British Isles there is a movement towards self-sufficiency and to have an allotment now is not solely associated with saving money but also with growing pure food. An allotment on the European continent has never been a place just to produce foodcrops. Individual plots usually have a small, carefully designed building incorporated within them, the style and scale of the structure varying from country to country. In parts of Germany, for example, the allotment is a private garden and the tool shed also acts as a weekend retreat in summer. Restrictions are placed, however, on electricity and other services to

ensure that the structure is not used as a second home. The areas surrounding these "chalets" are usually given over to a combination of vegetables, flowers for cutting and herbs for culinary use. Unfortunately, the USA has always lagged behind other countries in community garden projects.

Even a small garden can make a productive vegetable and fruit area, for most families need only what may be called "convenience" vegetables – that is, summer salad material, snap beans, some tomato plants and herbs. If you have the space, larger crops, such as squash, broccoli, cucumbers and corn,

Fruits of the earth *The object of vegetable gardening, which is often arduous, is to provide fresh home produce, preferably grown in soil enriched only with organic materials.*

A vegetable garden
This garden plot is approximately 10 m square (107 ft²) and contains not only vegetables but a herb bed (raised for easy cutting), a compost area, a work bench and potting shed, all arranged to be both practical and attractive. Given the space, two more vegetable areas of similar size would allow greater flexibility of cultivation and a wider range of vegetables but you can manage perfectly well in such a limited space with careful planning. The cultivation area in the foreground is surrounded by a low, clipped hedge of santolina, rosemary and box, an arrangement that would look appropriate even in a small town garden. Paths, edging and raised beds are all constructed in the same brick. Softwood fencing has been used to support a corrugated, clear vinyl roof, supported additionally by pointed metal verticals.

Summer crop bed
This area includes climbing beans and salad vegetables, such as lettuce, radish, miniature tomatoes and cucumbers.

Covered potting area and store
A roofed area can be used very successfully as a place for sowing into seed trays and potting. If you are careful to clean and oil your tools after use (see p. 248) so that they are protected against damp, you can also use this area for their storage. The corner structure also gives the vegetable area a permanent shape independent of the growing crops.

can be sited elsewhere, together with a soft fruit area perhaps, if desired.

But be warned before you embark on making a vegetable garden. However enthusiastic you are there are practicalities to face. If you wish to be self-sufficient through the cultivation of your garden, the planting, care and harvesting of food crops must dominate the time you spend outside. To provide sufficient vegetables for an entire family throughout the year requires an area larger than most gardeners possess. Furthermore, the labor is heavy, the time needed considerable if the vegetable garden is to be kept fully productive and in good order, and to be truly organic you will need space and time to maintain a compost cycle. The resulting vegetables are therefore not cheap. Most people,

of course, do not price their own time and it is certainly true that home-grown vegetables are more wholesome and fresher than those bought from a shop. A deep-freeze is a valuable piece of equipment for anyone growing more than the minimum, since whole crops invariably come to fruition at the same time and you can end up giving away the majority of your produce.

It is impossible to estimate the ideal size for a vegetable area, for it will depend on the size of your family, what you want to grow and how much time you have to tend it. However, a vegetable garden measuring 335 sq m (3600 ft²) should meet requirements of a family of four. The location of the garden will determine the plants that will grow best; the balmier the climate, the

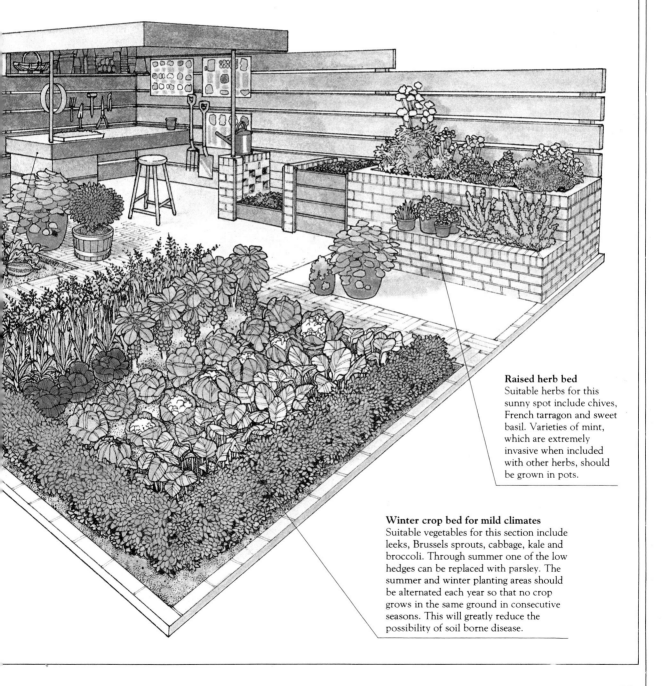

Raised herb bed
Suitable herbs for this sunny spot include chives, French tarragon and sweet basil. Varieties of mint, which are extremely invasive when included with other herbs, should be grown in pots.

Winter crop bed for mild climates
Suitable vegetables for this section include leeks, Brussels sprouts, cabbage, kale and broccoli. Through summer one of the low hedges can be replaced with parsley. The summer and winter planting areas should be alternated each year so that no crop grows in the same ground in consecutive seasons. This will greatly reduce the possibility of soil borne disease.

greater the yield. Production should increase over the years as you gain expertise and enrich the ground. It is always wise to look around at what other gardeners in your area are achieving and learn from their experience of various crops.

If, after considering all the factors, you decide to make a vegetable garden, ensure that its shape is strong and simple for it must be able to retain its character despite the constant change from bare soil to mature crop that occurs as you prepare the soil, grow the crop and harvest it. A bold, simple design is almost inevitable, since crops are traditionally grown in rows and should be served by hard paths for use throughout the year. The garden should also be divided into portions, so that different types of vegetables can be grown in different areas each year in rotation. In this way the soil will not become exhausted of any particular nutrient, nor will you encourage disease or pests to remain in the soil to feed a second year on a favored host plant. The vegetable area may be encompassed, and perhaps sub-divided, by some form of low surround. Edging box, a traditional garden surround, will har-

bor slugs which will feed on *Brassica* (the cabbage family) leaves, so it is better to use sage and rosemary for hedging, where hardy.

Traditionally, the vegetable garden was walled to keep out pests, and divided internally into four sections by wide paths, bordered with flowers for cutting, or with herbs or trained fruit trees, while other trained fruit trees lined the walls. There would be an adjacent potting-shed, a greenhouse, some frames and a place for storing sand and another for mixed soil, both for propagation and for making compost. One of the four working sections contained soft fruit or an asparagus bed or clumps of rhubarb, and possibly herbs, for its contents were semi-permanent. The other three cultivated areas housed crops which were rotated annually, both to deter soil-borne pests and to maintain a balance of nutrients in different parts of the garden.

The way such a traditional rotation works today is normally in the following manner. Planted in the first bed are leguminous crops (peas and beans), with onions, shallots, leeks, lettuce, celery and radish since they all need well-dug soil with plenty of manure or

Crop rotation

The object of rotating your vegetables is both to deter soil borne pests and to maintain a balance of nutrients in the soil. The two main enemies are clubroot disease in the cabbage family and nematode in potatoes, for these will rapidly infest the soil if cabbage family plants – the *Brassica* crops – and potatoes are planted in the same position in consecutive years. You must always ensure that when a crop is lifted the soil is suitable for the next growth you plant. Dividing your garden into four sections is ideal but fewer will suffice,

depending on what you want to grow. Here one section is planted with semi-permanent asparagus and seakale, a European favorite that has never caught on in the USA. Rhubarb can be substituted. Plot B contains leguminous vegetables and salad crops; *Brassica* crops occupy Plot C, while in the last quarter are found root crops.

This is the ideal arrangement, but if you do not wish to grow so wide a range you can still do very well provided that you keep vegetables in the groups defined here and plant them in a different location each year.

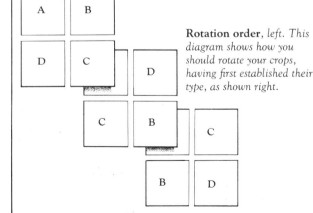

Rotation order, *left. This diagram shows how you should rotate your crops, having first established their type, as shown right.*

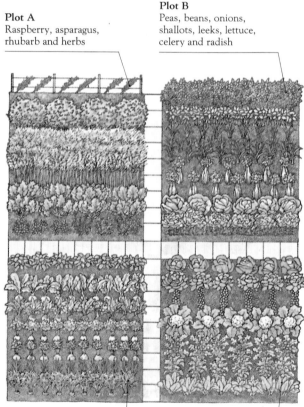

Plot A
Raspberry, asparagus, rhubarb and herbs

Plot B
Peas, beans, onions, shallots, leeks, lettuce, celery and radish

Plot D
Potatoes, turnips, rutabagas parsnip, salsify, celeriac and carrots

Plot C
Cabbages, Brussels sprouts, cauliflower, kale, broccoli and spinach

An established vegetable garden *The vegetable sequence in this garden has cabbages in the front, behind which are ripening peppers, strawed to protect them from damp. Farther back are French or snap beans, then Brussels sprouts and finally sweet corn. To the left of the growing area is a conveniently placed cold frame and a greenhouse at the rear.*

Vegetables with strong form and color *Useful vegetables can make very attractive planting. Below, green curly kale, left, and the dramatic ruby chard, center, and some ornamental cabbage, right, show the variety of stem and leaf textures and colors at your disposal. Such examples can be used in mixed planting throughout the garden and need not be restricted to the vegetable garden area.*

organic compost incorporated. The next quarter of the area contains mainly *Brassica* plants (cabbage, Brussels sprouts, cauliflower, kale, spinach and broccoli), and might need an inorganic feed to replace used minerals and possibly an application of lime if the ground is too acid. The third working quarter, where root crops are grown (potatoes, turnips, rutabagas, parsnips, salsify, celeriac and carrots) might need an initial application of inorganic fertilizer. Once the rotation is established, however, inorganic feed will not be necessary as the plots will remain in good health from the manure or organic compost they receive every third year. This traditional system of rotating the crops of the kitchen garden is as applicable now as it was in the old walled vegetable gardens that existed until 50 years ago, though few of us can practice the system on the large scale of a traditional fruit and vegetable garden. If a newcomer to vegetable gardening, you need to scale the system down and to adapt it, especially when space is limited, to more intensive ways of inter-cropping vegetables.

Start by selecting varieties of vegetables that are of small growth (though not necessarily small cropping), which can be planted

Decorative vegetable and herb garden design

These two decorative borders are shown in their early autumn prime. The areas will certainly look bleak in spring but no amount of planning and selection can make a vegetable arrangement look well throughout the whole year. Some thought, however, will reduce dull periods to a minimum except in very cold climates. An arrangement such as this would be quite possible in a small garden, provided it were open and sunny in aspect and the gardener did not require too many vegetables. A tomato plant could be substituted for globe artichoke, a perennial that rarely survives northern winters. Bay (*Laurus nobilis*), also not hardy, can be grown in a tub and wintered indoors in a cool room.

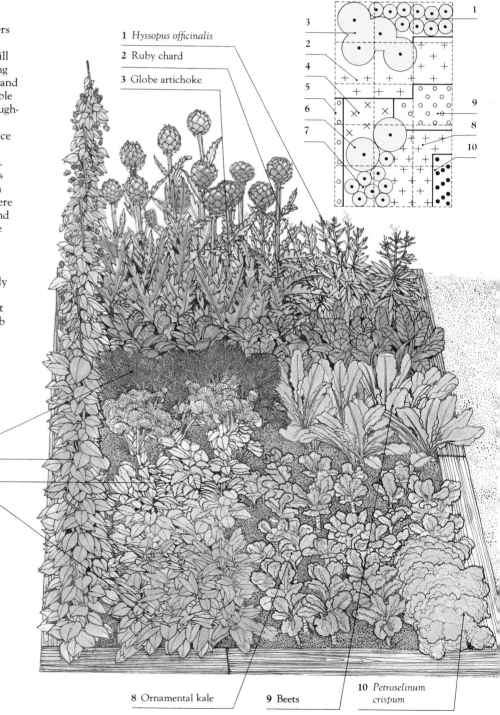

1 *Hyssopus officinalis*

2 Ruby chard

3 Globe artichoke

4 *Foeniculum vulgare*

5 Climbing snap beans

6 *Angelica archangelica*

7 *Rumex acetosa*

8 Ornamental kale   9 Beets   10 *Petroselinum crispum*

closer within the individual row. Then, between rows of slower, taller growing vegetables, plant quick-growing "catch" crops.

You will need to judge the different times of planting, rates of growth and size at maturity of your main crop vegetables, and then put in a quick-maturing crop before all the ground and light is used up. Quick-growing vegetables include radish, which reaches maturity within six weeks; kohlrabi and turnips, which grow in eight weeks, and Chinese cabbage and carrots, which take nine or ten weeks. Quick-maturing vegetables are also useful as "succession" crops to make use of well-prepared ground once the main crop for the year has been harvested. Succession crops should not be confused with "successional sowings", which are sowings of the same vegetable at intervals to avoid a glut at harvest.

During the growing season be ready to fill any ground vacated by a previous crop, for if you do not nature will. It is usually wise to abandon a row of seedlings where germination has been poor in a small area and start again with another freshly-planted crop.

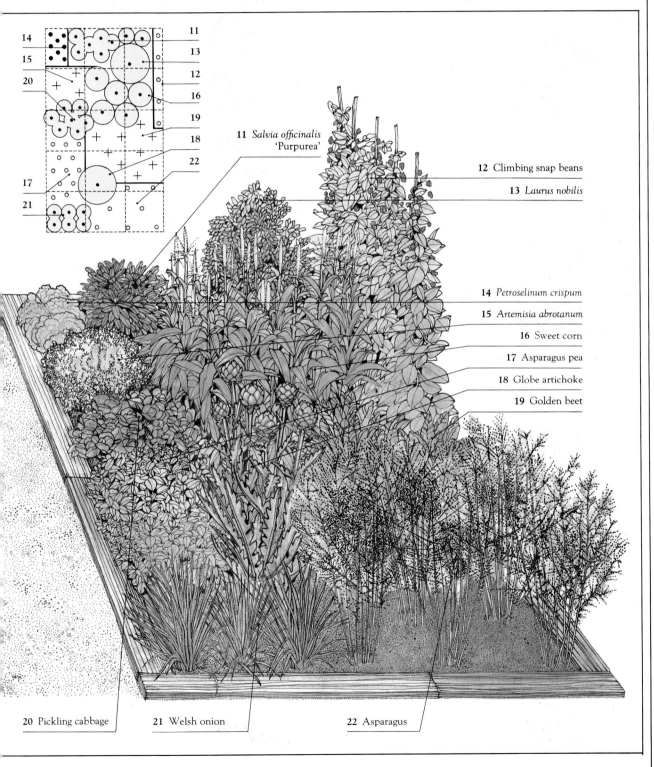

11 *Salvia officinalis* 'Purpurea'

12 Climbing snap beans

13 *Laurus nobilis*

14 *Petroselinum crispum*

15 *Artemisia abrotanum*

16 Sweet corn

17 Asparagus pea

18 Globe artichoke

19 Golden beet

20 Pickling cabbage

21 Welsh onion

22 Asparagus

Choosing vegetables

If you have space for a vegetable garden, and the time and enthusiasm to cultivate it, give careful thought to the choice of crops you grow and the growing area each will need. Details of 26 versatile vegetables are shown here. Sowing times given apply to most northern regions. Consult your county extension specialists for local recommendations. Yields in pounds are approximate as soil, climate and variety all affect results.

	Sowing time	Yield per 3 m row (10 ft)	Time to harvest (in months)
CHENOPODIACEAE			
Beets 	March–June	6.8 kg 15 lb	2
Spinach 	March, August	3.6–4.5 kg (8–10 lb)	From 2½
COMPOSITAE			
Lettuce 	March–May, August	15 lettuces	2
CRUCIFERAE			
Cabbages 	March, July	5–8 heads	4½
Cabbage (Savoy) 	April, May (plant June)	5–8 heads	From 6
Brussels sprouts 	March, July	5 kg (11 lb)	6
Kale 	March, August	5.4 kg (11.8 lb)	8
Broccoli 	March, July	5.4 kg (11.8 lb)	4
Cauliflower 	March, July	5–8 heads	From 11
Rutabaga 	June–August	3.6–6.4 kg (8–14 lb)	From 7½
Turnips 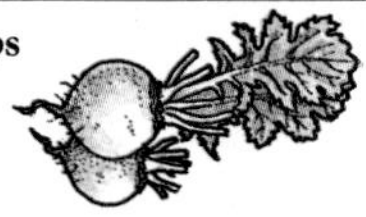	March–August	3.6–6.4 kg (8–14 lb)	5
Radish 	March, August	Plentiful	1½

	Sowing time	Yield per 3 m row (10 ft)	Time to harvest (in months)
GRAMINEAE			
Sweet corn 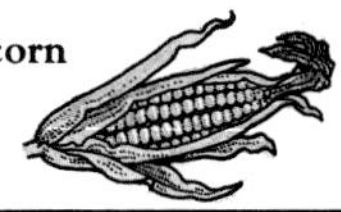	May	30–50 cobs	3
LEGUMINOSAE			
Beans (Broad) 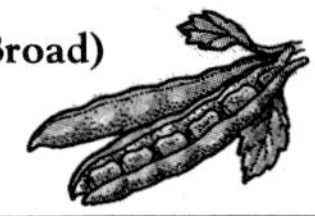	March	3.6 kg (8 lb)	3½
Beans (Snap) 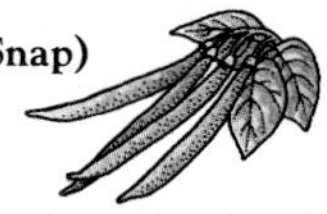	May–June	3.6 kg (8 lb)	From 3
Beans (Runner) 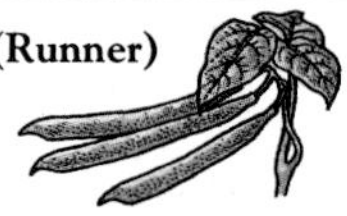	May–June	8–14 kg (17–30 lb)	From 4
Peas 	March, July	9 kg (19 lb)	From 3½
LILIACEAE			
Onions (from seed) 	March, April	3.6–4.5 kg (8–9 lb)	6½
Onions (from sets) 	Plant March, April	3.6–4.5 kg (8–9 lb)	5½
Shallots 	Plant March	3.6–4.5 kg (8–9 lb)	6
Leeks 	January indoors (plant March, April)	20 leeks	10
SOLANACEAE			
Potatoes 	Plant late February to May	11.3 kg (24 lb)	From 3½
Tomatoes 	February, March indoors (plant May, June)	9 kg (19 lb)	5
UMBELLIFERAE			
Carrots 	March–July	3.6 kg (8 lb)	From 5½
Parsnips 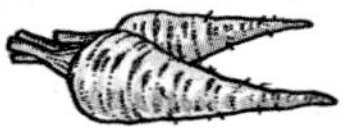	March–April	6.8-9 kg (15-19 lb)	From 7½
Celery 	February–April indoors (plant June)	5.4–6.4 kg (11-14 lb)	From 7

FINISHING
TOUCHES

Furniture, pots and containers, artificial lighting
and sculpture

Garden furniture

A garden seat is often the last thing that you add to a garden but it is often the first thing that catches the eye and provides the key to mood and style. A badly planned garden will seldom be rescued by adding attractive details but if a garden has been well-conceived and executed, the right finishing touches can make it special.

Choose your garden furniture much as you do that for your house, selecting pieces for specific purposes. Whatever you choose, however, should be relaxed in feel; few gardens are improved by overwrought little metal chairs. Another point to be remembered is that garden furniture should look decorative but be tough enough to stand outside throughout the year. The alternative is to buy furniture that can be stored.

Garden furniture is essentially of three types: tables and chairs for outside meals; chairs for relaxing and conversation, and, lastly, furniture for sunbathing, possibly beside a swimming-pool. There is a wide range of furniture on the market for each of these situations. Items may be of wood, which is attractive but heavy; of cane or bamboo; of metal, either painted or plastic-coated, or of molded fiberglass.

Purpose-built arrangement *A relaxed feel outside often stems from the compatability of seating areas with other areas for specific purposes. This happy arrangement consists of built-in seating adjacent to a barbecue.*

Metal

Metal furniture might look uncomfortable but, if well-designed, it can be quite the reverse, especially when combined with suitable removable upholstery. The lines of metal furniture should be crisp and its appearance lightweight, as opposed to the fussy, molded iron chairs and tables that are commonly sold.

The advantages of metal are its durability, which allows it to be left standing outside all year round, and its strength, which allows finely-detailed designs. Much metal furniture is plastic-coated to reduce the chore of re-painting that is otherwise required to maintain a crisp appearance. Indeed, the metal and plastic mix of materials is a useful combination for garden furniture, especially in urban and suburban locations where it is often in style.

Metal furniture as a year-round feature *This range of furniture is not only remarkably comfortable and practical when used outdoors, but it is also a decorative feature.*

Poolside furniture

Poolside furniture usually comprises tables and chairs for taking refreshment, and loungers for sunbathing. Poolside loungers must be able to withstand moisture and hot bodies covered in suntan oil and the frame must be tough enough to take children throwing themselves "aboard".

The plain-colored upholstery that you might choose for furniture positioned on a terrace would soon become soiled and probably rot if used at a poolside so many loungers are made with a covering of simple, fine-gauge nylon, or even woven plastic. These coverings have the advantage of allowing water to drain through while air circulates freely. If a lounger is upholstered in a textile, the design should be bold to disguise the inevitable stains.

Loungers range from simple canvas stretched over a metal frame, to more ornate metal or plastic-framed versions with backrests that adjust on the deck-chair principle. Most fold or dismantle for winter storage while the heavier types often have a pair of wheels for ease of movement.

Furniture for sunbathing is expensive and takes up a great deal of space. It demands a large terrace and this will look bare once the furniture is stored away for winter. In colder climates such furniture is best used on a large, sheltered balcony or in a sunny garden room where it can remain as a feature.

Wheeled poolside lounger *This sprung, metal-framed lounger has a removable floral-patterned mattress.*

Plastic

Reinforced plastic furniture is light and weather resistant and, since plastic can be molded into an infinite variety of shapes, is available in a wide range of styles. Some molded plastic furniture is perfectly comfortable without upholstery, while some (the chair shown below is an example) is designed to accept detachable cushions. Bold, plain colors are often ideal for sunny terraces in summer.

Stone and reconstituted stone

The function of stone and reconstituted stone furniture is quite different to that of the furniture discussed so far. It is certainly not for lounging on and it will be a permanent fixture. To be successful, stone furniture should be positioned to reveal any sculptural quality it might have. Well-sited, a piece of stone furniture can suggest a place to pause in a walk through the garden, or it might even be used as a focal point that is the culmination of your garden plan (see p 239).

Use of stone, because of its massive character, needs careful planning. Strong background planting is usually essential, so that plant detail will soften the stone in front of it.

It is possible to buy or construct simple stone slab benches that have attractive qualities. Much reconstituted stone furniture apes Renaissance styles. It is mostly too crude in its attempt to evoke "olde worlde" charm. Such furniture is part of the misconception that gardens should aspire to the uncomfortable grandeur of another age, although most people would think it strange to use anything but a 20th-century range in the kitchen and want a reasonably up-to-date car in the garage.

A pleasant place to pause *This bench is a successful sculptural addition to the garden. It is sited in front of an ingenious plant association of* Vitis coignetiae *and* Euonymus sp.

Wooden furniture

Wood, like stone and brick, is a material with natural attributes, such as bulk and grain, that are particularly suited to the garden. The detailing of unpainted wooden furniture should reveal these characteristics and, when sited, it should become a harmonious part of the whole garden scheme. When painted, however, wooden furniture has a completely different character. It instantly becomes part of the house rather than of the garden. It is also much more urban in feel. Softwood tables and chairs that were once used inside can often be bought cheaply in salerooms and at auctions. These can be stripped and then painted or stained to provide a far more attractive and cheaper seating arrangement for the garden than can be found on sale in garden centers and shops.

Wood is a very adaptable and readily available material so making your own furniture is another feasible economy if you are a reasonably competent carpenter. There are many existing designs for strong wooden furniture that you might choose to make. Simple designs are certain to be more successful than complicated ones. Alternatively, you might decide to design your own tables and chairs to complement your outside "room" perfectly. It is best to choose furniture that folds or dismantles for easy winter storage. Some such types are shown below. Choose a good quality wood such as redwood that has some natural weather resistance. Remember that hot sunshine can be as damaging to wood as damp and frost. Cedar, pine, spruce or similar softwoods are all adequate if seasoned and regularly painted or treated with preservative. A more resilient wood, such as oak, is ideal, if available, as it can be left untreated for longer periods and will weather to an attractive mellow tone.

A sturdy garden table, sited close to the house, is useful for much more than eating at. It is an ideal platform for potting house plants, flower arranging and so on. It is also useful for such incidental chores as cleaning shoes or grooming pets, if you cover it first.

Stowable wooden furniture *This style of furniture is designed for easy storage. The table folds flat and the chair pulls into two sections that interlock in a flat configuration for storing. Such furniture can be treated with a clear preservative, or one that stains the wood.*

Inventive wooden bench, *left. This substantial wooden bench is constructed from old railway ties. It is massive in scale but is in complete harmony with the planting and stone wall behind it. Bold planting of species with strong form and shape work with the bench to give a low-key sculptural arrangement.*

Oak and brick combination
Oak seating around an oak table is wholly in accord with the brick wall and paving on this terrace. Mature oak and mellow brick almost always work well together. The chairs are built to fit neatly up to the table top when not in use to keep the terrace tidy.

Stained softwood picnic table, *below. A well-designed, sturdy table of this sort can be invaluable with its built-in seating. You must be careful when buying or building furniture in this style, however, to choose a design that is substantial. Some examples are too lightweight and will not stand regular use for long before becoming unstable.*

Classic bench seat *If well-made and treated regularly with preservative, a bench seat should last almost indefinitely.*

Integrated furniture

Although most garden furniture should be considered a finishing touch and something that will attract the eye in its own right as well as providing a useful amenity, some very successful seating is built into the fabric of the garden as a permanent feature. Some of the gardens illustrated in this book make use of pre-cast concrete units that can be stacked or placed in a row to provide a bench. They might form steps or a retaining wall at the same time. In other gardens, wooden decking is built to include a bench section; alternatively a raised pool edge provides an inviting place to sit. Such "furniture" is part of the three-dimensional shape of many gardens. It is always low-key and harmonious compared with the eye-catching quality of some movable tables and chairs.

Built-in concrete seating corner *If the location is dramatic, even uncompromising reinforced concrete can provide a successful seating arrangement.*

Pots and containers

One of the ways of punctuating your garden layout is by grouping pots, tubs and other containers, either with or without plants, as incidental points of interest. You can also use color in containers to stabilize the mood of an area; pots around a terrace or pool can have this effect. Few groupings of this sort are large or important enough to become the focal point in a sizeable garden, but they can work well in a smaller area.

Having studied the various functions that a pot or collection of pots can perform, it is essential to choose a style that works for the particular spot on which you are to use them. The style of containers depends on the material of which they are made and also, of course, their shape.

Containers to enhance a terrace, *right. This splendid group contains daturas and lilies.*

1 Concrete dish
2, 4 Stoneware urns
3 Shaped concrete pot

Reconstituted stone, stoneware and china

Stoneware, including discarded sinks coated with a mix of mortar and moss or peat, are heavy and therefore difficult to move once filled with earth and planted. But they can look well in a traditional rural setting. Concrete or reconstituted stone can be as heavy as stone itself but containers exist which include lightweight materials. China pots for summer are often painted for a more refined effect.

Simple stoneware pot
The bold shape of this pot contrasts well with the agave backed by Coronilla **valentina glauca.** *Simple modern pots need a bold planting style to match.*

Gothic vase *The delicate tracery of this traditional container is complemented by the planting of a lacy species of pelargonium. Decorated pots need light planting styles.*

5 Stoneware "basket"
6–7 Lightweight containers
8 Glazed decorated vase

Terracotta

There is a vogue for using hand-made terracotta pots imported from Italy. They are often attractive, with patterns of swags and scrolls, but once on the ground, and especially if planted, it is difficult to see much of them. Moreover, the Renaissance form they ape is out of keeping in the average domestic garden. Far better to buy half a dozen cheaper containers, which will cost no more and can create a better effect.

Simplicity for success, *above and left. Simple containers are often the most successful. Here wood and terracotta containers are planted with pelargoniums and helichrysum.*

Wood

For a truly rural feel, you should use simple shapes in natural materials, such as wood. If you re-use wooden containers, such as old barrels, you must ensure that they have never contained poison and, if they were wine or beer barrels, treat the wood with paint or preservative, not omitting the hoops which will otherwise rust. Never let a barrel dry out, or the metal hoops that hold the planks together will become loose and ultimately drop off.

1 Half barrel
2 Versailles tub
3 Earthenware jar
4–5 Terracotta pots
6 Lugged terracotta pot

Hanging baskets

For the city gardener with little space, perhaps only a balcony, a hanging basket is an ideal way of containing summer color. Once established, however, a hanging basket is often difficult to water since it will be higher than eye level. Furthermore, being directly exposed to sun and wind it will dry out quickly. Plant hanging baskets with subjects that enjoy heat and exposure – pelargoniums, petunias, begonias and impatiens. In winter, you can fill the basket with ivies or in cold regions with cut evergreens.
It is essential to prepare your hanging basket properly, with a good mixture containing plenty of peat that will retain moisture.

Petunias and geraniums
This is how hanging baskets should look – full, colorful and overflowing.

Hanging baskets *The basket frame is traditionally lined with moss before being filled with soil. Today, however, it is possible to buy a porous composition pad, through which bedding plants may be grown.*

Moss lining

Composition lining

Plastic

The lightest materials for a container are plastic and fibreglass. The more simple shapes are attractive, but many are finished in unnecessarily bright colours which detract from anything planted in, or near, them. Plastic is well worth considering if you plan to move your containers during the growing season.

1
2
3
4
5
6
7
8
9
10
11

1, 4, 8–10 Tub containers
2, 5, 7 Pots and drainage dishes
3 Slatted container
6 Quadrant container
11 Split sphere container

Other materials

The variety of pots and containers on the market is considerable. It is possible to buy metal urns (right) which are specially made for plants and will last a lifetime, but you do not have to restrict yourself to these. Discarded objects of unusual shape, such as chimney pots (far right), can be extremely effective. Today there is also a wide range of man-made substitute substances (such as plastic and fiberglass) that are light, imitate many different styles of container and are almost indistinguishable from natural materials, such as china, clay and wood. When you require several containers it is best to have them all in the same material.

Containers of note, *left and above. This 19th-century metal urn (left) is wholly in character with the building behind. Old chimney pots make interesting containers if boldly planted.*

1 Plastic strawberry pot
2 Fiberglass panelled container
3 Plastic "wooden" container
4 Self-watering container
5 Plastic "pebble-dash" tub

Window boxes

The range of window boxes is enormous but the tougher and thicker their material the better. Boxes are often subjected to intense heat and wind, both of which dry out soil quickly, so the deeper and bigger they are the more the plants in them will thrive. Whatever their structure and material, boxes must have plenty of drainage holes to prevent waterlogging.

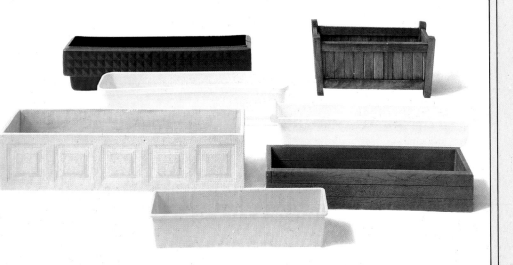

Artificial lighting

Garden lighting falls into two categories: useful illumination and decorative lighting. Necessary illumination includes the lighting necessary for seating and entertainment areas. It also covers the lighting that shows the way along a path to a log pile or illuminates your house number or name for the convenience of visitors. Such lighting should be subtle but strong enough to fulfil its function. It is especially important to illuminate steps used after dark.

Subtle decorative lighting can create a magical effect in the garden even when there is little growth to illuminate. The bare winter stems of a large tree, glistening with frost or decked with snow, can look even more spectacular than summer foliage. Successful decorative lighting must be low-key, directed away from the viewing point and usually from a low-level light source. You might choose to illuminate a scene – for example, a pond and its surround – or create a nighttime feature by illuminating a single subject such as a flowering tree, the arch of a gateway or a piece of sculpture, remembering that less attractive elements can be left in darkness.

Lighting fixtures are available in many shapes and sizes. It is imperative that all fittings are purpose-made for outside use. The design of a fixture provides either a spotlight effect or a more general floodlight effect. Generally, the simpler and more robust the design the better. Fixtures either screw to a wall, have a bracket that clamps to a convenient branch, have a bolt-down stand or a spike to hold the lamp in earth or gravel. Light fixtures on the external walls of a house can be connected to the internal main circuit; otherwise the fixture should be connected to the garden circuit (see p. 105) if you have one.

There are a number of illuminated decorative fixtures for the garden available where the light source itself provides the interest. These include Chinese lanterns and other low-wattage decorative lights for temporary decoration such as the very effective glowing spheres, or even imitation rocks, made in fiberglass and used to make sculptural groupings.

Spiked fixtures *The three types of spiked lighting fixture shown below include, from left to right: a low bollard, suitable for use by a path or drive; a shaded floodlight for siting among bushes or flowers, and a three-way spotlight for featuring shrubs and trees.*

Decorative bollard, *above. This column provides illumination and is a feature itself.*

Floodlit scene, *left. This magical scene represents the effect many seek to achieve when lighting trees and shrubs beyond water. Direct light on white blossom looks attractive, while deeper colors really glow. Note that the source of light is invisible, which should always be your aim. Visible light sources will detract from the lit area considerably.*

Attractive balcony, *right. On warm summer evenings, such a glowing table setting on a balcony is extremely inviting. The trees and shrubs beyond are illuminated from below the railings. Once established, such lighting greatly increases the usefulness of an outside entertaining area.*

Lighting a garden adjacent to buildings, *below. Here different points of light pick out elements of a building and terrace groupings. To achieve a balance between inside and outside lights you will need to experiment with the position and strength of your light sources.*

Flares

Night lighting attracts bugs, moths and mosquitoes in summer. One way to combat this is to use candles that are impregnated with insect repellent. This type of temporary lighting is useful for a summer party and has the advantage of not being dependent on an electricity supply. The lights illustrated below are large and fairly expensive but smaller versions are available. The pointed frames can be hung from trees or stuck into the earth; they are of bamboo and enclose a candle. The bucket type can be used again and again throughout summer.

Care must always be taken with any naked flame, for in summer dry wood, bamboo clumps and thatch will catch fire instantly. It is advisable always to have water to hand for emergencies.

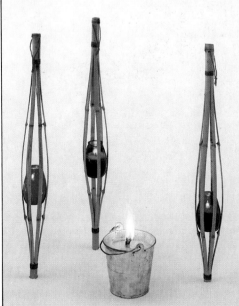

Sculpture

Sculpture may be the centerpoint of a garden or merely a side attraction, incidental to the whole. It may be overscaled for a dramatic effect or unobtrusive and in total harmony with the surroundings; it may be striking or incongruous, traditional in style or abstract. Groupings of pots or urns, boulders or stones, can all create a pleasing sculptural feature. Each location calls for a different style and treatment, although the dominating influence will be your personal preference.

As with all else in the garden, the selection of sculptural elements will depend on the style of your house, its setting and age, and of course on the style of your garden. Size is also important, for a large piece will always look pretentious in a small area.

The first question to answer, therefore, is whether you are designing a garden to show off a piece of sculpture or siting a sculptural object to enhance a portion of the garden.

For most people, sculpture is the last consideration in a garden, for usually an original piece is extremely expensive. Cast concrete sculpture, advertised in catalogues, is cheaper and you can always make your own arrangement in natural forms of wood and boulders. In any event, avoid mawkish sculpture, which is unsuitable for almost every kind of garden.

The ideal is a solid object, either representational or abstract, of simple shape, made in a durable material. This then needs sympathetic siting, either on a hard surround or contrasted by architectural plant forms. The final arrangement should be attractive at all times of the year and from all the angles from which it can be seen.

None of the sculptural groupings illustrated here could be described as extreme; you may like them or not but all demonstrate the importance of the correct siting of a piece. Sculpture must never be seen in isolation and it has to work visually within its paved or planted setting.

You can use a sculptural feature as a balance within your layout – to counteract a large tree, for instance, or on a roof terrace to detract attention from a neighboring eyesore. Not all sculpture has to sit in the middle of your site; move it around until you find it helps to create a satisfying and balanced composition.

It would be foolish to claim that much of the sculpture we incorporate in our gardens can be called great art, but there is no reason why it should not be attractive and fun.

Successful settings
Sculpture should give pleasure not only in itself but also in its setting. This Italian figure, of fiberglass impregnated with lead, would look well in either a modern or traditional garden. Here it sits on well-detailed brick paving, backed by a strongly architectural plant grouping.

Sphere in a courtyard, *above. This shining metal sphere is kept moist by a gentle central fountain. Water smothers the sphere, and then disappears into a reservoir below to be recycled by a pump. The arrangement is sited in a paved courtyard.*

Siting sculpture

The series of diagrams below shows how different styles of sculpture suit different locations and how the location changes a garden considerably. If the piece is located centrally and to the rear of an oblong plot it will demand instant attention and become the focal point of the whole garden. Placed to one side as a counterbalance to strong planting on the opposite side, a piece will become part of the incidental interest of the garden and encourage the eye to progrss from side to side. If you create a group, to which sculpture lends weight, to one side in the foreground, the garden space will seem to flow around the group.

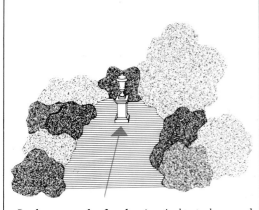

Sculpture as the focal point *A classical urn and plinth placed centrally dominate the garden and immediately draw the attention.*

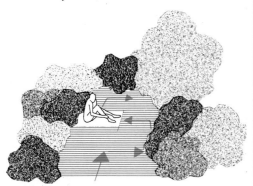

Sculpture to create a balancing feature *A modern seated figure strengthens one side of the garden to give it equal importance to planted masses on the other side.*

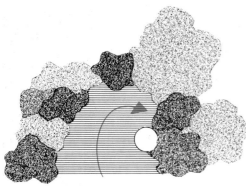

Sculpture to provide strong foreground interest *A sphere strengthens the foreground grouping considerably and encourages a feeling of movement around the group.*

Eye-catching arrangement, *above. A clever and humorous use of a number of sculptural pieces. The arrangement is on a roof terrace and disguises surrounding urban ugliness.*

Sculpture and water, *below. Water makes an ideal medium to offset sculpture. This landing swan has an ingenious fountain effect at its feet. Hosta leaves enhance the whole.*

Lion in a jungle
A terracotta lion placed within an arrangement of lush, tropical planting imitates the animal in its natural habitat. The grouping is intended to amuse and, in conjunction with the terrace, is highly effective and visually harmonious.

Importance of setting, *below. The setting for modern abstract sculpture has to be correct. This piece has a strength that blends with organic shapes. If the piece is minimal, however, it should be seen against the sky as strong plant forms will detract from a slight structure.*

Classic sculpture in a modern setting, *right. The main piece in this group sits well on a concrete plinth and the jar at the base of the plinth complements it. The bold foliage of Hedera colchica 'Dentata Aurea' forms a year-round backdrop.*

240

CARE AND
MAINTENANCE

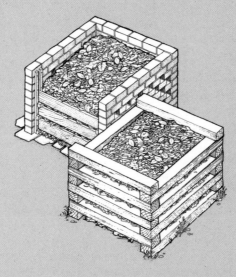

Looking after the structure of the garden and the
plants that fill it

Maintaining your new garden

Experienced gardeners know that there is no such thing as a completely maintenance-free garden, for even the simplest, those with large expanses of hard-surfacing, need periodic attention. The more subtle your garden plan, the more maintenance it will need. However, a good basic layout, well-designed and then well-constructed and planted, can greatly reduce subsequent maintenance throughout the year. For example, well-routed paths, laid to discourage weeds between the joints, save a great deal of seasonal upkeep.

We tend to think of garden maintenance solely as plant husbandry. This is far from so, for all structures will need attention. There are, in addition, certain seasonal tasks to be undertaken, such as maintaining soil fertility and cleaning garden pools.

I am not here seeking to describe essential day-to-day routines in the garden but rather to draw attention to the major seasonal duties which are necessary to maintain the initial standard of your garden throughout the years. Unlike most forms of design, gardening involves a constant modification of all the components of a garden.

Because of this, it is important that middle-aged people should realize that what they are capable of doing at present may be too much for them in 10 or 20 years time. For this reason, any alterations or improvements in the garden's layout should be directed towards ultimately reducing maintenance work. This is the last stage in a natural progression, for in the early years your garden can be more demanding when it serves the needs of a growing family.

For the reader's convenience, I shall discuss the maintenance of the elements that make up a garden in the order they were considered in the chapters on constructing and planting the garden. Reading through the maintenance necessary for the various elements of a garden before deciding on the sort of garden you want is a sensible step. This is especially so concerning your choice of plants.

Boundaries and enclosures

Walls
New brick walls, well-constructed on sound footings, should need little attention over the years. From time to time, however, a coping stone may become dislodged or frost may cause damage. Old boundaries of this material, on the other hand, have a habit of keeling over and some form of buttressing may be necessary. You may also find that older walls play host to seedlings. Buddleias, for instance, are great seeders in walls. As charming as the effect undoubtedly is, the woody roots will begin to destroy the wall as they mature and so they should be eradicated.

Extremely old walls may have a problem with ivy, which can bore its way into older, softer lime mortar. It is also true, of course, that ivy can support a wall, so have a care when pulling it out.

Fences
Wooden fences will need rather more maintenance over the years. All panel fencing must be given a coat of preservative from time to time, when all climbers to which it is playing host should be removed. It will then be some time before they grow back again, since most preservatives are toxic. When removing climbers, check that they have not broken any

Fence weaknesses
The diagrams below point out the inherent weaknesses of post and rail or panel fences, and those details that require regular replacement.

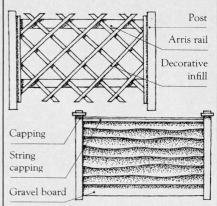

Post
Arris rail
Decorative infill

Capping
String capping
Gravel board

portion of the panel infill wood. Then check that the verticals to which your panels are attached have not rotted at ground level or been lifted by frost. Also check that the capping is sound and, most important of all, renew the gravel board running horizontal with the ground under the infill panel.

Fences with horizontal rails should be checked regularly, at the points where the rails join the posts. At the same time, check any gates through the fences and rehang any that have dropped.

All this type of maintenance work can be done during winter if there is no snow or immediately after it has cleared in spring if there is.

Buttressing
If you have a brick wall that is leaning or bowing you can stop further deterioration by adding buttresses, as in the diagrams below. The buttresses must be built on additional concrete foundations in materials that complement the existing walling. If the signs of weakness in a wall are advanced, you will have to demolish the offending section and rebuild it, including buttresses for increased structural strength.

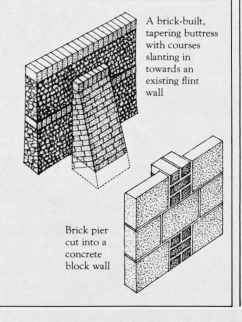

A brick-built, tapering buttress with courses slanting in towards an existing flint wall

Brick pier cut into a concrete block wall

Replacing a partly rotten post

Wooden fence posts sunk directly into earth or concrete will eventually rot at ground level. You can remedy this one post at a time without dismantling the fence, as shown below.

1 *Excavate beneath the post to remove existing foundations.*

2 *Saw the post back to sound wood and then square up a concrete spur against the post.*

3 *Drill the post and bolt it to the spur before backfilling with concrete and finishing.*

Replacing gravel boards

Gravel boards fit along the bottom of a fence, fixed to battens at the base of the posts. Simply unscrew the rotting boards, replace worn battens and screw on new boards.

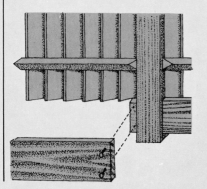

Changing levels

Retaining walls

Retaining walls in the garden should be inspected after heavy rain or snow for this is when they are supporting the maximum weight of wet earth. When there is any likelihood of collapse, excavate at the rear of the wall to reduce the pressure before rebuilding the offending section and backfilling with a good proportion of ash or hardcore behind the new construction to improve drainage. Also check that there are weep-holes at the base of the wall to allow any accumulation of water to escape. Depending on the structure of the wall, you should check its components and capping.

Steps

Stepped changes of level should be checked at the end of summer to ensure that treads have no movement in them and that there is a water run-off, either forward or to the side of the steps. Without this, water and then ice will form, which is extremely dangerous.

The precise nature of any wear in a flight of steps depends on the original construction material. Wooden steps need constant checking for signs of loosening, cracking or moss growth. Remove moss with a wire brush as this can make a very slippery surface. Poured concrete treads can chip away at the leading edges and you should consider construct-

ing new edges in a harder wearing material. Treads made from units, such as pre-cast paving slabs, can become unstable if the jointing around the units loosens. In this case, the offending units should be removed and relaid.

You might find that the original detailing of your steps has proven inadequate. If you are unhappy about an encroaching bank, for example, try one of the solutions proposed below.

Edging chipped treads

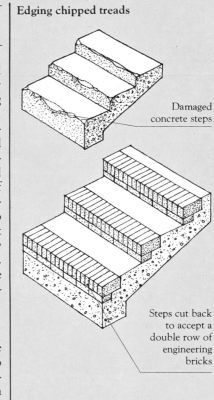

Damaged concrete steps

Steps cut back to accept a double row of engineering bricks

Rethinking step margins

After use, your step margins may have become difficult to maintain, either presenting a difficult mowing edge or over-spilling soil, as in the diagram, right. Two solutions are shown in the diagram, below right. A retaining wall now holds back the bank on one side of the flight, while "L"-shaped extensions to the risers contain the soil for successful planting on the other. A recessed brick edging makes mowing much easier.

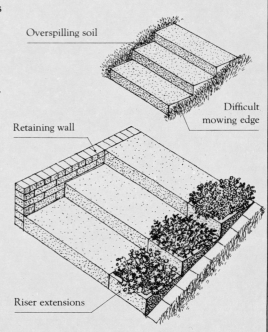

Overspilling soil

Difficult mowing edge

Retaining wall

Riser extensions

Banks

Changes of level divided by newly planted earth banks should be regularly checked. Ensure that the bank has not washed down after heavy rain or snow. To retain a new bank, especially one established at a steep angle, peg wire or plastic netting over the surface at regular intervals and plant ground cover through it to hold the bank with its roots.

Grassed banks which have been mown throughout the season should be examined in autumn for patches that the mower might have shaved too closely. Cut out any dead turf and replace with new, taken from another part of the lawn where a bare patch will not be so noticeable. Tamp the replacement turf down and keep it well-watered until the repair turf is established. Fill the gap left in the secluded part of the lawn with a mixture of soil and sand, incorporate a little grass seed in the surface and level off the patched area, similarly tamping it to match the surrounding turf.

Retaining an unstable slope

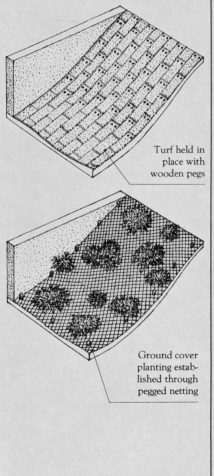

Turf held in place with wooden pegs

Ground cover planting established through pegged netting

Drainage

After wet weather you should also ensure that there is no standing water at the base of any contouring. If there is, a drain run should be dug which will direct surplus water to a convenient soakaway (dry well).

All drains should be checked in spring to ensure that they are doing their work properly. Temporary forms of drainage, mole or open trench drains, have only a short span anyway, but your type of soil, whether sticky or dry, will also make a difference. An open drain in clay soil will obviously last longer than one in sandy soil, which will quickly silt up or collapse.

When you have standing water or excessive moss in your lawn, you may need to drain it. Before going to this expense, however, ensure that there is not an impervious consolidated layer below the surface which might have formed during garden construction, especially if heavy machinery was used. If this is the case, you can cure the condition by forking straight down and working the fork about at regular intervals across the lawn, then brushing grit into the holes to facilitate drainage. You can pierce the lawn with your garden fork or use a purpose-built hollow-tined lawn perforator. There are many such tools available, of contrasting designs. They all cut out narrow cores of turf in a regular pattern across the lawn.

It is essential that any drainage you make is laid to a fall, and connected to a drainage outlet.

Surfaces

Hard surfacing

From time to time it is necessary to rethink your areas of hard paving. In autumn, consider whether the terrace area was large enough for your summer activities and whether you should increase it. If the terrace was planned with a specific purpose in mind, be critical as to how it fulfilled that function. A seating area, for example, should have provided a comfortable space for the garden furniture upon it. If it has not, you will have to go back to your original garden plan with its guiding grid (see p. 40) before revising the size of the terrace. Check, too, whether its surface is sound, whether any area has sunk and whether there is standing water after rain. Autumn is the time

for all this work, before the earth becomes wet and is therefore more difficult to work.

An existing terrace that falls short on any of these points might need to be taken up and relaid on a sound new foundation with new pointing between the paving elements. Sometimes, of course, only small areas need lifting and reinstating.

Check the pointing of any surfacing from time to time, and also check that the retaining brick or curb which holds a surface material together has not crept outwards, loosening other elements. It is into any weak joints in the surfacing that rain, then frost, infiltrates, causing

Re-planning a terrace

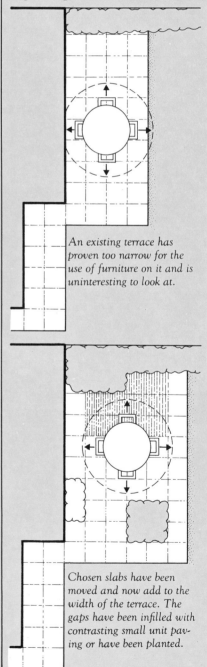

An existing terrace has proven too narrow for the use of furniture on it and is uninteresting to look at.

Chosen slabs have been moved and now add to the width of the terrace. The gaps have been infilled with contrasting small unit paving or have been planted.

the materials of which the surface is made to decompose rapidly.

You might also check whether pathways are wide enough to do their job and that they are routed correctly. Check that your stepping stones through grass or water are correctly distanced from each other.

Before winter, you may need to clean down brick or stone paving to prevent its becoming slippery. Use salt if there are no plants growing in the vicinity or a mild detergent. This operation may need to be done again in spring, when the surface should be hosed down.

Soft surfacing

Loose gravel surfaces will need weeding from time to time, either by hand or by the application of a weed killer. If using the latter method, the application must not be allowed to damage any plants growing in the medium. Weed killer may be applied as liquid from a watering-can or under pressure by spray. It can also be applied in granular form.

Decking

Wooden paving, or decking, when used in a moist climate that does not allow the material to dry out in summer, should be scrubbed with salt or a proprietary cleaner and hosed down, in autumn and spring, to prevent its becoming slippery. A wire brushing to roughen wooden paving surfaces is helpful. Wood will, however, wear relatively quickly in areas that take a high level of pedestrian traffic, such as steps. You should replace badly worn or split boards that might cause someone to trip. If you have room, it is a good idea to store some replacement decking timber outside so that it weathers at the same rate as the original deck and will make any necessary repairs a good match. Occasionally check the condition of the substructure of your deck to make sure that its boards are sound.

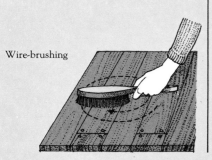
Wire-brushing

Features

Rockeries

You should have divided alpines after their spring flowering. Then, in autumn, give a more general clearance to the rockery outcrop. Study the configuration of rocks in your rockery and compare it with your experience of natural outcrops of rock. Make sure that there are no rocks sticking out of the ground vertically, nor groups of unnaturally small pieces of rock, nor areas where rocks are arranged in a random, unconnected way.

Lift rocks to dig out invasive weeds, cut back shrubby conifers and remove superfluous leaves and rubbish which invariably build up within a rockery. Ensure that paths and stepping stones are soundly bedded. A rockery is one of the first features in a garden to come to life in spring, with miniature bulbs and early alpine flowers, so have your clearance work completed in readiness for this.

Pools

A garden pool with clear water resulting from a well-balanced community of plants, fish, insects and amphibians should not need to be emptied during its first few years, but one which has not been cleared out for a long period, even if it has an oxygenating plant, fish and snail population, should be. This is because leaves will inevitably fall into a pool in autumn and will cause decay and pollution which the natural balancing elements of pond life cannot eradicate.

Netting a pool

Netting, or caging, over a pool always looks unsightly. If your pool is a regular shape, however, you can submerge netting just below the surface on a non-corrosive frame.

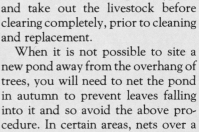

Nylon netting

Frame supported on blocks

Heavy non-corrosive frame

If there is no built-in outlet to the pool, you can syphon out the water to a lower part of the garden through a hose. If you have not first removed your fish, tie some gauze over the pipe outlet so they will not be sucked up. Lower the pool to a water level of 100 mm (4 in), then stop the syphon and take out the livestock before clearing completely, prior to cleaning and replacement.

When it is not possible to site a new pond away from the overhang of trees, you will need to net the pond in autumn to prevent leaves falling into it and so avoid the above procedure. In certain areas, nets over a pool, or just below the water's surface, are necessary to prevent herons and other predators from eating the fish and other pond life.

Draining a pool

If your pool does not have a purpose-built outlet pipe, the easiest way to drain it is to set up a syphon using a hose pipe. It is best to make a filter, shown right, using a funnel and gauze. Several meters (10 ft) of hose are required below the level of the pool.

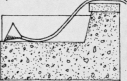

Gauze

Funnel

Hose

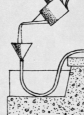

1 Plugging the emptying end, fill the hose with water through the funnel.

2 Fit the gauze, place the filter beneath the surface and unplug the emptying end of the hose.

Relining a pool

A poorly-constructed concrete pool may crack and present you with the alternatives of expensive re-building or lining the existing cracked pool with a heavy duty plastic (PVC) sheet. Technique for folding and disguising the liner is shown right and below.

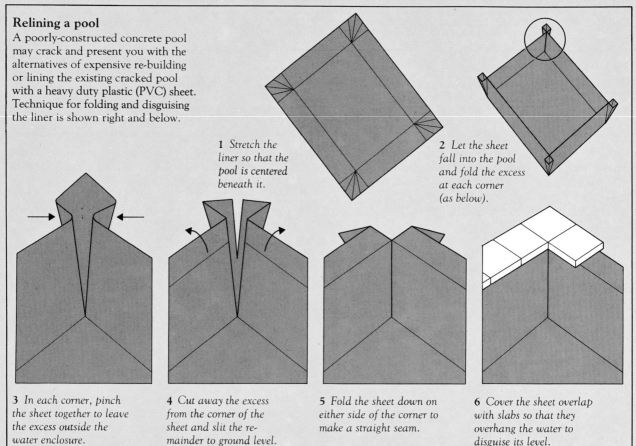

1 *Stretch the liner so that the pool is centered beneath it.*

2 *Let the sheet fall into the pool and fold the excess at each corner (as below).*

3 *In each corner, pinch the sheet together to leave the excess outside the water enclosure.*

4 *Cut away the excess from the corner of the sheet and slit the remainder to ground level.*

5 *Fold the sheet down on either side of the corner to make a straight seam.*

6 *Cover the sheet overlap with slabs so that they overhang the water to disguise its level.*

Ponds and pools constructed of concrete that has cracked are difficult to repair satisfactorily. It is sometimes better to empty the whole container and line it with heavy plastic (PVC) sheeting, which can be ordered to fit particular shapes. You may need to modify the coping surround to the pond to hide the edge of the plastic sheet. Any existing outlet and inlet pipes serving a cracked concrete pool that you decide to line in this way, will become defunct. You will have to remove protruding pipes and make sure that there are no rough edges that would puncture the plastic sheet. An existing onshore pump will also become inoperable once the pool is lined and will have to be removed or disguised.

Swimming-pools

Autumn is a good time to empty a Gunite swimming pool in order to clean it. However, this major project is only required every few years or so. Vinyl-lined in-ground pools are not emptied as without the water pressure the pool will collapse. All pools should be covered over winter. Furniture, umbrellas and loose cushions must be stored unless they are designed in waterproof materials to be left out over winter.

Recreational areas

In spring you should check the surfacing of your children's play area, add more peat bark where necessary and ensure that the area is dry and free of standing water.

Examine all the swings, slides and climbing frames, making sure that they are sound. Check that tree boughs with ropes attached are strong enough, and be sure that tree houses are secure. Wooden equipment should be sandpapered down to remove splinters and checked for splits that expand or contract under strain, since they can easily trap small fingers. This is especially true of sections of wooden climbing frame.

As your children grow, reassess the usefulness of purpose-built play equipment and play areas as a whole. Requirements change quickly and garden space is usually too precious to waste on unused areas and features. If you utilized a sawn tree trunk as a play frame (see p. 146) you can always retain it as a sculptural feature or saw it up for other constructional purposes or, as a last resort, for firewood.

In autumn, sandpits should be covered over. Then, in spring, ensure that drainage is satisfactory and fill the pit with fresh sharp sand.

Barbecue areas

The remains of a summer barbecue can look depressing in winter. Moveable barbecues should be cleaned, dried and stored, together with their equipment. Built-in barbecues should also be thoroughly cleaned. Barbecues are used for burning leaves and garden trash in Europe and England, but this practice is discouraged and in fact is illegal in most regions of the USA because of concern for the additional air pollution it will cause.

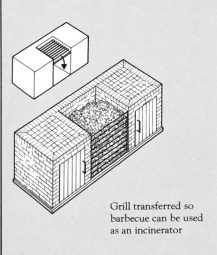

Grill transferred so barbecue can be used as an incinerator

Structures

Conservatories, greenhouses and cold frames

All wooden structures require regular maintenance. If they are painted, they will need recoating every two years or so and redwood houses should similarly be given an application of preservative. Metal structures need less attention, which is one of their attractions.

Glass should be kept clean so that it transmits as much light as possible. It should be thoroughly washed down in spring to remove grime that has built up through the winter. Do not attempt to crawl over a conservatory or greenhouse roof, however well it is supported, unless you can construct a safe ladder rest, as shown below. It is best to use a long-handled brush and a hose from the eaves. Always keep spare panes of glass in reserve: broken glass must be replaced immediately, since wind penetrating even a small aperture will reduce the temperature in the conservatory or greenhouse.

Before winter, check that glass fixtures are in order and that there are no leakages to dissipate your expensive heating. In spring, ensure that hinges to opening ventilation windows are sound.

Locating greenhouse leaks

Light a proprietary smoke pellet in your greenhouse (when it is free of plants), close the door and watch for escaping smoke.

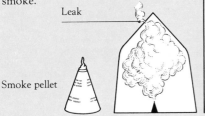

Leak

Smoke pellet

Climbing on to a greenhouse

It is not safe to rest a ladder directly on to a greenhouse roof. You must first tie planks across the entire width of the frame to distribute the weight of you and the ladder as widely as possible. Adjust the ladder so that it matches the slope of the pitch of the greenhouse roof and make sure that it cannot slip.

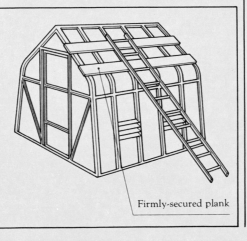

Firmly-secured plank

Replacing panes of glass

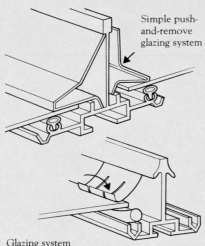

Simple push-and-remove glazing system

Glazing system using spring clips

Keep your structures clean and sound inside and out and check brickwork for any signs of dampness that might indicate a faulty damp proof course or leaking from above.

Snow can be a significant problem where structures comprise large expanses of glass. Clear falls of snow from roofs before the weight of snow builds up. Ensure there can be no sudden heavy falls of melting snow from overhanging foliage or masonry on to a glass roof.

In late autumn, clean out gutters, removing silt and leaves, and ensure that all gulleys are running freely. Blockages will result in leaks during the winter. Make sure that any drains that serve conservatories are free from debris and that greenhouse drainage systems are working well.

Pergolas

Let climbing plants down from pergolas in autumn so that you can check for any rotting sections in the structure. If you do find rot, replace boards as necessary. Treat the woodwork with preservative or paint. This is the time to prune climbing plants (see p. 358) before tying them back to their support. Freshly applied preservative will burn foliage.

Roof gardens

Roof gardens can take an enormous battering from snow, wind and rain throughout winter and it is essential to give them a thorough reappraisal before this. Furniture and fittings should go into storage; then thoroughly check the structure of the garden, including the planting areas, surrounds, any overhead structures, and electric wiring on walls. The most important task is to ensure that drainage is efficient, with good cross falls to outlet channels and then to clear downpipes.

After clearing your annuals planted for color and cutting back shrubs (for they should be low-growing and sturdy), either replace tired earth and compost in permanent beds or thoroughly feed them with an organic manure. Sacks of finely shredded horse manure, compost, peat moss or other organic feed are obtainable and their contents are both easy and clean to apply. This should then be lightly forked in.

Balconies

Much of the forementioned maintenance of roof gardens also applies to balconies. More attention will be necessary, however, to the plant containers for they are inevitably smaller than those on a roof garden and their nutrient will be exhausted. Replace growing mixes, incorporating plenty of fine organic matter to act both as a soil conditioner and as food. This will also help to retain moisture. All this should be undertaken in autumn if you are planting the containers for a winter effect, but if you seek a summer display do the work in the spring.

Spring is also the time to check decorative finishes for signs of frost damage. The glaze of ceramic tiles can be damaged by unexpectedly cold weather and lightweight flooring tiles can lift. Also check to see how paintwork and varnish finishes have weathered. However, if possible, it is best to leave painting and varnishing until late summer or autumn so that new coats will harden completely before facing the heat of the midsummer sun.

Cultivation

Gardeners seldom agree on the best methods of plant cultivation. Some, indeed, consider that none is necessary, since plants flourish naturally. It is true that once plants are established in a decorative garden, cultivation can be reduced to a minimum, often little more than the removal of unwanted weeds. However, most gardeners will agree that cultivation of some sort must be periodically undertaken to maintain plantings.

Autumn is the best time for a major clearance of the garden, for the application of organic compost and for a thorough dig-over before the ground becomes too heavy with moisture. Frost will break down the large clods of earth (organic feed will also help to do this) to provide a spring tilth for planting. Lighter soils will need a more gentle forking over in autumn, when organic compost or uncomposted soft organic waste can be incorporated to give the soil a more cohesive quality.

Most gardeners now dig only one spit deep (to the depth of the blade of the spade) and turn that over. In earlier generations, when labor was cheap and plentiful, gardens were dug two spits deep, which produced deeper cultivation. The system of digging you choose to employ must depend on your type of soil and the use to which you will put the land you are cultivating. Heavy soils (see p. 16) require more cultivation than light ones as they have to be encouraged to crumble and they hold perennial weed roots tightly. Soil that is to be used again and again for vegetable production requires more cultivation to replace soil nutrients than soil used for a perennial display. Digging also depends on the state of cultivation you inherit.

Hand-operated rotary cultivators working with rotary blades, it is claimed, can now penetrate the ground to one spit deep, but surfaces must be level since they are heavy and difficult to move.

Borders and beds should be lightly forked over in autumn and again in spring, turning in leaves and organic matter. If you dig these areas too deeply you will disturb the plants' small feeder roots.

Much cultivation is simply to tidy your garden when you have open beds and exposed earth, since newly turned earth looks fresh and attractive. By planting ground cover in bare areas, this chore is avoided.

Tools for the task

There is an abundance of garden equipment on the market but your needs are, in fact, very simple. Avoid too much gadgetry and choose only essential tools. However, it is advisable to buy the best, for good quality garden tools can last a lifetime even if given extremely hard use. Your basic equipment should include a spade, fork, rake, hoe, a trowel and hand-fork, a watering-can, pruners, a wheelbarrow and a hose.

It is important that you clean your garden equipment after use, particularly if you cannot afford stainless steel. Brush off all earth, clean blades with an oily rag and then store spades, forks and all other equipment in a dry place.

Spades

Spades vary in size. The largest may have a blade 290 × 190 mm (11½ × 7½ in) wide, while the smallest a mere 260 × 160 mm (10¼ × 6¼ in). If you are not strong, or have heavy soil, go for the smaller size. The best blades are made of stainless steel. These slice through the earth, are easy to keep clean and will not rust. Stainless steel is expensive, however. The shaft of the spade may be of a synthetic material for lightness but wooden shafts should be close grained and smooth. Handles will either be D- or T-shaped, so test them to see which suits you better.

A spade is the most important of all garden tools, for it is used not only for digging and trenching but for planting trees and large shrubs. It is therefore advisable to get the best, if you can. It is sometimes advisable to have more than one spade, not only of different blade sizes but also

---

The cultivation cycle

When land is used for vegetable and fruit growing, or for other plants grown on a seasonal basis, the soil needs tending so that it is ready for the planting of seeds or seedlings. This tending involves incorporating compost, digging to remove weeds and raking to a tilth. So as to make the best use of the good effects of frost on the soil, digging and composting is done in the autumn so that raking can follow in the spring immediately prior to planting. When you establish permanent planting this process is only necessary once. The soil between plants can thereafter be hoed and dressed with compost, if this is necessary.

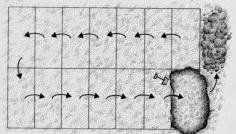

Single digging Bisect large areas and work down one side and up the other, moving earth from the first trench across ready to fill the final trench.

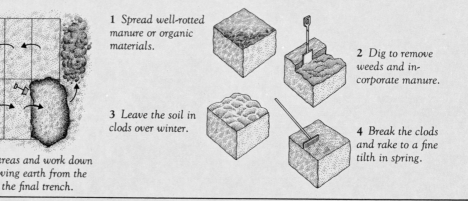

1 Spread well-rotted manure or organic materials.

2 Dig to remove weeds and incorporate manure.

3 Leave the soil in clods over winter.

4 Break the clods and rake to a fine tilth in spring.

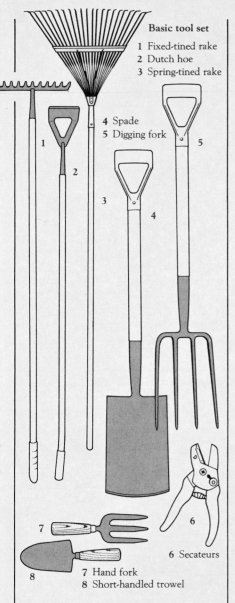

Basic tool set
1 Fixed-tined rake
2 Dutch hoe
3 Spring-tined rake

4 Spade
5 Digging fork

6 Secateurs

7 Hand fork
8 Short-handled trowel

of different construction. Most wooden-handled examples have a strapped socket with three rivets, but for heavier work, such as uprooting a tree, a stronger spade with longer straps and five rivets is better.

Forks
A digging fork usually has square tines, each narrowing to a point. Forks with flattened tines are specifically for digging potatoes. Like spades, the best forks are made of stainless steel with either a wooden or synthetic shaft and handle. The length of fork tines varies from 300 mm (12 in) to 260 mm (10 in), so select what you can manage. For forking through you will not need a large fork.

Rakes
A garden rake is invaluable for general clearance, though for raking leaves in autumn you will need a finer, more springy type than the

normal one with short rigid tines. Many gardeners also invest in a large, wooden hay rake, which can not only be used for clearing dead leaves but also for levelling ground.

In the vegetable garden, a rake will help you create a fine tilth for seed sowing. You can also use your rake to keep gravel areas looking fresh. Sizes vary from 400 mm (16 in), as do shaft lengths; try them and buy what suits you.

Hoes
We tend to overlook the old Dutch hoe, but it is extremely useful for keeping weeds down between rows of vegetables and elsewhere. You can also use this hoe to make seed drills, dragging it along a line of string stretched between pegs.

Other types of hoe include the draw hoe, the more modern scuffle hoe and, especially useful for awkward corners, the triangular hoe. It is important that you always keep your hoe blade not only clean but sharp.

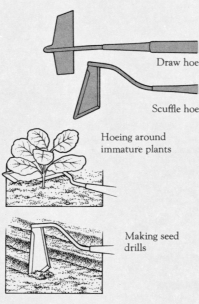

Draw hoe

Scuffle hoe

Hoeing around immature plants

Making seed drills

Trowels and handforks
These invaluable small tools for planting and hand weeding are best made of stainless steel. Quite apart from its greater efficiency, you invariably lose track of such small items in the garden and stainless steel will not rust when left outside for any length of time.

Pruners
There is an enormous range of pruners available. Always get the best, for cheap pruners do not cut cleanly and can cause damage to a branch, which in time may induce rot or disease.

Tool systems
Tool systems are available where a single handle locks on to a variety of attachments. The durability of the connection between handle and attachments is important.

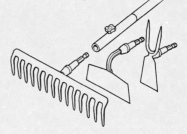

Other tools
When buying a wheelbarrow, get one that holds a reasonable amount and is strong but light enough for you to manage when loaded. The wheel should have a rubber covering.

Hoses should be of rubber or rubberized material for, despite manufacturers' assurances, plastic tends to buckle and block the flow of water.

Lightweight galvanized metal wheelbarrow

You may find that where you are growing crops of fruit or vegetables you need a pressure spray. Hand and knapsack versions are available.

There are also tools for specialist tasks. For example, if you have a number of fruit trees it is worth buying long-handled pruners and, where a lawn leads directly on to flower beds, edging clippers will eliminate stooping. Finally, a stiff garden broom is vital, particularly if you have a terrace, since hard areas will need to be cleared of moss and debris periodically.

Spray gun

Wind-up hose

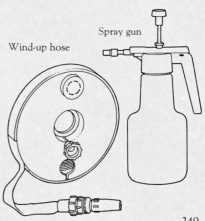

Plant care

Many gardeners make work by choosing plants and cultivation methods that need considerable attention; others prefer planting that requires a minimum of work. The choice is entirely yours. If you elect to grow plants that require regular replacement, such as vegetables or annuals, you will need to dedicate hours of work to gardening on a regular basis; on the other hand, a more casual treatment, with borders of shrubs and random planting through gravel, will only require periodic maintenance.

Trees, in most cases, fall between these two extremes. As a general rule, they require attention at the planting stage and many need care until they are established, which may be a year or two. After that, however, they should thrive with little or no interference until they are old, when special treatment may be necessary. Exceptions to this rule are the fruit trees, for they are usually trained for decorative purposes, for crop quality and ease of harvesting.

Tree maintenance

Newly planted trees
Careful maintenance during the period following planting is crucial if a healthy, vigorous specimen is to become established. The larger the tree, the more important the care. Semi-mature trees, newly planted, need regular watering, but the soil around their roots must not become waterlogged. Mulching the soil throughout summer to the extent of the trees' root runs will help to retain

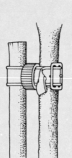

Support ties *Check support ties after windy and wet weather. Make sure the ties are neither too tight nor broken.*

moisture, and will help to keep down weeds which otherwise rob the soil of valuable nutrients. It is also vital that the guy ropes supporting a top-heavy specimen are regularly checked to ensure that there is no root movement. Such care is necessary for all newly established trees for at least two years. Certain conifers, such as pines, need longer attention.

Smaller trees, though staked rather than guyed, need to have their supports checked in spring to ensure that they are still firm after winter winds. Ties should be carefully examined to ensure that they are not too tight; if they are they will cut into the tree and weaken it. Nor should they chaff the bark in wind, for this will cause damage and encourage disease.

From time to time, look critically at the shape of your tree. Then, in autumn, prune by taking out limbs that are growing the wrong way.

Certain trees, particularly fruits and many weeping forms of tree, have been grafted on to another root stock. Usually the graft shows just above the ground. Suckers sometimes grow out from the root stock just below the original graft. These should be cut back flush to the trunk of the tree.

Older trees
Trees are living and as they get older need more specific attention, possibly tree surgery. Most gardeners do not understand the skill of tree surgery. Specialist firms practice this craft, however, employing skilled men with the correct equipment. Before employing such a firm, it is wise to ensure that they are covered by third party and public liability insurances if your trees adjoin a public right of way.

The work that a tree surgeon can perform (and you, to a lesser degree, on smaller trees) includes the pruning and removal of limbs, bracing of old limbs, treatment of hollows to avoid moisture settling and causing further rotting, and feeding trees.

Pruning and removing limbs are the most common operations necessary when a tree gets older. In either case, the limb or branch should be cut right back to the main trunk of its leader. When properly treated the remaining short stub will die and rot back into the tree, where the wound will heal naturally. The time for this in most regions is autumn and winter.

Extremely heavy branches are removed in two pieces to avoid the full weight of the branch, when partially cut, tearing the bark away on the lower parts of the tree.

All newly sawn surfaces should be cleaned at the edges with a sharp knife, and then painted with a commercial preparation which includes a bitumen emulsion with an added fungicide. This forms a seal until the raw area has grown over with callus.

Pruning free-growing trees, or any plant material for that matter,

Pruning for shape
The purpose of general autumn pruning is to create an attractive, open head to the tree. Drastic, clumsy cutting will produce a mass of unsightly new growth. Remove crossing branches, any dead wood and weak growth, then prune lightly to leave a predetermined framework.

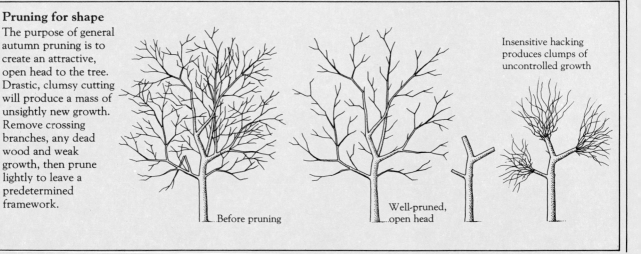

Insensitive hacking produces clumps of uncontrolled growth

Before pruning

Well-pruned, open head

seldom necessitates the severe clipping treatment so loved by the ill-informed gardener. When you clip a branch you substitute for one main growth half a dozen other lesser ones, which by the end of the following season will have compounded your problem.

Older trees, particularly when exposed to wind, may have grown in an unattractive way, probably due to having lost their leader growth in their youth. In high winds, different parts of the tree may sway in different directions, thereby causing stress and eventual cracking of the tree where the trunk forks. To prevent this, limbs may be braced together with wire bands, but this is work for a specialist. Failing this, the sensitive removal of one limb of the tree will reduce wind stress.

Removing limbs

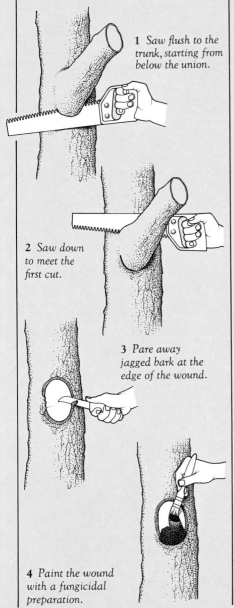

1 *Saw flush to the trunk, starting from below the union.*

2 *Saw down to meet the first cut.*

3 *Pare away jagged bark at the edge of the wound.*

4 *Paint the wound with a fungicidal preparation.*

Pleaching

The classic pleached screen of trees is started against supporting posts and wires. A row of young trees is encouraged to grow in one plane only, so that their branches can be intertwined. Each autumn, vertical growth is stopped above pairs of chosen buds that are left to grow horizontally along each wire, until the desired height is reached. Subsequent growth on this framework will merge to form a mass of foliage in the summer that is then clipped to shape.

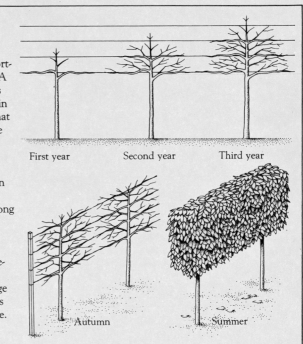

First year   Second year   Third year

Autumn   Summer

Where hollows develop in old trees they should be cleared out and any rotting wood removed. Clean with an antiseptic and then allow to dry. When possible, build up the hole with layers of the material used to seal tree wounds, mixed with sawdust or hardwood chippings. When weathered off, the tree callus will grow over the hole and its bung.

Old trees that have been neglected may benefit from root feeding. Into holes drilled about 230 mm (9 in) into the soil 600 mm (24 in) apart under the tree's overhang, apply a feed consisting of five parts by weight of sulphate of ammonia, five parts of superphosphate and one and a half parts of sulphate of potash. Pour this into each hole and cover with soil.

Special pruning

Pleaching deciduous trees to create a hedge requires considerable seasonal maintenance. This involves pruning, supporting and intertwining in autumn and clipping the overall foliage shape through the summer.

"Top-worked" fruit trees will not only make attractive forms (see p. 183) but will produce a quality crop and one that is easier to harvest. Training the trees is, however, time consuming. One method is fan training (see p. 252), in which the young tree is cut back to 600 mm (24 in). Then train the main branches on wires to the shape of a fan. Growth forwards and backwards from the plane of the fan is cut out. In time, subsidiary branches are trained to the same fan shape and unsuitable growth eliminated.

Another method, allowing many varieties of fruit tree to grow in a small area, consists of restricting a tree to one stem grafted on to dwarfing stock and trained obliquely. Every year, the tree (cordon) must be cut back as it grows longer, so that the entire crop is always within reach.

The espalier form (see p. 183) is perhaps the most effective for fruit trees but it, too, involves considerable yearly maintenance. An advantage of the espalier form is that it can be used for free-standing trees with the support wires strung between posts. In this way a row of espalier-trained fruit trees can be used to divide the garden. As with a pleached avenue of trees, growth away from the line of the supporting wires is removed annually.

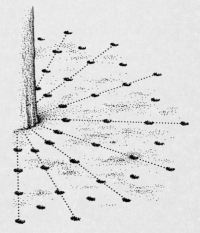

Root feeding 230 mm (9 in) bore holes, made at 600 mm (24 in) intervals.

251

Fan training fruit trees

Fan training is a useful form of top-working fruit trees, especially cherries, plums and peaches. The fan shape of growth is usually tied against wires and temporary canes attached to a wall. The main stem of a maiden tree is removed above two buds that will grow to form the chief pair of fan ribs.

Year one *Prune the main stem to about 600 mm (24 in), above two healthy opposing buds.*

Year two *Tie the ribs to canes and, in the winter, prune both to 450 mm (18 in), above a bud. Leave 4 buds on each rib.*

Year three *Tie subsidiary ribs to canes as they grow and, in winter, prune the 8 ribs to 750 mm (30 in), above a bud.*

Allow three shoots from each of these ribs to make the 32 ribs of a complete fan in the fourth year.

Hedges

Maintenance of a formal hedge varies according to type. Certain varieties, particularly the fast growing ones, such as privet (*Ligustrum* sp.), thorn (*Crataegus* sp.) and *Lonicera nitida*, need trimming from time to time throughout the year in order to keep them tidy. Other species should be trimmed during July or August and then again in October to remove the secondary growth made after the initial trim. This group includes box (*Buxus* sp.), hornbeam (*Carpinus* sp.), Lawsons cypress (*Chamaecyparis lawsoniana*), *Cotoneaster simonsii*, *Cupressus* sp., *Escallonia* sp., beech (*Fagus* sp.), holly (*Ilex aquifolium*), *Pyracantha* sp., rosemary (*Rosmarinus* sp.), yew (*Taxus baccata*) and *Viburnum tinus*.

Some hedges need to be trimmed only once a year. These include *Aucuba japonica*, *Berberis stenophylla*, *Elaeagnus pungens*, bay (*Laurus nobilis*), laurel (*Prunus laurocerasus*) and Portuguese laurel (*Prunus lusitanica*). The larger-leaved of these should be trimmed with pruners

Once established, it is important

that you feed and water your hedge from time to time. Where evergreens are packed extremely tightly to form a screen, they also provide a canopy that shields their roots from rain; in these cases leave a hose dribbling at their roots in high summer.

The shape that you hope your hedges will ultimately achieve is important, for they should be correctly trained from the start. Formal hedges should be trimmed to provide foliage right to the ground and be shaped so that the top is slightly narrower than the base, to prevent damage from wind and snow. A top-heavy hedge, with snow on it, will be pried open at the center and will ultimately collapse. Harder trimming will provide a denser hedge.

Informal and flowering hedges, which should have a much looser shape, are pruned to remove old and dead wood but should not be trimmed, as you will inevitably cut off flower buds. Therefore pick your time carefully. As with shrubs in a border, some hedging shrub flowers appear on young wood formed the same year. These should be pruned in winter or spring and include *Buddleia davidii*, *Cistus* sp., *Fuschia*

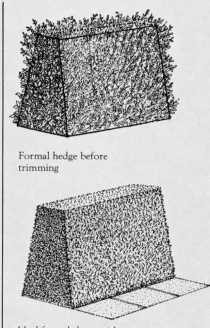

Formal hedge before trimming

Ideal formal shape with path for easy maintenance

sp., *Hydrangea paniculata* 'Grandiflora', *Hypericum patulum*, *Lavandula* sp., *Rosa rubrifolia*, *Rosa rugosa* and *Santolina chamaecyparissus*.

Others flower on wood formed during the previous year. These should be pruned immediately after flowering and include *Berberis darwinii*, *Berberis stenophylla*, *Ceanothus dentatus*, *Chaenomeles japonica*, *Forsythia* sp., *Hippophae rhamnoides*, *Mahonia aquifolium*, *Prunus × blireiana*, *Ribes* and *Weigela* sp.

The third and final group consists of those that flower on spurs or side shoots. These, which require little attention except for thinning and shaping, include *Berberis thunbergii*, *Cotoneaster franchetii*, *Cotoneaster microphylla*, *Hebe traversii*, *Rhododendron* sp., and *Skimmia japonica*.

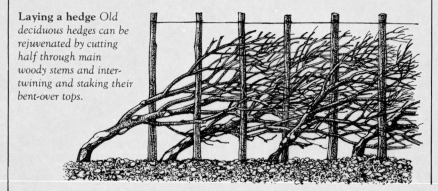

Laying a hedge *Old deciduous hedges can be rejuvenated by cutting half through main woody stems and intertwining and staking their bent-over tops.*

Shrubs

Transplanting

It is possible to transplant most shrubs, even when they are old, provided their roots are prepared and the plant itself cut back. Conifers, however, are notoriously difficult to move when large.

A plant's roots are composed of those which anchor it in the soil so that it is not blown over by wind, and by finer feeder roots located at the tip of the anchorage system. Some shrubs have one or two enormous tap roots, which grow to a considerable depth; most have a system not unlike their branches. As a general guide, you can assume that the shrub's underground feeder root system extends outwards at least as far as its overhead branch system.

By digging close to a shrub, prior to moving it, you will break both its feeding and its anchorage rooting systems. The larger and older the subject, the greater the problem. Up to two or three years of age, shrubs have a small root system and light anchorage since they have no bulk to hold. They can be moved easily, though the more earth you take with the root system the less root disturbance there will be.

Older, larger shrubs should be prepared a year before you propose moving them by slicing down hard around the shrub with a spade at a 500 mm (20 in) radius from the stem to encourage a tighter root ball of young feeder roots, which can be more easily moved the following spring. Older shrubs should also have their heads cut back to reduce loss of moisture through transpiration, since you are limiting their intake of water at the roots.

Temporary heeling in

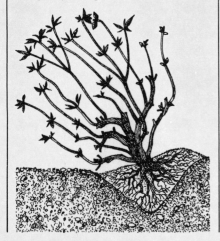

Before lifting a shrub of whatever size, dig the hole in which you are going to replant it. Make the hole wide and deep. It is most important that the moving operation is as swift as possible, so that the exposed root system does not dry out. Ideally, plant in overcast, windless weather, for both sun and wind are injurious.

Prepared for transplanting

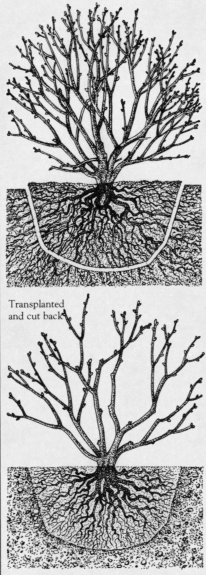

Transplanted and cut back

Heel the lifted shrub into a temporary trench if there is any delay in planting.

To lift a shrub, dig around the roots as gently as possible with a fork to ease them. You will then have to chop off extensive roots cleanly with a spade. Work your way around the plant, gradually loosening the soil underneath it and levering upwards.

When the shrub is free of its surround and you can examine its root system, adjust the size of the hole into which it is to be planted. Before replanting, fork into the base of the new position some organic manure or compost with a handful of bone meal. Transfer the shrub with as much earth attached to it as possible. Spread out its root system, cut broken roots cleanly with pruners and fork back the previously excavated soil. Shake the shrub up and down occasionally to allow soil to settle around the roots.

Before finally topping off, hammer in a stake but be careful not to damage the roots. Then complete the backfilling process, heeling down the earth as you go. The final earth height should be at the same position on the stem as it was in its original planting position. If the earth is dry, water the shrub heavily to ensure that earth has enveloped the root system. Finally, fix your shrub to its stake with a plastic tie.

Subsequent maintenance

Newly-planted shrubs need careful treatment. They must be regularly watered to ensure that roots do not dry out, evergreens being particularly susceptible to drought.

After frost or snow, newly planted shrubs should be firmed into the soil by treading around them. New beds should be kept clean and friable by hoeing or light forking through the growing season. This will also assist rain penetration. During early spring, more rotted manure or mulch can be spread on the soil.

The time of year at which you transplant shrubs, and their subsequent maintenance, will vary according to your location. In milder areas the work can be undertaken through autumn, winter and spring, provided the earth is not frozen. Transplanting is safer in spring in regions with short autumns and long severe winters and this is especially true for conifers. However, in most northern regions, gardeners can gain by moving plants in autumn. The weather is cooler and rainfall often more plentiful and plants are approaching their dormant period.

Weather may change in spring quite quickly, however; if the soil dries out, it is essential to keep shrubs well watered with a hose or a can without a fine nozzle. Wind will also dry your soil. Depending on species, you should be quite brutal in cutting back the head of the shrub to make it gain new growth quickly.

When you have moved shrubs in autumn, be sure to check the stability of the subject regularly and reheel in if necessary.

Pruning shrubs

Shrubs will generally flower quite well if left alone. Pruning should only be undertaken to regulate the height of the shrub, its shape and the thickness of its growth, and to establish the level at which you want its flowers. Therefore, decide upon your aims before you start.

Left to themselves, shrubs grow upwards and outwards with flowers early in the season formed on previous years' wood, or flowers towards the end of the season on the current year's wood. You should prune the shrubs to prevent the blossom getting higher and higher each year. Take care when you do this: it is no use pruning a spring flowering specimen in autumn for you will only cut off the next spring's flowers. Prune such shrubs after they have flowered in the spring so that they grow throughout summer to produce the wood on which the following year's flowers will grow. In autumn you should only prune shrubs which flower on the following year's growth.

You can shape your shrubs in the autumn but keep the outline relaxed and only clip dense shrubs, such as box (*Buxus* sp.) and holly (*Ilex* sp.). Use pruners to thin and prune shrubs, making clean cuts just above a node or joint, or cut back flush to the main stem.

Shrub roses need no pruning and floribunda roses only shaping and the removal of dead wood, but hybrid tea roses must be severely pruned back to the second or third bud on each major lateral stem. You must also prune to establish an open, well-shaped bush. New growth will extend from the buds you retain, so prune with ultimate shape in mind. In hard climates, this should be done in spring.

Pruning is a straightforward process but if you are in any doubt, do nothing. Then analyze your plant next season and ascertain what should be done to achieve a shape that will blend harmoniously with adjoining species. Remember that you will seldom kill a shrub by cutting it; you are much more likely to invigorate it. However, you can kill half-hardy roses by pruning too early in the season. You can take out or prune back the center of many shrubs, particularly those with a strong leader shoot, to achieve a more flattened shape.

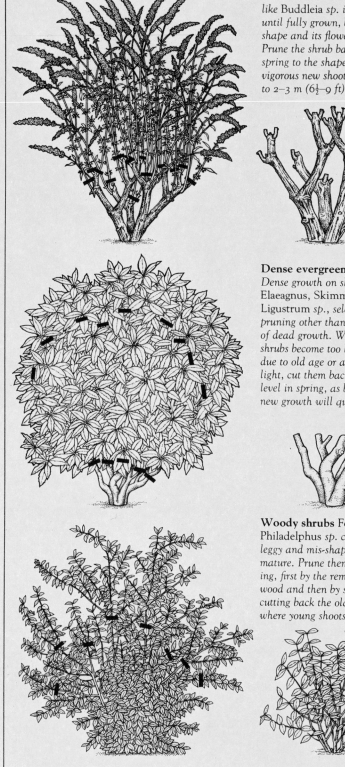

Soft-wooded shrubs *Shrubs like Buddleia sp. if left unpruned until fully grown, become loose in shape and its flowers too small. Prune the shrub back hard in spring to the shape below, and vigorous new shoots may grow to 2–3 m (6½–9 ft).*

Dense evergreen shrubs
Dense growth on shrubs such as Elaeagnus, Skimmia and Ligustrum sp., seldom needs pruning other than the removal of dead growth. When such shrubs become too large or leggy due to old age or absence of light, cut them back to ground level in spring, as below. Tight new growth will quickly emerge.

Woody shrubs Forsythia *and* Philadelphus *sp. can become leggy and mis-shapen when mature. Prune them after flowering, first by the removal of dead wood and then by selectively cutting back the old stems to where young shoots are growing.*

Pruning cuts

When pruning a stem it is important to make a clean cut close above a healthy bud, with the sloping face made away from the bud itself.

1 Too ragged   2 Too near bud
3 Too far from bud   4 Wrong slope
5 Correct cut

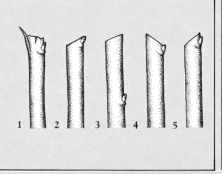

Perennials

Most herbaceous plants will grow in all but extreme soil conditions. They are cheap to buy but need rather more attention than shrubs. They grow quickly, however, and if you are just starting your garden they have the advantage of achieving their ultimate dimensions in one season. It is a mistake, however, to suppose that perennials live for ever; all vegetation ultimately dies of old age, but life span varies from one species to another. Lupines, for example, seldom enjoy more than two years of healthy life, while peonies can survive for 10 years or more. You can be fairly rough when dividing your herbaceous plants in autumn as there is little chance of your killing them. If you do not divide the plants until spring, you may not recognize them since they will have no foliage. You may also destroy their crown or growing point at that time of year.

Many herbaceous plants will self-seed and one of the pleasures of the mixed border is the casual appearance of something you had not intended. The results are invariably far more interesting than the designed areas. Unlike woody shrubs, herbaceous perennials have soft stems which tend to die down to the ground at the end of their growing season. These are the plants that form the mainstay of a flower border and they are the summer glory of the traditional cottage garden. Many herbaceous plants will flower quite happily alongside shrubs, and indeed their inclusion in a shrub border is easier than their cultivation in a strictly herbaceous border.

The herbaceous perennial border needs to be wider than twice the height of its tallest occupants, which are usually two meters (6½ ft) high. This arrangement will look correct in its proportions. These dimensions are often a surprise and to achieve them you may have to enlarge an existing bed in autumn. Perennials tend to·flop over and when this happens on to grass it makes lawn maintenance difficult. You may want to edge the area with paving stone or brick to avoid having to support the heads each time you mow.

The ground should be prepared several weeks in advance of planting perennials so that it can settle and consolidate. Cultivate the ground as deeply as possible, incorporating organic feed and some bone meal in the top spit of earth. Ideally, prepare your planting area in autumn to plant the following spring. On particularly light soil, with an equable climate, you can plant in autumn.

The planting hole for each specimen must be large enough to accommodate the root spread and the crown or growth point set to the correct depth. Planting distances within groups of plants should be 230–300 mm (9–12 in) between small species, like primulas, 300–380 mm (12–15 in) for medium species like *Erigeron* sp., while stronger-growing species, such as delphiniums, should be 460–600 mm (18–24 in) apart.

Subsequent maintenance of perennials involves staking the plants at the height of their growth, where wind is likely to blow them over. After flowering, dead heads must be cut off. Plants that flower early, such as lupines, may then produce a second crop of flower heads.

Divide your plants in autumn when they become too large, for herbaceous plants tend to grow outwards and a hole develops quite quickly in their center. Extract any invasive weeds and then, with two forks pushed back to back in the mass, force it apart by levering. Those with fleshy tubers, such as peonies should be lifted, then cut apart with a knife, allowing three to five buds per new division.

Dividing fibrous-rooted perennials

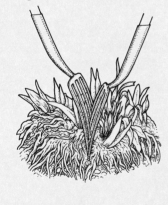

Dividing tuberous perennials

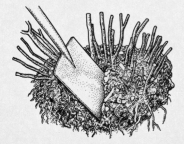

Annuals

Annuals are in general spectacular and, because their life span is short, require little attention once established. Many annuals are now sold as seedlings in spring. However, with a sterile growing medium and fluorescent lights, you can bring on annuals yourself from seed to be hardened off before planting out. Other, larger seeds, such as nasturtiums, can be sown where you want them to flower.

Prepare the ground by light cultivation, no deeper than 100 mm (4 in), and remove all surface weeds and weed roots. Where your seeds are small, as with *Eschscholzia* sp. for example, broadcast over the prepared ground by gently shaking the seed packet. For easier distribution, many seeds are now pelleted within a sterile medium. This not only makes them less subject to rotting but, since they are larger, more manageable. After sowing, gently rake over the ground and water, using a fine mist of water. Seedlings should appear after about 14 days or so, depending on your soil type and its temperature, and will probably need to be thinned.

If you have sown your annuals early in the year, cut them back with shears after they have flowered and you may well get a second flowering later in the growing season.

Broadcasting annual seeds

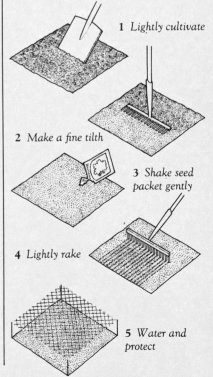

1 *Lightly cultivate*

2 *Make a fine tilth*

3 *Shake seed packet gently*

4 *Lightly rake*

5 *Water and protect*

Lawns

Grass makes a most attractive natural surface but has some disadvantages. In the first place, lawns need a great deal of attention during the growing season. Moreover, grass will not thrive in areas of heavy shade or in any situation where it is subjected to constant human traffic. During periods of drought, some grass species will dry out completely and go dormant. Excessive heat also wrecks many summer lawns. Lastly, grass can play host to organisms that are detrimental to its own growth; if the grass succumbs to disease it results in a poor sward.

If you are prepared to undertake the necessary maintenance tasks, however, there is no better garden surface. Essential maintenance, such as mowing, watering, feeding and weeding, will not only keep a garden looking trim and attractive but will increase the health and vigor of your grass, which in turn will inhibit invaders such as moss and weeds.

Mowing is an essential weekly task throughout the growing season. The blades of your mowing machine must be sharp, properly set and at the correct height, as shown in the diagram showing height of cut.

Watering will be necessary after about seven days of drought in summer and 10 days in spring, or your lawn will look brown and dull and lose its springiness underfoot. As with all watering, give the lawn a good soaking (see Irrigation, p. 105); too light an application will only encourage surface rooting, which compounds your problem.

Feeding your grass will be necessary, since constant cropping of the foliage drains the nutrient reserves in the soil. Do this in spring, when the grass starts to grow, using a lawn fertilizer, applied by a cyclone or drop-type spreader.

Raking with a spring-tined rake will remove surplus and dead surface foliage and open up the thatch of matted stems, which otherwise encourages moss and weed invasion and forms an impassable canopy for air and moisture. (Use a bamboo rake to remove light debris such as fallen leaves.)

Moss and weed eradication is a continuous process. Excessive moss is usually a sign that your lawn needs drainage; small areas of moss are not unexpected, however, after a period of heavy rain. Apply a weed and moss killer as soon as there is an obvious invasion.

Worm casts are a nuisance if your lawn takes much wear, for when crushed underfoot the bare earth makes a seed bed for weeds. When casts appear, scatter them with a bamboo rake before mowing.

Whether you edge your grass or not is an aesthetic consideration. A paved edging eliminates the need for

Maintaining features associated with lawns

Areas beneath trees
An area of lawn beneath a tree with dense leaves will inevitably suffer, for it will be deprived of food, water and sunlight. Removing the tree's lower branches will help but even so yearly reseeding of grass may be necessary. One solution is to turn the area into a bed and plant it with shrubs and perennials that welcome shade. Alternatively, surround the base of the tree with a pattern of brickwork.

Isolated beds
An isolated bed must be in proportion to the lawn. Wherever you site it, however, it will inevitably make the lawn appear smaller unless its shape is related to the surrounding pattern in which it sits. Reshape the bed if it is necessary.

Access areas
Ensure that the entry to your lawn is of generous proportions; if not, the area will quickly become worn and unsightly with constant use.

Banks
Modern machines make banked lawns easy to mow, provided the slope is not more than about 35°. Sharper gradients should be dug and planted with ground cover.

Bulbs
Daffodils look especially well in a lawn but the leaves must be allowed to die down if the next year's growth is to be vigorous. In a small garden it is better to site them within an overall pattern of rough grass.

Paths
Paths should run around a lawn rather than into it, for the junction of path and grass will otherwise rapidly become worn.

Edging
Much hard work will be avoided if you have a mowing edge around your lawn—that is, paving between the edge of the grass area and surrounding walls and buildings. Paths should be slightly below the lawn level for the same reason.

regular clipping but defines the lawn and whatever it abuts with an unnecessarily hard edge. Much clipping can be reduced if you ensure that your mower can get into all the corners and over the edge of the grass.

There are several other necessary but less frequent tasks. You can aerate the lawn with a spike or fork to break up the surface layer, which with use and mowing may become compacted. The spiking will also help aerate your grass and improve its drainage (see p. 244). This should be done at least once a year if moss becomes a nuisance.

Top-dress your lawn in autumn to improve the ground on which it feeds, particularly if your topsoil is poor. The dressing should be a mixture of peat, loam and sand. Minor hollows must be filled to give you an even surface for mowing. You should also feed your lawn in autumn with a balanced fertilizer, formulated for the season, to build

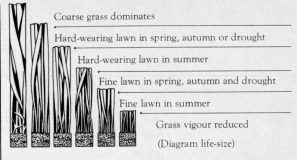

Coarse grass dominates

Hard-wearing lawn in spring, autumn or drought

Hard-wearing lawn in summer

Fine lawn in spring, autumn and drought

Fine lawn in summer

Grass vigour reduced

(Diagram life-size)

Height of cut
Maintain your lawn at the requisite height of cut according to the time of year, weather conditions and the type of grass established.

up the root system and increase resistance to disease. Autumn, in most sections of the country, is a good time to apply limestone, if soil tests show its need.

One task that is seldom necessary is rolling, which will compact your lawn if done at the wrong time of year. The only time to roll is in spring, when the surface of the lawn is dry although the soil beneath still damp, and you need to firm turf that has been lifted by frost.

Ground cover

As with all aspects of gardening, the secret of easy maintenance with ground cover is thorough preparation of the area to be planted. Once established, ground cover will largely eliminate weeding because no plant, however hardy, can survive if totally deprived of sunlight, but do not be deceived into thinking that ground cover will rapidly smother weeds for you. Much time and labor will be saved over the years if you first destroy all weeds by digging out or chemicals. If you can afford the time leave the area unplanted for two or three summer months to ensure that the eliminating process has been thorough.

Nevertheless, weeds will inevitably appear and from time to time plants will need to be lifted and the root systems cleared of pernicious weeds. Some plants will not only need to be lifted occasionally but also divided and replanted, for creeping plants, particularly perennials, such as *Thymus* sp., *Armeria* sp. (thrift) and *Stachys lanata*, grow away from their original center, which then becomes bare. Lift the whole plant, pull off the young growths (which will probably have developed their own root systems) and replant them. Other plants become invasive and their runners should be removed. An example is *Lamium maculatum*. If not held in check, this plant grows into,

and ultimately smothers, adjacent shrubs. Various species of *Rubus* also become invasive in this way, as do certain large-leaved forms of *Hedera*.

If you are not seduced into planting ground cover material that is too rampant for the area you wish to establish, maintenance tasks are not demanding. There are always slower-growing alternatives; the shrubbier junipers, for instance. So study your plants and their growth pattern before using them. You must also consider the site and its exposure. For instance, junipers will not grow in shade and shade is usually the reason why we seek plants other than grass. Both *Vinca minor* and pachysandra thrive with little care in shade.

Certain plants, such as *Hypericum calycinum* and bamboo (*Arundinaria* sp.), will need to be restrained, particularly if you are trying to establish a precise pattern. To do this, sink 300-mm (12-in) strips of slate into the ground to foil underground runners, though even this will sometimes fail to restrain coarse bamboo. In this case, sheet metal (preferably aluminium, which will not rust) provides a flexible, resilient and less penetrable guard, but it is expensive. If your ground cover is keeping within its bounds it will still need attention, either with shears or pruners, to keep the growth low and horizontal.

There are certain plants, such as ground cover roses and ivy, that need their runners directed to infill bare earth. Either pin the runner down with a stone or, more efficiently, make hoops of wire and use these to pin the stems firmly into the earth where you want them.

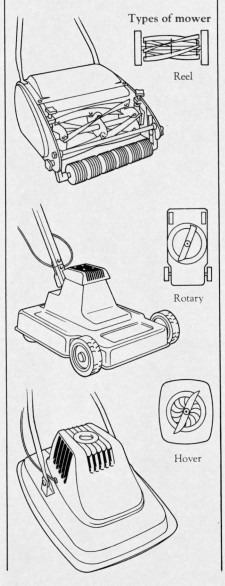

Types of mower

Reel

Rotary

Hover

Climbing plants

The manner in which climbers grow is the key to how they should be treated at the end of the season. The treatment you give will also depend on how high you want them to grow and flower, for you may want them to cover structures ranging from a low fence to the wall of a house. You can control the height at which flowers appear in that they generally appear on new growth. In general, the harder you prune a flowering climber, the lower new growth will appear and so the lower flowers will be. Flowering also depends on pruning at the right time of year. Prune spring-flowering climbers when they have finished flowering, for if you cut them in autumn, when the other climbers are pruned, you will cut off next spring's flowering buds.

Many tropical climbers, such as *Solanum jasminoides*, can be cut back each autumn, for they make enormous growth in the course of one year. In the same way, cut winter jasmine (*Jasminum nudiflorum*) in the spring. Outside decorative vines (*Vitis* sp.) should also be shortened to their main leader in autumn. Rambler roses must have all the year's growth removed in autumn. Tie new growth in a fan shape to make next year's pruning easier.

Woody climbers, such as *Solanum crispum*, are usually pruned in autumn, when they should also be shaped. Take out old and dead wood to encourage new growth. Be bold for you will get the best results by cutting back fairly hard. If you give a weak snip here and there, you will get a lot of fuzzy end growth that will neither flower nor be in the true character of the plant. To maintain the height of a climbing rose, for example, tie in all the vigorous old growth, take out dead portions and shorten the growths of intermediate length to encourage flowering lower down the plant. In autumn, remove any suckers and rogue growths from the root stock, taking them off with secateurs to the main stem.

Clematis, including the species and many hybrids, require mainly corrective pruning to cut back winter-killed wood or to restrict over-vigorous growth that is making the vines a tangle. For northerners, clematis varieties that bloom on new wood are safer. *Wisteria* sp. must have their rampant twining leaders shortened after flowering in July or August, and must then be trained, tied in and shaped during autumn. For detailed instructions on pruning and shaping a particular species, refer to specialist books on climbers and their maintenance.

Autumn is the ideal time to replace hardware, wires and trellises when pruning your climbers. You may need to let your plants down to give them thorough treatment, and it is sensible to do any replacement necessary then. At this stage, when a plant has a considerable amount of growth, you will see that, unless you have a particularly well-made trellis, it is uncertain whether the climber is holding your trellis up or the trellis the climber. It is for this reason that wires are a more efficient form of horizontal support.

Pruning deciduous climbing and clinging plants

Deciduous climbers must sometimes be cut back to prevent a mat of growth. Prune low to the ground above healthy buds. Clinging plants, such as climbing hydrangeas, should be detached from their supports before removing lateral growth back from the main stems and re-attaching to the support.

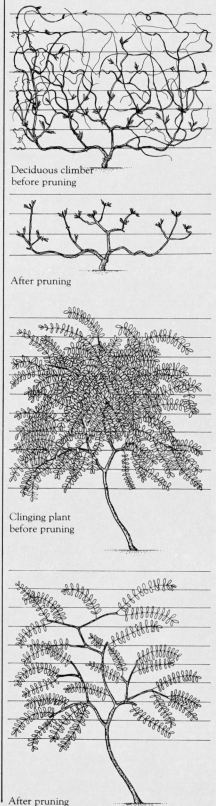

Deciduous climber before pruning

After pruning

Clinging plant before pruning

After pruning

Pruning roses

Cut out recent year's growth from rambler roses to leave a fan shape of vigorous, established wood. With climbing roses, take out dead wood and shorten new growth to leave a clear framework.

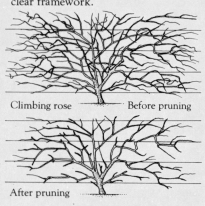

Climbing rose — Before pruning

After pruning

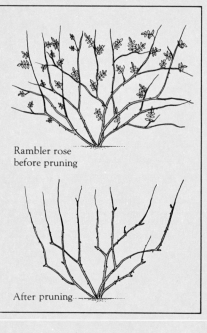

Rambler rose before pruning

After pruning

Water plants

It is neither necessary nor desirable to empty and clean a pool frequently, for every time you do it will need to re-establish a natural balance between water and pond life, including plants. A simple method of removing leaves from small ponds is to thread some wire netting into the tines of a digging fork and then use it like a ladle. You must remove leaves to prevent the choking of water plants. In full sun, algae growing in the water become a nuisance and must be cleared with a fine net, although proprietary chemicals are available that help.

When you do eventually need to empty and clean your pool, take the opportunity to divide your plants before replanting them, the best time being in late spring. Wash the plants thoroughly and cut out any weak or spindly growth. Strong stock should be divided and the tubers of water lilies cut into pieces, leaving one good crown to each plant. You need leave only a few inches of tuber to each crown and some of the old, fleshy roots must be cut away.

Plants and fish will be quite safe below ice during winter, provided your pool is deep enough (500–600 mm (20–24 in)). You should nevertheless maintain a hole in the ice 500 mm (24 in) across, admitting air to the water and enabling the fish to be fed. Tropical water lilies will not survive freezing and must be treated as annuals in the North. Hardy water lilies should survive if their roots are below the ice layer.

Very small ponds can quickly freeze solid in severe weather, injuring or even killing fish and lilies. Life within the pool can be protected by wooden boards, to which old mats

Wire netting in the tines of a digging fork used as a scoop for leaves.

Dividing water plants

When you come to divide water plants, use the method to suit the type of plant. Marginal plants with lower stems like celery are divided by pulling the elements of the root stock apart. Marginals with creeping rhizomatous roots should be cut to separate rooted sections and tuberous-rooted plants, such as water lilies, should be pulled apart.

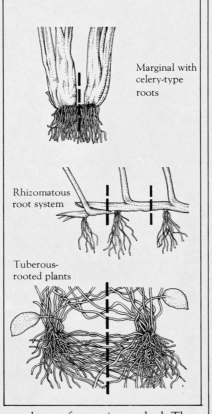

Marginal with celery-type roots

Rhizomatous root system

Tuberous-rooted plants

or a layer of straw is attached. These are then left to float on the surface but as soon as the weather improves in spring they must be removed or plants will be forced into premature growth. Alternatively, cover the pool with boards and place sacks or straw on top of them. Easier and almost a necessity in most northern regions is an electric immersion heater controlled by a thermostat.

Plants growing in damp soil at the edge of ponds and pools should be cut down during winter, much as you do with perennials and mixed border material. The crowns of the enormous *Gunnera manicata* can be protected by folding back one of its leaves over the crown and then covering this with evergreen boughs or with straw.

Herbs

Maintenance of herbs includes cutting back annual growth and dead heads and generally shaping bushes. In mild climates, do this in autumn but in the North spring is preferable. Sage, for example, becomes very straggly after two or three years and will need to be cut back to the main stem or dug up and replaced with new stock. Some climbing herbs, such as sorrel, will need to be lifted and divided or they will swamp the area. If you plant mints in open ground they must be dramatically restrained or their rampant growth will swamp the herb garden.

Many herbs, especially those with umbelliferous flowers, like lovage, seed extensively and the plants must be removed each year. Fennel and angelica, for instance, should always be treated in this way. If the ripe seeds are left to fall into the soil and germinate, they grow through other species and can then be very difficult to remove.

If you wish to collect herb seeds, remove the entire plant with its seed heads before they have dried out, then tie them in bundles and hang them upside-down from a stake over a prepared bed into which the seeds will drop. This method is especially successful with chervil, angelica, fennel and dill.

You must also remove annual herbs, such as dill and sweet basil, at the end of the season for they will not reappear the following year and you will need to utilize the space for new planting. Chives have an unfortunate habit of hosting grass roots, so lift the clumps when necessary, divide them and then replant after removing any entwined, foreign roots. The leaves of some herbs, such as basil and marjoram, may be harvested for immediate use. Remove the center tip, as this will produce bushy side growth. With herbs such as parsley and lovage you must take the outside leaves and their stalks, leaving the crown.

Other herbs need to be dried and stored after harvesting. Take only as much as you can manage to dry at one time, as delay after cutting reduces the strength of their essential oils. Annuals and perennial herbs will give two or even three crops in a season, but make your last cut in autumn to allow new growth to harden before the cold weather.

The organic cycle

In most conditions in the northern hemisphere plants will flourish without artificial additives, for nature has made adequate provision with her various cycles. The "water cycle", for example, is simply the process by which water evaporates from seas, lakes and rivers, is carried about the atmosphere by winds and is ultimately deposited as rain or snow to percolate through the earth and fill rivers and lakes again. In the same way, the "nitrogen cycle" (dead animal and vegetable tissue decomposing into the soil eventually releases nitrogen for the use of plants, which in turn provide food for animals) gives adequate soil nutrition. If you step in clumsily, adding synthetic, inorganic fertilizers and pesticides for instant results in your garden, you can easily ruin the long term fertility of your soil and disrupt the natural chains of life that will otherwise keep a rough balance. Establish your own compost heaps to re-use vegetable waste and introduce animal manures to increase the nitrogen content.

Leaf clearance
On still autumn days a regular task is to clear leaves from lawns, paths and plants. Do this regularly before they accumulate, as they can smother grass. Use the leaves for rotting down into leaf mold or include them in your compost heap. Beech and oak leaves, which take some time to rot, may be used directly, with other organic matter, as a mulch to protect tender perennials. Place the leaves around the base of the plants, leaving the tops uncovered if they are still green for only the crown of the plants and the roots need protection. Then place twigs over the mulch to hold it in place.

Compost heaps

A compost heap can be open or enclosed. In a well-composed heap, spring waste will be compost by summer and summer waste by autumn. An autumn heap will take longer to break down but will still be ready by spring.

You can build your own compost heap or buy a pre-shaped container. The decision will depend on how much waste you have, for bought containers tend to be small. When building your own, construct two areas so that you will have one area to contain vegetable waste as it is collected from the garden and kitchen while the other compost heap is decomposing. The heap should not be more than a meter (3 ft) or so high. The base of the heap should be slightly raised to allow for air circulation (a layer of twigs will suffice) and the sides of the container should also allow air through.

Build your compost heap in 150–200 mm (6–8 in) layers of waste. Poisonous leaves, including those of rhubarb, must be excluded. Spread farmyard manure, organic activator or sulphate of ammonia at rate of 15 g (.53 oz) to every square meter (10 ft²) over alternate layers and a sprinkling of lime over intervening ones. Water each layer as you build the heap. Finally, add a 200 mm (8 in) layer of soil.

Some gardeners prefer to leave the rotting process undisturbed, but there is some evidence to suggest that the rotting process is improved by turning the heap every month or so and watering any dry areas. Compost is ready for use when its components can no longer be distinguished, but can be used sooner.

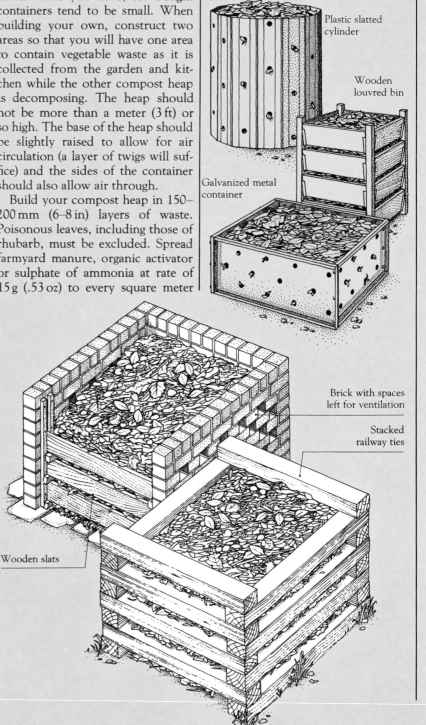

Plastic slatted cylinder

Wooden louvred bin

Galvanized metal container

Brick with spaces left for ventilation

Stacked railway ties

Wooden slats

APPENDIX

Plant lists and selection guides

Mortar mixes and concrete mixes

Paving coverages

Grass seed blends

Broad-leaved trees

The trees below are deciduous unless indicated evergreen. More than one entry under "size" in the selection guide indicates a wide size range.

Acer griseum (Paperbark Maple). Outstanding small tree for small properties. Shredding orange-red bark, compound foliage that colors to bright red and orange in late autumn.

Acer negundo (Box Elder). Spreading, open, fast-growing tree. Pinnate, irregularly-toothed leaves, which do not color in autumn. Drought- and cold-tolerant.

Acer platanoides (Norway Maple). Magnificent, round-headed, fast-growing tree. Sharply-lobed leaves turn yellow or red in autumn. Yellow flowers open April, before leaves.

Acer pseudoplatanus (Common Sycamore). Wide-spreading, densely-leaved tree. Deep green leaves.

Aesculus (Horse Chestnut). Handsome, wide-spreading, densely-leaved trees. Big, palmate leaves turn yellow in autumn. "Candles" of flowers in May. "Conkers" in autumn.

Ailanthus altissima (Tree of Heaven). Elegant, oval-headed tree with long, ash-like leaves. A "weed" tree but very useful in cities and at seashore.

Alnus (Alder). Fast-growing conical trees with leaves lasting long into autumn. Catkins in March before leaves, their buds conspicuous in winter.

Amelanchier canadensis (Shadblow). Lovely, round-headed tree, also grown as shrub. Leaves unfold pink and turn scarlet in autumn. Clusters of starry, white flowers in spring. Purple edible fruits ripen in July. Gray bark.

Betula (Birch). Graceful, open trees with white or brown bark in maturity. Yellow autumn leaves. Catkins in early spring.

Carpinus (Hornbeam). Beech-like forest trees. Beautiful gray, fluted bark. Strongly ribbed and toothed leaves, yellow in autumn, often persisting winter.

Catalpa bignonioides (Indian Bean Tree). Wide, low tree with big, heart-shaped leaves. White yellow and purple foxglove-like flowers, summer. Fruits like beans in autumn.

Cornus florida (Flowering Dogwood). Ever popular small tree with white or pink flowers in spring and autumn colors. Attractive winter form.

Crataegus (Hawthorn). Densely-leaved, very hardy trees. White flowers late spring. Profuse red berries lasting into winter.

Cytisus battandieri (Moroccan Broom). Open, many-branched tree with silky gray leaves, pineapple-scented flowers, July. For mild climates only.

Eucalyptus gunnii (Cider Gum). Fast, open, vertical tree with handsome bark. Silver-blue young foliage. Evergreen. For mild climates.

Fagus (Beech). Majestic, large-domed trees with silvery-gray bark. Leaves gold/copper in autumn as nuts produced.

Fraxinus (Ash). Open, fast trees with ascending branches. Pinnate leaves, green until they fall. Fruit ripens to brown in October and into winter.

Gleditsia Elegant foliage trees with barbed trunks and branches. Delicate, bipinnate leaves appear late and yellow in autumn. Most popular forms 'Moraine' and 'Sunburst'.

Koelreuteria paniculata (Goldenrain Tree). Rounded tree with long pinnate leaves, red in spring, turning slowly yellow, green and finally gold in autumn. Yellow midsummer flowers. Bladder-like fruit.

Laburnum (Golden Chain). Graceful trees with arching branches famed for their long racemes of bright yellow flowers, spring. Brown pods with poisonous black seeds.

Liquidambar styraciflua (Sweet Gum). Broad-domed handsome tree with maple-like leaves, which color richly in the autumn.

Liriodendron tulipifera (Tulip Tree). Fast, beautiful tree with distinctive squared-off leaves, gold in autumn. Mature trees have yellowish-green, tulip-shaped flowers.

Magnolia kobus Young trees cone-shaped, broader when mature. Shiny leaves. After 15 years, white, fragrant flowers appear profusely.

Malus (Flowering Crabs). Densely-crowned, wide trees with attractive pink/red/white flowers in spring. Some varieties color richly in autumn when most bear fruit which can be made into jelly.

Oxydendrum arboreum (Sourwood). Eastern USA native that is slow growing. Long lasting drooping "lily-of-the-valley" flowers in the summer.

Parrotia persica (Persian Ironwood). Wide trees with gray, peeling bark similar to the London plane's. Beech-like leaves, crimson/gold in autumn. Red, tufted flowers January/March before leaves.

Platanus (Plane). Particularly handsome, fast trees with high-domed crown. Distinctive flaking bark. Maple-like leaves sometimes color in autumn.

Populus (Poplar). Tall, slender trees ideal for screens. Young leaves red or bronze and often scented. Many have attractive catkins. Not to be placed near buildings due to thirsty roots.

Prunus cerasifera (Cherry Plum). Open tree with profuse small white flowers in February/March. Mature trees bear edible fruits.

Prunus dulcis (Almond). Open tree with ascending branches and pointed leaves. Large, pink flowers, March, before leaves. Nuts in autumn.

Prunus padus (Bird Cherry). Elegant tree, rounded in maturity with slender racemes of scented white flowers that appear in late May.

Prunus persica (Peach). Shrubby tree with pale pink flowers, April. Edible fruits. Must be sprayed against peach leaf curl and other pests.

Prunus serrulata (Japanese Cherry). Stiffly-branched tree with profusion of white or

Acer platanoides

Ailanthus altissima

Catalpa bignonioides

Eucalyptus gunnii

Gleditsia triacanthus

pink flowers in spring. Young leaves often bronze. Some forms color in autumn.

Pyrus (Pears). Very hardy, round-domed trees with plentiful white flowers, April. Apart from fruiting forms, there are ornamental varieties with good autumn color.

Quercus (Oak). Tall, wide, stately trees needing a lot of space. Some varieties color richly in autumn. Most produce acorns.

Robinia Very hardy, fast trees with light, open crown, noted for beautiful foliage (pinnate). Fragrant, white flowers in June.

Salix (Willow). Diverse, vigorous genus. Early slender leaves, often silvery. Many have colorful bark and stems in winter. Catkins.

Sorbus aria (Whitebeam). Compact tree with ascending branches. Attractive gray-green foliage turns red/gold autumn. White spring flowers. Conspicuous red berries.
Sorbus aucuparia (Rowan or Mountain Ash). Irregularly-shaped, oval-headed tree with delicate pinnate leaves and

Liquidambar styraciflua

Liriodendron tulipifera

Pyrus communis

Robinia pseudoacacia

Sorbus aria

SELECTION GUIDE
Broad-leaved trees

	SOIL TOLERANCE				LOCATION		SIZE			
	Acid	Alkaline	Well-drained	Damp	Full sun	Semi-shade	Over 60 ft	35–60 ft	15–35 ft	Provides dense shade
Acer griseum	●		●		●	●			●	
Acer negundo	●	●	●		●	●		●		
Acer platanoides		●	●		●	●	●			●
Acer pseudoplatanus	●	●	●	●	●	●	●			
Aesculus	●	●	●		●	●	●			
Ailanthus altissima		●	●		●	●	●			
Alnus	●	●		●	●	●	●			
Alemanchier lamarckii	●			●	●	●			●	
Betula	●	●	●		●	●		●		
Carpinus	●	●		●	●	●	●	●		
Catalpa bignonioides		●		●	●	●		●		●
Cornus florida	●		●	●	●	●			●	
Crataegus	●	●		●	●	●			●	
Cytisus battandieri	●	●	●		●				●	
Eucalyptus gunnii	●		●		●			●		
Fagus		●	●		●	●	●			●
Fraxinus	●	●	●		●	●	●			
Gleditsia	●	●	●		●	●		●	●	
Koelreuteria paniculata		●	●		●	●			●	
Laburnum		●	●		●	●			●	
Liquidambar styraciflua	●			●	●	●		●		●
Liriodendron tulipifera	●	●	●		●	●	●			
Magnolia kobus	●	●	●	●	●	●		●		
Malus	●	●	●	●	●	●		●		
Oxydendram arboreum	●		●	●	●	●	●			
Parrotia persica		●	●	●	●	●			●	
Platanus	●			●	●	●	●			●
Populus	●	●	●	●	●	●	●			
Prunus cerasifera	●	●	●		●	●			●	
Prunus dulcis	●	●	●		●	●			●	
Prunus padus	●	●	●	●	●	●		●		
Prunus persica	●	●	●		●	●			●	
Prunus serrulata	●	●	●		●	●			●	
Pyrus	●	●			●	●		●		
Quercus	●			●	●	●	●			●
Robinia		●	●		●	●		●		
Salix	●	●	●	●	●	●		●	●	
Sorbus aria	●	●	●		●	●			●	
Sorbus aucuparia	●	●	●		●	●			●	
Tilia	●	●			●	●	●	●	●	●
Ulmus	●	●			●	●	●		●	●

white, scented flowers in May. Bright autumn berries.

Tilia (Lime or Linden). Narrow-crowned trees with ascending branches and glossy, green, heart-shaped leaves. Scented yellow flowers hang in cymes, June.

Ulmus (Elm). Tall, elegant trees, now greatly reduced due to Dutch elm disease.

Conifers

My selection of conifers, below, is largely restricted to the larger growing genera. Forms of conifer are included in many other classifications.

Abies (Silver Fir). Handsome, conical trees whose name refers to their imposing, lofty stature. Erect cones, in some species blue when young. Dislikes pollution.

Cedrus (Cedar). Conical at first, spreads later. Huge trees with barrel-shaped cones. Leaves in rosettes, in some species blue or silvery-blue. There are dwarf forms.

Chamaecyparis (False Cypress). These differ in their flat branches and small cones from the true Cypress, which has rounded branches and large cones. A varied genus, often with attractive foliage. Recommended: the range of cvs of *C. lawsoniana*.

× Cupressocyparis varieties. Columnar, extremely vigorous trees, ideal as hedge or screen. Some have unusual and attractive leaf color.

Cupressus (Cypress). Handsome, conical trees with wide variety of colors.

Ginkgo biloba (Maidenhair Tree). The only survivor of a group of trees flourishing 200 million years ago. Beautiful, slow tree with lovely fan-shaped leaves, yellow in autumn. Long lived.

Juniperus (Juniper). Large genus. Most forms have gray-green berries and aromatic leaves, poisonous to cattle.

Larix (Larch). Fast, deciduous trees with bright green leaves in spring, yellow in autumn. Dense linear leaves.

Metasequoia (Dawn Redwood). Beautiful, conical, deciduous trees becoming rounder in maturity. Fern-like foliage, coloring pink and gold in autumn.

Picea (Spruce). Dense, conical trees with sharp, pointed leaves. Pendulous cones. Genus includes Christmas Tree.

Pinus (Pine). A large and varied genus with long, sharp leaves. Many forms have handsome, colored bark.

Taxodium distichum (Deciduous Cypress or Swamp Cypress). Conical trees with reddish bark. Feathery green foliage, bronze before falling.

Taxus baccata (Yew). Long-lived, dark green-leaved tree, particularly useful for hedges.

Tsuga canadensis (Canada Hemlock). Native over wide area of Northeast. Large, handsome tree with soft needles, small cones. Many dwarf forms.

Hedges

I have selected both deciduous and evergreen hedge plants below. The flowering species will only produce blooms if trimmed at the right time of year (see p. 252).

Berberis (Barberry). Large and varied genus of prickly shrubs, both evergreen and deciduous. Yellow/orange spring flowers. Most have autumn fruits.

Buxus (Box). *The evergreen hedge where winters are mild to moderate. B. sempervirens best but hardier forms exist.*

Abies alba

Ginkgo biloba

Metasequoia glyptostroboides

Taxodium plicata

Thuja plicata

SELECTION GUIDE
Conifers

	SOIL TOLERANCE				LOCATION			SIZE		
	Acid	Alkaline	Well-drained	Damp	Full sun	Semi-shade	Total shade	Over 60 ft	35–60 ft	15–35 ft
Abies	●	●		●	●	●		●	●	
Cedrus	●	●	●	●	●	●		●		
Chamaecyparis	●	●	●		●	●		●	●	
× Cupressocyparis	●	●	●	●	●	●		●		
Cupressus	●	●	●		●	●			●	
Ginkgo biloba	●	●	●		●			●		
Juniperus	●	●	●		●	●			●	●
Larix	●	●	●		●			●	●	
Metasequoia	●	●		●	●			●	●	
Picea	●	●	●	●	●			●		
Pinus	●	●	●			●	●	●	●	
Taxodium distichum	●			●	●	●		●		
Taxus baccata	●	●	●		●	●	●		●	●
Tsuga Canadensis	●	●	●	●	●	●		●		

SELECTION GUIDE
Hedges

	Soil Tolerance				Location			Size		
	Acid	Alkaline	Well-drained	Damp	Full sun	Semi-shade	Total shade	Over 10ft	5–10ft	3–5ft
Berberis	●	●	●		●	●		●	●	●
Buxus	●	●	●	●	●	●			●	●
Carpinus	●	●	●		●	●		●		
Cotoneaster	●	●	●		●	●	●	●	●	●
Escallonia		●	●		●				●	●
Euonymus	●	●	●			●	●	●	●	
Fagus		●	●		●	●		●		
Hebe		●	●		●	●			●	●
Hippophae	●	●	●	●	●			●	●	
Ilex	●	●	●	●	●	●	●	●	●	
Ligustrum	●	●	●	●	●	●	●	●	●	●
Lonicera	●	●	●		●	●		●	●	
Potentilla	●	●	●			●			●	●
Pittosporum	●	●	●		●	●		●		
Prunus laurocerasus	●	●	●	●		●	●	●		
Prunus lusitanica	●	●	●			●	●	●		
Pyracantha	●	●	●		●	●		●	●	
Rhamnus	●	●	●		●	●		●	●	
Syringa	●	●	●		●				●	
Coniferous hedges										
Chamaecyparis	●	●	●	●	●	●		●	●	
× Cupressocyparis	●	●	●	●	●	●		●	●	
Cupressus	●	●	●		●	●		●	●	
Taxus baccata	●	●	●		●	●	●	●	●	
Thuja occidentalis	●	●	●	●	●	●		●	●	

Berberis × stenophylla

Cotoneaster lacteus

Escallonia illinita

Euonymus alatus

Pyracantha 'Watereri'

Rosmarinus officinalis

Taxus baccata

Thuja occidentalis

Carpinus (Hornbeam). Deciduous trees whose yellow-brown, oval leaves remain throughout winter when clipped as hedge.

Cotoneaster These are deciduous and evergreen shrubs noted for spring flowers, bright berries and, in some forms, autumn foliage.

Escallonia Generally evergreen shrubs (semi-evergreen in colder districts) with profuse summer flowers. Good coastal plant in California.

Euonymus (Spindle). Most varied genus of evergreen and deciduous shrubs, often with conspicuous fruits and, in deciduous forms, provides autumn color.

Fagus (Beech). Deciduous tree useful as all-year screen. Retains brown leaves all winter as clipped hedge.

Hebe (Veronica). Slightly tender evergreen shrub with plentiful flowers carried in small spikes through summer.

Hippophae Silver or sage-green-leaved shrubs with profuse berries throughout winter. Ideal on coast.

Ilex (Holly). Prickly, evergreen genus, many forms with bright berries. Most are tender.

Ligustrum (Privet). Either evergreen or semi-evergreen fast-growing shrubs. Grow in all conditions.

Lonicera (Honeysuckle). Dense, evergreen and deciduous shrubs of the same family as the better-known climbers. All have fragrant, usually cream, flowers.

Pittosporum Dense, evergreen shrubs; elegant, oval foliage. Small, fragrant flowers in May.

Pontentilla (Cinquefoil). Compact, long-flowering shrubs with pretty, white/red/orange/yellow flowers.

Prunus laurocerasus (Cherry Laurel). Vigorous evergreen shrubs with glossy leaves, white spring flowers and black fruits. Good for shade, tender.

Prunus lusitanica (Portuguese Laurel). Similar to Cherry Laurel, with purple fruits and, though hardier good in shade.

Pyracantha (Firethorn). Handsome, thorny evergreens with white spring flowers and profuse red/orange/yellow autumn berries.

Rhamnus frangula 'Columnaris' (Tallhedge). A superior deciduous hedge plant because of its hardiness, fast growth and neat form. Does not need as much pruning as privet.

Syringa (Lilac). Where space is ample the common lilac makes an informal screen and windbreak.

265

Coniferous hedges

Chamaecyparis (False Cypress). Hardy genus with fan-like foliage. *See Conifers*

× **Cupressocyparis** varieties. Adaptable, very vigorous. × C. *Leylandii* is fast growing in Washington, D. C. area.

Cupressus (Cypress). Fast-growing genus, including forms with blue-gray, green, gold and blue foliage.

Taxus baccata (Yew). Slow tree, excellent as clipped hedge, with dark green foliage (there are also gold and variegated forms). Poisonous seeds.

Thuja occidentalis (American Arborvitae). Adaptable tree which makes good, thick hedging. Foliage forming fan-like sprays.

Shrubs

My selection of shrubs provides a range of mild climate as well as hardy kinds. Note the column denoting "architectural form" in the selection guide.

Abelia × **grandiflora** Graceful shrub with glossy, green leaves and abundant, tubular, white/pink flowers, late summer.

Acacia dealbata (Mimosa). Beautiful shrub with fern-like foliage and yellow, fragrant flowers, winter. Tender and requires considerable protection from frost.

Acer japonicum Handsome shrubs with palmate leaves. Glorious purplish-red autumn color. Recommended: A. *j.* 'Aureum' a slow-growing form with soft yellow leaves growing to form a rounded bush.

Acer palmatum (Japanese Maple). Similar to *Acer japonicum* with elegant, 5/7-lobed leaves, splendid purplish-red autumn colors. Recommended: *Dissectum* group, all having deeply-cut leaves and dense, round habit. Green, purple or bronze-tinted leaves, all with autumn color.

Aesculus parviflora A shrubby relative of the Horse Chestnut, with similar leaves. White "candles" with red anthers, late summer.

Amelanchier canadensis *See Trees.*

Aralia elata (Japanese Angelica Tree). Spiny, many-stemmed shrub with huge, palm-like leaves. White flowers in plumes show through autumn. Often treelike.

Arbutus (Strawberry Tree). Evergreens with white, pitcher-shaped flowers and red, strawberry-like fruits. Recommended: A. *unedo* bears flowers and fruits simultaneously in autumn.

Aronia arbutifolia (Red Chokeberry). Hardy, dependable, tolerant of moist soil. Red berries, leaves in autumn.

Arundinaria (Bamboo). Fine evergreens for shade. Recommended: A. *nitida* has arching, purple canes, contrasting well with delicate, narrow leaves that rattle in the wind.

Aucuba japonica Handsome, rounded evergreens with red berries. Some forms have attractive gold-splashed foliage.

Berberis A variable genus with evergreen and deciduous members, noted for its profuse flowers (usually yellow) and autumn berries. Evergreens are spiny and have dense, glossy leaves. Deciduous forms have fine autumn foliage. Recommended: B. *thunbergii* 'Rose Glow'. Leaves start purple, turning silver-pink, then purple again. Deciduous.

Buddleia (Butterfly Bush). Graceful shrubs, whose long racemes of scented flowers (June/July) attract butterflies. Recommended: B. *davidii* offers red, white, violet or blue flowers; B. *fallowiana* 'Alba' has silver-gray leaves and highly-scented white flowers with an orange eye. Tender.

Camellia japonica Beautiful, evergreen, winter/spring-flowering shrubs. Glossy green leaves and sumptuous flowers. Hardy, to Washington, D.C. and like climates.

Caryopteris (Blue Spiraea). Aromatic, gray-green, low shrubs with blue flowers in late summer. Recommended: C. × *clandonensis*, hybrid with several cultivars.

Ceanothus (Californian Lilac). Large family of evergreen and deciduous shrubs, usually with bright blue flowers from July onwards. Recommended: C. *thyrsiflorus repens* is mound-forming ground cover with light blue flowers. Tender.

Ceratostigma (Hardy Plumbago). Autumn-flowering, low shrub with blue flowers and often rich autumn foliage color. Recommended: C. *willmottianum.*

Cercis siliquastrum (Judas Tree). Slow-growing, half-hardy large shrub with pink pea-flowers, spring. Red seed pods from July. According to legend, the tree from which Judas hanged himself.

Chaenomeles (Japonica or Flowering Quince). Very hardy, spiny shrubs invaluable for their lovely, very early flowers. Recommended: C. 'Cameo', which has apricot flowers.

Chimonanthus (Winter Sweet). Sweetly-scented, winter-flowering shrubs. For mild climates. Recommended: C. *praecox* has yellow flowers with purple or red centers.

Choisya ternata (Mexican Orange Blossom). Glossy, aromatic, tender evergreen shrub with fragrant, white flowers, late spring.

Cistus (Sun Rose). Half-hardy, evergreen shrubs with masses of very pretty, short-lived, saucer-shaped flowers. Recommended: C × *corbariensis* is a hybrid form with crimson-ringed buds, opening white.

Clethra alnifolia (Summersweet). Very hardy native shrub with fragrant white flower panicles in summer.

Cordyline australis (Cabbage Tree). Palm-like evergreen with trunk and long, sword-like leaves. Small, scented, cream flowers, summer. Tender.

Cornus (Dogwood). Large, mainly deciduous family. Attractive foliage, often richly colored in autumn, and bright stems through winter. Recommended: C. *stolonifera* 'Flaviramea' has yellow stems, white flowers.

Arbutus unedo

Aucuba japonica

Choisya ternata

Cotoneaster horizontalis

Euonymus japonica

Cortaderia (Pampas Grass). Evergreen perennial with tall autumn plumes and arching, narrow leaves. Recommended: *C. argentea* has silvery-white plumes.

Cotinus (Smoke Tree). Handsome, foliage shrubs with rich autumn colors. Best in poor soil. Recommended: *C. coggygria* has smooth, green leaves and fawn/pink, wispy inflorescences in summer.

Cotoneaster *See Trees and Hedges* Mainly evergreen genus. Recommended: *C. horizontalis* 'Variegatus' is a ground cover form with spreading, "herringbone" branches, small, cream, variegated leaves, bright fruit and autumn foliage.

Cytisus (Broom). Free-flowering shrubs with yellow, pea-shaped flowers, spring. Recommended: *C. scoparius* includes many unusual colors.

Daphne Very fragrant, deciduous and evergreen shrubs, spring flowering. Recommended: *D. odora aureomarginata* has early, purple-pink flowers and large, lanceolate leaves which are variegated yellow and green.

Deutzia Pretty, June-flowering shrubs with narrow leaves and profuse clusters of white flowers along stems. Recommended: *D. discolor* has scented, rose-tinted flowers.

Elaeagnus Vigorous, very hardy, deciduous and evergreen shrubs with small, fragrant flowers and fine foliage. Recommended: *E. ebbingei* has silvery flowers, autumn, orange, silver-speckled fruits, spring.

Escallonia *See Hedges* Recommended: *E.* 'Iveyi' has large, glossy leaves and white autumn flowers. Not hardy.

Eucalyptus gunnii *See Trees*

Enkianthus campanulatus (Red-vein Enkianthus). Hardy, elegant shrub. Background or specimen. Red autumn color.

Euonymus *See Hedges* Tender. Recommended: *E. alata* has corky, winged branches and good autumn color; *E.*

fortunei is evergreen ground cover with some lovely variegated forms.

Fatsia japonica Exotic-looking evergreen with large, palmate leaves and globular, cream flowers on stalks. Not hardy.

Forsythia Hardy shrubs with plentiful, golden-yellow flowers in early spring on bare branches. Recommended: *F. suspensa* is a vigorous, handsome wall shrub.

Fothergilla. Southeastern natives hardy to Boston. Fuzzy white flowers in spring. Fragrant. Good autumn leaf color. Use in woodland garden.

Fuchsia Hardy summer/autumn flowering shrubs with handsome, pendulous blooms. Recommended: *F.* garden hyb. 'Riccartonii' has scarlet and purple flowers.

Garrya elliptica Graceful evergreen with handsome, midwinter catkins on male plants. Vigorous. Not hardy.

Gaultheria Evergreen ground cover with white, urn-shaped flowers, spring/summer. Recommended: *G. procumbens* has bright red autumn berries.

Genista Broom-like shrubs with yellow, summer flowers. Recommended: *G. aetnensis* is a vigorous, free-flowering form to 6 m high.

Griselinia littoralis Leathery-leaved evergreen, not hardy. Small, green flowers and apple-green leaves. Some variegated forms.

Hamamelis (Witch-hazel). Lovely shrubs with fragrant, spidery winter flowers. Usually fine autumn foliage. Recommended: *H. mollis* 'Pallida' has dense clusters of sulphur-yellow flowers.

Hibiscus Syriacus (Rose of Sharon) Splendid, hardy summer/autumn-flowering shrubs with hollyhock-like flowers of blue, red or white. The last color is particularly recommended.

Hippophae *See Hedges* Recommended: *H. rhamnoides*

has masses of orange-red berries and silver leaves.

Hydrangea Varied genus with domed or flat flowering heads. Pink, red, blue or white flowers, summer/autumn. Recommended: *H. villosa* (Lacecap) has large lilac-blue flowers. Also *H. serrata*.

Hypericum (St. John's Wort). Evergreen, deciduous shrubs with bright yellow flowers, summer/autumn. Recommended: *H. androsaenum* has black berries and often good autumn color.

Ilex (Holly) *See Hedges* Recommended: *I. aquifolium* includes variegated forms and interesting berry colors.

Kalmia latifolia (Mountain-laurel). Outstanding native evergreen noted for late spring flowers. Prefers part shade and needs acid soil.

Kerria japonica Attractive shrubs with bright yellow, buttercup-like flowers on arching stems. Recommended: *K. j.* 'Variegata' has creamy-white variegated leaves.

Kolkwitzia amabilis (Beauty Bush). Hardy, dependable. A fountain of beauty in early summer with its pink flowers. Pretty, soft green foliage.

Laurus nobilis (Sweet Bay). Aromatic, oval-leaved evergreens with small, yellow flowers, April. Not hardy.

Ligustrum (Privet) *See Hedges.* Recommended: *L. ovalifolium aureum* has rich yellow leaves with green blotch, semi-evergreen.

Lonicera (Honeysuckle) *See Hedges* Recommended: *L. nitida* 'Baggensen's Gold' has gold-yellow leaves, turning greenish in autumn.

Magnolia Varied genus with evergreen and deciduous forms and magnificent flowers. Recommended: *M. grandiflora* has long, glossy leaves and big, scented, cream flowers, summer/autumn.

Mahonia Prickly, compound-leaved evergreens with racemes of fragrant yellow, winter flowers. Blue/black berries.

Garrya elliptica

Griselinia littoralis

Kerria japonica

Laurus nobilis

Ligustrum ovalifolium

APPENDIX

Foliage burns in winter north of Washington, D.C.

Myrica pensylvanica (Bayberry). Leathery aromatic foliage that gives a billowy effect. Gray berries. Seaside subject.

Myrtus communis (Myrtle). Aromatic, tender leafy evergreens with profuse, white summer flowers and purple berries. *M.c. lechleriana* has white berries.

Nandina domestica (Sacred Bamboo). Erect shrub with white summer flowers and red autumn berries. Pinnate foliage crimson in spring and autumn. Half hardy.

Pachysandra terminalis Evergreen ground cover with diamond-shaped leaves and greenish-white winter flowers.

Paeonia (Tree Paeony). Handsome foliage shrubs with glorious flowers when established. Recommended: *P. lutea ludlowii* has saucer-shaped, golden flowers. May/June.

Parrotia persica *See Trees*

Pernettya mucronata Evergreen ground cover with profuse, white spring flowers and white berries. Some forms have pink/red berries.

Perovskia Aromatic shrubs with gray, deeply-cut foliage and panicles of blue flowers, autumn. Recommended: *P. atriplicifolia* 'Blue Spire'.

Philadelphus (Mock Orange). Invaluable, fragrant, white-flowered shrubs. Recommended: *P. coronarius* has richly-scented summer flowers, and some variegated forms with cream-margined green leaves.

Phlomis fruticosa Semi-evergreen shrubs, like giant sage. Bright yellow flowers, late summer. Tender.

Phormium tenax Handsome evergreens with sword-like leaves and bronze-red flowers in panicles, late summer. There is a form with bronze-purple leaves. A New Zealand native for California and like climates.

SELECTION GUIDE — Shrubs

	SOIL TOLERANCE				LOCATION			SIZE			
	Acid	Alkaline	Well-drained	Damp	Full sun	Semi-shade	Total shade	Over 10ft	5–10ft	Under 5ft	Architectural form
Abelia × grandiflora	●	●	●		●				●	●	
Acacia dealbata	●		●		●			●			●
Acer japonicum	●		●		●	●		●		●	●
Acer palmatum	●		●		●	●		●		●	●
Aesculus parviflora	●	●	●		●	●		●			●
Amelanchier canadensis	●			●	●	●		●			
Aralia elata	●	●	●		●			●			
Arbutus		●	●	●	●			●			●
Aronia arbutifolia	●			●	●	●			●	●	
Arundinaria	●	●	●	●		●	●	●			●
Aucuba japonica	●	●	●		●	●	●	●	●	●	●
Berberis	●	●	●		●	●		●	●	●	
Buddleia	●	●	●	●	●	●		●	●		
Camellia japonica	●			●		●	●		●		●
Caryopteris		●	●		●	●				●	
Ceanothus		●	●		●				●	●	
Ceratostigma		●	●		●					●	
Cercis siliquastrum		●	●		●			●			●
Chaenomeles	●	●	●		●	●			●	●	
Chimonanthus		●	●		●					●	
Choisya ternata	●	●	●		●	●	●		●		
Cistus		●	●		●				●	●	
Clethra alnifolia	●			●	●	●			●		
Cordyline australis	●	●	●		●	●		●			●
Cornus	●	●	●	●		●	●	●	●		
Cortaderia	●	●	●	●		●	●	●	●		
Cotinus		●	●		●	●		●	●		●
Cotoneaster	●	●	●	●		●	●	●	●	●	
Cytisus	●	●	●		●			●	●	●	
Daphne		●	●		●	●				●	
Deutzia	●	●	●		●	●			●	●	
Elaeagnus	●	●	●		●			●	●		
Escallonia		●	●		●			●	●	●	
Eucalyptus gunnii	●	●	●	●	●			●			●
Enkianthus campanulatus	●		●	●		●		●			●
Euonymus	●	●	●		●	●		●	●	●	
Fatsia japonica	●	●	●							●	
Forsythia	●	●	●	●	●	●		●			
Fothergilla	●		●			●		●		●	
Fuchsia		●	●		●	●			●	●	
Garrya elliptica	●	●	●	●	●	●		●			●
Gaultheria	●	●	●	●	●	●				●	
Genista	●	●	●		●			●			
Griselinia littoralis		●	●		●			●			●
Hamamelis	●		●		●	●		●			●
Hibiscus		●	●		●			●	●		
Hippophae	●	●	●	●	●			●			●
Hydrangea	●	●		●		●	●	●	●	●	

	SOIL TOLERANCE				LOCATION			SIZE			
	Acid	Alkaline	Well-drained	Damp	Full sun	Semi-shade	Total shade	Over 10ft	5–10ft	Under 5ft	Architectural form
Hypericum	•	•	•	•	•	•			•	•	
Ilex	•	•	•			•	•	•	•		•
Kalmia latifolia	•		•	•	•	•			•	•	
Kerria	•	•	•	•	•				•	•	
Kolkwitzia amabilis	•	•	•		•			•			•
Laurus nobilis	•	•	•		•				•		•
Ligustrum	•	•	•	•	•	•	•	•	•	•	
Lonicera	•	•	•	•	•				•	•	
Magnolia	•	•	•	•	•			•	•		•
Mahonia	•	•	•		•	•			•	•	•
Myrtus communis		•	•		•				•	•	•
Nandina domestica		•	•		•					•	•
Pachysandra terminalis	•	•		•			•			•	
Paeonia		•	•	•	•				•		
Parrotia persica	•		•		•	•		•			•
Pernettya mucronata	•		•				•			•	•
Perovskia		•	•		•					•	•
Philadelphus	•	•	•		•	•			•	•	
Phlomis fruticosa		•	•		•					•	•
Phormium tenax		•	•		•				•		•
Pieris	•		•	•		•			•		
Pittosporum	•	•	•		•			•			•
Potentilla	•	•	•		•	•	•		•	•	
Prunus	•	•	•	•	•	•		•	•	•	
Pyracantha	•	•	•	•	•	•		•	•		
Rhamnus alaterna	•	•	•	•	•	•	•	•	•	•	•
Rhododendron (inc. Azalea)	•			•	•	•	•		•	•	
Rhus typhina	•	•	•		•	•			•		•
Romneya		•	•		•				•	•	
Rosa	•	•	•	•	•	•			•	•	
Rosmarinus		•	•		•				•	•	
Rubus	•	•	•	•	•				•	•	
Ruta graveolens		•	•		•					•	•
Salix	•	•	•	•	•			•	•	•	
Sambucus	•	•	•	•	•	•			•	•	
Santolina		•	•		•					•	
Sarcococca humilis	•	•	•			•	•			•	•
Skimmia japonica	•	•	•		•	•	•			•	•
Spartium junceum	•	•	•		•				•		•
Spiraea	•	•	•		•					•	
Stephanandra incisa	•	•	•		•	•			•	•	•
Symphoricarpus	•	•	•	•	•	•			•	•	
Syringa	•	•	•		•				•	•	
Teucrum fruticans		•	•		•				•	•	
Ulex europaeus		•	•		•				•	•	
Viburnum	•	•	•	•	•	•			•	•	
Vinca	•	•	•			•				•	
Weigela	•	•	•		•	•			•	•	
Yucca		•	•		•				•	•	•

Pieris Lovely evergreens with white lily-of-the-valley-type flowers in spring. Bright red young foliage. Recommended: P. 'Forest Flame', leaves turn red, pink, cream, green. P. floribunda most hardy.

Pittosporum See Hedges Recommended: P. tenuifolium has dark purple, honey-scented spring flowers. Not hardy.

Potentilla See Hedges Recommended: P. fruticosa.

Prunus laurocerasus Prunus lusitanica See Hedges

Pyracantha See Hedges Recommended: P. angustifolia, orange-yellow berries all winter; P. crenato-serrata.

Rhamnus alaterna Narrow, densely glossy evergreens with yellowish-green flowers and red fruits. Hardy to Washington, D.C.

Rhododendron (including **Azalea**) Huge group of beautiful deciduous and evergreen shrubs with glorious flowers. Some have fine foliage and some deciduous forms have autumn color. Recommended: Azalea pontica (Rhododendron luteum) has funnel-shaped, fragrant, yellow flowers, May, and fine autumn color; A. 'Palestrina' is an evergreen, flowers white with faint green stripes.

Rhus typhina (Stag's Horn Sumach). Easily-grown shrub with fine pinnate foliage and glorious autumn color. Dark red spikes of fruit persist all winter.

Romneya (Californian Tree Poppy). Fine foliage shrubs with large, white, late summer flowers with gold stamens. Slow to establish and needs protection. Recommended: R × hybrida, more vigorous.

Rosa (Shrub Rose). Easily cultivated, very varied shrubs which can offer abundant flowers over a long season, decorative foliage and colorful hips. Broadly divided into modern garden, old garden and wild types.

Rosmarinus See Hedges Recommended: R. officinalis

has a dense habit and gray-green leaves. Tender.

Rubus (Ornamental Bramble). Prickly, deciduous and evergreen shrubs, offering attractive foliage and flowers. Fruits edible but generally flavorless. Recommended: *R. × tridel* 'Benenden' is a vigorous, spineless, arching form to 3 m (10 ft) with large, white, scented flowers, May.

Ruta graveolens (Rue). Low, aromatic evergreen with fern-like leaves and small, yellow summer flowers.

Salix *S. purpurea* 'Nana' is a very low-growing form with blue leaves.

Sambucus (Elder). Handsome foliage/fruit shrubs with ornamental pinnate leaves. Recommended: *S. nigra* 'Aurea' has cream flowers, June, black berries, autumn.

Santolina (Cotton Lavender). Delicate, silvery evergreens with button, yellow flowers, July. Half hardy. Recommended: *S. virens* has vivid green, filigree leaves.

Sarcococca humilis Dense, evergreen ground cover with glossy foliage and small, white, fragrant flowers in winter.

Skimmia japonica Easily-grown, ornamental evergreens with white fragrant spring flowers and bright red fruits on female plants.

Spartium junceum (Spanish Broom). Almost leafless, rushlike stems bears fragrant, yellow pea-flowers all summer.

Spiraea (Spirea). Large genus with white, pink or rose flowers, mostly in summer. *S. × arguta* is very hardy, bears white garlands of shortlived flowers in spring.

Stephanandra incisa (Cutleaf Stephanandra). 'Crispa' is low-growing, mounding, with indifferent flowers but fernlike foliage. Fine on banks.

Symphoricarpus Range of ornamental shrubs with white/pink berries, autumn/winter. Recommended: *S. × doorenbosii* 'White Hedge' is vigorous.

Syringa (Lilac). Lovely, spring-flowering shrubs, often fragrant. Recommended: *S. vulgaris* 'Miss Ellen Willmott' has large panicles of scented, pure white flowers.

Teucrium fruticans (Shrubby Germander). Tender evergreen with terminal racemes of pale blue flowers in summer.

Ulex europaeus (Gorse). Spiky, dense shrub, ablaze with golden flowers in spring and intermittently thereafter.

Viburnum Evergreens have ornamental leaves, deciduous have rich autumn color. Fragrant, white and/or pink flowers. Recommended: *V. × carlcephalum*, white fragrant flowers in spring; *V. × burkwoodii* (evergreen), dark shiny leaves and flowers January–May; *V. davidii* (evergreen), bright turquoise berries when grown in groups; *V. plicatum*, double rows of florets May/June; *V. rhytidophyllum* is a vigorous form with red fruits, turning black; *V. tinus* has metallic blue berries.

Vinca (Periwinkle). Evergreen ground cover with blue flowers. Recommended: *V. minor* has bright blue flowers, spring then intermittently.

Weigela Shrubs with fresh green leaves and funnel-shaped flowers June/July. Recommended: *W. florida* 'Eva Supreme' has a compact habit with attractive leaves and deep red flowers.

Yucca Arresting, half-hardy shrub with sword-like leaves and spectacular panicles of cream-white flowers, late summer. Recommended: *V. gloriosa* has a trunk-like stem and sharp leaves.

Perennials

By the term "perennials" most gardeners refer to the hardy herbaceous perennials used in borders and mixed planting schemes. My selection emphasizes "architectural form" and color.

Acanthus (Bear's Breeches). Stately plants with dark green, deeply-cut leaves

and mauve, white-lipped summer flowers. Recommended: *A. mollis*.

Achillea (Yarrow). Yellow, flat flowering heads and feathery, pungent leaves (60–80 cm/24–30 in). *A. millefolium* 'Moonshine' has clear yellow flowers, May–August, and silver foliage.

Agapanthus (African Lily). Clumps of long, slender leaves with 80 cm (30 in) flower stems towering above them. Blue/white, lily-like flowers, July/August. Not hardy. In North store in cool, frost-free room over winter.

Alchemilla (Lady's Mantle). Mounds of lovely, gray-green leaves and feathery sprays of yellow-green, starry flowers (30 cm/12 in). Recommended: *A. mollis*.

Anemone japonica (× hybrida) (Japanese Anemone). Clumps of dark green, vine-like foliage and lovely autumn flowers in white or pink (60–90 cm/2–3 ft). Recommended: *A.j.* 'September Charm'.

Anthemis Parsley-like leaves, daisy-like white/yellow flowers, summer (75 cm/30 in). Recommended: 'Moonlight' has yellow flowers.

Artemisia (Wormwood). Silver, fern-like foliage and insignificant flowers, late summer (60 cm–1.5 m/2–5 ft). Recommended: *A. ludoviciana* 'Silver King'.

Aster Late summer-flowering, bushy plants (30 cm–1.2 m/1–4 ft). Blue/pink, daisy flowers, including Michaelmas Daisies. Recommended: *A. amellus* 'Triumph' has light blue flowers and low, woody stems.

Bergenia (Elephant's Ears). Round, evergreen leaves. Spikes of pink/white flowers, (30–45 cm/12–18 in). Recommended: *B.* 'Silberlicht' is slightly smaller and has white flowers. Autumn foliage is tinged pink.

Brunnera macrophylla Blue, flowers like forget-me-nots, through spring/summer. Large, soft heart-shaped leaves. Good ground cover (45 cm/18 in).

Pyracantha atalantoides

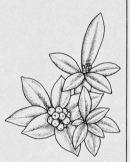

Skimmia japonica

Viburnum opulus

Campanula (Bellflower). Large genus of lovely plants with purple/blue/white funnel or bell-shaped flowers, summer (15 cm–1.5 m/½–5 ft). Recommended: *C. latifolia* has long blue funnels of flowers, July, and is one of the tallest varieties; *C. l. alba*, white flowers.

Chrysanthemum Very varied, summer-flowering (60–90 cm/ 24–36 in). Single or double daisy flowers, toothed leaves. Recommended: *C. uliginosum.*

Crambe Big (1.8 m/6 ft), eye-catching plant with huge, dark, limp leaves and clouds of white, scented, starry flowers, summer. Recommended: *C. cordifolia.*

Cynara Tall (1.8 m/6 ft), handsome, purple flowers, late summer, and gray, decorative foliage. Tender. Recommended: *C. cardunculus.*

Dianthus (Pink). Pretty, carnation-like flowers with bluish foliage (15–45 cm/ 6–18 in). Recommended: *D. deltoides* has scarlet/pink/white flowers.

Dierama Half-hardy plant with sprays of pink, summer flowers and long, rush-like leaves (75–90 cm/2½–3 ft).

Digitalis (Foxglove). Tall spikes (60 cm–1.5 m/2–5 ft) of trumpet-like, pink/purple flowers. Recommended: *D. ambigua* has soft, yellow flowers. Short lived. Self sows.

Echinops (Globe Thistle). Prickly plants with statuesque, round, blue flowers, summer (1–1.4 m/3–4½ ft). *E. ritro* has steel-blue flowers.

Euphorbia (Spurge). Bushy plants (15 cm–1 m/½–3 ft) with greenish/yellowish flowering heads, spring. Recommended: *E. wulfenii* has handsome, glaucous foliage.

Gaillardia Hardy with yellow/ orange/brownish-red, daisy flowers, profuse all summer (90 cm/35½ in).

Geranium (Cranesbill). Indented foliage and plentiful, blue/pink, spring/summer flowers (45–90 cm/18–35 in).

SELECTION GUIDE **Perennials**	SOIL TOLERANCE				LOCATION		
	Acid	Alkaline	Well-drained	Damp	Full sun	Accepts shade	Architectural form
Acanthus	●	●	●		●	●	●
Achillea	●	●	●		●		●
Agapanthus	●	●	●		●		●
Alchemilla	●	●	●	●	●	●	
Anemone japonica	●	●	●		●	●	●
Anthemis	●	●	●		●		
Artemisia	●	●	●		●	●	●
Aster	●	●	●		●		
Bergenia	●	●	●			●	●
Brunnera	●	●	●			●	
Campanula	●	●	●	●	●	●	
Chrysanthemum	●	●	●		●		
Crambe	●	●	●	●	●		●
Cynara	●	●	●		●		●
Dianthus	●	●	●		●		
Dierama	●	●	●	●	●		
Digitalis	●	●	●	●	●	●	
Echinops	●	●	●		●		●
Euphorbia	●	●	●	●	●	●	●
Gaillardia	●	●	●		●		
Geranium	●	●	●	●	●	●	
Helenium	●	●	●	●	●		
Helleborus	●	●	●			●	●
Hemerocallis	●	●	●	●	●	●	
Hosta	●	●	●	●		●	●
Iris	●	●	●	●	●	●	●
Kniphofia	●	●	●		●		●
Lavandula	●	●	●		●		
Ligularia	●	●	●	●	●	●	
Macleaya	●	●	●		●		●
Oenothera	●	●	●		●		
Paeonia	●	●	●	●	●	●	●
Papaver	●	●	●		●		
Phlox	●	●	●	●		●	
Rheum	●	●	●	●	●		●
Rudbeckia	●	●	●		●		
Salvia	●	●	●		●		●
Sedum	●	●	●		●		
Sisyrinchium	●	●	●		●		●
Stachys	●	●	●		●		
Veronica	●	●	●	●	●		
Zantedeschia	●	●	●	●	●	●	●
Grasses							
Arundo	●	●	●	●	●		●
Carex	●	●	●	●	●		●
Festuca	●	●	●		●		●
Helictotrichon	●	●	●		●	●	●
Lasiagrostis	●	●	●		●	●	●
Miscanthus	●	●	●	●	●		●
Pennisetum	●	●	●		●		●
Stipa	●	●	●		●	●	●

Acanthus mollis

Agapanthus umbellatus

Crambe cordifolia

Dierama pendulum

Macleaya cordata

Helenium (Sneezewort). Useful daisy-like, summer and early autumn flowers with pronounced centers, yellow/orange/copper/mahogany. The last is particularly recommended (60–90 cm/24–36 in).

Helleborus Fascinating family of winter/early spring-flowering plants with attractive foliage (30–60 cm/12–24 in). Recommended: *H. corsicus* has pale green flowers, February; *H. orientalis* (Lenten Rose) has white/pink/purple flowers, November/March.

Hemerocallis (Day Lily). Mound of strap-like, bright green leaves and, above, plentiful though short-lived, lily-like flowers, red/orange/yellow (60–90 cm/24–36 in).

Hosta (Plaintain Lily). Beautiful foliage plants (60–120 cm/2–4 ft) with lily-like flowers, summer. Recommended: *H. plantaginea* has fragrant, white flowers; *H. sieboldiana* has bluish-gray leaves and lilac-white flowers.

Iris A vast range of glorious flowers generally blue/purple/white but also pink, red and copper in bearded varieties. There are many worthy species but most practical for today's gardens are Siberian, Japanese and bearded types.

Kniphofia (Red-hot Poker). Striking, red/orange flowers, summer/autumn, above grass-like mounds of evergreen leaves (60 cm–1.8 m/2–6 ft). Slightly tender. Recommended: *K.* 'Springtime' has yellow flowers with red tips.

Lavandula (Lavender). Evergreens with fragrant, blue or purple flowers in spikes, summer. Recommended: *L. angustifolia* 'Munstead' has dark blue flowers.

Ligularia (Ragwort). Vigorous, sturdy plants with bright yellow/orange flowers, summer (60 cm–1.5 m/2–5 ft). Recommended: *L. dentata* has huge leaves and daisy-like flowers.

Macleaya Tall (1.8 m/6 ft) plants with gray, lobed leaves and plumes of buff flowers. Recommended: *M. cordata*.

Oenothera (Evening Primrose). Bright spring shoots and saucer-shaped, yellow summer flowers (20–45 cm/8–18 in). Recommended: *O. cinaeus* has bronze-pink shoots.

Paeonia (Peony). Glorious spring flowers, attractive foliage (60–90 cm/2–4 ft). *P. mlokosewitschii* has yellow flowers, April.

Papaver (Poppy). Deeply-cut, usually hairy foliage and big, fiery flowers (60–90 cm/2–3 ft). Recommended: *P.* 'May Sadler'.

Phlox Broad panicles of bright flowers all summer (60–90 cm/2–3 ft). Recommended: *P. divaricata* has pointed leaves and fragrant, lilac flowers, in spring.

Rheum Tall (1.5 m/5 ft), red flower spikes, early summer. Deeply-cut foliage. Recommended: *R. palmatum* 'Rubrum' has young leaves, pink/purple, green later.

Rudbeckia (Coneflower). Drooping-petalled, yellow/orange, late summer flowers (60 cm/2 ft). Recommended: *R.* 'Goldsturm'.

Salvia officinalis (Sage). Aromatic, semi-evergreen herb with blue flowers in whorls, summer. Variegated forms include *S. o.* 'Tricolor'.

Sedum (Iceplant). Glaucous, fleshy foliage plants (30–60 cm/1–2 ft), with broad flowering heads, pink/yellow. Recommended: *S. maximum atropurpureum* has maroon leaves and dark pink flowers, autumn.

Stachys Evergreen ground cover with woolly leaves and pink/purple/white flowers, summer (30–60 cm/1–2 ft). *S. lanata* (Lamb's Ears) has silvery leaves and small, pink flowers.

Veronica (Speedwell). Blue spikes flower for long summer season above leaf mats/mounds (30–60 cm/1–3 ft). Recommended: *V. spicata*.

Zantedeschia (Arum Lily). Beautiful, white/yellow/red, spring flowers, tender. Can be grown in water. Recommended: *Z. aethiopica* has dark, arrow-shaped leaves.

Grasses

Arundo Magnificent form, with bamboo-like stems and large, arching leaves. Recommended: *A. donax* is one of the longest of the grasses (1 m/3 ft). Native to S. Europe. Clump forming, non-invasive.

Carex Striped, gold-green evergreen leaves. Flowers in spikes (30–90 cm/1–3 ft).

Festuca Blue, dainty grass, erect growth. Recommended: *F. amethystina* is a densely-tufted perennial, grayish blue/green (up to 45 cm/18 in).

Helictotrichon sempervirens Blue clumps with flower spikes above, June (75 cm/30 in).

Lasiagrostis Handsome, buff-colored plumes with clumpy growth (90 cm/3 ft). Recommended: *L. splendens* is one of the largest species (2 m/6½ ft); drought resistant, evergreen perennial. Purplish flowers May–July.

Miscanthus Upright, slow-spreading grasses (1 m/3–5 ft). *M. sinensis* has narrow, graceful leaves with a white central stripe.

Pennisetum Soft, gray-white leaves below flower spikes (30–90 cm/1–3 ft). *P. orientale* has purple-green flowers, late summer.

Stipa Handsome plumes above dark evergreen foliage (90 cm/3 ft). *S. gigantea* has purple plumes, turning golden. Gray foliage.

Annuals

Annuals are those plants that are planted afresh in the spring. Examples from my selection, below, will infill mixed borders and decorate boxes and hanging baskets.

Ageratum Superb bedding plants, generally blue (some pink), fluffy flower heads and soft, hairy leaves (23 cm/9 in).

Alyssum (Lebularia). Edging plants with profuse white/purple summer flowers. Recommended: 'Carpet of Snow', (4 in).

Paeonia mlokosewitschii

Sisyrinchium striatum

Arundo donax

Pennisetum orientale

Antirrhinum (Snapdragon). Bright, often bi-colored, half-hardy bedding plants with dark, narrow leaves (30–90 cm/1–3 ft). *A. majus*, most cvs, rust resistant

Calendula (Pot Marigold). Hardy bedding/edging plants with pale green leaves and, generally, bright yellow/orange flowers over a long season. Recommended: C. 'Pacific Beauty' is most drought resistant.

Callistephus (China Aster). Bedding and cut flower source. Rich colors on low to tall plants. Midsummer.

Cheiranthus (Wallflower). Hardy, spring-flowering biennials, white/yellow/red/rust (30 cm/12 in). Recommended: *C. cheiri* acts as a perennial in mild areas.

Cosmos. Single or semi-double daises and fine-cut foliage. Pink, white or yellow to orange range.

Dianthus (Pink). *See Perennials* Recommended: *D. chinensis* has fringed petals and dark centers. Many varieties.

Dimorphotheca (Cape Marigold). Hardy, daisy flowers, yellow/orange/pink/white, summer (30 cm/12 in). Sow seed early.

Eschscholzia (Poppy). Brilliant, flame-flowered, hardy bedding plants (30 cm/12 in). *E. californica* has fern-like leaves and yellow flowers. Scatter seeds in early spring.

Gazania Handsome foliage – evergreen when grown in mild areas as perennials – with yellow/orange/red daisy-flowers (30 cm/12 in). Recommended: G. 'Sunshine' has big, sun-loving flowers and is heat resistant. Likes dry soil.

Helianthus (Sunflower). Giant, golden, daisy-like flowers up to 3 m (10 ft) high, late summer. Recommended: *H. annuus* has flowers 30 cm (12 in) wide.

Heliotropium (Heliotrope). Bedding plants with flat heads of scented, violet flowers, summer/autumn. Can be grown as perennials in frost-free districts (90 cm/3 ft).

Iberis (Candytuft). Hardy, edging, bedding or cutting annuals. White/pink/red, bushy flowers, summer (30–40 cm/12–16 in).

Impatiens (Busy Lizzie). Fast-growing, generally pink/red-flowered plants which can overwinter indoors for following year.

Limnanthes Small annuals, native to West Coast. *L. douglasii* has saucer-shaped, yellow/white flowers, spring and summer.

Lobelia Lovely edging/rockery plants with bright blue flowers over a long season (15 cm/6 in). 'Sapphire', trailing; 'White Lady'; 'Crystal Palace', dark blue with dark leaves.

Lunaria (Honesty). Mauve-flowered biennials with large, coarse leaves and very attractive, silver-transparent seed heads (60 cm/2 ft). Plants will self-sow.

Matthiola (Stock). Spikes of scented, colorful flowers, spring. Hardy bedding plants (40 cm/16 in). Recommended: *M. bicornis* has heady-scented flowers, opening at night.

Mesembryanthemum Daisy-like half-hardy edging/rockery plants for sunny position (8 cm/3 in). Very popular on the West Coast.

Molucella (Shell Flower). Shell-shaped sepals surround tiny, white flowers on these unusual bedding plants (50 cm/20 in). Popular as cut flowers.

Calendula officinalis

Gazania × splendens

Mollucella laevis

Nicotiana affinis

Papaver alpinum

Zinnia elegans

SELECTION GUIDE **Annuals**	SOIL TOLERANCE				LOCATION	
	Acid	Alkaline	Well-drained	Damp	Full sun	Semi-shade
Ageratum	●	●		●	●	
Alyssum	●	●	●		●	
Antirrhinum	●	●	●		●	
Calendula	●	●	●		●	
Callistephus	●	●	●		●	
Cheiranthus		●	●		●	
Cosmos	●	●	●		●	
Dianthus	●	●	●		●	
Dimorphotheca	●	●	●		●	
Eschscholzia	●	●	●		●	
Gazania	●	●	●		●	
Helianthus	●	●	●		●	
Heliotropium	●	●	●		●	●
Iberis	●	●	●		●	●
Impatiens	●	●	●		●	●
Limnanthes	●	●	●		●	
Lobelia	●	●		●		●
Lunaria	●	●	●	●	●	●
Matthiola	●	●	●		●	●
Mesembryanthemum	●	●	●		●	
Molucella	●	●	●	●	●	
Nicotiana	●	●	●		●	
Nigella	●	●	●		●	
Papaver alpinum	●	●	●		●	
Pelargonium	●	●	●		●	●
Petunia	●	●	●		●	
Reseda		●	●		●	
Tagetes	●	●	●		●	
Tropaeolum	●	●	●		●	
Zinnia	●	●			●	

273

Nicotiana (Tobacco Plant). Strongly-scented, long-flowering bedding plants in many colors, including lime-green. Half-hardy (90 cm/3 ft). Recommended: *N. affinis*, white flowers.

Nigella (Love-in-a-mist). Hardy bedding plants with pale blue flowers, spring, and lovely ferny foliage (30 cm/12 in).

Papaver alpinum (Poppy). Colorful, summer-flowering annuals with lovely saucer-flowers and delicate foliage (30 cm/12 in). Scatter seeds early.

Pelargonium (Geranium). Free-flowering bedding plants which will winter indoors for following year. Big heads of varied color (60 cm/2 ft).

Petunia Showy bedding plants for hot, dry position. Innumerable colors of funnel-shaped, scented flowers In mid-summer, pinch back plants to force new bushy growth and flowers until frost.

Reseda (Mignonette). Yellow stars of scented, summer flowers on annuals which can be perennial in mildest areas (60 cm/2 ft). Recommended: *R. alba* has white flowers.

Tagetes (Marigold). Mainstay of annual garden and long-lasting cutflower. Yellow, orange, rusty red and near white ('Snowbird').

Tropaeolum (Nasturtium). Trailing, sometimes climbing, hardy annuals with pretty, round leaves (edible in salads) and bright orange tubular flowers (Spread 1.2 m/4 ft). Recommended: *T. majus* offers a variety of shades of yellow and red.

Zinnia Dahlia-like, summer flowers in bright colors. Versatile annual in wide range of forms and heights.

Ground cover

In this category, I include some shrubs that, despite their height, grow down to ground level in addition to the usual ground-smothering plants.

Ajuga (Bugle). Carpet of bright blue flower spikes from leaf mat. Recommended: *A. reptans* 'Atropurpurea'.

Alchemilla *See Perennials* Recommended: *A. mollis* (Lady's Mantle) forms mounds of light green leaves with sulphur-yellow flowers in loose sprays, summer.

Anthemis *See Perennials* Recommended: *A. marshall-iana*, gray foliage, daisy flowers.

Artemisia *See Perennials*

Recommended: A. 'Silver Mound' has attractive gray foliage forming a low mound.

Aubrieta Spring flowers with long season. Blue/pink/red/purple. Recommended: *A. deltoidea*.

Asperula odorata (Sweet Woodruff). Whorled foliage.

Berberis *See Shrubs* Recommended: any low-growing forms. *B. candidula* (evergreen) makes glossy mounds with purple berries; *B. thunbergii* (deciduous) has red berries and good autumn foliage color.

Bergenia *See Perennials* Recommended: all forms.

Choisya *See Shrubs* Recommended: *C. ternata* (Mexican Orange Blossom) has scented white flowers. Tender.

Alchemilla mollis

Bergenia cordifolia

Hypericum calycinum

SELECTION GUIDE
Ground cover

	SOIL TOLERANCE				LOCATION			SIZE		
	Acid	Alkaline	Well-drained	Damp	Full sun	Semi-shade	Total shade	Over 5 ft	2–5 ft	Under 2 ft
Ajuga	●	●	●	●	●	●				●
Alchemilla	●		●	●		●	●			●
Anthemis	●	●	●		●				●	
Artemisia	●	●	●		●	●			●	●
Aubrieta	●	●	●		●					●
Asperula	●		●			●	●			●
Berberis	●	●	●		●	●		●	●	
Bergenia	●	●	●			●	●			●
Choisya	●	●	●	●	●	●	●	●	●	
Cornus	●	●	●	●	●	●		●	●	
Cotoneaster	●	●	●		●	●		●	●	●
Dianthus	●	●	●		●					●
Elaeagnus	●	●	●		●			●	●	
Epimedium	●	●	●		●	●	●			●
Erica	●									●
Escallonia		●	●		●	●			●	●
Euonymus	●	●	●		●	●		●	●	●
Euphorbia	●	●	●	●	●	●				●
Festuca	●	●	●		●					●
Gaultheria	●		●	●		●	●		●	
Genista	●	●	●		●					●
Geranium	●	●	●	●	●	●				●
Hebe			●	●	●				●	
Hedera	●	●	●			●	●			●
Helianthemum		●	●		●					●
Helleborus	●	●		●		●	●			●
Heuchera	●	●	●	●	●	●			●	●
Hosta	●	●		●		●	●			●

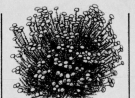

Santolina chamaecyparissus

Stachys lanata

Tiarella cordifolia

Cornus *See Shrubs* Recommended: *C. alba* (Red Barked Dogwood) has many interesting forms with rich autumn color. Stems red in winter months.

Cotoneaster *See Shrubs* Recommended: all prostrate to medium-sized varieties, especially *C. dammeri*.

Dianthus *See Perennials.*

Elaeagnus *See Shrubs* Recommended: all evergreen forms. *E. pungens* 'Maculata', gold/green variegated leaves.

Epimedium (Barrenwort). Heart-shaped, evergreen leaves with small, yellow/pink/white, May/June flowers.

Erica (Heath). Large evergreen family with variable leaf and flower colors and flowering seasons.

Escallonia *See Shrubs* Recommended: *E. iveyi* has dark, glossy leaves and white autumn flowers.

Euonymus *See Shrubs* Recommended *E. fortunei* has some brilliantly colored variegated forms.

Euphorbia *See Perennials* Recommended: *E. myrsinites* has silvery foliage in rosettes and light green flowers; *E. wulfenii* has larger, yellowish flowers (1.3 m/4 ft).

Festuca (Fescue) *See Grasses* Tufted, glaucous grass. There is a blue-green variety.

Gaultheria *See Shrubs* Recommended: *G. procumbens* has scarlet berries and dark green leaves.

Genista *See Shrubs* Recommended: *G. hispanica*

(Spanish Gorse) is a prickly shrub with bright yellow, early summer flowers.

Geranium *See Perennials* Recommended: all forms.

Hebe Recommended: all forms where hardy.

Hedera *See Climbers* Recommended: all forms.

Helianthemum (Rock Rose). Lovely, small, profuse flowers in summer. Protect in North.

Helleborus *See Perennials*

Heuchera (Coral Flower). Low, heart-shaped leaves, often mottled with tall spikes of pink/red bell flowers above them, summer.

Hosta *See Perennials*

Hydrangea *See Shrubs* Recommended: *H. petiolaris* has flat heads of greenish-white flowers, June.

Hypericum *See Shrubs* Recommended: *H. calycinum* (St. John's-wort) has big golden flowers.

Juniperus *See Conifers* Recommended: *J. horizontalis* are wide-spreading, low shrubs with many vareties offering blue-green/gold/yellow/bright green, ferny, evergreen foliage.

Lamium (Deadnettle). Nettle-like perennial for shade with interesting leaf variegations. Purple, yellow, white flowers.

Liriope Blue spikes of flowers, late summer.

Lonicera *See Shrubs* Recommended: *L. pileata* has cream flowers and violet berries.

Pachysandra *See Shrubs* Recommended: *P. terminalis* is evergreen, likes shade.

Polygonatum (Solomon's Seal). Arching stems with broad leaves and, hanging beneath them, tiny white bells.

Potentilla *See Shrubs* Recommended: all forms.

Prunus laurocerasus *See Shrubs* Recommended: *P. l.* 'Zabelliana' has profuse white flowers with narrow leaves.

	SOIL TOLERANCE				LOCATION			SIZE		
	Acid	Alkaline	Well-drained	Damp	Full sun	Semi-shade	Total shade	Over 5 ft	2–5 ft	Under 2 ft
Hydrangea	●	●		●	●	●		●		
Hypericum	●	●	●		●	●			●	●
Juniperus	●	●	●		●			●	●	
Lamium		●	●		●	●	●			●
Liriope	●		●		●	●				●
Lonicera		●	●		●	●		●	●	
Pachysandra	●		●	●			●			●
Polygonatum	●	●		●		●				●
Potentilla	●	●	●		●	●				●
Prunus laurocerasus	●	●	●	●		●		●	●	●
Rhododendron	●			●		●			●	●
Ribes	●	●			●	●			●	●
Rosmarinus		●	●		●					●
Ruta		●	●		●					●
Salix	●	●		●		●		●	●	●
Sambucus	●	●	●			●		●	●	●
Santolina		●	●		●					●
Sarcococca	●	●	●			●				●
Saxifraga	●	●	●			●	●			●
Sedum	●	●	●		●	●				●
Senecio	●	●	●		●				●	●
Stachys	●	●	●		●	●				●
Symphoricarpus	●	●	●		●	●		●		●
Teucrium		●	●		●					●
Thymus	●	●	●		●					●
Tiarella	●	●	●	●		●				●
Viburnum davidii	●	●	●	●	●	●		●	●	●
Vinca	●	●	●			●	●			●

Rhododendron *See Shrubs* Recommended: all forms especially low, small-level.

Ribes (Flowering Currant). Evergreen and deciduous shrubs with yellow or pink spring flowers.

Rosmarinus *See Hedges* Recommended: *R. officinalis* has blue summer flowers.

Ruta *See Shrubs* Recommended: *R. graveolens* has mustard-yellow flowers, pungent leaves.

Salix *See Shrubs* Recommended: *S. repens argentea* is very good for coastal areas; *S. hastata* 'Wehrhahnii' has silvery male catkins in spring, slowly turning yellow.

Santolina *See Shrubs* Recommended: all forms.

Sarcococca *See Shrubs* Recommended: *S. humilis* has dark shiny leaves, white/pink flowers and black berries.

Saxifraga (Saxifrage). Rosettes of leaves with pink, starry, summer flowers.

Sedum *See Perennials* Recommended: all forms.

Stachys *See Perennials*

Symphoricarpos *See Shrubs* Recommended: *S. albus* has oval leaves, pink flowers and white berries.

Teucrium *See Shrubs* Recommended: *T. fruticans* has downy leaves and blue summer flowers. Requires winter protection.

Thymus (Thyme). Aromatic, gray foliage with pink/white/mauve summer flowers. Used in cooking.

Tiarella Round, pale green evergreen leaves, bronze in winter. White/pink, starry spring/summer flowers carried on stems high above leaves.

Viburnum davidii *See Shrubs*

Vinca *See Shrubs* Recommended: *V. minor* spreads easily and has attractive blue spring flowers.

Bulbs

You will see below that my selection of bulbous plants provides flower color and form for spring, summer and autumn. The selection guide indicates "architectural form".

Allium This family includes onions, shallots and garlic, generally having strap-leaves with clusters of summer flowers (blue/white/purple) on long stems (15–60 cm/6–24 in). Choice: *A. giganteum* for its spectacular, violet flower heads, July.

Anemone Delightful spring flowers (white/blue/purple/red), with attractive foliage (15–30 cm/6–12 in). Recommended: *A. blanda* flowers in early spring. Good for naturalizing.

Arum Extraordinary, spiky flowers held in a leaf-like shield or spathe (15 cm/6 in). Recommended: *A. italicum* has bright red, autumn berries.

Chionodoxa (Glory of the Snow). Starry, bright blue, very early flowers. Strap-like leaves. At their best when naturalized in rough grass (15 cm/6 in).

Colchicum (Meadow Saffron). Pink/lilac autumn flowers, similar to crocus (often known as Autumn Crocus). Leaves appear in spring, die back in summer (25 cm/10 in). Recommended: *C. speciosum*, lilac-rose to red-purple range and also white.

Crinum Handsome, lily-like flowers (white/red/pink), generally hardy in south-facing bed. Strappy leaves (90 cm/3 ft). Recommended: *C. × powellii* 'Album'.

Crocus Large and varied genus of spring and autumn flowering bulbs. Main colors purple/gold/white, (10 cm/4 in). Recommended: *C. tomasinianus* has rich purple flowers.

Eranthis hyemalis (Winter Aconite). Bright yellow, early spring flowers. Pale green, finely-cut leaves. Ideal for naturalizing (5–10 cm/2–4 in).

Eremurus (Foxtail Lily). Tall spikes (1.2–2.4 m/4–8 ft) of star-shaped summer flowers. Strappy leaves.

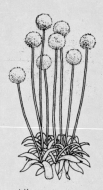

Allium giganteum

Crinum x powellii

Fritillaria imperialis

Galtonia candicans

Leucojum aestivum

SELECTION GUIDE **Bulbs**	SOIL TOLERANCE				LOCATION		
	Acid	Alkaline	Well-drained	Damp	Full sun	Semi-shade	Architectural form
Allium	●	●	●		●		
Anemone	●	●	●	●	●	●	
Arum	●	●	●		●		
Chionodoxa	●	●	●		●	●	
Colchicum	●	●	●		●		
Crinum	●		●		●		●
Crocus	●	●	●		●		
Eranthis hyemalis	●	●	●		●	●	
Eremurus	●	●	●		●		●
Fritillaria	●	●	●		●	●	
Galanthus		●	●		●	●	●
Galtonia candicans	●	●	●		●		●
Hyacinthus	●	●	●		●		
Leucojum	●	●	●	●	●		
Lilium candidum	●	●	●		●		●
Muscari	●	●	●		●	●	
Narcissus	●	●	●		●		
Nerine	●	●	●			●	●
Scilla		●	●		●	●	
Tulipa	●	●	●		●		●

Fritillaria Pendulous spring flowers on leafy stems. Recommended: *F. imperialis* has imposing red/orange/yellow flowers, hanging beneath a whorl of leaves (1.2 m/4 ft).

Galanthus (Snowdrop). Charming, very early white flowers (10–20 cm/4–8 in). Force in pots. Recommended: *G. nivalus* is particularly good for naturalizing in grass.

Galtonia candicans (Summer Hyacinth). Long, narrow leaves and white, hyacinth-like flowers, summer (1.2 m/4 ft).

Hyacinthus (Hyacinth). Ideal for garden or indoor forcing, bright blue/purple/white/pink/yellow spring flowers with heady scent.

Leucojum (Snowflake). White snowdrop-like flowers spring, some species in autumn. Recommended: *L. aestivum* flowers in late spring.

Lilium candidum (Madonna Lily). Large, white, delightful flowers, fragrant, summer (60 cm–1.8 m/2–6 ft).

Muscari (Grape Hyacinth). Clusters of tiny blue flowers, late spring (15 cm/6 in). Recommended: *M. armeniacum* has tight clusters of blue flowers, April–May.

Narcissus (Daffodil). Bright yellow/white, trumpet flowers, spring. Hardy and easy to grow, there are thousands of cultivars of this genus.

Nerine Handsome, pink/red, late summer flowers, hardy only in mildest areas but otherwise need greenhouse protection (30–60 cm/1–2 ft).

Scilla (Bluebell). Lovely blue spring flowers (also white/pink), naturalizing well in half-shade (15–30 cm/6–12 in). Many varieties. Recommended: *S. (Endymion) campanulata* (Wood Hyacinth) flowers early in mixed colors.

Tulipa Innumerable varieties of brightly-colored, spring flowers, often bi-colored. Recommended: Lily-flowered has tall (60 cm/24 in) flowers with petals bent inwards or outwards.

Climbers

Some climbers cling without help, some ramble and need to be tied, others will grow against a support if trained. The selection guide, below, separates them under the heading "nature".

Abutilon Unusual, handsome wall shrubs with bell-shaped, hanging flowers. Recommended: *A. megapotamicum* has red and yellow summer flowers. Tender.

Actinidia Vigorous climbers. Recommended: *A. chinensis* (Chinese Gooseberry) has cream, late summer flowers and produces fruit in full sun. This is the "kiwi" from New Zealand and it is tender in the North.

Akebia Purple/red-flowered climber with handsome foliage. *A. quinata* occasionally produces dark purple fruits. Fragrant flowers.

Aristolochia Pipe-shaped, yellow, summer flowers and heart-shaped leaves. Recommended: *A. macrophylla* (Dutchman's Pipe) is vigorous.

Campsis Eye-catching, red/orange trumpet flowers, late summer. Recommended: *C. radicans* (Trumpet Vine) has strikingly bright flowers.

Ceanothus *See Shrubs* Recommended: *C. thyrsiflorus* has light blue flowers, early summer. Mild climates only.

Chaenomeles *See Shrubs* Recommended: *C. speciosa* has a wide choice of colors.

Clematis Huge range of species and hybrids with handsome flowers and often attractive seed heads. Recommended: *C. montana* 'Alba' has pure white, early summer flowers and, being vigorous, is ideal for growing into the branches of established trees.

Eccremocarpus Tender climbers. Recommended: *E. scaber* is hardy in mild districts and very vigorous. Red/orange/yellow tubular summer flowers. The leaves are small and fern-like.

Clematis montana

Hydrangea petiolaris

Jasminum nudiflorum

Wisteria sinensis

SELECTION GUIDE
Climbing plants

	SOIL TOLERANCE				LOCATION			NATURE		
	Acid	Alkaline	Well-drained	Damp	Full sun	Semi-shade	Shade	Clinger/twiner	Wall shrub	Rambler
Abutilon		●	●		●				●	
Actinidia	●	●	●		●			●		
Akebia	●	●	●	●	●	●		●		
Aristolochia	●	●	●	●	●			●		
Campsis	●	●			●			●		
Ceanothus		●	●		●				●	
Chaenomeles	●	●	●		●				●	
Clematis	●	●	●		●					●
Eccremocarpus	●	●	●		●			●		
Euonymus fortunei	●	●	●			●				●
Garrya elliptica	●	●	●	●		●	●		●	
Hedera	●	●	●	●		●	●	●		
Humulus lupulus	●	●	●		●	●		●		
Hydrangea petiolaris	●	●	●		●	●		●		
Jasminum	●	●	●		●	●				●
Parthenocissus	●	●	●		●	●		●		
Passiflora	●	●	●		●				●	
Polygonum	●	●	●		●	●	●	●		
Rosa	●	●	●		●	●				●
Solanum		●	●	●	●				●	
Wisteria	●	●	●	●	●				●	

Euonymus fortunei *See Shrubs*

Garrya elliptica *See Shrubs*

Hedera (Ivy). Easy, hardy evergreens with great variety of leaf color and shape. Recommended: *H. colchica* 'Dentata Variegata' has very large, cream-edged leaves.

Humulus lupulus (Hop). Small flowers followed by hops in late summer. Recommended: *H. l.* 'Aureus' has handsome, yellow leaves.

Hydrangea petiolaris Large, flat heads of white flowers, June. Vigorous.

Jasminum (Jasmine). Small, white/yellow, fragrant flowers. Recommended: *J. nudiflorum* (Winter Jasmine) has scentless, yellow flowers on bare branches, November–March.

Parthenocissus (Virginia Creeper). Handsome-foliaged climber with glorious autumn color. Recommended: *P. quinquefolia* has large leaves and spectacular autumn color.

Passiflora (Passion Flower). Large, exotic flowers. Vigorous, but tender. Recommended: *P. caerulea* has blue, purple and white, fragrant flowers. Semi-evergreen.

Polygonum Hardy, very vigorous climber, any situation. Recommended: *P. baldschuanicum* (Russian Vine) has cream, pink-tinged flowers, summer/ autumn.

Rosa Innumerable varieties, broadly divided into climbing and rambler roses, from the three types: modern garden, old garden and wild.

Solanum Handsome, late-summer flowers, usually blue/purple. Tender. Recommended: *S. crispum* 'Glasnevin' has purple, yellow-centred flowers; *S. jasminoides* (Jasmine Nightshade) has gray-blue flowers.

Wisteria Lovely blue/pink/white flowers in long racemes, spring. Recommended: *W. sinensis* bears fragrant, lilac racemes on bare branches, late spring.

Water plants

I have subdivided this list into submerged aquatics (oxygenators), floating aquatics and bog and waterside plants, that need various degrees of moisture.

Bog and waterside

Acorus calamnus (Sweet flag). Greenish-white flowers, sword-leaves. There is a handsome variegated form.

Alisma Hardy perennials, sprays of white/pink flowers.

Aponogeton distachyus (Water Hawthorn). Fragrant white flowers, floating leaves.

Butomus umbellatus (Flowering Rush). Umbels of pink flowers, June, Narrow, twisted leaves tinted purple when young.

Calla palustris (Bog Arum). Flowers very similar to Arum *See bulbs*, including red, autumn beries. Dark green, heart-shaped leaves.

Caltha palustris (Marsh Marigold). Golden, spring flowers, heart-shaped leaves.

Juncus (Rush). Stately plants with insignificant flowers.

Mentha aquatica (Water Mint). Blue, late summer flowers, lemon-scented leaves.

Menyanthes trifoliata (Bog Bean). Lovely, pink-budded white flowers, bean-like leaves.

Myosotis scorpiades (Water Forget-me-not). Sky-blue summer flowers.

Sagittaria (Arrowhead. *See Submerged Aquatics* Recommended: *S. lancifolia*.

Typha latifolia (Great Reed Mace). Also called Bulrush. Very tall (2.4 m/8 ft).

Floating aquatics

Azolla (Fairy Moss.) Floating perennial forming carpet of red-tinted moss-like growth. Tender.

Eichornia (Water Hyacinth). Glossy, heart shaped leaves, lilac flowers with gold. Winter indoors.

Nymphae (Water Lily). Glorious, exotic summer flowers, generally divided into:
a) Extra strong growing (75 cm–1 m/2½–3 ft). Recommended: *N. alba*.
b) Strong (50–75 cm/19–30 in). Recommended: *N. gloriosa*.
c) Medium (30–50 cm/12–19 in). Recommended: *N. odorata alba*, white flowers.
d) Small (10–30 cm/4–11 in). Recommended: *N. pygmaed*.

Submerged aquatics

Callitriche (Water Starwort). Some varieties grow completely submerged, some prefer shallow (15 cm/6 in) water, producing rosettes of foliage on the surface.

Elodea (Canadian Pondweed). Excellent oxygenators.

Hottonia (Water Violet). Lovely, ferny foliage. Whorls of pale lilac flowers, May.

Myriophyllum (Water Milfoil). Finely-cut foliage, some varieties with red stems.

Potamogeton Wavy-edged, reddish-green, translucent leaves, like seaweed.

Sagittaria (Arrowhead). Arrow-shaped leaves 60 cm (24 in) above surface.

Butomus umbellatus

Calla palustris

Caltha palustris

Sagittaria lancifolia

SELECTION GUIDE Bog and waterside	SOIL TOLERANCE				SIZE	
	Acid	Alkaline	Full sun	Semi-shade	Over 1 ft	Less than 1 ft
Acorus calamnus	●	●	●	●	●	
Alisma	●	●	●	●		
Aponogeton distachyus	●		●	●		●
Butomus umbellatus	●	●	●		●	
Calla palustris	●	●	●	●		●
Caltha palustris	●	●	●	●	●	
Juncus	●	●	●	●	●	
Mentha aquatica	●	●	●	●		●
Menyanthes trifoliata	●	●	●	●	●	●
Myosotis scorpiades	●	●	●	●		●
Sagittaria	●	●	●		●	
Typha latifolia	●	●	●	●	●	

Mixes and coverages

Gardeners interested in do-it-yourself will need to know what quantities of materials to order when constructing the garden. If you have drawn up your garden layout to scale, however (see pp. 40–41), you can easily calculate the quantities required by taking measurements from your scale drawing, but the charts below and overleaf give a useful guide to coverages. They will also help you to decide on the exact mix of constituents for mortar, concrete and lawn depending on location, climate and expected wear and tear.

It is always cheaper to buy constituents separately and to mix them yourself. Weigh this saving against the savings in time and labor offered by ready-mixed products.

Paving coverages

The chart on the right will help you to work out the number of paving elements you require to cover a particular area. If you intend to mix more than one material, there is really no substitute for counting the numbers required from a scale drawing. If the area has odd corners (something to avoid), you will need more elements to allow for cutting. Thinner elements tend to break during unloading so you should allow for this. It is anyway a good idea to have a few spare elements that can weather at the same rate as those laid, to replace breakages due to frost damage.

A   Paving slabs (700 mm²/28 in²)
B   Paving slabs (460 mm²/18 in²)
C   Paving slabs (305 mm²/12 in²)
D   Granite blocks (240 × 110 mm/ 9½ × 4.4 in)
E   Paving bricks (220 × 110 mm/ 8.8 × 4.4 in)
F   Tiles (150 mm²/6 in²)

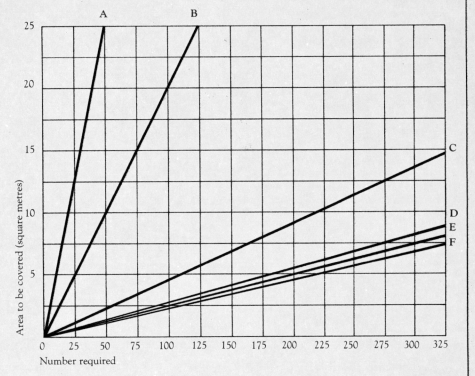

Mortar mixes

Mortar consists of sand and a binding agent. The binding agent is cement or lime, or a mixture of the two. Using all cement makes a strong mix that dries quickly but is liable to crack, while using all lime makes a weak mix that dries slowly but is less likely to crack. Mortar should not be stronger or weaker than the material it joins. Aerated mortar is made with cement and a proprietary plasticizing agent that forms air bubbles in the mortar, making the mix more workable and resistant to frost. Add plasticizer as indicated by the manufacturer.

Use	Cement mortar	Cement-lime mortar	Aerated mortar
Retaining walls, engineering bricks	1 part cement 3 parts sand		
Cappings, step treads and risers	1 part cement 3 parts sand	1 part cement ½ part lime 4½ parts sand	1 part cement 6 parts sand Plasticizer as indicated
Exterior walls, work below damp proofing	1 part cement 3 parts sand	1 part cement 1 part lime 6 parts sand	1 part cement 6 parts sand Plasticizer as indicated
Exposed walls above damp proofing		1 part cement 1 part lime 6 parts sand	1 part cement 6 parts sand Plasticizer as indicated
Internal walls		1 part cement 2 parts lime 9 parts sand	1 part cement 8 parts sand Plasticizer as indicated

Concrete mixes and coverage

The thickness and mix of concrete you use depends on its function – mainly the weight of the traffic upon it. You have the choice of buying aggregate and sand separately or paying a little more for mixed aggregate and sand. Aggregate is available in different grades from fine to coarse. In general, the thicker the concrete required, the courser the aggregate you should use. Finer aggregate is required, however, for smooth surface finishes.

Sharp sand is required for mixing concrete as opposed to the soft builder's sand used in mortar mixes. If a large quantity of concrete is required, for say a driveway, consider contacting a firm that supplies ready-mixed concrete to you direct. Ready-mixed concrete has the advantage of being aerated (see p. 279) and so is more resistant to frost than hand-mixed concrete. It is essential, however, that you are well-prepared for the delivery with curbs or temporary forms in position, since ready-mixed concrete starts to harden within an hour and a cubic meter (35.31 ft³) equals 40 wheelbarrow loads. You will need assistance.

Use	Cement	Aggregate	Sand
Foundations, driveways, garage floors, surfaces for heavy wear	1 part cement	4½ parts all-in aggregate (max. size 20 mm/0.8 in)	
(Separate aggregate alternative)	1 part cement	4 parts coarse aggregate (max. size 20 mm/0.8 in)	2½ parts sand
Paths, surfaces for pedestrian traffic	1 part cement	3½ parts all-in aggregate (max. size 10 mm/0.4 in)	2½ parts sand
Bedding for slabs	1 part cement		3 parts sand
Pond linings	1 part cement	4 parts aggregate (max. size 10 mm/0.4 in)	

Grass seed mixtures

You can buy grass seed mixes to suit most locations. Broadly there are six grasses that have various qualities of wear and appearance. Most grass seed is sold in mixes formulated for various uses and climates and often contains perennial rye grass. Ryegrass is a coarse, fast growing tufted plant that will take heavy wear and is useful for lawns on which children will play. In the USA, state and federal regulations control the formulations of grass seed and label information. St. Augustine and Zoysia are available as sod or plugs rather than seed.

Grass type	Disease Resistance	Winter Hardiness	Drought Resistance	Shade Tolerance
Bent	poor	good	poor	fair
Fescue	good	good	very good	good
Perennial Ryegrass	good	good	good	poor
Kentucky Bluegrass	good	very good	fair	poor
St. Augustine	poor	poor	very good	fair
Zoysia	very good	fair to good	very good	fair

Index

Acknowledgments

Author's acknowledgments

I must thank those that have helped me in this compilation: Hilary Bryan-Brown, who has typed up my appalling script so patiently, David Lamb, who has edited it so knowledgably and Steven Wooster, who has presented it so handsomely. I would also like to thank Ivan Ruperti for the use of his photographs.

Dorling Kindersley would like to thank the following for their help in producing this book:

Michael Runge (landscape designer) and James Seymour of Seymours Garden and Leisure Centre, Ewell, who provided most of the materials photographed in *Constructing your garden* and *Finishing touches*.

Peter Morter, for the color illustrations in the *Garden-by-garden guide*.

Alison Chappel; Geoff Dann for special photography; Polly Dawes; Debbie Lee; George Perkins (Cement and Concrete Association) and Anna Selby.

Ben Knott, Ron Phillimore and Geoff Owens of Adroit Photo Litho.

Photographs were provided by:
Molly Adams: 136
Architectural Association: 22T
A–Z Botanical Collection Ltd: 124T
Michael Boys: 2, 6, 39TR, 50, 62, 100, 131, 149B, 150T, 212L, 217, 235TL (Susan Griggs Agency): 9T, 24, 27, 90, 130B, 151, 155L, 156, 164B, 182BL, 213B, 228B, 231B, 237T, 237BL
John Brookes: 18B, 118, 149T, 158T, 173B, 188T, 189T, 229B, 232BL, 232BC, 238L
Karl-Dietrich Bühler: 4, 11T, 13B, 19T, 43, 44, 47, 48, 54, 74, 88, 120, 121, 140, 141T, 143T, 145T, 145B, 154, 157R, 169, 192, 201, 206T, 211T, 214, 216B, 230B
Camera Press: 14, 15, 19B, 26T, 33, 39B, 45, 46, 56, 66, 70, 72, 76, 80, 86, 94, 110, 119, 128, 130T, 137, 142, 148, 159B, 170, 172, 175, 179, 202T, 212R, 228T, 236B, 240T
Michael Crockett (EWA): 82
Cam Culbert (Susan Griggs Agency): 23
Geoff Dann: 30, 109, 114, 115, 132, 133, 230T, 231CL, 232C, 232BR, 233B, 234B, 235C, 235B, 236TL, 236TR, 237BR, 229TL, 229TR
Richard Davies (EWA): 26B
Michael Dunne: 127C, 144
EWA: 134T

Roberta Frateschi Bosetti: 147, 161TR
Iris Hardwick Library of Photographs: 117C, 139, 157L
Pamela J. Harper: 12BR, 22B, 58, 60, 96, 107B, 111B, 112B, 116, 117B, 123, 126, 134BL, 153T, 155R, 163T, 195, 206BL
Peter Hayden: 21
Clive Helm (EWA): 98
Ann Kelly (EWA): 166
Landscape Institute: 112T
Georges Leveque: 12BL, 37, 186B, 203, 207
Neil Lorimer (EWA): 9B
Michael McKinley: 10, 28T, 34, 111T, 122, 125T, 127T, 127BR, 129T
Tania Midgley (Vision International): 17CL, 17CR, 36B, 52, 125L, 138T, 143BR, 152, 158B, 181BR, 185, 198, 199B, 200, 205R, 234T
Michael Nicholson (EWA): 160, 162, 239T
Ian O'Leary: 150B
George Perkins: 130C, 134BR, 240BL
Spike Powell (EWA): 145C
Ivan Ruperti: 49
Scala: 20
John Sims: 235TR
Harry Smith Agency: 8, 36T, 143BL, 164T, 168, 189B, 215T, 223T, 232T
Anthea Sieveking (Vision International): 146
Tim Street-Porter (EWA): 25, 28B, 124B, 135R, 159T
George Taloumis: 13T

Friedhelm Thomas (EWA): 84
Pamla Toler: 17T, 17BL, 17BR, 18T, 35, 64, 68, 117T, 127BL, 141B, 163B, 165, 171, 174, 178, 180, 182BR, 183, 184, 186T, 193, 194, 197, 205L, 206BR, 208, 210, 211C, 215B, 223BR, 233T, 233C
Jerry Tubby (EWA): 11B, 108, 135L, 153B, 161B, 202BL, 231T
Steven Wooster: 39TL, 106, 107T, 129B, 138B, 161TL, 181TL, 181TR, 181BL, 188B, 202BR, 213T, 213C, 216T, 231CR, 238R, 239B, 240BR
George Wright: 78, 92, 173T, 199T, 220, 223BL, 223BC

T = top, B = bottom, L = left, R = right, C = centre

Illustrations by:
David Ashby
Will Giles
Jim Robins
Saxon Artists
Les Smith
Eric Thomas
Venner Artists
John Woodcock

Typesetting
MS Filmsetting